virgin film

OLIVER STONE

Stephen Lavington

Dedicated to
Jim Smith – a better man than Richard Nixon

First published in Great Britain in 2004
by Virgin Books Ltd
Thames Wharf Studios
Rainville Road
London
W6 9HA

A catalogue record for this book is available from the British Library.

ISBN 0 7535 0975 X

Typeset by TW Typesetting, Plymouth, Devon
Printed and bound in Great Britain by Mackays of Chatham PLC

Contents

Acknowledgements iv

Introduction 1
Seizure (1974) 7
Midnight Express (1978) 16
The Hand (1981) 23
Scarface (1983) 33
Year of the Dragon (1985) 41
Salvador (1986) 51
Platoon (1986) 67
Wall Street (1987) 85
Talk Radio (1988) 103
Born on the Fourth of July (1989) 116
The Doors (1991) 134
JFK (1991) 153
Heaven and Earth (1993) 174
Natural Born Killers (1994) 193
Nixon (1995) 211
U Turn (1997) 230
Any Given Sunday (1999) 244
Alexander (2004) 263
Bibliography 272
Index of Quotations 276
Index 295

Acknowledgements

Special thanks to Jeni and Tony Fisher (for keeping me going), Martyn Lavington (for giving me a *Hand* . . . a *Year of the Dragon* and *Eight Million Ways to Die*) and Kirstie Addis at Virgin.

Thanks for help and encouragement to: Nick Edwards, Dan Doyle, Pete Gray, Nik Haley, Jeremy Lenearts, David Mullins, Darren Rhymes, Rowan Searle, Matthew Symonds, Helen Taylor and Tom Whitehead. Also Mark Clapham, Eddie Robson and Jonny Miller at Shinyshelf.com and Rose and Barnaby at Eland.

Vital materials were made available by the BFI Library, the British Library, the Laura Cook Collection, the James Clive Matthews Memorial Archives and the Ben Williams DVD Index.

This book would have been sorely lacking without information from www.thenumbers.com, www.mrqe.com and, inevitably, www.imdb.com.

To everyone who asked me who Oliver Stone was . . . I hope this answers your question.

Introduction

In 1965 the first American combat troops landed at Danang in South Vietnam. That same year a young American, disillusioned with, and on sabbatical from, conservative Ivy League Yale, arrived in Saigon to teach English at a local school. Within a year he had tired of this and taken employment on a merchant vessel to pay his way back to the States. Within two years he had finally quit university and returned to Vietnam, this time in the uniform of a private in the 25th Infantry; Oliver Stone was about to begin his tour of duty.

As well as the baptism of fire of a life and death struggle in the sweltering jungle, Stone was turned on to the radical counterculture of acid rock and dope. He returned to America in 1968, deeply affected by his experiences in Vietnam. Like many other veterans he found himself uprooted in a culture largely indifferent, if not actively hostile, to the war and those who had participated in it. After a spell in a Californian jail on drugs charges (see **Midnight Express**), Stone drifted north to New York. Previously a novelist by inclination, Stone took advantage of the GI Bill to enrol on a film course at New York University – from now on his creative endeavours would be exercised in writing and creating for the cinema.

An affinity for writing and performance can be traced back to Stone's childhood. Lou Stone (born Silverstein) was a straight-laced Jewish stockbroker, who served out the last years of World War II on the staff of General Eisenhower. On VE day, Lieutenant-Colonel Stone chased down an attractive French girl on the streets of Paris and begged for her address. The girl in question, Jacqueline Goddet, married Lou in November 1945 and returned with him to New York. It was there that Oliver Stone was born on 15 September 1946.

Moderately successful professionally (if not personally – James Riordan, Stone's biographer, commented that 'The standing joke was that everybody who took Lou Stone's advice became wealthy except Lou Stone'), Stone Sr was a frustrated writer, his desk full of unpublished plays and poems. He eventually found an outlet in a widely respected financial periodical, *Lou Stone's Investment Letter*, which grew to enjoy a circulation of over 100,000. Writing became a love, indeed a vocation, passed by Stone to his son. The young Oliver would be set weekly writing assignments to earn his allowance. When holidaying with family in the south of France he would write plays and charge older relatives to perform in them. Even when playing with cousins, Stone would develop elaborate scenarios based on the stories of his grandfather, a veteran of the 1914–18 Great War. The daily entry in his diary became a vital ritual, so important that Stone diagnosed his later drug problems through a lapse in his diary-keeping (see **Scarface**). Stone acknowledges a debt, both in learning the basics and the commitment required: 'My father taught me how to write. He said writing is ass plus seat. Basically it's very hard work.'

In contrast to his serious, withdrawn father was Jacqueline, Stone's sensuous, exotic and socially outgoing mother. Spontaneous and irrepressible, Jacqueline would happily let Stone play truant and would sometimes accompany him on these illicit days out to the cinema. Together they would sit in picture houses watching matinees and double bills. This early connection with film can also be attributed to his father: 'We could have done it better, Huckleberry' would be the refrain of the elder Stone whatever the movie seen.

A somewhat unconventional but comfortable childhood came to an abrupt end in 1962. Despite a growing rift between them, the divorce of his parents came as a total shock to Oliver Stone, who was unhappy at his enrolment in a high-pressure boarding school in Illinois. The sudden shock, coupled with isolation from both of his parents, threw Stone into a deep depression, leaving him with the feeling that 'everything had been stripped away. That there was a mask on everything, and underneath there was a harder . . . more negative truth.' Almost simultaneous with this was the revelation that his superficially prosperous father was deeply in debt and unable to guarantee any support for his son beyond a college education.

It was an embittered and troubled 18-year-old who entered Yale in 1964, and who swiftly became disillusioned with another high-pressure education factory on the American upper-middle-class production line. His work declined, interest waned and, inspired in part by Conrad's *Lord Jim*, Stone took a year out and headed to the Orient.

Stone did return to Yale, prior to enlisting in the army, but his work did not improve: it actually deteriorated. Instead of studies and term papers he chose to devote this fresh start to a novel-in-progress – *A Child's Night Dream*. After this stream-of-consciousness semi-autobiographical work had been rejected by every publisher to receive the submission, Stone tore the manuscript in half and threw part of it into the East River (see **A Child's Night Dream**, p. 243).

If the sudden shock of his parents divorce had caused the inner turmoil that sparked his militant non-conformism, Vietnam was a second turning point, spurring the transition from books to film. Unable to write in the sweltering jungle heat, Stone had turned to photography. This was a symptom of a wider change of perspective: 'I was a novelist . . . gave up the idea because the nature of warfare was very uncerebral,' said Stone. '[I]t's about sensuality, the six inches in front of your face. That translated to me into movies.' He had moved from introverted intellectual writing to the immediate, the visceral, the visual.

Early days

Though Stone had completed one screenplay, *Break* (see **The Doors**), prior to starting his studies, NYU would fix this career choice. While there he would study the work of influential directors such as Orson Welles, Jean-Luc Godard, Alain Resnais and Luis Bunuel under the tutelage of the young Martin Scorsese (see **The Doors**). He would also meet a future collaborator, Stanley Weiser (see **Wall Street**). *Last Year in Viet Nam*, the film he directed as part of his course, would foreshadow his later work. It is refreshingly free of pretension for a student film – a short (just over ten minutes) semi-autobiographical narrative on the subject of a Vietnam veteran, played by Oliver Stone. There are some arch touches – the narration is in French and some rather heavy-handed parallels are drawn between the concrete and the tropical jungle, while the veteran himself is explicitly compared with a caged animal. But it is touching both in the long shots of a drably attired man plodding through the streets and in the central conceit – that he bundles together his citations and medals and hurls them over the side of the Staten Island Ferry, in an attempt to release himself from the burden of the past. A direct attempt at exorcism completed in *Platoon*. Another project he developed at college was *Mad Man of Martinique* in which Stone's own father played a man killed on a subway platform.

After studies had been completed, Stone was left in something of a void. Without the contacts to get his ideas produced, he drifted for some time in the New York party scene, living off a succession of low-paid menial jobs: copy boy, messenger and cab-driver. He was also supported by Najwa Sarkis, a girl he had met at NYU and who worked for the Moroccan mission to the UN – they were married in 1971. However, her ability to provide support to Stone dried up with the appointment of a new Moroccan ambassador and a corresponding cut to Najwa's bonus.

Despite this, Stone kept up a steady output of film scripts. *Dominique: The Loves of a Woman* was an eerily biographical piece about the erotic life of a middle-aged divorcee (not a million miles removed from his own mother) and the relationship with her 18-year-old son. *The Wolves* was a loose adaptation of a Greek myth telling of a young prince returning home to kill his mother and her lover – the man who has usurped the throne, throwing in the complicating addition of a younger brother who vows to find the killer. The undertone of incest remained dormant through most of Stone's later career but can be glimpsed in *Scarface*, *The Doors* and *U Turn*, as well as the dysfunctional child–parent relations in *Born on the Fourth of July*, *Natural Born Killers* and *Nixon*. It was while working on these screenplays that Stone was offered a job on *Sugar Cookies*, kick-starting his career – see **Seizure**.

This book will examine the career of Oliver Stone film by film, using the method of other guides in this Virgin series: a system of categories to break the story of each film down into smaller parts ready for analysis. These categories are:

SUMMARY: A synopsis of the film in question.

ADVANCE PUBLICITY: Details on specific trailer and poster campaigns and distinctive taglines as well as less orthodox marketing techniques.

PRODUCTION HISTORY: Tracks the making of the films from inception to release.

CASTING: An analysis of the key players in each film. Also tackles questions of casting, such as 'Why was a Welsh thespian chosen to play a president of the United States?'

OLIVER'S ARMY: Not just recurring casting choices, such as Charlie Sheen or James Woods, but long-term collaborators, such as director of photography Robert Richardson and other significant behind-the-camera contributors.

CUT SCENES: Significant scenes that failed to make the final cut.

MEMORABLE QUOTES: 'Greed, for want of a better word, is good' (*Wall Street*).

GOOD VS EVIL: A discussion of morality, from black/white idealism to grey ambiguity and outright cynicism. In many cases this clash is made flesh with the characterisation of 'Good' and 'Evil' as competing influences on the protagonist.

REDEMPTION OR DAMNATION: A similar topic to the above but focussing on what judgement the film passes on its protagonist. Concentrates on the various choices made by the lead character (or characters) and his or her eventual fate.

HISTORY 101: Gives a brief historical background to Oliver Stone's work, specifically the many cases where his films are set in the context of a real historical event. Also a discussion of any manipulation of history; for example, the compression of events and/or personalities in a film for narrative reasons rather than polemical emphasis.

CONSPIRACY THEORY: Partly a look at Stone's instinctive anarchy in the context of the film – his unwillingness to believe those in authority or the established view of history. Conversely, the book will also look at instances where Stone himself makes questionable claims or assertions, where the truth is bent in the telling of a good story, or the making of a questionable point.

STARS AND STRIPES: Many of Stone's films have distinctively American settings – not just in historical terms (see above) but in other ways too: the small desert town of *U Turn*, the world of professional sports in *Any Given Sunday* and the all-American shock-jocks of *Talk Radio*. This category, where applicable, explains the film in the wider context of America.

BEING OLIVER STONE: The book is not a biography, but this category gives a chance for examination of Stone as a person in the context of his films and also to see the dynamics of his films in relation to their director.

REAL PEOPLE: In several cases, Stone bases his characters on historical figures – Richard Nixon, Jim Morrison and reporter Richard Boyle (*Salvador*), for instance. This section will look at these figures, the accuracy of their cinematic portrayal, their involvement (if any) with the filmmaking process and what they represent in the context of Stone's vision.

INSPIRATION AND INFLUENCE: Materials that inspired the films, be they in the form of books, articles or other movies, coupled with an assessment of the impact of the film upon the wider world.

REEL TIME: The technical side of Stone's filmmaking.

MUSIC: A discussion of music in his films.

BOX OFFICE: It is widely true, and especially so in the case of Oliver Stone's films, that financial success is achieved or lost in the United States. With this in mind, this category concentrates on US box office receipts.

CRITICS: A brief overview of critical reactions to the film at the time of release.

CONTROVERSY: Closely linked to, but separate from, critical judgement are issues of controversy surrounding the content or conclusions of the films. Stone has received bouquets and brickbats aplenty. Celebrated for *Platoon*, condemned in the British tabloids for *Natural Born Killers*, and regarded as both a teller of truth and arch-dissimulator for *JFK*, one thing you can't say is that people are indifferent towards him. This category focuses on media coverage of his films outside the world of film criticism.

AWARDS: Oscars, Golden Globes and other major awards. Also records nominations.

TRIVIA: Any interesting facts that do not quite fit anywhere else.

THE BIG PICTURE: How does this film fit into Stone's portfolio? It might be part of a mini-sequence; it might at first seem incongruous only to relate closely with other work on closer examination.

FINAL ANALYSIS: An unashamedly subjective view of the film in question.

This will be a comprehensive review of Oliver Stone's career, but concentrates primarily on those films he directed, from 1986's *Salvador* to 1999's *Any Given Sunday* (with a glance at 2004's *Alexander*). Shorter chapters will deal with those films on which he worked solely as screenwriter; these will include a category called **AT THE HELM**, a

OLIVER STONE Seizure

brief general look at the director of that particular film. Individual box-outs will examine Stone's work as a novelist, his production companies, his documentary work, his brief excursion into TV drama and those films for which he is credited on the screenplay but on which he had little effective influence.

Seizure (1974)

Euro-American Pictures presents
Director of Photography: Roger Racine CSC
Art Director: Najwa Stone
Wardrobe and Jewellery Design: Alexis Kirk
Edited by Nabuko Oganesoff and Oliver Stone
Music by Lee Gagnon
Music Produced by Theme Variations (Montreal)
Executive Producers: Harold Greenberg and Donald Johnston
Original Screenplay by Oliver Stone and Edward Mann
Produced by Garrard L Glenn and Jeffrey D Kapelman
Directed by Oliver Stone

CAST: Jonathan Frid (*Edmund*), Martine Beswick (*the Queen*), Joe Sirola (*Charlie*), Christina Pickles (*Nicole*), Herve Villechaize (*The Spider*), Anne Meacham (*Eunice*), Roger de Kovan (*Serge*), Troy Donahue (*Mark*), Mary Woronov (*Mikki*), Richard Cox (*Gerald*), Timothy Ousey (*Jason*), Henry Baker (*Jackal*), Lucy Bingham (*Betsy*)

SUMMARY: Edmund Blackstone is a successful writer of horror novels, plagued by bad dreams in which three strangers invade his house and kill the occupants. His wife, Nicole, has arranged a party to help him relax. Gradually the guests arrive at the house, buried deep in the forests of 'Juliet County'. Mark, a playboy friend of the couple, is first. Then Charlie Hughes, one of Edmund's old business partners, an arrogant middle-aged man with his bitchy bimbo wife Mikki. Last to arrive are Serge, an old European aristocrat (a baron) of indeterminate nationality and troubled finances, and his wife Eunice, still deeply attached to her long-dead first husband. Also present are Nicole's brother Gerald, a drunken WASP-y slacker, Jason, Edmund and Nicole's young son, and Betsy, a local girl who helps out around the house.

Around the pool, Charlie clashes with the other guests while a radio reports the escape of three inmates from a local psychiatric hospital. Edmund heads off into the woods to search for his missing dog Aziz and the audience sees Mikki and Mark together. Mikki, tired of Charlie, agrees to go to Mark's bedroom after dinner. Charlie is downstairs trying to finalise a deal in Libya, but the deal falls through. Edmund finds the dog. It is dead, hanging from a tree just as in his dream.

Dinner is tense, with Mikki and Mark flirting and Charlie taunting Serge with a cheque for $50,000, a cheque Serge humiliatingly accepts. Edmund sees a strange face at the window and drops his glass – again events prefigured in his dream – and asks Serge to see him privately. Mark retires to bed, with a pointed look at Mikki. Nicole goes to say goodnight to Jason, who is cowering with fear at his father's strange behaviour. Serge sits in Edmund's study, and tries to assure him that the dream is not coming true. Eunice goes to bed early (it is her habit to 'talk' with her dead husband). She is upstairs, brushing her hair, and talking to the mirror, addressing it as her dead husband. Suddenly a voice answers back, telling her to use the ointment a visitor will bring her to become young again in preparation of meeting her dead husband. She turns to see a strange dwarf who rubs the ointment on to her face. She laughs hysterically. Meanwhile Mark hears someone enter his darkened room. He assumes it to be Mikki, and a woman jumps on to the bed; a light reveals her as a stranger, who strangles him. Downstairs, Betsy leaves the house but, on her way through the woods, is chased by a huge man. The camera cuts away as his hand moves to her face.

Charlie, Nicole, Mikki and Gerald are in the drawing room. Suddenly, the strange dwarf from Eunice's room crashes in. He beats Charlie unconscious then turns on Nicole and Mikki. Gerald attempts to break into the study, but Edmund shoots the lock out with a revolver, accidentally killing Gerald. He and Serge run to the drawing room and while Edmund is frozen with fear, Serge attacks the dwarf but is soundly beaten. The huge man from the woods appears behind Edmund and throws him against a wall, knocking him out.

When he comes to, the guests are tied up on the floor. Mark's killer, an elegant woman in a black cloak, walks into the room. She orders that no one should ask the identity of the intruders but that everyone should do as they are told, 'though nothing will make sense', assuring them that, by the next morning, all save one will be dead. She tells them that Mark, Gerald and Eunice are dead or dying already and the others will be

killed. As the survivors are led out of the room, the camera cuts to
Eunice being shown her hideously scarred and aged visage by the dwarf,
who tells her that her first husband will no longer want her. She jumps
out of the window to her death.

Outside, Mikki, Nicole, Serge, Charlie and Edmund are lined up for a
five-lap race around the house – whoever finishes last will be killed. Serge
assures them all that he will lose, but Charlie, despite a sprint start,
collapses and clutches his chest. Mikki leaves him behind, while Nicole
and Edmund make an abortive attempt to escape in their car, before
being dragged back by the giant. Serge staggers to the line first, and sees
the body of his wife in the bushes. Charlie begs for mercy but the giant
crushes his head between his bare hands.

Nicole is taken upstairs to her room, while Serge and Edmund are
locked in the study. Mikki has made an escape bid but is quickly
retrieved. While the search for her is going on, Serge and Edmund
discuss their captors. Serge has heard what the woman calls the other
two. The dwarf is addressed as the 'Spider', and Serge believes this refers
to a nickname for the diminutive eleventh-century French king Louis the
Cruel, a madman and torturer. He thinks the huge black man – Jackal –
is named for the mute Arab slaves, taken by eighteenth-century Russians
for use as executioners. He suggests that the woman, a 'Queen of Evil', is
the embodiment of Kali, the murderous Indian goddess, simultaneously a
beautiful temptress, a mother figure and a woman of darkness. The
Spider interrupts and leads Edmund off to knife-fight Mikki in front of
the Queen. He wins, though fighting reluctantly, and the Queen attempts
to seduce him. He resists and, impressed, the Queen grants him two
hours with his wife, before taking him back.

Edmund finds her in the attic, comforting their son who has remained
hidden. Nicole holds Edmund responsible for the appearance of the
strangers, but sleeps with him one last time. Edmund awakes to the last
minute of his two hours ticking away, and to a bathroom with a farewell
message penned on the mirror in lipstick and a bloody razor blade by the
sink. Distraught, he runs downstairs to see Serge being led to his
execution by the Spider. Serge rationalises it as being 'his time' and goes
willingly after ripping up Charlie's cheque. This leaves just Edmund . . .
and Jason. He eventually betrays his son, in exchange for his own
survival, but the boy has escaped. Furious, the Queen orders the Spider
and Jackal in pursuit of Edmund, who manages to kill Jackal with an
axe. The Queen finds Jason, but the ghost of Nicole scares her off. She
promises to claim Edmund instead. In the forest, the Spider has tackled

Edmund and is throttling him when . . . the writer wakes up. Relieved at the slumbering form in bed beside him, he sleepily strolls to the bathroom. But as he splashes water on his face, he notices the lipstick farewell still on the mirror; horrified, he staggers to the bed as the Queen rips off the covers and envelops him in her cloak.

Back outside Nicole plays with Jason, telling him to wake Edmund, as the guests will soon arrive. In the bedroom Jason recoils in terror from his father's corpse, a radio voice-over tells of the death of 'the Edgar Allan Poe of modern American literature' Edmund Blackstone from a heart attack, aged 47.

PRODUCTION HISTORY: Stone was searching for a way into the film business and Lloyd Kaufman, a classmate from his early schooldays, contacted him with an offer of work. Kaufman would go on to found the Troma production house, responsible for schlocky sub-B-movies such as *Toxic Avenger* (Michael Herz, Samuel Weil, 1985), *Class of Nuke 'Em High* (Richard W Haynes, Lloyd Kaufman, 1986) and *Tromeo and Juliet* (Lloyd Kaufman, James Gunn, 1996), but in 1971 he was working with Theodore Gershuny, a similarly low-brow director, on *Sugar Cookies*, a soft-core porn film. Stone was offered a job as production assistant.

Prior to this, Stone had been polishing his latest screenplay, *Seizure*, based on a nightmare he had experienced. He worked with Santos Alcacer (a Spanish veteran of horror movies, working under the pseudonym Ed Mann) on a script, creating a surreal 'haunted house' horror film with psychological overtones. With the connections he made on the set of *Sugar Cookies*, Stone became convinced that he could put together the backing for *Seizure*. Garrard Glenn and Jeffrey Kapelman had also worked on *Sugar Cookies* and agreed to raise some money from their families. Stone himself borrowed a few thousand dollars from his father and more from some of Najwa's wealthier friends. As he recalls, 'We raised about fifty grand and made a deal with the Toronto company for the other half.' Canada had been chosen as the destination – it was and still is a cheap choice for film and TV crews on a tight budget – and cast and crew headed north. But they discovered a Toronto funding company in bankruptcy. Fortunately for them, Harold Greenberg, a Canadian mogul, agreed, with Donald Johnston, to put up the rest of the money in exchange for what amounted to total ownership of the film.

Stone wrote a broad comedy script titled *Horror Movie* that told the story of *Seizure*'s chaotic, crazy and eventful production. This had included: Herve Villechaize threatening Stone over his expected pay, at one point grabbing a knife and locking himself in a cupboard; the crew tying up the producers and rowing them to the middle of a lake, again over pay; one of the crew coming at Stone with a machete in a jealous rage, thinking that Stone was flirting with the actress the crewmember was then sleeping with. The culmination was a raid on the studio, led by a Canadian Mountie, to retrieve the print of *Seizure* that was being held hostage by the belligerent director of photography.

A planned title change to *Queen of Evil* was dropped, and *Seizure* eventually received a very limited release on New York's 42nd Street in 1974.

CREW AND CASTING: The majority of the cast were stalwarts of the B-movie horror genre. Jonathan Frid had been a key cast member of cult horror soap *Dark Shadows*, while Martine Beswick enjoyed a degree of fame based on her work with the Hammer production house. In addition she had appeared in two James Bond movies, *From Russia With Love* (Terence Young, 1963) and *Thunderball* (Terence Young, 1965). Herve Villechaize was a diminutive French actor who would go on to play Nick-Nack on another Bond film, *The Man with the Golden Gun* (Guy Hamilton, 1974). He also found fame as Ricardo Montalban's sidekick in the long-running TV series *Fantasy Island*. Mary Woronov played Mikki, and had also appeared in *Sugar Cookies*. The crew were largely amateurs, like Stone, with no vast backlog of experience and have since done nothing of note.

GOOD VS EVIL: Despite the name of the lead villain, this film cannot really be described as a clash of good and evil. At heart it is a simple exploitation horror film with psychological pretensions. A group of people meet a variety of gruesome fates, largely dictated by the individual vices of their characters. This is not morality so much as irony (see **REDEMPTION OR DAMNATION**), and the Queen's verdict on the two characters best described as 'good' (Serge and Nicole) is rendered largely meaningless as the final twist reveals the whole thing to be a dream.

Indeed, even if Serge and Nicole are seen as good, how do their actions constitute a conflict with evil? Ultimately both die. In a way this is a forerunner to American horror films of the late seventies and early eighties, films such as *Halloween* (John Carpenter, 1978), *Friday the Thirteenth* (Sean S Cunningham, 1980) and *A Nightmare on Elm Street* (Wes Craven, 1984). The forces of evil in all of these are absolute, and opposing them is little more than a struggle for survival. It could be argued that *Seizure* is a more bleakly existential film. In the last three, salvation/survival can be reached through a simple moral code of abstention from pre-marital sex, drugs and alcohol. In *Seizure*, death is inevitable, but posthumous judgement is more lenient if your conduct merits it.

REDEMPTION OR DAMNATION: This is a more fruitful theme with two layers in the film. On an individual level, the manner of each death roughly corresponds with the demeanour of the victim. Lustful Mark is lured into sex then death at the hands of the Queen. For Eunice, vanity is fatal – the ointment supposed to restore her youth disfigures her and leads to suicide. Charlie pushes himself so hard in the race, just as he pushes himself against other men in business, that he collapses. Then, pathetically, he tries to buy his way out and is killed. Mikki shows a selfish, atavistic survival instinct all the way through, kicking away her pleading husband, making a run for escape and finally attacking Edmund in the knife-fight so brutally that she pretty much falls on the blade herself. Serge and Nicole receive praise from the Queen, the closest the film ever gets to any form of redemption. Both accept the inevitability of death, rather than trying to fight it (Eunice with desire for eternal youth, Charlie with money, Mikki with animal desperation) – Nicole kills herself (it is implied) rather than fall into the Queen's hands, and Serge goes to his execution with grace, reasoning that death is near for him and believing not so much in God as his own dignity. This leaves loose ends in Betsy (whose death exists to prove Edmund's dream predictions) and Gerald, whose death is pretty much purposeless, unless one reads it as being a consequence of his cowardice.

This also leaves Edmund, whose own redemption/damnation is the second layer of interpretation. It is possible to read the whole film as a fight for Edmund's soul in the moments before his death: his dreams as a battleground. In this there is the final betrayal of his son (a betrayal foreshadowed in his eagerness to escape by car rather than try to save the other guests) as leading to a verdict of damnation. The other characters have shown him various alternatives, with Serge and Nicole putting forward the virtues of dignity in the face of inevitable death or self-sacrifice rather than betrayal, but he still takes the path of damnation. So, in the first twist the audience sees the verdict, as the Queen comes to take his soul. Finally they see his actual death.

This is just one reading of a somewhat confused film. There are unanswered questions, such as why the long exposition about the origin of the trio of evil, or why the appearance of Nicole's ghost to protect her son (which would be pointless if this were just Edmund's dream)? It is likely that these are just narrative glitches, plot-holes that few films are without. The best proof for this interpretation is in the story's origin: it began as a nightmare for Stone, involving the betrayal of an imagined son. The theme of judgement is strong in his later work, and such a betrayal would demand the highest punishment.

STARS AND STRIPES: There is something archetypal in *Seizure*'s setting, if not in its idiosyncratic and rather confusing plot. Elements of *Psycho* (Alfred Hitchcock, 1960) can be seen in the isolated house, far from civilisation and outside help. Similarly the idea of the 'escaped maniac', though a red herring here, crops up in many later films, most famously *Halloween*. It is probably not going too far to link the final dash through the woods with the primal fear of the forest, exploited in *The Blair Witch Project* (Daniel Myrick and Eduardo Sanchez, 1998). *Seizure* bears the hallmarks of a certain type of American horror film, one not relying on the supernatural by itself but on broader themes, of violation of the home (*Poltergeist*, Tobe Hooper, 1982; *Halloween*), of dreams (*A Nightmare on Elm Street*) and of the threat of the oppressive wilderness to a lone outpost (*Evil Dead II*, Sam Raimi, 1987; *Friday the Thirteenth*'s camp Crystal Lake; *Psycho*).

This is not to suggest *Seizure* is a hugely influential film, more to present it as tapping into an early trend for those looking to shock and terrify their audiences, the idea of bringing unstoppable, deadly evil into areas that a materialist modern society might assume were safe. These simple, blunt attacks on the complacency of modern America might lack the complexity of existentialist horror, such as *Nosferatu* (FW Murnau, 1921), and do owe a level of debt to the exploitative cinema of the Hammer production house, but at their best they could be greatly effective and, as the genre of slasher movie, they are fundamentally American.

BEING OLIVER STONE: This film is of the greatest interest as the only one of Stone's early screenplays to be filmed (save *Last Year in Viet Nam*). It displays the themes of over-analysis and excessive psychological pretension that mark out the plot of these films, as well as a dreamlike surrealism and a tendency to fatalistic pessimism. These common factors could be interpreted as an attempt to process the immense impact of Vietnam, before he reached a point where he could make the war itself the subject.

It is a fairly impressive achievement, demonstrating the iron will he would show in the industry proper, as well as a predilection for the guerrilla filmmaking that would ensure completion of *Salvador*. In this can be seen the commitment to his work that kept the young artist (28 at the time *Seizure* was made) going through the years of rejection that preceded *Midnight Express*.

INSPIRATION AND INFLUENCE: The timing of *Seizure* technically qualifies Stone as a participant in the Hollywood New Wave. This was an informal phenomenon that struck Hollywood in the late 1960s, beginning roughly with *Bonnie and Clyde* (Arthur Penn, 1967). The earlier French New Wave (directors such as Jean-Luc Godard, Alain Resnais and Luis Bunuel) had its roots in theory – the film criticism of *Cahiers du Cinema* and the teachings of newly established university courses in film – specifically *auteur* theory. The exact definition of this theory remains contested even today, but broadly nominated the director as the heart of a film, its guiding, shaping force.

This period in American cinema saw the first generation of directors to have been educated at film schools, and several adopted a similar approach – shaping daring personal visions that went against the grain of conventional Hollywood movies, reinvigorating a moribund industry. Several directors who would later work with Stone can be identified in this movement: Michael Cimino, Hal Ashby and John Milius, as well as former lecturer Martin Scorsese. Though there was nothing necessarily new in what they were doing (and that is part of the point; even the French directors had declared inspiration from earlier Hollywood directors such as Howard Hawks, Orson Welles and Alfred Hitchcock), it was the convergence of talent at a point where movies were losing their lustre, which was significant. For a time these individuals brought a spark to movie production, until they were brought down by the hubris of their increasingly excessive demands, for instance, the box office disaster of *Heaven's Gate* (Michael Cimino, 1980).

Stone came from this stable: an intellectual, educated in the medium, who set out to make an eccentric and challenging (if flawed) film. He did not, at this point, have anything near the status or backing of a Francis Coppola or a Scorsese, but it is interesting that this similarly distinctive filmmaker had his origins, be they ever so humble, in this cinematic era.

REEL TIME: The editing and photography of *Seizure* is primitive but broadly effective, though too sluggish to produce the knee-jerk shocks that normally characterise the slasher flick (*The Hand* was similarly afflicted). There are some nice sequences: the disjointed cutting and different filters used in the strangling of Mark look good, as do a sudden freeze frame on Eunice's withered face, the killing of Charlie conducted in silhouette and a rapid montage of shots just before Edmund's death, all of which help break up the rest of the film.

MUSIC: The score for the film is absolutely terrible. The credits list it as 'composed' by Theme Variations (Montreal), probably a company specialising in providing cheap ready-made scores for low-budget films. The music is intrusive, has a tendency to cut out suddenly between scenes and shifts drastically in mood. Each surprise is accompanied by a bellowing orchestral chord, to leave no one in any doubt that something *very significant* has happened. It is a bad oversight that handicaps the film.

BOX OFFICE: When it came to financing *Seizure*, Stone and his partners struck a most unfavourable deal. They received funding as part of a tax scam from a company basically uninterested in any commercial marketing of the film. A consequence has been the relegation of the film to a sort of limbo – box office returns remain a mystery and the movie itself is only available in a limited way (it finally saw video release in the wake of *Born on the Fourth of July* in 1989) even to its director: 'When I get contacts about getting the film to show in England, there's not a thing I can do about it.'

CRITICS: The film had a very limited run in New York as part of a double-bill programme. As such, there was precious little critical coverage, though Vincent Canby wrote favourably in the *New York Times*: 'the screenplay includes two or three too many twists but there is some genuinely funny, waspish dialogue.' Others were less complimentary. The *New York Daily News* critic wrote of it as 'a sadomasochistic ditty that ought to have an aspirin break'. A brief review in *Variety* described it simply as a 'stylishly filmed but . . . murkily plotted horror film'.

THE BIG PICTURE: As mentioned above (see **BEING OLIVER STONE**), *Seizure* is relevant primarily for what it says about Stone as a filmmaker at the time of its release. However, it has little in common with work from *Salvador* onwards. The one film it could be compared with is *The Hand*. Both are rather muddled efforts, with superficial ambitions to profundity in conflict with the structure and appearance of exploitative horror movies.

FINAL ANALYSIS: This is not a great horror film, nor a great psychological thriller. Its shocks are not shocking, its twists a little predictable and its drama overwrought (and not helped by the off-the-shelf soundtrack). It remains interesting as a curio, and quite entertaining thanks to some good acting from a stable of genre veterans and a snappy script – Stone's potential is clearly visible here – though it does tail off into pretension towards the end.

There is something endearing about its cheap surrealism and the seriousness with which it regards itself. It is also amusing to note that, with all the pretensions stripped away, this is ultimately the sort of slasher film derided in *Talk Radio*.

Midnight Express (1978)

Columbia Pictures presents
A Casablanca Filmworks Production
Music by Giorgio Moroder
Editor: Gerry Hambling
Production Designer: Geoffrey Kirkland
Executive Producer: Peter Guber
Based on the book by William Hayes with William Hoffer
Screenplay by Oliver Stone
Produced by Alan Marshall and David Puttnam
Directed by Alan Parker

CAST: Brad Davis (*Billy Hayes*), Irene Miracle (*Susan*), Bo Hopkins (*Tex*), Paolo Bonacelli (*Rifki*), Paul Smith (*Hamidou*), Randy Quaid (*Jimmy Booth*), Norbert Weisser (*Erich*), John Hurt (*Max*), Tranco Diogene (*Yesil*), Mike Kellin (*Mr Hayes*), Michael Ensign (*Stanley Daniels*), Gigi Ballista (*Chief Judge*), Kevork Malikyan (*Prosecutor*)

SUMMARY: 'The following is based on a true story. It began October 6 1970 in Istanbul, Turkey.'

Billy Hayes is caught trying to fly back to America with 2 kilos of hashish. Initially promised leniency in exchange for identifying the dealer, he attempts to flee his police shadow and is thrown in jail. He steals a blanket for his bare bed but is discovered and beaten by the thuggish chief guard Hamidou.

Later he is moved to the foreigners' wing where he meets volcanic American Jimmy, calm Swede Erich and half-crazed Englishman Max, who advises that Billy catch the 'midnight express' – break out. They point out Rifki, a spiv and snitch who hoards money and informs on the other prisoners whenever he gets the chance. Billy is reunited with his father and meets the American consul and a lawyer, Yesil, recommended by Max. Yesil has Billy's charge downgraded from smuggling to possession, and he gets four years' jail.

Prison life is harsh and brutal and made worse by Rifki. One night, irritated by Max, he hangs the man's pet cat. Escape plans are mooted, one by Yesil, another by Jimmy (to go through subterranean tunnels). Billy rejects both, choosing to sit out the sentence. Jimmy is caught going over the roof and beaten. Billy and Erich become close, but Billy gently rejects the Swede's homosexual advances – Erich is later released.

With 54 days to go, the Turkish Supreme Court extends Billy's sentence to thirty years. Billy is stunned, and elects to go ahead with Jimmy's escape plan. They break into the catacombs but the tunnels are blocked. Rifki finds the entrance and tells the guards, who haul off Jimmy, who is never seen again. Max is enraged, and he plots with Billy to destroy Rifki's beloved stash of money. They burn the cash and Rifki is left penniless. But on the day of his release Rifki frames Max by planting hashish in his pocket. Billy cracks under the pressure, savagely tearing into Rifki, gouging his eyes and biting his tongue off.

'Section 13 for the criminally insane. January 1975, 7 months later.' Billy is slowly going insane, while Max has lost his mind completely. Billy's girlfriend Susan visits with a photo-album packed with hidden hundred dollar bills. Billy tries to bribe Hamidou, who tricks the American, taking him to a deserted room for a beating. But in a freak accident the guard is killed, with his head impaled on a coat hook. Billy grabs his uniform and strolls out of the front gate. A closing caption, 'On the night of October 4 1975, Billy Hayes successfully crossed the border to Greece. He arrived home at Kennedy Airport three weeks later.' The film finishes with a black-and-white photomontage of reconciliation with his family.

PRODUCTION HISTORY: *Seizure* caused barely a ripple in the film industry, and Stone was back to the same odd-jobs that had sustained him on his graduation from NYU, pounding out screenplays in his spare time.

One of these was titled *The Cover Up*. Completed in 1975 it dealt with a wide-ranging conspiracy (including the intelligence community) to discredit left-wing radical groups. A criminal is bust out of prison by a secret group and given instructions to kidnap the daughter of a rich businessman. After distributing the $3million ransom to the poor he is ordered to kill the child, but disobeys and goes on the run. The film ends with the unmasking of the conspiracy but also the deaths of the criminal anti-hero and the young girl.

A product of mid-1970s paranoia like *Three Days of the Condor* (Sydney Pollack, 1975) or *The Parallax View* (Alan J Pakula, 1974; see **JFK**), *The Cover Up* was Stone's first work to have the advantage of contemporary resonance. It came to the attention of producer Fernando Ghia, who passed it to screenwriter Robert Bolt. Bolt was riding high off three highly respected scripts: *Lawrence of Arabia* (David Lean, 1962), *Doctor Zhivago* (David Lean, 1965) and *A Man for All Seasons* (Fred Zinnemann, 1966), the last two winning Academy Awards for best adapted screenplay. And now he wanted to meet Oliver Stone.

They worked together on a final draft of *The Cover Up*, but the film failed to arouse much interest. However, Stone had gained invaluable experience from the working relationship with Bolt and the regular trips to Los Angeles, including an entrée to the William Morris agency, who took him on as a client.

Stone returned to New York, where his marriage to Najwa Sarkis was on the verge of break-up. The couple eventually parted amicably and he went back to writing, turning out several (currently unfilmed) screenplays: *The Rascals* (semi-autobiographical account of decadent young artists in 1970s New York), *Brazil Run* (CIA agents hunting Nazis in South America) and *The Life and Times of Deacon Davis* (government conspiracy based around the life of Black Panther activist George Jackson). It was this period that also saw the writing of *Platoon*. In 1976 Stone went back west, returning to the contacts made on his earlier expedition in an attempt to sell this Vietnam movie.

In January the previous year, William Hayes had returned to the US after over four years in a Turkish prison. His account was published as *Midnight Express*, and attracted the interest of top British producer David (now Lord) Puttnam, who asked his friend Alan Parker to direct. They needed a script and took the project to Columbia. Peter Guber, head of Casablanca Filmworks and a man with contacts at Columbia, had seen the script for *Platoon* and loved it; Stone was hired to write *Midnight Express*, which he did over the winter of 1977. After shooting on location in Malta, the film was released in 1978.

AT THE HELM: Sir Alan Parker was a key member of the British invasion of Hollywood, an ephemeral movement of the 1980s characterised in the hubristic cry of 'The British are coming!' by Colin Welland after *Chariots of Fire* (Hugh Hudson, 1981) took the Oscar for best screenplay. This was followed by the brief appointment of David Puttnam as chairman of Columbia in 1986 (an appointment that delayed production of *The Doors*).

For a short time British film seemed on the verge of a major breakthrough, and Parker was on the front line. In addition to *Midnight Express*, he directed *Bugsy Malone* (1976), *Fame* (1980) and *Mississippi Burning* (1988). In truth though, this was just an import of talent; the money and power remained (with the exception of Puttnam) in American hands.

Parker's work with Stone is comparable with that of Brian De Palma. Both stick closely to a brutal and bloody script, there is a feeling of integrity and no evidence of the compromise that would blunt *Year of the Dragon* or outside intervention that would dilute later films (see **The Ones That Got Away**, p. 47). It is perhaps no coincidence that *Midnight Express* and *Scarface* were Stone's most successful films as screenwriter. Given the overblown, violent and racist undertones of both films, of which the script is a key part, some might find reason to object to their success. Both films are undeniably coherent, cogent visions.

Parker's main difference is a dramatic earnestness that De Palma translates into broad burlesque. The opening sequence of *Midnight Express* is incredibly tense and the violence is presented with unflinching savagery. It has the power of a punch to the stomach, while *Scarface*, for all its bloodletting, is fantasy – criminal excess turned to self-parody: both are different interpretations of Stone's relentless writing style.

MEMORABLE QUOTES: For all its admirable structure, there are some sentiments expressed in this film that can be interpreted as nothing other than racist. The worst comes in the second courtroom scene:
Billy: 'You know, for a nation of pigs it sure is funny you don't eat them.'

GOOD VS EVIL: In a simple reversal, quite common to the genre of prison movies, the moral status of criminals and prison wardens are flipped – the basically good prisoners struggling against a corrupt, repressive regime.

This is complicated by the racial element, which leaves a nasty taste in the mouth. All Turkish characters – prisoners, guards, police, legal staff – are portrayed as corrupt, brutal, stupid, vicious and dirty. By comparison, the whites are clean and decent. They pull together, are kind, compassionate and earnest. Even the mysterious embassy official who recaptures Billy after an escape attempt at the start of the film has a compassionate side. Thus the real delineation is not between the establishment and those who fall foul of it but between whites and Turks. In *The Blood Poets* Jake Horsley described *Midnight Express* as 'an exploitative, masochistic fantasy of incarceration in a strange land, every white man's worst fear of the Dark Continent'.

If one can ignore this racism, the film is powerful in its condemnation of arbitrary jail terms for offences whose severity is contingent on the spirit of the time. But this is a weak message swamped by the movie's heavy racial stereotyping. There is no attempt on the film's part to make allowances for the customs of a foreign land, for a different culture with different priorities and beliefs. Racial origin becomes shorthand for good and bad. World War II POW films went further to present a balanced view of Nazis than this film does with Turks.

REDEMPTION OR DAMNATION: Billy's personal journey is to hell. He is condemned to this within twenty minutes and the rest of the film tells of his return. At its most powerful, this mythic form relies on a wrongfully convicted innocent – *The Shawshank Redemption* (Frank Darabont, 1994). Here, a quirk of the factual inspiration for the film necessitates that the protagonist be found guilty, but this is so downplayed as to become negligible guilt, heightening the sense of vicious injustice. This is repellent logic. The film makes Billy's imprisonment an issue of punishment relative to the scale of the crime. The script goes out of its way to qualify this crime: the airport police were searching for explosives, not drugs, they mock Billy's stash, it is suggested that he is a political prisoner, detained as a result of Nixon's clash with Turkey, that bigger smugglers have purchased their freedom. Never does the issue of personal responsibility arise – Billy knowingly carried drugs out of the country and, if he had the slightest degree of sense, would know the risk he took. But this isn't the focus of the film. Stone wanted to make Billy a martyr to a vicious prison system, whereas he comes across as a rather stupid American teen who can't take responsibility for his own actions.

In a sense, the trajectory is one of moral redemption but only at the cost of vilifying the Turks to the point of xenophobia, and turning Billy into a tragic hero out of all proportion to his adolescent dope-smuggling antics.

BEING OLIVER STONE: On return from Vietnam, Stone had drifted down America's west coast, ending up in Mexico, where he remained for just a few days before heading back north. He still had a small amount of the marijuana he'd spirited out of Asia, just enough to land him in a San Diego jail on smuggling charges when he was busted at the border. He spent nearly two weeks in an overcrowded jail (3000 beds for some 15000 inmates at his estimation) before calling up his father who arranged for Stone's release.

Though scarcely on a scale with Hayes's own experiences, Stone could employ a degree of empathy. In addition, and given his justified reputation for hard partying, it is unsurprising that the screenwriter imbued the script with his own sense of distaste for draconian drug-smuggling legislation. One detail found its way into the script: Stone compared the public defender (whose interest in Stone's case was suddenly enlivened by Lou Stone's money) with the greedy Yesil.

Though Stone's script was largely stuck to by Alan Parker, the screenwriter got little chance to see his work being filmed – he was never invited to the Maltese set.

INSPIRATION AND INFLUENCE: The book, published in 1977, tells a different tale from the film. Broadly speaking the circumstances of arrest and original imprisonment are the same, even down to the intimidating figure from the US embassy (though Billy had more than one girlfriend – one he was hoping to meet after his return to the States and an older girlfriend who supported him during his prison term).

The book better spells out the conditions of Sagmalcilar jail, where Billy was imprisoned, and the wider range of fellow foreign occupants: Jimmy is a composite of a variety of nationalities, Arne was recreated as Erich, while Max appears very much as in the film – though he did not end up in the wing for the mentally ill. The relationship with Scandinavian prisoner Arne was implicitly physical in the book and rejected in the film (though not in a homophobic way). Stone has since said that, in the current climate, such obfuscation could be avoided. In *Alexander* he is set to back up this suggestion on screen.

But these details are cosmetic compared with the alteration of Billy's time in jail. Though he did spend time in a prison for the mentally ill

(Bakirkoy), this was due to his American medical records listing exemption from service in Vietnam on psychological grounds, and part of a deliberate escape plan. He was eventually returned to his original place of imprisonment. Other escape attempts are mentioned in the course of the book, but most involve bribery; none mention digging into the catacombs and the only one with which Billy was involved was a scheme to file through the bars of their window.

His opportunity actually came after transfer to a labour camp on Imrali, an island in the Sea of Marmora (between the Dardanelles and the Bosphorus). He managed to swim out to a fishing vessel and steal the rowing boat, landing on Turkey's European shore. He then underwent a tense journey to Istanbul. From there he made an arduous trek to the Greek border.

In fairness to the film, accurately re-creating such sequences, as full of dramatic potential as they appear on the page, would have shifted emphasis from the prison movie storyline in a disorientating way. However, this has left a ripe seam of material to be mined and, in late 2003, Miramax announced its intention to film a sequel to *Midnight Express* titled *Escape*. It is to be directed by Russell Mulcahy – *Highlander* (1986), *The Shadow* (1996) – and based on Billy Hayes's own sequel to his prison memoirs, *The Return*.

A few other films have dealt with the premise of *Midnight Express*. *Brokedown Palace* (Jonathan Kaplan, 1999) told of three Westerners imprisoned in a Thai jail. *Return to Paradise* (Joseph Ruben, 1998) took a more intriguing tack, posing a question to two young Americans: would they return to Malaysia to help a friend facing the death penalty, and so run the risk of being imprisoned themselves? This is not as original as it seems, being a remake of the French film *Force Majeure* (Pierre Jolivet, 1989).

The circumstances of Billy's escape may have been fabricated for the film but have become popular for later films. The female assassin in *La Femme Nikita* (Luc Besson, 1990) makes her getaway from a foreign embassy in the uniform of a guard. Most recently *Welcome to Collinwood* (Anthony and Joe Russo, 2002) almost exactly copied this means of escape to allow criminal Luis Guzman back on the streets after a prison guard suffers a heart attack.

AWARDS: The film picked up a smattering of awards at the Golden Globes and the BAFTAs. Giorgio Moroder won an Oscar for his score. Of the greatest importance to Oliver Stone, however, was the Academy

Award he won for Best Screenplay Adapted from Another Medium. It wasn't a strong field; he beat out *Blood Brothers* (Robert Mulligan, 1978), *California Suite* (Herbert Ross, 1978), *Heaven Can Wait* (Warren Beatty and Buck Henry, 1978) and *Same Time, Next Year* (Robert Mulligan, 1978). On reception of the award, Stone made a typically outspoken speech, hoping that it would lead to 'some consolation for all the men and women who are still in prison tonight'.

THE BIG PICTURE: Manipulative, distasteful melodrama this may be, but it also bears the hallmarks of Stone's later films – the blunt uncompromising approach, brutal violence and critical judgement on society, all conveyed with an unmitigated certainty. This was also the first to find its basis in a true story – all his movies post-*Salvador* (save *U Turn* and *Natural Born Killers*) would employ a certain amount of factual source material.

The racism bears some comparison with *Scarface* and *Year of the Dragon*. However, in this case the offence is exacerbated by the bleeding-heart true-story credentials that the movie trades on, an approach that exaggerates cruel prison treatment to a national characteristic.

THE FINAL ANALYSIS: *Midnight Express* attempts to preach a sermon on injustice, but it launches too strident a lecture from too shaky a foundation. But the film is powerful on a purely emotional level, and part of the credit belongs to Stone's script. The script must also bear the blame for one of the film's major shortfalls – Billy's courtroom speech, which aspires to be a great movie monologue, but ends up a crude diatribe.

It is best to appreciate this film on a purely visceral level, and not to dwell too long on the ethical muddle at its core.

The Hand (1981)

An Edward R Pressman/Ixtlan Production
Casting: Barbara Clemen BCI
Music Composed by James Horner
Editor: Richard Marks
Production Designer: John Michael Riva
Director of Photography: King Baggot
Executive Producer: Clark L Paylow

Based on the book *The Lizard's Tail* **by Marc Brandel**
Screenplay by Oliver Stone
Produced by Edward R Pressman
Directed by Oliver Stone

PRINCIPAL CAST: Michael Caine (*Jon Lansdale*), Andrea Marcovicci (*Anne Lansdale*), Annie McEnroe (*Stella Roche*), Bruce McGill (*Brian Ferguson*), Viveca Lindfors (*Doctress*), Rosemary Murphy (*Karen Wagner*), Mara Hobel (*Lizzie Lansdale*)

NOTABLE CREDITS: Medical and Psychiatric Consultant: Stuart Lerner MD. Oliver Stone's use of expert consultants dates back to this early film.

The opening credits are rendered in a handwritten calligraphic style – pretty, but in places almost impossible to read.

SUMMARY: Jonathan Lansdale is the illustrator and writer of the comic strip *Mandro*, a derivative clone of *Conan the Barbarian*. He is also the father of a young daughter, Lizzie, and husband to wife Anne, who is unhappy with their home, deep in the countryside of Vermont, and discontented with her life. She has little independence from her husband.

They argue about her desire to buy a small flat in New York. She wishes to study yoga and, on a drive to the city, it becomes clear that she wants to spend time separate from Jon. They argue and both are distracted, leading to an accident; Anne is fine but Jon loses his right hand. Anne searches the fields with police but they are unable to find it.

Jon recovers, but is unable to continue drawing *Mandro* left-handed. He also begins to suffer hallucinations about the severed hand and disturbing blackouts. Meanwhile, his life is crumbling around him, despite a powerful new prosthetic limb. The couple move to New York, where Anne is attracted to her lithe young yoga instructor, Bill Richman, and Jon is feuding with his agent. She suggests a younger artist take over the strip but Jon is enraged with the idea. He bellows at Anne and, at a meeting with the agent the next day, he discovers the artist's sample boards disfigured with ink. On his way back to the apartment he encounters a tramp who is also missing a limb. The tramp is then attacked and apparently killed by the rogue hand.

Jon moves out to take up a lecturing post in a run-down west coast college, where he meets a psyche professor, Brian Ferguson. Anne advises that he 'meet new people', promising to travel out to California come Christmas. He begins sleeping with Stella Roche, one of his students. One night he discovers an obscene drawing in her sketchbook, a drawing that he apparently made without either the ability or any memory of doing so. He tells Ferguson, who warns him that this was an act of his subconscious, that his inner desires have been released making him capable of anything, even murder.

Stella becomes more distant as Christmas approaches, and Jon discovers that she intends to spend the holidays with Ferguson in an LA motel. Later that night Stella returns to Jon's house where she is strangled by Lansdale's hand. Jon drives to Reno where he spends time alone, drinking.

Lizzie and Anne arrive for Christmas, but Anne shows no intention of staying for any length of time – she means to start a new life with Bill Richman. Jon becomes angry, especially over the fate of their daughter, and when his wife drives out to a supermarket he hallucinates her death at the hand of his renegade limb. However, she eventually returns safely.

Jon bumps into Ferguson, who is drowning his sorrows after apparently being stood up by Stella. The psychology professor becomes suspicious of Jon and threatens to go to the police. The hand attacks him in his van, choking Ferguson to death. Jon returns to his house and has another row with his wife, who intends to take Lizzie with her. As Jon beds down in a spare room, the hand creeps into Anne's room and attacks her. He hears the struggle and rushes after the hand. He tracks it into the garage where it attacks him, strangling him until he passes out. However, when awakened by police, it is his own left hand around his neck. Anne will be fine, but the cops appear suspicious, especially about a bad smell coming from the boot of Jon's car – the decomposing bodies of Stella and Brian.

In a coda, Jon is hooked up to an elaborate ECG machine, being interviewed by a female doctor. She tells him that he tapped into an ancient evil, that he committed all the crimes as a manifestation of his own hate, anger and desires – Ferguson was killed because 'his actions were threatening, interfered with your will.' The women also went against his will, leading to the attacks in the midst of blackout. Anne only survived because 'love [for Lizzie] brought you consciousness.' Then, Jon's scans go haywire and the hand leaps upon the doctor's throat, killing her. Jon cackles maniacally as he loosens his restraints and the film ends on a freeze-frame.

PRODUCTION HISTORY: *Midnight Express* had been a big hit, and Orion offered to fund a modestly budgeted film directed by Oliver Stone.

Stone had worked with Ed Pressman on *Conan the Barbarian* (see **The Ones That Got Away**, p. 47) and asked him to come on board as producer. Initially, the plan was to develop *Baby Boy*, a story about a prison relationship between two men, similar to *Midnight Express*. Stone had been working on the idea with Richard Rutowski, carrying out research trips to high-security prisons across the US, and the two had become close friends, Rutowski would work on later films, from *The Doors* through to *U Turn*. However, Stone decided to ditch this idea, choosing instead to develop a script based on a novel by Marc Brandel, *The Lizard's Tail*, a psychological thriller about a cartoonist whose severed limb might be killing people on his behalf. Stone gave his screenplay the less ambiguous title *The Hand*. There was a fundamental disparity from the very start: a book where the main question was whether the hand had actually taken on a murderous life of its own or whether the protagonist is unconsciously murdering those who oppose him, and where the limb in question was never directly seen, was replaced by a bizarre monster movie, where the hand would play a visible – if still peripheral – part.

Nearly $1 million of the $6.5 million budget was spent on a batch of eight mechanical hands, put together by special effects legend Carlo Rimbaldi, each one specially designed for a different action, crawling, walking, strangling, etc. Stone was perfectly happy with the working of the models but, as he said at the time, '[Rimbaldi] worked so hard and long on those mechanicals that he let the make-up go a bit.' Renowned make-up specialists Stan Winston and Tom Burman were recruited to work on the appearance of the models.

Stone explains the shift to a more traditional horror film because of external forces: 'There was a lot of studio pressure, I wanted the picture to succeed, so I bowed. The trouble was the studio wanted more hand.' The result is a somewhat uneasy hybrid of schlocky horror and tense psychological thriller. It is this attempt to have its cake and eat it that is the film's main fault.

The shoot lasted nearly 80 days (including 20 set aside for filming sequences with the hand) and was shot on location and sound stages around LA, culminating in a session in the San Bernardino Mountains. It was released on 29 April 1981.

CASTING: Jon Voight, Dustin Hoffman, and Christopher Walken all turned down the part of Jon Lansdale. Into the breach stepped Michael Caine, who boasts perhaps the most varied CV of any actor still working. He has made some great films, such as *Alfie* (Lewis Gilbert, 1966), *Get Carter* (Mike Hodges, 1971) and, more recently, *The Quiet American* (Philip Noyce, 2002), and some terrible films, such as *The Swarm* (Irwin Allen, 1978), *Jaws: The Revenge* (Joseph Sargant, 1987), and has won two Oscars – *Hannah and her Sisters* (Woody Allen, 1986) and *The Cider House Rules* (Lasse Hallström, 1999). In his autobiography, Caine gave two reasons for taking the film: 'one, it was a horror film and I had never done one before and, two, the director . . . impressed me.' The overriding impression, however, is that this was the sort of film Caine became infamous for in the 1980s – a case of just turning up to collect the money. This is perhaps a little harsh. Caine is actually quite good, with the same slit-eyed lizard glare he used for Jack Carter, and an explosive rage. He is reliably watchable, even in mediocre performances, and is the best thing in the film.

Andrea Marcovicci was a respected stage actress (she played Ophelia opposite Sam Waterston's Hamlet – he played Richard Helms in *Nixon*) whose few screen credits include *The Concorde: Airport '79* (David Lowell, 1979). She is also a trained singer, and 1993 saw her solo Carnegie Hall debut, with the American Symphony Orchestra. Her Anne Lansdale is a fairly undemanding and unsympathetic character – despite Jon's rage, possessiveness and that he's a control freak, the script and film still manage to paint her as in the wrong. This taints a perfectly adequate performance. Bruce McGill has, along with Caine, the most prolific career of the main stars. His biggest role was as crazed biker fraternity member D-Day in fraternity comedy *National Lampoon's Animal House* (John Landis, 1978) but he has also appeared in a wide range of movies, including the socially conscientious melodrama *Silkwood* (Mike Nichols, 1983), gross-out juvenilia *Shallow Hal* (Bobby Farrelly, Peter Farrelly, 2001) and con-trick comedies such as *Matchstick Men* (Ridley Scott, 2002) – anywhere where a stocky figure of pomposity or insanity is needed. He provides solid support here, his Ferguson the embodiment of slacker West Coast academia – drunk, lazy and prone to over-analysis.

Dr David Maddow was played by Charles Fleischer, who is probably most famous for a film in which he did not actually appear – he provided the voice of Roger Rabbit in *Who Framed Roger Rabbit?* (Robert Zemeckis, 1988).

OLIVER'S ARMY: Annie McEnroe (Stella) appeared in several of Stone's later movies, though never as more than a cameo. In *Wall Street* she played a guest at Gekko's dinner party, Muffie Livingston; in *Born on* *the Fourth of July* a passer-by at the Democratic Convention; a secretary in *The Doors* and a Thanksgiving dinner guest in *Heaven and Earth*. In *The Hand* she plays the treacherous whore to Anne Lansdale's treacherous harpy – it is not a good film for strong female characterisation. Oliver Stone made his first acting cameo as the murdered tramp.

Edward Pressman was, and is, one of the most important independent producers in contemporary American cinema. He has had a hand in many movies, but few are regarded as classics – exceptions include *Badlands* (Terrence Malick, 1973) and *Das Boot*, a.k.a. *The Boat* (Wolfgang Petersen, 1981). Instead, he has been most significant in championing the early projects of individuals who would later rise to prominence, including Malick and Petersen but also Brian De Palma and Oliver Stone. He has enjoyed the longest, if a rather intermittent, professional association with Stone, having been the best man to Stone's second wedding (to Elizabeth), helping him with this movie, producing *Wall Street* and *Talk Radio* and then becoming involved with films made through Ixtlan. Most recently he was involved in *American Psycho* (Mary Harron, 2000) – see **Any Given Sunday**.

None of the other major crewmembers on *The Hand* would work with Stone again, but several would go on to enjoy successful careers. This hugely experienced crew was not the boon to Stone that it may appear. He commented in a 1987 interview, 'I'd been advised to hire a very experienced colleague for each job, and I was miserable during all the filming. I didn't like working with them.' He described his preferred method thus: 'I find it much more interesting to work with new people who share the joy of discovery with you.'

The biggest name among the crew is James Horner, now one of the most successful composers in Hollywood – Oscar winner (*Titanic*) and six-time nominee (*A Beautiful Mind*, *Apollo 13*, *Braveheart*, *Field of Dreams*, *An American Tail* and *Aliens*). The fairly undistinguished jittering of *The Hand* represents an early period in his career.

Respectable careers would be enjoyed by Richard Marks (editor – *Serpico*, Sidney Lumet, 1973; *The Godfather – Part II*, Francis Ford Coppola, 1974; *Apocalypse Now*, Coppola, 1979; and *Broadcast News*, James L Brooks, 1987, for which he was Oscar nominated) and J Michael Riva (production designer – *The Color Purple*, Steven Spielberg, 1985; *Lethal Weapon*s I, II and IV and, most recently, the bombastic mayhem of *Charlie's Angels*, McG, 2000, and *Charlie's Angels: Full Throttle*, McG, 2003).

After this point Stone would tend to work with a select crew who would return from film to film. When they moved on, he would usually find their successors from within the ranks – establishing a loose form of apprenticeship.

Respected comic-book artist Barry Windsor-Smith provided Jonathan Lansdale's illustrations for *Mandro*. At various times he wrote and drew artwork for several Marvel titles, including *X-Men*, *Daredevil* and *Fantastic Four*. Intriguingly, Windsor-Smith was also the original artist on the *Conan the Barbarian* comic book (1970–3), based on the novels from which the film of the same title had drawn its influence.

MEMORABLE QUOTES:
Lansdale: 'You don't cut the balls off Superman.'

GOOD VS EVIL: As with several later films, *Scarface*, *Natural Born Killers* and *U Turn,* there is little objectively good (or, indeed, likeable) about the protagonist. In a sense the film is a study of selfishness and control – Lansdale loses the ability to shape his cartoon world and flies into a rage over a similar impotence to control reality.

Michael Caine plays him well, but the man is ultimately a thug, with none of the warped ideals of the anti-hero (such as Stanley White in *Year of the Dragon*), nor the attractive flamboyance of a vaudeville villain (such as Tony Montana in *Scarface*), nor any sense of development or growing consciousness throughout the story (like Mickey and Mallory in *Natural Born Killers*). The only good in him is a love for his daughter and that is an obsession too. Everyone else is, as the psychiatrist points out at the end, an obstacle to his desires.

This in itself would not be bad, if the desires were identifiable and suitably grand as to allow for ultimate hubris, but there is little indication of what the character wants, beyond a fling with an attractive co-ed and access to his daughter. However, there is an interesting association between the fate of the character Mandro and that of his creator. Lansdale denounces the introduction of abstract psychology into the strip, specifically, the desires of the unconscious (as he says, 'Mandro knows what he wants. Mandro doesn't think'); he even makes an explicit reference to the redesigned character by showing unhappiness at the introductions of hallucinations – an experience he appears to be going through.

Ultimately, these are gimmicky touches that do little to resolve the more fundamental flaw: it's difficult to care about such an unsympathetic character in such a tawdry scenario, especially when the monstrous 'supernatural' force, though psychologically understandable (it drew fantasy now and, through it, Lansdale subconsciously achieves his fantasies), is, well, a bit rubbish.

Stone is often criticised for his treatment of female characters. This film is a prime example why. Not so much a dogged misogyny (though he comes close at times), but a tendency to draw them as needy obstacles to the protagonist. In this case, however, the move is deliberate: to the self-obsessed control freak Lansdale, they are obstacles.

REDEMPTION OR DAMNATION: As with *Seizure*, there are a couple of ways to read this film, not so much due to deliberate subtlety in composition as ambiguity in its messy conclusion. On the one hand the audience is asked to believe that Lansdale is saved from killing his wife by the redemptive power of love for his daughter. On the other, the man has already killed three people out of blind rage – little sense of salvation here. The viewers are led to believe that the darkness in his soul has been banished and that 'love . . . brought you to consciousness', but this turns out to be untrue, and for no other reason than to provide a shock finish.

Perhaps this is the ultimate triumph of his urges over any remaining semblance of reasonable humanity, but it is more likely simply to indicate a rather muddled attitude towards the movie, resulting in a compromise finish: unsatisfying if one is looking for a psychological reading of the movie, and rather weak if one seeks more visceral thrills.

BEING OLIVER STONE: This was Stone's first shot at a major production and he blew it. To be fair, this does not so much appear to have been through technical incompetence as misjudgement, studio interference and a bad choice of genre. Biographer James Riordan, on the subject of abandoning development of *Baby Boy,* says, 'because of his desire to become established as a director as quickly as possible, he didn't listen to his instincts.' Instead of a tense prison melodrama he would choose a potentially more marketable horror film.

In the light of *Seizure* and *The Hand* it is perhaps understandable that Stone has never returned to this genre. In addition, while the former was a manifestation of his more deliberately abstract phase (one of his first, ambitiously psychological, semi-autobiographical scripts), the latter was a more cynical project all together; Stone had moved on, had already written *Midnight Express, Born on the Fourth of July* and *Platoon* and had found a direction, just not the studio muscle to back it. The failure of this movie would make such backing even less likely for the foreseeable future. One further episode in Stone's life is noted in the credits. In 1979 Stone had met and fallen in love with Elizabeth Cox, described as Assistant to the Director. Their relationship would last until the late 1990s (see **Natural Born Killers**).

INSPIRATION AND INFLUENCE: *The Lizard's Tail* was a psychological novel, with supernatural traces, published in 1980. Broadly speaking, Stone's adaptation was very close. Some changes were cosmetic. Jon Lansdale was originally Martin Trask, illustrator of a successful comic strip detailing the misadventures of Mexican peasant *Miguel* – social commentary more than a fantasy strip. It is likely that *Mandro* was created as more visually effective on film – it is easy to understand the concept from a brief glimpse of one frame. Elements of the book were lost and some details simplified to fit the 287 pages into a film. Also dropped was a detailed account of the fate of Jon/Martin's wife. Brandel makes it clear that she has been paralysed from the waist down. This dovetails with the book's conclusion, where Trask is acquitted of Stella's murder (Brian does not die in the book) as all evidence is superficial. Instead he learns to draw with his left hand and returns to a state of dominance over his invalid wife, but having always to keep a close handle on his emotions.

This is the key difference: the hand exists only in Trask's suspicions. He believes it (the book is written in the first person) but the audience is given only ambiguous evidence – far from Rimbaldi's multiple mechanical prosthetics. The result is a balanced subtlety of tone largely lost in the film. The ongoing interior monologue gives a better idea of Trask/Lansdale's state of mind. What appears as blind rage in the film is, in the book, an agonised dichotomy between fear of isolation (a clinging neediness with regard to family and lovers) and desire for control – a control lost in the opening accident. The hand in the book (if it exists) is the outlet for powerful, atavistic desires triggered by the subconscious. This terminology is bandied about in the film, but there the hand acts out of instant gratification, a simple removal of 'obstacles'.

REEL TIME: Though not outstanding, the camerawork is solid and efficient. It's difficult to single out any particular moments, but there is a foreshadowing of things to come in Stone's work, as the stock drops into black-and-white for sequences with the hand – as if to further muddy the distinction between hallucinatory rage and real supernatural menace.

There is a rather weak effort at 'hand-cam' with the camera stalking Lansdale across a field at ground level, and later (with unintentional hilarity) attacking a tramp in an alleyway. More successfully, one quite impressive point-of-view shot has the camera represent Lansdale as he walks through a crowded bar. Otherwise it's rather predictable stuff and attempts to jazz up the action with some shaky camerawork just come across as messy – there is none of the precise intent with which a similar technique is used on *Salvador*.

MUSIC: Though James Horner is credited with the score it is heard little in a film dominated by oppressive silence. It tends to come into play over sequences of the hand, and takes the form of a strange multi-track composition of a pulsing heartbeat, ominous bellows-wheezing and a skittering electronic keyboard track (in later murder scenes it adopts the more typical orchestral thrashing of a horror movie). It's actually rather effective and does more to conjure suspense than the camerawork.

The movie also has a selection of songs on the soundtrack, albeit rather limited. Pride of place goes to the new-wave Blondie classic *Union City Blue*, which plays on Lansdale's car radio during his flight to Reno. The bar in the film has its own resident band, a fairly anodyne combo called the Country Bumpkins, two of whose songs are featured.

BOX OFFICE: Off a budget of $6.5 million, the film grossed a mere $2 million. Though not the biggest box-office upset of his career (see **Heaven and Earth**), this was a disappointing result and a setback for Stone.

CRITICS: There was little fanfare surrounding the release of this film, but reception was, at least, lukewarm rather than actively hostile. The *New York Times*' Vincent Canby thought it 'a clever horror tale – a suspenseful horror film of unusual psychological intelligence and wit'. *Village Voice*'s Andrew Sarris, a noted critic, agreed, describing it as 'one of the more intelligent efforts to combine psychological analysis with scary spectacle'. It is odd for a film that has become so mocked in retrospect that it received such praise at the time.

THE BIG PICTURE: As noted above, this was the second and, to date, last attempt on the part of Stone to make a horror film, though some of Lansdale's obsessive rage might be traced to *Talk Radio*'s Barry Champlain, and also *Nixon*.

FINAL ANALYSIS: In a technical sense, this is an interesting film. It shows the early origins of thematic concerns that haunt Stone's later work, such as the developing stages of a fine visual mind and the ability to get a sound performance from a leading man. Sadly, it is not very good. There is no real suspense (save very briefly at the end), it sags dramatically in the middle and is, ultimately, very dull. There are glimmers of potential, however. The idea of a man who is unsure whether he is killing people or whether this is due to some supernatural force is a sound one. Here, however, the protagonist does not seem concerned so much as indifferent. This, coupled with heavy hints about blackouts and their potential release of subconscious rage, explains away the hand before it even appears – it comes as little surprise when the bodies of the victims are found, and the final appearance of the killer limb is really just a bit silly.

As with *Seizure*, Stone had the wrong genre. The movie just doesn't work.

Scarface (1983)

A Brian De Palma Film
Casting by Alixe Gordin
Music by Giorgio Moroder
Executive Producer: Louis A Stroller
Visual Consultant: Ferdinando Scarfiotti
Edited by Jerry Greenberg and David Ray
Art Director: Ed Richardson
Director of Photography: John A Alonzo ASC
Screenplay by Oliver Stone
Produced by Martin Bregman
Directed by Brian De Palma

CAST: Al Pacino (*Tony Montana*), Steven Bauer (*Manny Ray*), Michelle Pfeiffer (*Elvira*), Mary Elizabeth Mastrantonio (*Gina*), Robert Loggia (*Frank Lopez*), Miriam Colon (*Mama Montana*), F Murray Abraham (*Omar*), Paul Shenar (*Alejandro Sosa*), Harris Yulin (*Bernstein*)

NOTABLE CREDITS: 'This film is dedicated to Howard Hawks and Ben Hecht' – director and writer of *Scarface* (1932).

SUMMARY: Opening caption: 'In May 1980, Fidel Castro opened the harbour at Mariel, Cuba with the apparent intention of letting some of his people join their relatives in the United States. Within seventy-two hours, 3,000 U.S. boats were headed to Cuba. It soon became evident that Castro was forcing the boat owners to carry back with them not only their relatives, but also the dregs of his jails. Of the 125,000 refugees that landed in Florida, an estimated 25,000 had criminal records.'

One of these is Tony Montana, who pleads asylum but is considered an undesirable and sent to a nearby processing facility. He is offered a way out – a green card and legal citizenship arranged by a wealthy Cuban ex-pat who hires Tony, and his close friend Manolo 'Manny' Ray, to carry out a hit on a former secret policeman, which they do during the chaos of a prison riot. They secure release from the camp but are stuck in low-paid menial work. Their earlier benefactor, drugs boss Frank Lopez, offers them further employment through his shifty subordinate Omar. Tony rejects the first offer – unloading smuggling boats for $500 a night – so Omar gives them a tougher assignment, overseeing a drug deal. The deal goes sour, but Tony retrieves the drugs and the money. He and Manny are taken to see Lopez, who gratefully welcomes them into his organisation. During this visit Tony also meets, and becomes attracted to, Frank's junkie trophy wife Elvira.

Three months later, Tony visits his mother and his sister Gina – resident in Miami – with news of his success. Gina is excited but his mother, who sees Tony as a bad influence, throws him out. He travels to Bolivia, nominally as an assistant to Omar, to discuss a deal with cocaine producer Alejandro Sosa. Omar is unveiled as a snitch and is killed. Tony goes on to arrange a deal unilaterally, much to Frank's anger. Frank attempts to assassinate Tony, who survives and comes back to kill Frank, take over his organisation and marry his wife.

In an attempt to cut what he sees as exorbitant costs, Tony employs a new money launderer who turns out to be part of an FBI sting operation. Tony is desperate to avoid prison at any cost and contacts Sosa, who can arrange leniency (it is never stated how but the implication is that he has links with the CIA). In exchange Tony has to help with the assassination of a UN official who is hindering Bolivian cocaine production. Tony refuses to do this when it becomes apparent that the man's wife and children would be killed too, shooting dead the man Sosa sent to carry out the hit.

Gina becomes increasingly embroiled in the sordid underworld life, something Tony did not want. He returns to Miami and discovers that

Gina is engaged to Manny. In a cocaine frenzy Tony kills Manny and drags Gina back to his mansion. An enraged Sosa promises revenge and a swarm of fanatical killers overwhelm Tony's defences and kill Gina, herself in the act of trying to kill her brother. Tony goes down in a hail of bullets, a victim of the American dream.

PRODUCTION HISTORY: Though discredited as a director, Stone was still much sought after for his writing and received many offers of work. One of these was an update of Howard Hawks's classic 1932 gangster film conceived by previous acquaintance Marty Bregman (see **Platoon**) for direction by Sidney Lumet (whose name had been linked with attempts to shoot *Born on the Fourth of July*). The intent was for prohibitionist beer runners of the earlier movie to be updated to flashy drug smugglers of modern America. Stone travelled through Miami and Latin America, visiting real drug gangsters to research the film. In one anecdote, Stone talks of how close he came to death. He claims to have been talking with drug runners in Bimini, when he 'dropped the name of a guy I knew who was a defence lawyer, but it turned out he used to be a prosecutor who nailed one of these guys'. Stone was terrified: 'I figured this was it: they were going to blow me away.' Fortunately they backed down, Stone swiftly made his excuses and left.

In December 1981 he flew to France with new wife Elizabeth (they had married earlier that year) where Stone pounded out a script for which he was paid $200,000. A sensationalist account of 1930s gangsterism became a gaudy paean to 1980s style and values. A tale suitably dedicated to excess – material, chemical and emotional. Lumet turned the film down when he saw the script that Stone had cooked up, and the project was offered to Brian De Palma. Stone worked closely with the director and has expressed himself 'very pleased with the movie'.

AT THE HELM: Brian De Palma's reputation for excess and bluntness is a match for Stone's own. He has combined visual flair with a style that tends towards the bloody and gruesome (rooted in his childhood – he was the son of a surgeon and used to watch his father perform operations). De Palma has work spanning five decades, progressing from cheap underground films in the 1960s through to suspense melodrama (including *Sisters*, 1973, helped along in its production by Edward Pressman). *Carrie* (1978) has become notorious for its bloody finale; *Dressed to Kill* (1981) and *Body Double* (1986) scored him critical respectability; *The Untouchables* (1987) has been equally praised, especially for its solid ensemble cast that includes Oscar-winning Sean Connery, and condemned as somewhat simple-minded. He even has a Vietnam film under his belt – the underwhelming *Casualties of War*. In recent years De Palma has hit the skids. *Bonfire of the Vanities* (1990) and *Mission to Mars* (2000) were heavily panned, while works such as *Mission: Impossible* (1996) and *Snake Eyes* (1998) were dismissed as efficient but undistinguished Hollywood thrillers.

De Palma has received much attention for his role as arch-pasticheur, whether in general imitation of style (a 'Hitchcock' period, lasting from 1973 to the mid-1980s) or specific homage. For instance, the staircase shoot-out in *The Untouchables* is directly lifted from the Odessa Steps massacre in *Battleship Potemkin* (Sergei Eisenstein, 1925). In *Scarface*, Pacino's outrageous death scene comes from the finale of *Throne of Blood* (Akira Kurosawa, 1957), where an evil nobleman (Toshiro Mifune) is pin-cushioned by a myriad of arrows.

MEMORABLE QUOTES: Stone has frequently spoken of how often he hears lines of *Scarface* quoted at him and it remains a favourite source of drunken pub declamations, and slogans for student posters. For good reason – the combination of insanely bombastic script and Pacino's frenzied delivery puts it on a level with the nihilism and deadpan psychosis of De Niro speaking Paul Schrader's lines in *Taxi Driver* (Martin Scorsese, 1976).

Tony: 'In this country you've got to make the money. Then when you got the money, you get the power. Then when you get the power, then you get the women.'

Tony (to assembled society types): 'You don't have the guts to be what you want to be . . . You need people like me so you can point your fucking fingers and say, "That's the bad guy." So what does that make you? . . . You're not good, you just know how to hide, how to lie . . . Me, I always tell the truth, even when I lie.'

Tony: (wielding machine gun/grenade launcher assault rifle): 'Say hello to my little friend!'

GOOD VS EVIL: *Scarface* is brutal cynicism. The protagonist is a drug-addicted, violent, foul-mouthed, vulgar and borderline incestuous thug. However, he is somehow more attractive than those who surround him – the bumbling, pathetic Lopez, the greasy, snobbish Sosa and the obsequious, treacherous Omar. Tony has his own integrity, and gets by through his own hard work – unlike the parasitic lawyers and bankers he is forced to deal with. Even the wealthy citizens of Miami are lambasted in the last restaurant scene for their cowardice, complacency, hypocrisy and lack of drive. As Stone said, 'Tony Montana is a nut, but he's *funny*.'

But there is a greed to the character, insatiable greed for power, for money and for drugs, and it is this greed that both creates him and destroys him. In this film the good (such as it is) and the evil are the same. In this respect it brushes up against some of the concerns of *Wall Street* – greed can be good, in encouraging efficiency, but also harmful, in prompting unbridled avarice: hunger for money leads to the FBI sting, hunger for drugs leads to the psychosis in which he kills Manny, hunger for power leads to a fatal challenge to Sosa.

Elvira fits into this scheme in a satirical sense. Just as Tony's material possessions are tacky and vulgar, his 'perfect' woman is a junkie, unable to conceive children. This is not grounds to further condemn Stone's treatment of women. No one in this film comes out well save, perhaps, Gina. She exists to represent the innocent, corrupted through association with Tony and his money. She is also the subject of a discomforting incestuous fascination, which provides a catalyst for the murder of Manny and thus Tony's final sin, betrayal of his friend.

REDEMPTION OR DAMNATION: Ironically it is Tony's one unquestionably good act – preventing the assassination of a man and his children – that finally leads to his downfall. At least, it does in an immediate causal sense. The drive of the film points towards a 'rise and fall' narrative from early on. Such an unpleasant character, even in the context of the company he keeps, has to get his comeuppance.

HISTORY 101: The Cuban community has been a major constituent of Miami's society since the Cuban revolution of 1959 caused a vast exodus of those unprepared for, or fearful of, Castro's government. Perhaps unsurprisingly, this community has solidified into a tight knot of anti-Castroism deep in the southeast of the USA. According to Stone it was originally Sidney Lumet's idea to transplant the immigrant narratives of Italians in the earlier Hawk film to the Cubans of Florida.

There is also a natural association between Miami and the drug culture. In the same way as the ghettoes of New York and Los Angeles were seen as hotbeds of crack use in the 1990s, and San Francisco and the west coast of the 1960s were big areas for marijuana and LSD, Miami in the 1980s was the nexus of 'specialist imports' from the coca fields of Latin America. Such an impression was reinforced through portrayals in the media by works such as *Scarface* and, later, *Miami Vice*.

The movie, though an update, rather cleverly takes a real historical event – the mass flight from Cuba in 1980 – as its inciting incident.

STARS AND STRIPES: Tony Montana is entirely sincere with his devotion to America and his hatred for Communism. He demands human rights, in keeping with the policies of then President Jimmy Carter, but his true hero is the incoming President Ronald Reagan, a keen proponent of the free market.

This phrase, free market, is perhaps the best summation of the American Dream: that a man, purely through his own merit, effort and perseverance, can achieve greatness. The myth of the presidency – that any man (born in the US) can attain its office – is one manifestation of this, as are images of lonely prospectors striking gold or oil, or the wagon trains that snaked out west in the nineteenth century. A variant of this is found in the immigrant experience, the image of a poor boy landing at Ellis Island with nothing and rising to become great. *Scarface* is hardly unique in the adaptation of this last theme and the substitution of crime for lawful, productive endeavour – it was fully taken on board in the earliest gangster movies, and further refined by *The Godfather – Part II*.

As *The Godfather* had in the 1970s, *Scarface* came under heavy criticism for its representations of immigrants. It was said that all Latin Americans were presented as criminals, though this ignored the fact that *every* character in the film was a criminal (bar the Cubans Gina and Mamma Montana).

BEING OLIVER STONE: At the time of writing the film, Stone was a self-confessed cocaine junkie and *Scarface* was written off the back of an attempt to go straight. While in Paris, he went cold turkey and he has since described the movie as his 'farewell to all drugs'. There is an oddly ambiguous tone. The morality of the drug trade is not directly criticised, nor are there any lectures on the damage cocaine does to the body; the increasingly maniacal and paranoid behaviour of Tony says all that one needs to know – cocaine turns you into a dangerous jerk.

INSPIRATION AND INFLUENCE: This is the only straight remake Stone has scripted. In several ways it is faithful to the 1932 original. Tony Carmonte begins as a henchman to a gang boss, exceeds his remit, the boss tries to assassinate him so he kills the boss and takes over. His closest friend becomes involved with Tony's sister – the subject of her brother's incestuous obsession – leading to his death. This directly leads to Tony's downfall – his own sister testifies against him and he is shot down by the police in an attack on his fortified compound.

Some details are directly borrowed: several lines are retained, the way in which Tony proves his boss's treachery through a phone call is the same, and in both versions he becomes obsessed with a sign, 'The world is yours'. Thematically there is also continuity, the smuggling of illegal contraband, the corrupting influence of money on the innocent, the gaudiness of gangsters' tastes. One important difference is in the attitude to ethnicity. The 1932 film condemns the Italian community of Chicago as a bad influence, whereas De Palma and Stone concentrate more on the act of immigration – America as a land of opportunity. Stone also built in the political subtext, issues of the UN and American involvement with Bolivian drug producers. It is interesting to note, in context of criticism, that the 1983 film was overly violent and racist, that Hawks's movie was banned for some time as a result of its violence and that pressure from Italian-American groups forced the inclusion of a scene where a representative of their community denounces the gangsters.

Tony Montana's impact fed back into the media. The film influenced a new sort of cinematic gangster, where the criminals were not intellectually appealing existential rejects, such as Travis Bickle in *Taxi Driver,* nor tragically cool, such as *Bonnie and Clyde,* nor smooth and possessive of a twisted honour, such as in *The Godfather,* but were loud, brash, violent and sprayed money around with an ebullience that made up for their lack of taste. The film *New Jack City* (Mario van Peebles, 1991) revolved around a coterie of these new flamboyant young killers, and actually featured a clip of the film, while Christopher Walken played a white Tony Montana with a hip-hop crew in *King of New York* (Abel Ferrara, 1990). TV was also affected; *Scarface* directly inspired the flashy aesthetic ethos and celebrated superficiality of *Miami Vice.* Most recently the video game *Grand Theft Auto: Vice City* sold millions on the back of a broad pastiche of the gangster genre, with *Scarface* at its centre, while the recent DVD special edition of the film included a documentary on its influence among rap musicians.

AWARDS: Giorgio Moroder's score was nominated for a Golden Globe, as were the lead performances of Al Pacino and Steven Bauer. Less prestigiously, Brian De Palma was nominated for the Golden Raspberry for Worst Direction. Set up in direct opposition to the Oscars, this is an attempt to puncture the pomposity inherent in mainstream award ceremonies (see also **Year of the Dragon** and **U Turn**). Stone has been linked with a fair few of them in his time.

THE BIG PICTURE: Stone's movies tend to lean either towards grim pessimism or glossy bombast. The particular perspective of *Scarface* marks it among his darker works – *U Turn, Natural Born Killers, Year of the Dragon* and *The Hand*.

FINAL ANALYSIS: *Scarface* is reviled by cinephiles and critics, slated as the nadir of Stone's screenwriting career in its racism, misogyny and perceived right-wing populism. It has also seen great commercial success and gathered a huge popular following.

It is perhaps time to re-evaluate it. It is broad, crude and outrageous but is also, in its own way, a witty and successful commentary on American corporate culture. Indeed, in its use of metaphorical (rather than literal) 'hostile takeovers', it might be said to do this more effectively than *Wall Street*. On one level it's trashy exploitation, on another a slapdash satire verging on burlesque and on yet another a perfect condemnation of 80s excess – Stone's later film is put to shame for its comparative sobriety. But how much of this is down to the writer? His interviews lend the impression that this was one of the more successful of his post-*Midnight Express* collaborations, and the general style is stock-car Stone – intellectual adornment stripped out for a leaner, simpler, more violent ride. Unsurprisingly, a lot of this baggage marks out his personal touch in later films and, with another director at the helm, it is less obviously Stone at the typewriter.

This is not necessarily a bad thing – in later films the continual pounding in of the 'message' can get a little tiresome. But there is something unique about Stone's earnest bluntness; in later films he comes across as a director with concerned knitted brow pummelling morality and truth into his viewers. De Palma does something else. There is a light, frivolous touch to the story, undercutting the script's faux-operatic gravity and bringing the film closer to satire than Stone could claim with *Natural Born Killers*.

Different and enjoyable (though guiltily so), the writer and director compliment each other nicely – a team of experienced vandals being more efficient than just one. It's both a shame and a blessing that they never worked together again.

Year of the Dragon (1985)

Dino De Laurentiis presents
A Michael Cimino production
Costume Designer: Marietta Ciriello
Production Designer: Wolf Kroeger
Music Composed and Conducted by David Mansfield
Editor: Francoise Bonnot
Photographed and Operated by Alex Thomson BSC
Based on the novel *Year of the Dragon* by Robert Daley
Screenplay by Oliver Stone and Michael Cimino
Produced by Dino De Laurentiis
Directed by Michael Cimino

CAST: Mickey Rourke (*Stanley White*), John Lone (*Joey Tai*), Ariane (*Tracey Tzu*), Leonard Termo (*Angelo Rizzo*), Ray Barry (*Louis Bukowski*), Caroline Kava (*Connie White*), Joey Chin (*Ronnie Chang*), Victor Wong (*Harry Yung*), Eddie Jones (*William McKenna*)

SUMMARY: Stanley White, the most decorated cop in New York, is assigned to a new beat in Chinatown. The tough racist White comes down hard on the local gang bosses, who run the place like their own private fiefdom. But there is dissent in their ranks as young immigrant under-boss Joey Tai foments a fake gang war as a way of seizing power. White is thrown out by his wife and starts an affair with a beautiful Chinese-American reporter (Tracey Tzu), using her to cast light on the criminal activity that many in the NYPD are keen to keep covered up.

Tai arranges a major heroin deal with his Thai suppliers, and White sets out to track it down. Enraged by White's campaign, and unable to buy him off, Tai murders his wife, kills the undercover cop infiltrated into the Triad operation, and arranges for the rape of Tracey, as well as trying to kill White himself on a number of occasions. White is transferred back to Brooklyn for his lack of procedure, but sets out to bust Tai anyway. He confronts the gangster at the docks and severely wounds him in a shootout. Tai confesses the location of the heroin before committing suicide. At the end of the film, the big bosses are still at large and the film ends with White plunging into a funeral procession in an attempt to arrest them, only to be beaten to the ground, before being gently led off by Tracey.

PRODUCTION HISTORY: Though critically reviled, *Scarface* did big business, and Stone had cemented his status as a professional screenwriter, at the cost of burdening him with a reputation for right-wing exploitation flicks similar to that attributed to *Conan* director John Milius and notorious schlock merchant Joe Eszterhas – the 'talent' behind films such as *Flashdance* (Adrian Lyne, 1983), *Basic Instinct* (Paul Verhoeven, 1991) and *Showgirls* (Paul Verhoeven, 1995).

But Stone was soon at work on other projects including a script based on the Los Angeles-based Hillside Strangler murders and one based on a pulp thriller he had personally optioned (*8 Million Ways to Die* – see **The Ones That Got Away**, p. 47). Then Stone had a call from Michael Cimino, a Vietnam film veteran from *The Deer Hunter* who had read the script for *Platoon* and liked it. He offered Stone a *quid pro quo* through mega-producer Dino De Laurentiis (the big money behind *Conan the Barbarian*) – collaboration on an adaptation of the novel *Year of the Dragon* at a lower than usual wage, in exchange for De Laurentiis's guarantee to back *Platoon*. The subject of the book, *Year of the Dragon*, was the closed world of Chinese immigrants and specifically their involvement in crime and drug dealing. There was more than a passing resemblance to *Scarface*, though the story this time would be told from the perspective of a cop, and a similar course of research was followed as Cimino and Stone hurled themselves into the New York Chinese underworld. They dined at lavish banquets and interviewed anyone who was prepared to say anything about Chinese gangsters but learned little until they spoke with what Stone described as 'a dissident gangster group. Very on the outs and very unhappy . . . [they] showed us what was going on in Chinatown.' Cimino and Stone reached these groups through Alex Ho, a young man just starting out in the film business. Stone would work with him again on *Platoon*.

The script was completed, and filmed by Cimino, but De Laurentiis did not keep up his end of the bargain (see **Platoon**). Stone had another screenwriting credit under his belt, but seemed no nearer to filling the director's chair again.

AT THE HELM: Michael Cimino had written and directed the well-received Clint Eastwood vehicle *Thunderbolt and Lightfoot* (1974) but enjoyed the greatest acclaim for *The Deer Hunter* (1978). A moving, beautiful melodrama, it featured great performances from Robert De Niro, Frank Cazale (Fredo in Coppola's *Godfather* movies) *Salvador*'s John Savage and a young Christopher Walken (who picked up an Oscar) and followed the experiences of blue-collar Pennsylvanian steelworkers before, during and after the Vietnam War. Since the 1970s, this film's stock has fallen. Cimino has come under fire for the infamous sequence where North Vietnamese prison guards force Americans to play Russian roulette, sequences that have been pretty much debunked as fiction.

His second film, *Heaven's Gate* (1980), chronicled a land-war in Wyoming between landowners and immigrant workers and has become a byword for cinematic disaster. Whatever its qualities, and critical opinion has improved over time, the sheer scale of the flop (the film's cost increased more than threefold from the original budget of $12 million to $38 million) destroyed a great deal of the independence from studio control that directors such as Cimino, Martin Scorsese, Francis Ford Coppola and William Friedkin had built up over the 1970s (see **Seizure**). Cimino was, unsurprisingly, the worst affected, and *Year of the Dragon* was his first film since *Heaven's Gate*. He has been intermittently busy since, but with no significant success. Cimino's style is similar to Stone's: brutal, unsubtle and sentimental. He also has a tendency to let his films overrun (the original cut of *Heaven's Gate* was a whopping 219 minutes – 7 minutes more than the mammoth director's cut of *Nixon*). He has also suffered (as on *The Deer Hunter*) from criticism of his historical rigour. Stone differs in two key ways – he has never gone significantly over budget or missed a deadline by more than a few days.

MEMORABLE QUOTES:
Stanley White: 'I'd like to be a nice guy, I would. I just don't know how to be nice.'

GOOD VS EVIL: Stanley White is an anti-hero, but in a much more conventional sense than Tony Montana. Indeed, it's difficult to imagine a greater cop cliché – the maverick who gets the job done, whatever it takes and despite the interference from bureaucrats in City Hall (it's perhaps not surprising that Cimino had co-written *Magnum Force* (Ted

Post, 1973), which featured the archetype of this character, 'Dirty' Harry Calahan). He is 'good' but at the grey end of the scale, an undeniable racist (like Calahan), a sexist, hard-drinking, hard-smoking, shoot-first-and-damn-the-consequences kind of guy. His moral force comes from his convictions, his decorations and his single-minded commitment to the bringing of brutal, simple (and somewhat arbitrary) justice.

The 'evil' is not so much bureaucratic inertia (as was more markedly the case in the Dirty Harry films) but a single figure, Joey Tai. Tai is an interesting character, more so, in fact, than White. An immigrant who works his way up the ranks of the gangs, who kills to get to the top and who represents a raw form of naked capitalism through the drug trade – all characteristics of Tony Montana.

Tai is also a cliché, the slickly suited villain, ruthless, smooth and successful. He is as unrelenting as White, letting nothing get in his way, but is obviously evil (using the morality of this sort of cop movie) because he is rich – he is rewarded for his brutality and single-mindedness. White is penalised for employing a similar approach in the name of justice.

It's all fairly banal melodrama, but there is one interesting sequence at the end – a literal clash of good and evil as these two men hurl themselves at each other, guns blazing. It's bloody stuff but not the ending imagined by Stone and Cimino, who had White arrest Tai for bigamy, as in the book. De Laurentiis forced the more conventional ending on the film. A sly twist would have seemed wrong somehow – better for the two characters to duke it out like men in this sort of movie are supposed to.

REDEMPTION OR DAMNATION: Inconclusive. White would seem to have triumphed, but soon finds that Tai is just one gang boss among many; the crime and corruption goes on. White's uncompromising approach can win a battle, but there is no end to the war. The love of Tracey is some consolation, but White has lost his wife, a colleague, received serious wounds and had his career shattered. It's a downbeat ending, and clumsily handled.

STARS AND STRIPES: At first glance there appears to be a developing trend in Stone's screenplays to denigrate immigrant communities (see **Scarface**). This runs counter to a basic tenet of America – the idea of the melting pot. Stone refutes these suggestions and, in a 1987 interview, he argued that 'The Chinese are the biggest importers of heroin in the country . . . yet nobody knows about it – they do it quietly.' But the film itself carries a better defence. At several points the script refers to the sufferings of immigrant Chinese in the nineteenth and early twentieth centuries, and the injustices done them by the American government (government injustice being a subject Stone would return to). Additionally there is a second important immigrant presence in the Poles, of whom Stanley White is a member (having changed his name from Wyzynsky) with his friend, boss and neighbour Bukowski and even a third, the Irish, represented by the cop McKenna and the customs guard at the dock.

The film's real target is the criminal element of *any* nationality (the film has a brief appearance from Italian Mafiosi – a fourth but entirely negative ethnic grouping). There are several Chinese (such as the old man who tells the police the location of two dead gangsters, or the shopkeepers victimised by the gangs) who are good American citizens to be protected, even by the racist White (who also, it should be noted, forms a relationship with a woman of Asian descent). This might come across as a somewhat chauvinist idea, but it is an American belief, that one can come to America from abroad and leave the old ways behind – it is suggested in the script that it is these old ways that are the problem.

Ultimately the film is not totally fair and balanced in its presentation of race (and nor is it particularly good). However, to totally disregard it as a slur on the Chinese people is to oversimplify.

INSPIRATION AND INFLUENCE: The source novel is a fairly uninspired, stodgy affair that combines an attempt at sociological analysis with a weak narrative built around maverick cop Arthur Powers (Stone changed this to Stanley White, after an LAPD detective he had met while researching the proposed film on the Hillside Strangler murders) and his attempts to bring down alleged gangster Jimmy Koy. Much of it is taken up with dull, half-baked lectures on Chinese gang crime and the opium trade. It is needlessly padded out with a tedious subplot on Powers's affair with TV reporter Carol Cone, which ends unresolved. It is suggested that Powers will stay with his wife (who is not killed in the book) but the affair looks certain to be revealed after Powers travels to Hong Kong to track down Koy. There he and Cone are almost killed by henchmen of the Chinese villain. In a manner as stripped of drama and excitement as the rest of the book, the viewers are informed that the infidelity will emerge through the resultant court case.

The detail of the affair is peppered with nasty, casual chauvinism, while the book as a whole is rife with racist views – early on, Chinese dialogue is written in a stunningly insensitive way: 'You want nice dlink [sic] please, maybe?' There are points in which Daley tries to compensate for this, but they are wholly inadequate. By comparison, the screenplay is sensitive.

There are changes to the cop character in the film. It is suggested that Powers is a maverick who gets results, but it is difficult to see what results he actually gets – he sort of stomps through the book and the grand stand-off with the villain is notably lacking in solid accusations. The attempt to paint Koy as an Al Capone figure who is convicted for a technicality (bigamy) falls flat. The movie may rely on movie cop cliché, but at least this makes White interesting. Importantly, the racial element is played up, with the addition of Polish heritage for White, and Stone's first incorporation of Vietnam into a character's back-story.

The book itself draws heavy inspiration from *The French Connection* – itself a book, filmed by William Friedkin in 1971. The elements are the same: a huge shipment of heroin, a maverick cop in a race against time and bureaucracy, time-consuming stakeouts and a suave foreign villain. The only difference is an attempt to incorporate the origins of the drug, far more successfully handled in the Channel 4 drama *Traffik*. Daley also expands the drug-trade concept to embrace gang warfare, but it is clear that the earlier book and film of *The French Connection* were hugely influential on *Year of the Dragon*, without lending any of the tension, drama or critical success.

AWARDS: *Year of the Dragon* picked up the Best Film award at the Flanders Film Festival. American awards were thinner on the ground, with only two Golden Globe nominations – for the score and John Lone's turn as Tai. One award ceremony handed out a swathe of nominations: Ariane, Michael Cimino, Oliver Stone and the film as a whole were all recognised by the Golden Raspberry awards.

THE BIG PICTURE: Similarities with *Scarface* have been noted, as has the somewhat dubious treatment of race – echoes of *Midnight Express* here too. In addition, the character of Stanley White is a Vietnam Veteran, whose experiences abroad are implied to be the cause of his racism (there is similar banter between White and his Korean War veteran boss – as would later feature in the bar scene of *Born on the Fourth of July*). Aside from this, there is little that was used again in later scripts, though some of the politically charged speeches, especially on the plight of Chinese coolies, have a resonance with Boyle's awkward monologue in *Salvador*.

FINAL ANALYSIS: Bog standard at best and stodgy, clumsy and a little offensive at worst, *Year of the Dragon* has rightly faded into insignificance. In script terms it is a lukewarm reworking of *Scarface* and *The French Connection*, and has no profound or pertinent new developments on any of the themes explored in this film. It is noteworthy that Stone's career intersected with Cimino's while one was in the ascendant and the other in decline, but there is little else of interest here.

The Ones That Got Away

As well as projects abandoned during production (*Noriega, The Mayor of Castro Street*) and films with which Stone was for a time linked as director (*Planet of the Apes, American Psycho*), there were several movies on which he is credited for work on the screenplay but which had been altered to such a degree by later writers as to render his own contribution of minor significance. A good comparison here would be Quentin Tarantino, credited for the writing of *Natural Born Killers* but without any control over the eventual film. Nonetheless, these films are still of enough interest in the context of Stone's career to merit a brief look.

Conan the Barbarian (1981)
The character of Conan is familiar enough to require little by way of explanation. Creation of eccentric novelist Robert Howard in the early twentieth century, the Cimmerian warrior battled through a series of pulp adventure stories telling of his numerous adventures through foreign lands.

Ed Pressman (see *The Hand*) had struggled for the rights through the late 1970s, finalising the deal in 1980. He also acquired an actor to play the role – Arnold Schwarzenegger, best known at the time for the bodybuilding documentary *Pumping Iron* (George Butler, Robert Fiore, 1976). Impressed by *Midnight Express*, Pressman went through the William Morris agency to contact Oliver Stone, asking him to rewrite a script originally penned by Edward Summer and Roy Thomas (a former comic-book writer). An initial plan was for Stone to direct, in tandem with an experienced action director Joe Alves, who had assisted Steven Spielberg on *Jaws* (1975). This deal proved difficult to sell, and eventually it was agreed that Stone should stick to the writing.

Stone showed the unrestrained flamboyance that would characterise later films such as *The Doors*. He envisaged a conflict of epic scale between the forces of light and darkness set in a post-apocalyptic future. Armies of mutants versus Conan, with lavish effect work done on the hideous armies of evil and an arc for the hero following his rise from slave to king, before refusing the throne and galloping off towards an anticipated sequel (Stone foresaw a long-running series akin to the Bond films). A hint of Stone's grand intentions might be seen from his plans for the shoot: 'I wanted to shoot it in Germany or Russia – and to get the whole Russian Army, thousands of people in the green fertile fields.' Outside the source novels, Stone was heavily influenced by heroes of medieval romance – in epics such as *Beowolf* or *Chanson de Roland*, warriors would often see off overwhelming hordes single-handedly.

For a brief time it looked as though Ridley Scott would helm the project as written by Stone, but he turned the script down and was replaced by John Milius, a strong libertarian with a reputation for excess, like Stone, but with a right-wing mindset in contrast to the liberal Stone. He had been responsible for post-*Bonnie and Clyde* crime biopic *Dillinger* (1973), surfer movie *Big Wednesday* (1978) and would go on to direct *Red Dawn* (1984), a notorious Reagan-era fantasy imagining a Soviet invasion of the USA. He was also a writer, having contributed to *Dirty Harry* (Don Siegel, 1971) and *Apocalypse Now* (Francis Ford Coppola, 1979) and rejected Stone's draft, relocating the film to a more subdued setting, more realistic in aspiration. Stone's involvement was minimal, as he put it, 'I criticised some changes he had made to my script, and once I did that . . . my shadow would never darken his door again – so I was told.' The movie was shot in Spain, and by the time it was released Stone was hard at work on *The Hand*.

From Stone's comments on his early draft it is possible to note some similarities – Conan as the archetypal noble savage, akin to Mickey Knox and his assertion to being 'God of his [own] world'. Having said this, such attributes are rooted within the character, and are better credited with being the lure that drew Milius and Stone to the project in the first place, rather than a product of either writer's imagination. A fundamentally similar approach of writing for the character would explain Stone's credit on the film – he helped flesh out the Conan of the novels for the big screen.

Like horror, Stone has yet to return to fantasy, though *Alexander* will employ the epic scale he imagined for Conan, while the genre itself has enjoyed a revival through Peter Jackson's *The Lord of the Rings* adaptations (2001–3).

OLIVER STONE Year of the Dragon

Digital technology has only just reached the stage where fantastic environments can be effectively re-created. Given rumours of a new Conan film (*King Conan*) in development, and dependent on *Alexander*'s success, perhaps Stone will see his vision realised.

Eight Million Ways to Die (1986)

Lawrence Block, like John Ridley (see *U Turn*), was a writer of contemporary noir novels, and one of his recurring characters was the alcoholic private eye Matt Scudder, star of colourfully titled mysteries such as *The Sins of the Fathers*, *Time to Murder and Create* and *In the Midst of Death*. In the book *Eight Million Ways to Die* Scudder investigated the mysterious death of a prostitute who had become the target of Colombian emerald smugglers seeking vengeance for a scam played on them by one of their fences. An atmospheric novel, interested as much in the demons haunting its protagonist as any unfolding of the plot, and incorporating an interesting subplot on the motivation behind prostitution, its appeal to Stone is understandable – a flawed hero, intense internal struggle, a shady morality and, perhaps, a smidgen of borderline misogyny (or at least the opportunity for salacious plotting around glamorous hookers).

He optioned the Lawrence Block novel with his own money and did a deal with Steve Roth to produce. He intended to direct the resultant screenplay himself, but could not get enough studio backing, and the project was taken to Hal Ashby. Ashby had been a participant in Hollywood's new wave and was the director of brilliant low-fi escort movie *The Last Detail* (1973), paraplegic veteran drama *Coming Home* (1976) (see *Born on the Fourth of July*) and Peter Sellers's vehicle *Being There* (1979), *Eight Million Ways to Die* would be his last movie before his death in 1988. David Lee Henry heavily rewrote the script with later amendments by Robert Towne, renowned in Hollywood as a freelance script doctor.

Little remains of its source. Emeralds become cocaine, a new villain – a drug lord – was created to replace the book's machete-wielding assassin (unseen until the last few pages), while the potentially fascinating alcoholism subplot was almost totally lost – Jeff Bridges (the film's Scudder) blacks out once after a drink binge, but afterwards little is made of his affliction. The movie becomes a bog-standard noir thriller, distinguished only by its utterly predictable plot, complete lack of tension and character delineation based entirely upon cliché (the tart with a heart, the ex-con made good – but still a rough diamond – and the smooth drug baron with impeccable taste).

Stone had little else to do with the production, save a visit to the production's Malibu set. There is nothing in the final version in terms of narrative flair or stylistic tone to link it with its original writer. As Rand Vossler would later lose *Natural Born Killers*, so Stone had lost this movie, eventually released (to little fanfare) in the same year as *Salvador* and *Platoon*.

Evita (1996)

Of the three, this is the closest to a 'missing' Stone film. He had been looking to direct a cinematic adaptation of Andrew Lloyd Webber's musical, based on the life of Eva Peron, wife to populist Argentinian dictator Juan Peron, since 1987, off the back of a proposal by Robert Stigwood that had been circulating since the 1970s. Madonna was initially up for the title role but clashed with Stone, who claims she demanded approval over the script, something that as writer and director he was not prepared to give. Meryl Streep was touted as a replacement, and location scouting was carried out in Argentina and southern Europe. However, in 1989 Streep dropped out and the project foundered.

But Stone did not give up on *Evita*. In the wake of *Natural Born Killers* he returned to work on the musical, this time with Michelle Pfeiffer in the lead. However, things did not go smoothly. Costs were approaching $32 million before shooting had even commenced and, according to a *Daily Mail* story, Stone had 'failed to charm Argentina's president Carlos Menem . . . [who] denounced the Evita film as "a total infamy"'. Additionally he clashed with Pfeiffer and the budget had become such a cause for concern that the project was suspended in late summer 1994. It was eventually released under the direction of Alan Parker, who cameos as a put-upon film director, and with Madonna once again in the lead.

The reason for Stone's credit is obvious from watching the film: save about ten words, the entire spoken script takes the form of Tim Rice's lyrics. As the creative talent to express Stigwood's proposal of the musical in cinematic form, and on the basis of his long-term role in shaping the production, Stone would be due recognition. However, as with *Eight Million Ways to Die*, this is not to read active involvement on Stone's part in Parker's movie.

It would be interesting to see the emphasis Stone would have put on the story. In interviews he has spoken of his intentions for the character in the context of Parker's film: 'She was too sedate in the first half. She should have been hungrier for power, more lascivious, more of a "hooker".' He added, 'In the second half I wanted to see a real transition into what I think she became, which was a hero to the masses.'

Salvador (1986)

Hemdale presents
An Oliver Stone film
Associate Producers: Bob Morones and Brad H Aronson
Editor: Claire Simpson
Director of Photography: Robert Richardson
Original Music Composed and Conducted by Georges Delerue
Production Design: Bruno Rubeo
Executive Producers: John Daly and Derek Gibson
Screenplay by Oliver Stone and Richard Boyle
Produced by Oliver Stone and Gerald Green
Directed by Oliver Stone

PRINCIPAL CAST: James Woods (*Richard Boyle*), James Belushi (*Dr Rock*), Michael Murphy (*Ambassador Thomas Kelly*), John Savage (*John Cassady*), Elpedia Carrillo (*Maria*), Tony Plana (*Major Max*), Colby Chester (*Jack Morgan*), Cynthia Gibb (*Cathy Moore*), Will MacMillan (*Colonel Hyde*), Valerie Wildman (*Pauline Axelrod*), Jose Carlos Ruiz (*Archbishop Romero*), Jorge Luke (*Colonel Julio Figueroa*), Juan Fernandez (*Army Lieutenant*)

NOTABLE CREDITS: Juan Fernandez's character is occasionally known as 'Smiling Death' in secondary literature.

SUMMARY: Washed-up war journalist Richard Boyle is unemployed in San Francisco. He heads to El Salvador, hoping to make use of his contacts there to dig up stories on the escalating civil war and takes his DJ buddy Dr Rock along for the ride. They are arrested at the border and fear the worst after witnessing the murder of a student for lack of a *cedula* (ID papers that double as voter registration; non-possession can result in execution on assumption of being linked with guerrilla forces). The pair are freed after meeting Boyle's Salvadorian army contact Colonel Figueroa. He goes on to be reunited with photojournalist colleague John Cassady, civil-rights campaigner Ramon Alvarez, old friend and Catholic lay worker Cathy Moore and Maria, his Salvadorian lover. He also learns of the growing power of 'Major Max', an ultra right-wing political leader with connections to the paramilitary death squads.

Boyle and Rock attend a reception to mark the 1980 US presidential election where Jimmy Carter loses to Ronald Reagan – a robust proponent of military aid to Salvadorian government forces. Boyle schmoozes with preppy CIA representative Jack Morgan, bullish military attaché Colonel Hyde and liberal Ambassador Kelly in attempts to get leads, but Kelly ignores him, Hyde berates Boyle for his Vietnam coverage while Morgan is obsessed with the idea that Cubans, Soviets and/or Nicaraguans are backing the rebels. Depressed Boyle trades insults with obtuse television anchorwoman Pauline Axelrod (under the table, Rock spikes her drink with LSD). Elsewhere, at a dinner party, Major Max arranges for the assassination of radical Archbishop Romero.

Dr Rock and Maria's brother Carlos are arrested for possession of marijuana. Cathy and Boyle bribe the police to let Rock go, but Carlos is kept in jail. Boyle and Cathy go to see Ambassador Kelly who offers a much warmer reception than previously, as he is a friend of Cathy. However, he can offer little help: there are no records of Carlos's arrest and he cannot provide a *cedula* for Maria. Boyle, out of desperation, offers to wed Maria. She is initially reluctant to contemplate marrying the divorced, amoral Boyle but eventually agrees to think about it if Boyle confesses and takes communion.

At San Salvador's cathedral the Archbishop's latest sermon, preaching against the repression, is in full swing. Boyle confesses and takes communion next to Maria. A few seconds later, however, Archbishop Romero is shot by one of Major Max's henchman. In the confusion Alvarez is arrested by the military.

The Major holds a press conference to announce his candidature for president and Boyle attends, shouting accusations of death squads. Later Carlos's corpse is discovered, and Maria throws Boyle out, blaming him for her brother's death. After a bar-crawl he bids farewell to Cathy – off to collect nuns flying into the country from Nicaragua – and is ambushed by the same officer (Smiling Death) who detained him at the border, who shot the student, who arrested Alvarez – a close associate of Major Max. John Cassady narrowly prevents Boyle's murder.

Cathy meets the nuns at San Salvador airport but on the way back they are waylaid by a gang of drunken thugs, raped and murdered. Boyle, Rock, Pauline Axelrod and Ambassador Kelly are all present as the bodies are dug from their shallow graves. Kelly suspends military aid. Alvarez had managed to secure access to the guerrilla camp for Boyle and Cassady. They take photographs, witness the simple village life and hear plans for a 'final offensive' from a Guevara-esque rebel leader.

Later, Boyle tries to exchange his photographs of the rebel camp for a *cedula* for Maria, but Hyde and Morgan are unimpressed. After a lengthy argument the journalist leaves in disgust, though not before Hyde has warned him that he is now a target of the far right.

Cassady hears news that the rebels' 'final offensive' has commenced, and he begs a lift from Boyle, who insists on reconciliation with Maria first. They rush to Santa Ana where the rebels have taken over; Smiling Death is killed in the battle. At the American embassy the embattled Kelly (with only a few days left before his Reaganite replacement arrives) refuses to be rushed into restoring aid despite reports of Sandanista troops landing from Nicaragua. At Santa Ana, Boyle and Cassady trawl through the rubble. A disgusted Boyle witnesses the execution of government troops at the hands of rebel forces – Cassady manages to take some surreptitious photographs. Kelly agrees to restore aid and Figueroa's tanks roll into battle, sending the guerrillas into a rout. A lone fighter-plane swoops down, strafing the town and mortally wounding Cassady, who passes his film to the injured Boyle.

In hospital Rock hands Boyle a badly forged exit visa and counterfeit *cedulas* for Maria and her children. They run for the border, though Rock decides to stay behind. The brawny border guards spot Boyle's forgery and check with the capital: he is to be executed. In the nick of time, Kelly arranges for Boyle's release as his last ambassadorial act. The guards had destroyed Cassady's film, but Boyle reveals one last roll hidden in his heel. Boyle and Maria cross the US/Mexican border in a bus. They appear to have been successful but the coach is subject to a random immigration check. Maria and her two children are hauled off while Boyle watches in anguish. Closing caption cards tell of the continued lack of arrests for the murder of Archbishop Romero, of Rock's return to the US, of the publication of Cassady's photographs and of Boyle's ongoing search for Maria, last seen in Guatemala.

PRODUCTION HISTORY: Oliver Stone met journalist Richard Boyle in the late 1970s while in talks with Ron Kovic (see **Born on the Fourth of July**) and they quickly became friends. In late 1984, disillusioned after the fallout with Dino De Laurentiis over *Platoon*, Stone travelled to San Francisco where he met with Boyle. As Stone later recalled, 'On the back seat of his car was this oily manuscript . . . I picked it up and read it . . . Immediately . . . I loved it.' This manuscript was a collection of stories compiled by Boyle from his time in El Salvador, and Stone decided to adapt it into his next screenplay. Over three months they thrashed out the script together: three months of travel (Honduras, Costa Rica, Belize Mexico, El Salvador) culminating in Boyle's prolonged period of residency in Stone's own house (much to the consternation of Elizabeth Stone – Boyle would drink everything in sight, once polishing off a can of baby formula meant for young Sean Stone). The finished version combined Boyle's notes with elements of Raymond Bonner's book *Weakness and Deceit*.

With the screenplay complete, Stone set about trying to raise money. Initially he intended to fund it personally, mortgaging his house and borrowing heavily from banks. In addition, he returned to El Salvador with Boyle in an attempt to secure government backing. The macho military commanders welcomed Stone with open arms – they were huge fans of *Scarface*. Stone and Boyle presented a Spanish script, celebrating the achievements of the army against Communist insurgency. It was popular, it was officially approved, it got them a military adviser . . . and it was a complete lie – the intention was to 'con them into giving us all their tanks and all their troops for nothing . . . then we would go to Mexico . . . and would rebalance the film there'.

In the end this arrangement fell through after their government liaison, Colonel Ricardo Cienfuegos, was shot dead on a tennis court, his body draped with a rebel flag. President Duarte, nominal head of the government junta, stepped in to stop support for the film, claiming it would harm tourism to the country.

Stone had shown the screenplay to a number of producers. One of these was Englishman Gerald Green, who passed it on to John Daly, co-founder, with veteran actor David Hemmings, of Hemdale – a small British production house responsible for some surprisingly big hits such as 1984's *Terminator*. Stone claims that the English management of Hemdale saw potential for *Salvador* in the humour: it had been written with comedy very much in mind (especially in the Rock/Boyle double act) and he claims to have promoted it as a 'sort of road movie . . . a bit like *Abbott & Costello go to Salvador*, along with some social realism'. Daly had also seen the script for *Platoon*, liked it and asked Stone to choose which film he wanted to make first. Stone chose *Salvador*: a lot of the groundwork had already been laid and he was simply too tired of seeing plans for *Platoon* come to nothing. Nominally Hemdale were to shoot an Arnold Schwarzenegger picture, tentatively titled *Outpost*, in the Mexican desert. But this movie did not exist beyond the concept, even though funding had already been arranged through a suspicious Belgian deal (later the subject of a criminal investigation). The money

($4.5 million) and the location instead went to Salvador, and shooting began in the spring of 1985. The project was guerrilla filmmaking in its purest form: the budget was a lie, the crew were perpetually on strike and the film was financed and produced in the shadiest of circumstances. But things went well – they received a warm reception from the mayor of Tlayacaplan, the village that stood in for Santa Ana, who allowed them to virtually tear the town to pieces. In addition he let his office stand in for Figueroa's orgy chamber, where Boyle and Rock first meet the Colonel. He was so pleased with the lurid décor that he insisted on keeping it.

Robert Richardson captured the last shot (Maria's departure) with the last light of the last day of scheduled filming in the desert outside Las Vegas. After editing, *Salvador* was released in March 1986.

CASTING: Stone initially intended to have Boyle and Rock play their respective screen counterparts. This fitted with the original ultra-low budget, and Stone even sent Boyle to receive acting lessons. For a while this remained the plan for the Hemdale production, and footage remains of initial screen tests. Frankly Rock and Boyle are lousy actors without a trace of screen charisma. In addition Boyle was a heavy drinker, and Director of Photography Robert Richardson complained of his constantly changing complexion – in one shot it would be red, in the next green – making colour matching impossible. In the end the substantial rise in budget allowed for the hiring of some respectable names.

James Woods would be signed up as Richard Boyle, after beating out Martin Sheen for the part (Woods had been suggested for Rock). He had few scruples about casting doubt on Sheen's suitability for the role, saying to Stone, 'He's kind of religious, isn't he . . . Gee, I'm surprised he didn't have a problem with some of the language here. It's pretty strong.' Woods compounded Stone's confirmations of the actor's doubts: 'Oh . . . I see, I thought you were going to do this thing for real . . . so then he decided to cast me for the lead.' It's difficult to imagine Sheen (who appears in *Wall Street*) as the jumpy, weasel-like Boyle seen here. The character of Boyle rests on a knife-edge between decent yet misunderstood and atavistic self-interest. Woods portrays his neuroses and his sharp features emphasise this vital ambiguity, and his performance brings humour, slyness and the right touch of frenzy to the character.

With the part of Rock vacant, Stone was pointed in the direction of James Belushi by Hollywood's Creative Artist's Agency (both actor and director were clients). Brother of the more famous John Belushi, who had died in 1982, Jim had little on his CV save a stint on *Saturday Night Live*, the comedy academy of the 80s and early 90s, but it was his performance in a skit entitled 'White man's rap' that got him the part. It was a sound bit of casting, the pudgy Belushi a Hardy-esque figure for the razor-thin Laurel of Woods (but psychologically reversed – Rock is the hapless buffoon, constantly arousing Boyle's ire). The banter between the two is a valuable addition, amusing in the opening montage as the duo make their way south of the border, and raising the already high tension once in El Salvador. This bickering was rooted in conditions on set, as it was here that Oliver Stone's reputation for needling performances out of his actors began. Woods was already an established actor, with eighteen films to his credit (including a fine performance in Sergio Leone's 1984 swan-song *Once Upon a Time in America*). This was only Belushi's fourth film, and he was constantly aware of the experienced Woods's scene-stealing tendencies. Stone played on this, feeding Belushi's paranoia, while warning Woods of the up-and-coming comic actor out to upset his career. Woods probably gets the upper hand – he is, after all, the lead – but there is chemistry when they appear together, a real tension and edginess, as one would expect given their circumstances. Mention of Stone's 'pressuring' technique became less common in his later work, but some of the best performances in his earlier films, such as with Woods, came about as a result of this constant aggressive pressure (see **Platoon, Talk Radio** and **Wall Street**).

The tousel-haired, square-jawed John Savage is best known for playing the crippled veteran in *The Deer Hunter* (Michael Cimino, 1978). He also appeared in *The Onion Field* (Harold Becker, 1979) with James Woods. He does a good job with Cassady, especially as there is little help from a script that seems unsure of how to present the character. He veers from a somewhat hard-nosed journalist ('Come on, take some pictures. There are fresh bodies up there') to dreamy artist, discussing Capa, to prissy loner (fiddling with his lenses) to drinking buddy, boozing with Rock and Boyle, to heroic captor of the 'magic' image of war. To be fair, Cassady exists as simultaneously a colleague, to underline the fact that Boyle does have a job in El Salvador, and as an example of journalistic integrity, of altruism, of dependability – of all the virtues that Boyle does not possess. Savage keeps the character ticking on a level somehow not quite human – he seems to go unnoticed by everyone except Boyle. One reading could be of Cassady as Boyle's guardian angel.

Elpedia Carrillo has appeared as 'the Latin American woman' in several other Hollywood movies, most notably *Predator* (John McTiernan, 1987). It has been argued that Stone fails to create good parts for women in his films, that they are presented in an actively hostile way or, at best, as bland love interest for the male lead. Maria falls into the latter category. She is never at the forefront of any scene and it could be said that the film revolves around Maria's importance to Boyle, with her own opinions and life of little concern. However, this might be explained better as the total importance of Stone's protagonist: the cinematic world does revolve around him. Mitigating Maria is the character of Cathy Moore (ably played by Cynthia Gibb), well rounded and effective.

OLIVER'S ARMY: Stone had developed a preference for working with newcomers (see **The Hand**) and the low budget of Salvador dictated that the crew would be composed of new faces. Most of these would stay with Stone to work on *Platoon* and one would go on to have an especially productive relationship – Bob Richardson, who would work with Stone on all his films up to *U Turn*.

Richardson was raised in New England and took an oceanography major at the University of Vermont. However, he left after two years to attend Rhode Island School of Design, studying in the film department from where he went on to the American Film Institute. He took jobs on a number of documentaries after finishing at the Institute, including work for the BBC on *Crossfire*, filmed in El Salvador. Though Richardson had a number of movies on his CV – including *Repo Man* (1984) for Alex Cox – it was this documentary work that interested Oliver Stone and led to his recruitment.

CUT SCENES: A clumsily satirical scene was cut – in it a pair of marketing yuppies speak of their success selling the Shah, Nixon and then helping Save the Whales while Major Max smirks at them. Footage of Alvarez's funeral was dropped, in which direct comparisons were drawn with real-life leaders of the left-wing Democratic Revolutionary Front (FDR) killed by paramilitaries in 1980. The battle of Santa Ana was trimmed, removing the guerrillas' flight to the hills as well as a brief scene of reconciliation between Boyle and Axelrod.

Several scenes in the original screenplay were never even filmed, including a sequence that builds on Boyle's claimed 'carte blanche' with Figuerola's elite unit. He arranges to join them on a patrol but is reviled by the men, especially an American mercenary who almost kills him. In another, a Dutch camera crew explicitly pay off Boyle for leading them to the guerrilla camp. A handover of money takes place in the movie, but with no explanation.

There are two scenes which appear neither in the screenplay nor the film, but have often been spoken of, an example of Stone's tendency to let the spirit of the film – in this case an improvisatory guerrilla feel – influence his direction. The orgy at Figueroa's office went on for much longer. Rock receives a blow-job from one prostitute and Boyle has sex with another, while simultaneously trying to interrogate the colonel, who drops a severed ear in a champagne glass before declaring a toast. The other is a longer confessional sequence improvised by Woods after being told by Stone to reach deep into his 'weasel soul'. One exchange that remained on the cutting room floor:

> **Priest:** Have you had carnal knowledge?
> **Boyle:** Well, yeah, I'm not a saint or anything, but I'm not bad, it's not like I've been out fucking quadrupeds.
> **Priest:** You had sex with a quadriplegic?
> **Boyle:** No, with a quadruped, like a goat or a Shetland pony or something.

This improvisation did not go all Stone's way. In the script, the Salvadorian border guards are supposed to destroy all of Cassady's film. But Woods thought Boyle ought to complete at least one act of redemption, and so persuaded a member of the prop department to fit a false heel to his boots. When he sprung this surprise on Stone, it was the afternoon of the last day of the Mexican shoot, and the director could do little about it.

MEMORABLE QUOTES:
Boyle: 'Take this, be dumb, act cool, all right?' [Hands Rock a pill]
Rock: 'A tranquillizer?'
Boyle: 'A permanent one. Cyanide.'
Rock: 'I'm not taking that shit.' [Throws it away]
Boyle: 'You know something, you're really going to regret that when they fuckin' cut off your balls and stick one in each ear!'

Major Max: 'Who will rid me of this troublesome Romero?'

GOOD VS EVIL:
This is a deeply earnest film, and at first inspection the moral demarcation seems pretty clear – the poor, oppressed villagers are

good, the brutal military regime is bad. Despite the blunt partiality, however, there is a fair amount of middle ground.

Broadly speaking, the embassy represents the 'evil' of complicity, the support lent by Reagan's administration to the far-right government and the military. Even so, there is the figure of Kelly, a liberal disgusted by the actions of the death-squads but unprepared and lacking the official support to back the left-wing alternative. Conversely, the guerrillas are portrayed sympathetically, yet this is offset by their execution of government prisoners – included in the film at Richard Boyle's insistence. Though it does not change the orientation of the film, there is the suggestion that the real answer to Salvador's problems lies not in some ideological extreme but in providing practical help for the people, as the aid groups do, a simple humanist solution. The guerrillas are good in that they don't harm the people to nearly the same degree as the military. Were they to achieve power, things might be different. As with *Heaven and Earth*, the downtrodden ordinary villagers are most clearly deserving of our support.

Boyle and Rock exist in the middle. Attached to the villagers but initially driven by self-interest, they essentially come to deliver a moral commentary on the situation, condemning the American military aid, criticising the guerrilla executions and trying to help out the aid groups. They act as a proxy for the audience, uncovering the horror of Salvador and revealing the actions of the US government.

REDEMPTION OR DAMNATION: The literal translation of Salvador is 'salvation' and the film is presented as one long path of redemption: Boyle comes to appreciate the problems of El Salvador, the real plight of its people, how this is more than some juicy story for the gringo press (indeed, it is anything but a juicy story – no one north of Mexico has any interest in what Boyle has to say). Atrocities in which he had nothing but professional interest are brought home personally. Ironically, there is little chance in the film for Boyle to redeem himself, beyond an intangible spiritual sense. He speaks of saving over 1000 refugees from the Khmer Rouge in Cambodia but fails to save just one family from Salvador.

This is mirrored in the collapse of the country – the death of the reforming archbishop, the hardening of attitudes of the American embassy, and the suppression of the guerrilla revolt. A situation has gone from bad to worse and there seems to be little hope.

Boyle's tribulations are one thing but, expressed on the wider canvas of misery and oppression, there is little doubt where the real tragedy lies, or that the film is ultimately pessimistic. In this sense the title, initially so full of hope, is ironic. There can be no salvation, even on an individual level.

HISTORY 101: One of the best features of Oliver Stone's *Salvador* is the appreciation of the limits of political filmmaking – it is impossible to create a popular, successful film based on a complex situation without cutting some corners. Ultimately, criticism is unavoidable – either from a cinemagoing public turned off by wordy ideological tracts or keen-eyed critics unimpressed by populist dumbing-down. Stone, by and large, treads the line carefully. In the case of *Salvador* exposition is seamlessly incorporated into the script, or simply passed over, the emphasis being on simple graphic representation of the murder and violence of the time. This simplification did have its critics – some complained that Stone's representation of Latin American affairs lacked subtlety and that the deeper rifts between landed wealth and landless poverty went uncommented on. This is fair, but misses the point: Stone aims at the story of Americans caught up in the chaos, as oblivious to deeper factors as the viewer; the Salvadorian civil war was and is as complex to grasp as the Arab–Israeli conflict, the Troubles of Northern Ireland and many other internecine political struggles of the late twentieth century.

Salvador was ruled by a strict authoritarian government from 1932 to 1979, dominated by an oligarchy of landlords backed by the military. In 1979 an idealistic group of young officers led a coup against then dictator General Romero. However, their aims for land reform and greater political freedoms were corrupted by older authoritarian elements in the army. The moderate and leftist civilian parties, which had participated in the formation of a governing junta, left in disgust and a fledgling resistance of leftist groups arose in the hills, politically represented by the persecuted Democratic Revolutionary Front (FDR). It was here that the interests of the USA came into play.

The industrial, economic and military dominance of the USA in the Americas led to Latin America being judged as an exclusively US sphere of influence. In the 1970s and 80s this jealous defence of outside interference took the form of stalwart opposition to perceived Communist incursion from Cuba and Nicaragua. The reference in the film to Sandanistas (Marxist rebels who had overthrown the Nicaraguan dictator Somoza in the 1970s) invading across the Gulf of Fonseca was a real piece of disinformation spread in an attempt to bolster support for military aid. The Americans viewed any leftist government with deep suspicion. Richard Nixon and Henry Kissinger supported the coup against President Allende in Chile in 1973 (see **Nixon**), putting Augusto Pinochet in power, and right-wing regimes were sponsored in Honduras (a neighbour and traditional enemy of El Salvador – the film's Boyle speaks to Figueroa of the 1969 'Soccer War', a conflict sparked by a disputed World Cup qualifying game between the two countries) and Panama.

The election of Ronald Reagan made prevention and containment of Communism a priority. By 1982, Salvador had become the fourth highest recipient of American financial and military aid, after Israel, Egypt and Turkey. The elections referred to in the film were held in 1984 but were massively handicapped by a lack of participation from leftist parties, paramilitary intimidation and the abuse of the *cedula*. Those who chose not to vote as protest against the limited range of candidates could be identified by their unendorsed *cedula* and 'punished'. The far right ARANA (Nationalist Republican Alliance) party, led by Roberto D'Aubuisson (see **REAL PEOPLE**), was a favourite to win, but his policies were too extreme, even for Washington, and American hostility to 'Major Bob' persuaded the dominant military to 'suggest' the choice of a moderate substitute. Power stayed in the hands of the military and civil war continued beyond the nominal end of the film and until the early 90s when both sides, exhausted, declared a ceasefire. At the time of writing, a slightly more moderate ARANA is the party of government.

CONSPIRACY THEORY: *Salvador* may appear a biased take on Latin American affairs, but all of the major events here did take place in one form or another, and pretty much in the manner represented on screen. It is true that the film has a degree of fiction to it; one critic commented on 'the improbability of Boyle's knack of witnessing every key moment of the Salvadorean tragedy' and the time scale is greatly compressed, but this is not so much a subjective interpretation or an alternate history as a necessary use of dramatic licence to shape a narrative. The lack of overt manipulation makes the facts all the more repulsive.

STARS AND STRIPES: In the representation of its protagonist, *Salvador* borrows from an American tradition of crusading journalism. The twist here is that Boyle is not a successful journalist – it is never made clear in the film whether he ever actually files a report (though the cut scenes suggest complete failure) – and in reality it was Raymond Bonner who published the account of El Salvador's horrors (see **INSPIRATION AND INFLUENCE**, below).

The film itself fitted in with another strand of literature – a close cousin to investigative journalism. This genre found its origins in Upton Sinclair's *The Jungle* (1906), a novel set in the very real world of the Chicago meatpacking trade. Though nominally a work of fiction, it raised questions on the terrible working conditions of the trade, questions that were seriously considered at the highest levels. Though not nearly so influential, the intent of *Salvador* was the same – using a fictionalised form to criticise the policies of the US.

BEING OLIVER STONE: This is a film about Richard Boyle's experiences, not those of Oliver Stone, and more is revealed about the character of the director from the turbulent story of the film's production than in the movie itself. Having said this, Stone had displayed an interest in the shadier areas of American policy in South America, going back to *Contra* (see **Talk Radio**) and even further to *Brazil Run* (see **Introduction**). It would also make appearances in *JFK* and *Nixon*.

On a personal note, Lou Stone died as filming on *Salvador* was starting up. After seeing his son drop out of Yale, fight in south-east Asia, arrested on drug charges and continually borrow money while pursuing a faltering film career, he would not live to see Stone's first true directorial effort.

REAL PEOPLE: There are several characters in *Salvador* directly comparable to real-world equivalents. Some are thinly veiled fictionalised versions. Tom Kelly is based on Robert White, the American ambassador to the country from March 1980 to February 1981 (White refused permission to use his name). As represented in the film, he was not a blind liberal, but was less than happy with the actions of the military and the government.

Archbishop Romero was a real cleric, seen as a powerful reforming force in the country. He gave speeches similar in style and content to the one seen in the film, itself based directly on earlier sermons, one of which finished in a similar fashion – 'I beg you, I ask you, I order you in the name of God: stop the repression.'

'Major Max' was based on the leader of ARANA, Robert 'Major Bob' D'Aubuisson. All accusations levelled at Major Max were said of 'Bob' – involvement in the death squads, organisation of the murder of Romero and intimate involvement with Reagan's representatives.

Then there are the two central figures – Richard Boyle and Dr Rock. Simultaneously they are accurate representations and fabrications. Rock was a slob, a DJ from San Francisco, and the story of his lost dog is rooted in a real event, but he never went to El Salvador and exists in the film as a figure of ignorance with whom the audience can identify. The case with Boyle is more complex. A photojournalist with a career covering Northern Ireland, Cambodia, the Yom Kippur War of 1973 and Vietnam, where he completed a book mentioned in this film (*Flower of the Dragon*, telling of cases of mutiny in American forces), Boyle briefly quit journalism, returning to cover first the civil war in Nicaragua and then El Salvador. The film is based on his experiences and has all the unreliability inherent in this, but also, on the wider sweep of history, placing Boyle at battles and events (such as the assassination of Romero) where he was not actually present. The need for drama also adds a fictional comrade, Cassady, loosely based on photographer John Hoagland.

INSPIRATION AND INFLUENCE: As well as Boyle's unpublished notes, Stone would consult the work of another Latin-American correspondent, Raymond Bonner, the *New York Times* reporter who published his account of El Salvador in the early 1980s under the title *Weakness and Deceit*. Simultaneously a scathing indictment of official US policy (especially that of the Reagan administration) and a disturbing record of the torture and political intimidation practised by the military and right-wing organisations, the book's general tone of despair at the tyranny and repression contributes as much to the film as do the specific accounts of atrocities that are replicated on screen. *Salvador* marked the start of an important trend in Stone's filmmaking, foreshadowed by *Midnight Express*. From here on, the majority of his work would be anchored in the reality of autobiography, biography and reported history. Even his fiction would often have 'real-life' elements (see **Talk Radio** and **Any Given Sunday**).

An influence on the screen relationship of Boyle and Rock is Hunter S Thompson's 1971 book *Fear and Loathing in Las Vegas*, itself a fictionalised account of real events. In the book, Thompson writes of a drug-fuelled road trip through Nevada. His companion was a chicano lawyer, Oscar Acosta, who travelled as Dr Gonzo, and the byplay between the equally stoned compatriots – one a tall, thin, nervy journalist, the other a squat, fat, lecherous hanger-on – mirrors that of Richard Boyle and Dr Rock. The homage goes deeper, as *Fear and Loathing . . .* was a work of gonzo journalism, a tricky term that basically involves the reporter becoming a part of the narrative. This clearly describes Boyle's role in the film. That gonzo journalism frequently involves some blurring of exact details in search of a greater truth is of further interest in the context of Stone's subsequent work.

The proximity and comparative poverty of Latin America to the USA has also created its own genre of literature, which the film riffs on. This varies from thrill-seeking Bohemian or Beatnik northerners seeking cut-price thrills in the South (Jack Kerouac's *On the Road* or Tom Wolfe's *The Electric Kool-Aid Acid Test* to the worthier, more serious explorations of the subsistence-level existence endured by the peasantry – for instance in the books of Moritz Thomsen, a North American who lived alongside villagers in 1960s Ecuador. *Salvador* is a synthesis of these approaches, the hedonistic urges of Dr Rock and Boyle counterpointed with the more conscientious representation of a desperately poor society.

Salvador was and remains a little-known low-key film. It shares characteristics with *The Killing Fields* (Roland Joffe, 1984) and *The Year of Living Dangerously* (Peter Weir, 1982), which feature journalists caught up in the chaos of Cambodia and Indonesia respectively, and it is probably best to think of them as a tiny sub-genre, a brief flowering of genuinely conscientious filmmaking relating to atrocities in foreign lands. *Salvador* is the only American picture (*Killing Fields* was British and *The Year of Living Dangerously* Australian), and this is also revealing. However you choose to analyse it – a right-wing political shift in domestic politics, obsession with a perceived communist threat or just sheer indifference – the subject matter was just not popular in the American market.

REEL TIME: Robert Richardson's influence on *Salvador* becomes clearer in comparison with *Platoon*, *Wall Street*, and *The Doors*. The calm of a static shot occasionally cutting to close-up is suddenly broken in moments of action, the camera frantically darting around the fray as if handheld (as in fact it was for several sequences). There are no fancy visual effects (none are needed, even had there been the budget) but the print is astonishingly clear, even taking into account the crispness that DVD lends to older films. A great example of what can be achieved with a little money and a lot of skill: the end result is of the highest quality but without the high-tech prices.

MUSIC: The least coherent aspect of the film. It begins with the insistent dramatic pounding that accompanies an opening montage of documentary footage. This drops into a couple of mellow 60s/70s hippie-rock tracks for the San Francisco/travel montage sequences. The body of the soundtrack is a pretty derivative yet effective sinister orchestral composition but the mood bizarrely shifts when Boyle travels to the guerrillas' hideout, the score replaced by some jaunty Latin rhythms performed by Yolocamba. These run through the battle of Santa Ana and Latin guitar plays over the closing scene. There is nothing wrong with any one of these tunes, more with the inconsistency that they bring. The accompaniment to the guerrilla scenes lends a certain mawkish tone: the message of the film is far from obscure, and the music adds unneeded emphasis.

BOX OFFICE: As of 30 November 2003, *Salvador* had grossed $1.5 million. It was never released on a sufficient scale to make back its budget from box office receipts but has enjoyed good business in the home DVD and VHS market.

CRITICS: Roger Ebert praised the lead performance: 'This is the sort of role James Woods was born to play, with his glibness, his wary eyes and the endless cigarettes.' The critic for the *New Socialist* went furthest, saying that 'it is that performance which is central to the film and, I think, one of the cleverest acting feats in contemporary cinema.'

Another popular view was to see the film as 'a radical riposte to the *Rambo* school of thick eared jingoism', in the words of Nigel Andrews, or as 'a salutary antidote for films like *Top Gun*', as noted by William Parente in the *Scotsman*. Another writer for the same paper was more complimentary of the structure to the film: 'Stone does a fine job of condensing fact and incident . . . and of recreating the madness, fear and brutality.' Philip French also thought the film was well observed, describing it as 'sensational but not unduly sensationalised'. Derek Malcolm saw balance: 'The film does not romanticise the actions of the rebel troops', and a wholly appropriate ending: 'This aura of despair, extended into an ironically downbeat ending . . . seems very much in keeping with Salvador's style of provocation.'

There was some disagreement: Walter Goodman wrote in the *New York Times* that 'viewers . . . will be hard put to tell whether the events on screen are actually known to have occurred in quite the way they are pictured.' Another noteworthy criticism was aired in the *New Statesman*, which suggested that 'the film is unable to treat women as equals' and therefore that 'on a deeper level it recycles the ideologies that underlie what it purports to condemn.' This is a valid point, and it would not be the last time that a critic would question Stone's attitude towards women. Nevertheless, there was a prescient note in the review in the *NME*: 'By the end of 1987 Oliver Stone will undoubtedly be seen as one of America's most creative and politically forceful directors.'

CONTROVERSY: *Salvador* had a low-key release, though it caused some fuss south of the border: the film was banned by Honduran authorities, according to the *New York Times* 'on the ground that its grim portrayal of El Salvador's civil war threatened state security'.

AWARDS: Because of the release schedule and quick turnaround of both films, *Salvador* found itself facing *Platoon* at the 1987 Academy Awards – Stone and Boyle were nominated in Best Original Screenplay category. James Woods was also nominated for best actor, though he lost out to Paul Newman in *The Color of Money* (Martin Scorsese, 1986).

Woods was awarded best actor at the Independent Spirit awards in the same year. Salvador also picked up five nominations – cinematography, director, film, screenplay and female lead for Elpedia Carrillo, flying in the face of those who criticised her performance. The screenplay was also nominated for a Writers Guild of America award.

THE BIG PICTURE: To all intents and purposes, this represents Oliver Stone's first film as director. *Seizure* was a post-student experiment while *The Hand* was Stone cashing in on post-Oscar kudos. Here a screenplay and direction are unimpeded by big studio interference, a low-budget is expertly managed and there is skilled handling of a temperamental lead. Most importantly, Hemdale had already given Stone a second picture, so he could afford not to take *Salvador*'s poor box-office performance to heart: *Salvador* was a project born of opportunism in every way; *Platoon* would be the fruit of a decade's work, straight from the heart, and represented another precious chance to break into the mainstream.

It is also important to note a change in attitude to foreign nationalities. In this film Stone treats the ordinary Salvadorians and the guerrillas with a degree of respect and compassion. Even the villains, while vicious, are not portrayed as universally brutish and stupid (though their foot-soldiers are). From here on, none of Stone's films could be regarded as racist in the way that his early scripts are. This is perhaps most due to the leeway provided by the material: *Midnight Express* and *Year of the Dragon* are both xenophobic in their original form, while *Scarface* relies heavily on the idea of a criminal immigrant element. From here on in Stone would be dealing with matters of great personal interest, and – say what else you like about him – his personal interests do not extend to casual racism.

FINAL ANALYSIS: Many people name this as their favourite Oliver Stone film, and it is easy to see why: the polemic aspects of the script and story are offset by the acerbic Woods, the style is perfectly matched to the subject, and the handling of the film accomplished, both in scenes of intimacy and outbursts of violence. This is the most balanced of Stone's 'message' movies, and it helps that the subject was not personally close to the director's heart (the same applies to *Talk Radio*). It does not batter the viewer into submission and so, paradoxically, is better able to make its point – there was something deeply wrong with US attitudes to Latin America, a point that is all the more powerful for its lack of coverage in mainstream media.

Salvador sends a strong political message through the medium of a single man's experiences and own personal journey. It is very much James Woods's film and fits him like a glove – contrast his final expression of frustrated angst with the devious chancer first seen in San Francisco. It is a transformation and performance unmatched in Stone's canon – superior even to Tom Cruise's work on *Born on the Fourth of July* – and any praise for the film must be equally shared between the director and his lead.

Salvador is a witty, compelling and gripping work, shrouded in obscurity when compared with the high-profile *Platoon* but a minor classic in its own right.

Platoon (1986)

Hemdale Film Corporation presents
An Arnold Kopelson production
An Oliver Stone Film
Executive in charge of Production: Graham Henderson
Special Make-up and Visual Continuity: Gordon J Smith
Special Effects Supervisor: Yves de Bono
Military Technical Adviser: Captain Dale Dye, United States
Marine Corps (Retired)
Sound Mixer: Simon Kaye
First Assistant Director: H Gordon Boos

Film Editor: Claire Simpson
Production Designer: Bruno Rubeo
Director of Photography: Robert Richardson
Production Executive: Pierre David
Co-Producer: A Kitman Ho
Executive Producers: John Daly and Derek Gibson
Producer: Arnold Kopelson
Written and Directed by Oliver Stone

CAST: Tom Berenger (*Sergeant Barnes*), Willem Dafoe (*Sergeant Elias*), Charlie Sheen (*Chris*), Forest Whitaker (*Big Harold*), Francesco Quinn (*Rhah*), John C McGinley (*Sergeant O'Neill*), Richard Edson (*Sal*), Kevin Dillon (*Bunny*), Reggie Johnson (*Junior*), Keith David (*King*), Johnny Depp (*Lerner*), David Neidorf (*Tex*), Mark Moses (*Lieutenant Wolfe*)

NOTABLE CREDITS: Special thanks to Michael Cimino (see **PRODUCTION HISTORY**).

SUMMARY: Caption card: 'Rejoice, O young man in your Youth – Ecclesiastes'. Chris Taylor arrives in Vietnam in September 1967 to join Bravo Company of the 25th Infantry on the Cambodian border. At the airbase he passes two sets of troops leaving Vietnam – one group who have finished their tour and are on their way back to the States, the other in body bags.

He slogs through the dense jungle with the other soldiers of Bravo Company. Platoon Sergeant Barnes snarls at Chris for lagging behind. Sergeant Elias takes pity and lightens his load. At camp, black troopers King and Harold discuss schemes for dodging frontline duty while another black soldier, Junior, mocks Chris. The platoon head off on a night patrol. Chris completes his sentry duty and wakes Junior, who goes straight back to sleep. Chris spots Vietcong creeping up on their position but is frozen to the spot and unable to set off the protective perimeter of Claymore mines. A firefight ensues, in which machine-gunner Tex is badly wounded and new recruit Gardener is killed. Chris is lightly wounded and goes to hospital.

When he returns to base-camp, loudmouth Sergeant O'Neill, a friend of Barnes, sets him to clean the latrines with surfer boy Crawford and King. The two high-school dropouts can't believe college boy Chris's reasons for volunteering – he felt it was unfair for rich kids to dodge the draft. King introduces Chris to the 'heads' – dope-smoking, urban laid-back soldiers such as barely sane Rhah, iron-pumping Manny, translator Lerner, Big Harold, quiet Francis and Elias, who 'shotguns' marijuana smoke to Chris. Their neon-lit hedonistic bunker is contrasted with the cold austerity of the barracks home of beer-drinking rednecks like the psychotic Bunny, quiet, religious Rodriguez, 'Lifers' (career soldiers) such as O'Neill and Barnes and the whiny Junior: a disparate group united in their disdain for the pot-smoking heads. Lt Wolfe makes an abortive attempt to fraternise with the barracks dwellers but creeps away in embarrassed failure.

On patrol Chris is already a better soldier, but still he is oblivious to an elaborate bunker complex spotted by Barnes. The platoon scatters around the site while Elias infiltrates the tunnels, but a booby-trap is set off topside, killing two men and bringing him back to the surface. Manny goes missing and Elias is left to guard the bunker, awaiting the arrival of engineers to disarm the booby traps while Barnes takes the others to investigate a nearby village. On the way they find Manny strung up, his throat cut. Inflamed, they hit the village hard and without mercy, beating, shouting and intimidating. Weapons are found and a crazed Chris almost kills a villager who fails to obey him. Bunny bludgeons the hapless man to death. Outside, Barnes rails at a village leader who claims to have nothing to do with the North Vietnamese. His wife protests and Barnes coldly shoots her, threatening to do the same to the man's daughter. Elias arrives and throws himself at Barnes. They grapple and Wolfe breaks them up – Elias is enraged that the lieutenant did not stop Barnes. They are ordered to torch the village and force the villagers out. Back at base Elias promises to submit a report. O'Neill suggests to Barnes that Elias be fragged – assassinated.

The next day the platoon returns to the bunker complex, but is ambushed. Wolfe calls in an artillery bombardment that hits his own men, including Lerner. Harold sets off a booby trap and is also wounded. Elias leaves Chris, Crawford and Rhah to cover him while he goes in search of enemy positions. They successfully ambush a VC patrol but Crawford is injured. Barnes calls a retreat and orders Chris, Rhah and Crawford to an evacuation point. He tracks down Elias and shoots him three times in the chest. As the choppers lift off, the men see the wounded Sergeant Elias run to the landing zone, only to be cut down by a horde of pursuers. Later, after interrupting the heads' discussion over his guilt, Barnes is attacked by, and nearly kills, Chris, who blames Barnes for Elias's death.

The platoon is to guard a battalion HQ from impending heavy attack. As night falls, King's leaving papers come through and he is choppered out. Less successful are O'Neill, who pleads with Barnes for early R&R, and Junior, who burns his feet with caustic mosquito repellent. Neither ruse is successful. Chris is stationed with Francis but the line of defence collapses as soon as the attack begins. In the chaos Junior, Bunny and Wolfe are all killed. O'Neill survives by hiding under a corpse. Chris charges the enemy troops and Barnes lays waste to anyone who comes near. As total annihilation looms, an air strike is called in, right on the Americans' own position, preventing Barnes from killing Chris. The dust clears and Chris pulls himself up. Badly wounded, he grabs a Vietnamese AK 47 and staggers over to the prone Barnes, who first calls for a medic and then for a quick death when he sees the look in Chris's eyes. Chris shoots him.

An armoured brigade arrives bringing military and medical support. O'Neill is made Platoon Sergeant – to his dismay. Chris is flown out with Francis and looks down on Rhah as the helicopters lift off.

A closing caption – 'Dedicated to the men who fought and died in the Vietnam War'.

ADVANCE PUBLICITY: The poster for *Platoon* has become one of the most iconic images of any Vietnam War film, on a level with *Apocalypse Now*'s powerful sunset motif.

The title, in blocky military font, is splayed across the image of Elias, arms raised Christ-like, in his death pose. A powerful image with a powerful tagline: 'The first casualty of war is innocence.'

Stone's own war record was much publicised. Press releases mentioned his infantry service, and contemporary interviews make much of autobiographical elements. Some saw it as excessive – David Denby wrote in the *New York Times* that 'the IWT [I Was There] factor is being used to bully a presumably reluctant, uninterested audience into seeing the movie.'

In addition, a reunion of Stone's old platoon was televised, and an advance screening of the film was held for veterans at the suggestion of military adviser Dale Dye.

PRODUCTION HISTORY: The first draft of *Platoon* dates back to 1976. Stone was pushing thirty, with little to show for his efforts at filmmaking save an increasing stack of debts and the break-up of his first marriage. Somehow, the American bicentennial celebrations, then in progress in New York harbour, inspired him to write up his experience in Vietnam. With eight years' distance from the events of which he wrote, Stone hammered out a draft in four or five weeks, combining his personal experiences and relationships with a plot focussing on internal conflict that he saw as central to the American involvement in Vietnam. Gone was the metaphorical musing of *Break* (see **The Doors**) and other early screenplays in favour of a simpler narrative, imbued with raw power and honesty. Unfortunately, no one wanted to make it. Producers were interested and Martin Bregman – responsible for other American new wave films such as *Serpico* (Sidney Lumet, 1973) and *Dog Day Afternoon* (Sidney Lumet, 1975) – hawked the screenplay around the major studios, but as he puts it, 'I banged on every door in California to get it done, but at that time Vietnam was still a no-no.' The war was just too recent – it would be at least two years before the Vietnam films of the American new wave would be released: Michael Cimino's *The Deer Hunter* (1978), Hal Ashby's *Coming Home* (1978), Francis Ford Coppola's *Apocalypse Now* (1979).

Stone's skill as a writer shone through and he was offered other work in the meantime, including the task of adapting *Midnight Express*. By 1984 he had carved out a fairly successful career as a writer and was asked to script *Year of the Dragon*, to be directed by Michael Cimino. It was Cimino who suggested that Stone pull *Platoon* out of mothballs and do a deal with producer Dino De Laurentiis, to write his script in exchange for backing Stone's Vietnam picture (it was this encouragement that Stone thanked with Cimino's credit on the film). The Italian mogul agreed, and Stone set to work. With *Year of the Dragon* finished, Stone returned to *Platoon*, carrying out rewrites – including the addition of Barnes's death at the hand of Chris – and location scouting in the Philippines. However, De Laurentiis reneged on the deal after he failed to find a distributor. To rub salt in the wound, the producer claimed ownership over the rights to the film, in lieu of payment for money spent on the Philippines trip. It would be two years until this conflict was resolved – essentially De Laurentiis handed the rights back over for fear of legal action that might delay the release of *Year of the Dragon*. By the time Stone had regained ownership he was heavily involved with Hemdale (see **Salvador**), which agreed to take on *Platoon* with Arthur Kopelson (who had played a vital role with foreign distribution of *Salvador*) producing.

Funding was hard to come by, but the $6 million budget was eventually scraped together – an impressive commitment by Hemdale considering that they had yet to recoup their expenditure on *Salvador*. By October 1985 the film had a green light, but even then things did not go totally smoothly. A successful revolution against Ferdinand Marcos, ruler of the Philippines, took place while the details for the shoot were being finalised – in fact Willem Dafoe and Bob Richardson were already in Manila. To prevent disruption, it helped that most of the filming would take place away from the capital and last-minute pay-offs to key members of the new government – specifically to secure use of military equipment, which had been refused them by the American armed forces – ensured that the production could take place. In 54 days, the film was in the can. It was released in December 1986.

CASTING: As the title indicates, this film is built around the actions of one platoon, and so casting of its members was of great importance. The nature of the project required a group of skilled actors who could work as individuals and gel not only as part of a military unit but also as members of one of the two 'tribes' – the redneck/lifer/juicer establishment and the radical heads. This cast was drawn from a pool of young actors. Some would go on to successful careers (Forest Whitaker and Johnny Depp for instance) and others would not, but they represented a largely untapped range of talent for whom this would be the first big break. Indeed, the part of Chris Taylor was the first lead role for Charlie Sheen. Sheen's brother Emilio Estevez had been suggested for the role when the film was being discussed in 1984 but Sheen was considered too inexperienced. In the two intervening years Sheen corrected this with a role in the right-wing militaristic fantasy *Red Dawn* and a cameo in *Ferris Bueller's Day Off* (John Hughes, 1984) and successfully re-auditioned.

Barnes and Elias are key roles, as much for what they represent as for their direct contributions to the plot, and great care had to be taken with finding actors. Curiously, Tom Berenger and Willem Dafoe were cast against type. Stone saw a beauty and gentleness in the features of Dafoe, better known for his 'bad guy' roles before and since *Platoon* (most recently as the Green Goblin in Sam Raimi's *Spider-Man* (2002) and an eerie turn as a vampiric Max Shreck in E Elias Merhige's bizarre 2000 comedy/horror *Shadow of the Vampire*) and also for his performance as Jesus in *The Last Temptation of Christ* (Martin Scorsese, 1988). Tom Berenger, meanwhile, was possessed of attractive, rugged matinee idol features. With the addition of a gruesome prosthetic scar, this translated into the hardness and intransigence of Sergeant Barnes. For comparison, look at his clean-cut Marine-recruiting officer in *Born on the Fourth of July*, a film in which Dafoe also appears, displaying his corrupt, reptilian side.

To bond these actors as fighting comrades, military adviser Dale Dye devised a two-week boot camp. Each performer adopted their character name and rank, learned to set ambushes, dig foxholes, handle weapons and carried out long marches with full gear. Stone basically wanted to create an impression of a year without sleep in two weeks.

The net result was to give a great impression of camaraderie and the feel of real military cohesion to the platoon, supporting the quirks of the individual soldiers. The leads are equally competent. Berenger oozes a dark menace, a man who revels in the darkness of Vietnam but who takes care of those men who unquestioningly follow his orders, while Dafoe's Elias has an ethereal quality, seeming to float through the jungle contrasted with a sense of humanity that seems naïve in the circumstances. Sheen's Chris is dreamily absent at times, fiercely intense at others, an observer forced to become an actor by what he sees. Another example of a great performance needled out of an actor by Stone, Sheen was taunted and teased over his soft Californian lifestyle. All in all a great ensemble cast, and a great example of (admittedly imposed) method acting.

OLIVER'S ARMY: Most of the crew moved straight from the set of *Salvador* to the Philippines. Bob Richardson and Claire Simpson were there, as was production designer Bruno Rubeo – responsible for the impressive Vietcong bunkers that seem to melt into the jungle – and composer Georges Delerue, this time working with Barber's *Adagio for Strings* rather than Latin American folk music. There would be two important debuts. Captain Dale Dye made his first appearance as technical adviser (assisted by Stanley White – see **Year of the Dragon**). After 20 years in the Marines, including 30 months on the front lines in Vietnam, Dye offered his services to Hollywood producers and directors in an attempt to promote a more realistic representation of the military. This appealed to ex-serviceman Stone, who has used Dye in all of his Vietnam pictures. He even appears in front of the cameras, putting in a decent turn as Captain Harris who takes charge of the beleaguered battalion after the death of the lieutenant colonel, a cameo by Stone.

Another important addition to the roster was A Kitman Ho, who had previously helped out on the production of *Year of the Dragon*. He had become involved with Stone afterwards, hawking *Platoon* around the studios, and had a role in Dino De Laurentiis's abortive attempts to get this Vietnam movie made. He would stay with Stone for years afterwards, working on every film up to *Heaven and Earth*. Many of the actors would also make appearances in later Stone films and John C McGinley would become a Stone regular.

CUT SCENES: Around 15 per cent of the initial script was not shot. Some miscellaneous details were lost; for instance, Gardner was originally seen to arrive on the same transport as Chris but Johnny Depp's Lerner and Francesco Quinn's Rhah are the greatest victims of the cuts.

Lerner gets more time on the page as an easygoing head, while Rhah is painted as a mystic and shaman, an impression that is briefly sketched in the film. At one point he illustrates the Barnes/Elias dynamic with tattoos on his knuckles reading 'Hate' and 'Love'. This is referred to in Chris's closing monologue ('fighting . . . for what Rhah called possession of my soul').

The starlit conversation between Elias and Taylor was greatly shortened. In the original script, Elias asks Taylor to make sure the truth of Vietnam gets told, apparently foreseeing his own death – at which point he dreamily suggests he would like to return as a deer, adding another dimension to the film's close: Chris sees a deer in the immediate aftermath of the battle. The scene also featured a brief indictment of US policy in Vietnam from Elias, similar to the critique Boyle delivers in *Salvador*. In a rare show of restraint, Stone left this out of the film – 'I just thought it would be enough to document exactly what happened and let people draw their own conclusions.'

There is one inconsistency that is not resolved: as the heads debate fragging Barnes, Rhah recalls the 'first time you came in here, Taylor . . . telling me how much you admired that bastard'. There is no mention of this admiration in the film or the published screenplay – the closest Chris gets is to say that Elias is 'as crazy as Barnes'.

Perhaps the most interesting omission, in light of Stone's treatment of Richard Nixon, is a throwaway line from King shortly before he is shipped out: 'Somewhere out there man is the Beast, and he hungry tonight' (see **Nixon**).

MEMORABLE QUOTES:
Barnes (over Gardner's corpse): 'Y'all take a good look at this lump o' shit . . . You fuck up in a firefight and I guaran-goddamn-tee you a trip

out the bush – in a body bag. Out here, assholes, you keep your shit wired tight at *all times . . .*'

Elias (on Gardner): 'Man'd be alive if he'd had a few more days to learn something.'

O'Neill: 'Excuses are like assholes, Taylor – everybody got one.'

Elias (on dope smoking): 'First time?'
Chris: 'Yeah.'
Elias: 'Then the worm has definitely turned for you man.'

Barnes: 'You smoke this shit to escape reality? Me, I don't need that shit. I am reality.'

GOOD VS EVIL: The concept of a clash between good and evil is important to all of Oliver Stone's films, but nowhere is it more directly expressed than in *Platoon*. What is especially interesting is that in this film's scheme of 'good' and 'evil' the nominal enemies of the American troops – the Vietcong and NVA forces – have no place, existing as lifeless bodies or as vengeful jungle ghosts. Stone related the film's perspective on Vietnamese soldiers to his real experiences: 'We didn't really *see* the North Vietnamese very much.' Even the murder of Manny, strung up by a riverbank, is presented in retrospect, a thing already done, and not so much a deliberate action. Instead the divide lies within the ranks of the US troops, as Stone himself perceived had actually been the case: 'On the one hand there were the lifers, the juicers [heavy drinkers] and the moron white element.' On the other, 'a very progressive, hippie dope-smoking element made up of black guys and whites from the cities . . . Indians, random characters from odd places'.

There is a clear delineation between those judged to be 'good' – the latter group in Stone's description, led by Sergeant Elias – and the 'bad' – best described as everyone else and led (dominated would be more accurate) by Sergeant Barnes. It is the contrast between these two that acts best as the gauge to any moral judgement made by the film.

Some rather clumsy Christian allusions are made with regard to Elias, a 'water-walker' who 'thinks he's Jesus Christ' and who dies in full crucifixion pose. Barnes is demonic in an ancient sense, his facial scars marking him as evil. In the most basic way the position of these characters can be seen by their actions – Elias takes pity on the newly arrived Taylor, Barnes chastises him, Barnes shoots the village woman, Elias challenges Barnes. But Barnes is also realism, orthodoxy versus the idealistic rebellion of dope-smoking Elias – who has been three years in the country and, while talking with Chris, questions the righteousness of his actions. Barnes does not question anything, and despises those who do – 'Don't tell me how to run my war!' he shouts at one point. Both are still fighting, but Elias is doing so only really to survive and to protect his men, his dominant emotion being love. Barnes uses combat as a release for his immense rage. He has become consumed by the fighting, and can express only anger at the death of his men – whether this is directed at innocent villagers or the incompetent Lieutenant Wolfe. He has no compassion for the dead, such as Gardner, or for those trying to cheat death: 'Everybody's got to die,' he tells O'Neill, who is trying to wheedle an extra few days' leave.

Barnes's 'reality' is dog-eat-dog, kill-or-be-killed, with no compromise, and this blind loyalty to a murderous cause is the film's evil. Elias sees what the war has become and rejects it; he joins the heads in smoking pot 'to escape this reality', looking just to stay alive and keep his men alive. It is debatable if this urge for self-preservation exists in Barnes's soul beyond the level of animal reflex. Stone has described his sergeants as 'The angry Achilles versus the conscience stricken Hector fighting for a lost cause on the dusty plains of Troy' and there is a powerful emotional and mythological feel to either path, pure, unfettered rage versus a more mystical, conscientious spirit. This is the choice Stone presents to his alter ego Chris Taylor.

REDEMPTION OR DAMNATION: In his memorable closing voice-over, the Chris character says, 'The war is over for me now, but it will always be there . . . As I am sure Elias will be, fighting with Barnes for . . . possession of my soul . . . there are times when I have felt like the child born of those two fathers . . .' In keeping with the spirit of clear delineation between Barnes and Elias, it is this closing voice-over that sums up the journey of its protagonist – into the war, through it and out of it without losing his soul. Initially Chris volunteers for the same reasons as Oliver Stone himself (see **BEING OLIVER STONE**) but he soon realises his mistake. What is left is a choice: to wire himself into a survival trip, like Elias and the heads, or to sink into the rage that war inspires in Barnes. Ultimately the question rests on his execution of Barnes. Some have interpreted this as a counter-productive act of murder, identifying Chris with Barnes over Elias. This is flawed. It fails to consider the suicidal impulse of Barnes, the idea that at some level he does not want to go on living, or whether it is right that Barnes be allowed to go on sating his rage by waging his own war in Vietnam. It is not an act of good in conventional morality, but perhaps in terms of the film. However, Taylor is returning to a world of conventional morality and it is not Stone's intention to let him leave Vietnam with a clean moral slate: 'I wanted to show that Chris came out of the war stained and soiled.' His justification for this? 'I think that we all did, every vet ... So what if there was some bad in us? So what? That's the price you pay.' Barnes is dead, the animal impulse to violence is dead, but the act of killing carries its own opprobrium.

It is worth briefly noting the third group of soldiers – those lifers and juicers who reject Barnes's raging fatalism – specifically O'Neill and Junior. They do not really fit into the Elias group either – their dislike for the war is total and selfish, stopping short of comradely loyalty. For Chris to choose this third way would amount to a pathetic form of damnation from the film's viewpoint.

HISTORY 101: This is not a factual historical documentary. Nor is it dramatised or condensed in the manner of *Salvador*. Indeed, it almost exists in isolation from the greater narrative of the Vietnam War, with recognisable weapons, uniforms, opposing forces and locations but without any reference to specific events (in comparison, the latter part of *Full Metal Jacket* (Stanley Kubrick, 1987) is staged against the backdrop of the 1968 Tet offensive). The move away from political and historical factors seems deliberate. Over the course of the film, the soldiers accomplish no meaningful directive, are shot and killed or injured in apparently purposeless patrols and missions. With no reference to wider political goals this makes the activity of the grunts doubly pointless, as one imagines it could have been from their perspective at the time.

CONSPIRACY THEORY: The film is free of polemic or proselytising, beyond Chris's voice over. Condemnation of the decisions to enter Vietnam or the prosecution of the war is not within Stone's remit, beyond the implied criticism of the savagery of certain soldiers. This feels the most honest of Stone's films, perhaps because it comes from such a personal place.

STARS AND STRIPES: If there is an antithesis of the American dream, it might be sought in Vietnam. Especially in this Vietnam, free from ideology, with reality composed of the 'six inches in front of your face', the heat, humidity and death, and presented from the perspective of those on the front line to whom the war appears mystifying, futile and pretty much unwinnable. There are those who defend the war, but here it is devoid of any glory, of any higher purpose and without any connotation of a great battle to defend democracy and freedom. In later films (see **Born on the Fourth of July**) Stone develops and deepens this idea of the Vietnam war as the dark side of America.

BEING OLIVER STONE: It is difficult for anyone who did not fight in Vietnam to judge what *Platoon* as a film represents for Oliver Stone. It is largely autobiographical in nature, and explores a deeper interpretation of what time in Vietnam meant for the young soldier, but it also exists as a cathartic work, a way of expressing feelings bottled up for some years. Stone (and Dale Dye) were not always able to remain composed on set, during the village raid scene for instance.

It is possible to draw a tentative comparison, a guide to how the experiences of Private Bill (he signed up under his middle name) Stone mirror those of Private Chris Taylor.

Both arrived in-country (in the same month – September 1967) from a privileged upbringing, with similar attitudes to this privilege and a similar desire to test themselves in this conflict from a certain perspective (it might have seemed equivalent to World War II for those sons whose fathers had fought in Europe, North Africa or the Pacific) and both soon realised the enormity of their misconceptions and their mistakes. Stone recalls the straight swap of fresh recruits, 'cherries', for body bags and returning veterans at the military airbase – even this highly symbolic image is rooted in reality. Assigned to the real-life equivalent of Taylor's platoon, he was thrown straight into front-line work, given a machete and told to cut point, with little help offered from the experienced short-timers. With just a few months left of their tour they were disinclined to put their neck out for a rookie. In his second week Stone fell asleep on his watch and awoke to a Vietcong attack; paralysed with fear, he was unable to act and was wounded in the back of the neck.

Shortly after his return to the platoon, Stone found himself involved in the Battle of Firebase Burt (firebases were concentrations of artillery, allowing heavy fire support to front-line units). Two battalions were defending the firebase over the Christmas and New Year period during which a truce was supposed to be in effect. But early on the morning of 1 January over 2000 Vietnamese attacked the 700 American guards. The perimeter was overrun and the platoons were split up and surrounded, the Vietcong having, according to Stone, sketched maps of positions.

Eventually a last-ditch counterattack was backed up by a heavy air raid, with bombs dropped almost directly on top of the firebase. In the morning the 500 dead North Vietnamese were buried in huge pits by military bulldozers. It is clear where Stone drew the inspiration for *Platoon*'s climactic battle.

Just two weeks later, Stone was caught in an ambush near a Vietcong bunker complex, tying in with the third major battle of the film. Like Big Harold in the fictional ambush, he was wounded by flying shrapnel from a satchel charge, triggered by one of his fellow soldiers. Taken off to hospital ('like the end of *Platoon*'), Stone missed the Tet Offensive of 1968, a broad North Vietnamese push on all fronts in the middle of another truce, to mark 'Tet' – Vietnamese new year. The 25th Infantry were caught in the middle of this and suffered heavy casualties. Stone's second wound saw him posted to a military police battalion based in Saigon. But he couldn't stay away from combat and, after a fight with one of the rear echelon lifer sergeants he so disparaged, he volunteered for front-line duties. He even turned down his father's efforts to pull strings and have him assigned to the CIA for intelligence work. Instead, in April 1968, he was assigned to a long-range reconnaissance unit, part of the 1st Cavalry, which worked far behind enemy lines. One member of this unit was a Sergeant Juan Angel Elias; another was Ben Fitzgerald (see **REAL PEOPLE**). In August 1968, Stone won his Bronze Star after charging an enemy foxhole, but not long after was transferred to a mechanised unit, driving Jeeps under the command of Platoon Sergeant Barnes.

Both Stone and Taylor were introverts, constantly writing to their grandmothers, both took a while to be accepted, but became heads, partying, listening to rock music and smoking dope, sometimes dangerously near the combat zone. And both had dalliances with the dark side of combat – Taylor's machine-gunning of a peasant man's feet was an experience drawn straight from Stone's recollection of the war – being complicit with acts of savagery committed by American forces, though neither man totally crossed the line; Stone speaks of breaking up an attempted rape, another act attributed to Chris Taylor.

When Stone shipped out, in November 1968, he did so with a Bronze Star, a Purple Heart with Oak Cluster, and experiences and memories that would drive the rest of his life.

REAL PEOPLE: The majority of characters in *Platoon* find their inspiration in Stone's Vietnam comrades. King was known in reality as

Ben Fitzgerald, who became his close friend. Both were large black men from small-town Tennessee, though Fitzgerald was not quite the mentor that King was to Chris Taylor. Bunny is based on a real soldier too, and his beating to death of a villager is based on a real event that Stone describes as taking place 'in an isolated part of the village. Nobody saw it. It was just like a really quiet thing.' Junior is based on a soldier whom Stone blames for falling asleep on watch during the ambush in which he was first wounded, while the real O'Neill was also a sergeant who tormented Private Stone and continually assigned him to unpleasant duties.

Sergeant Elias served in the long-range patrol unit, and Stone describes him as a handsome half-Spanish, half-Native American 23-year-old, 'like a rock star to me, the Jimmy Morrison of that time'. The real Elias was, to the young soldier, an inspiration as a warrior, who valued instinct over analytic thinking, and also as a rebel, a charismatic dope-smoking head. In the film this is built into a philosophy of non-conformism, of regard for life and comrades over political imperatives. He was later killed in a grenade accident that Stone suspects to have been a fragging. Platoon Sergeant Barnes, of one of the 1st Cavalry's motorised infantry units, was a great warrior, deformed by a bullet wound like his cinematic counterpart. Though Stone talks of the real Barnes as a man with warmth and humanity, he also speaks of the man's intensity and almost inhuman skill. Stone hangs a demonic significance on this toned-down humanity.

Of course, the central 'real person' is Stone himself, and to a significant degree the film exists as autobiography.

INSPIRATION AND INFLUENCE: In its almost tangible realism and its basis in personal experiences, *Platoon* marks itself out as different from the herd of Vietnam War films. *Apocalypse Now* is similar in theme, the descent of nominally civilised man to brutal savagery, but more overblown and pretentious in execution (though it shares one eerie similarity in this respect, the voice-overs by father and son Martin and Charlie Sheen that tie their respective films together). *The Deer Hunter* explores similar ground in the change that war can bring to a man, and the danger of addiction to the adrenaline high of combat. But it remains curiously impersonal, despite some great performances, and the representation of the North Vietnamese as directly responsible for the psychological damage of the protagonists is easy vilification that indirectly justifies the war – something Stone is keen to avoid, preferring to represent the conflict as a pointless struggle against a hostile environment: it is the pressure, fear and futility that drives the platoon to its violence and infighting, not directly the Vietcong or NVA.

Having said this, there are elements of what appears to be homage to the conventions of the war film; it is difficult otherwise to explain the old cliché of a new recruit proudly showing off a photograph of his sweetheart and then, soon after, being shot and killed. The movie departs from the niceties of earlier war films in its chilling indifference. There is none of the rose-tinted solidarity or respect for the dead rookie that other films display: 'Take a look at this piece of shit,' says Barnes.

Indeed, this is probably the greatest thematic impact of *Platoon,* beyond such cultural scavengers as *The Simpsons,* which borrowed the image of the field of dead with Barber's Adagio playing over the top for a barroom brawl scene (a motif widely recycled in popular culture – it has also cropped up in hospital drama *ER*). *Apocalypse Now* comes close, but is more quest than straight war flick. The impact of *Platoon*'s unflinching realism can be detected in the most high-profile revision of the WWII genre, *Saving Private Ryan* (Steven Spielberg, 1998). Its influence lies in its depiction of the common soldier's desperate struggle. Perhaps in some battles the fight will rise to embrace higher, ideological ends, but in the wholly believable way Stone presents it, it is first and foremost a battle for survival.

There were rumours of a sequel. Dale Dye (who wrote a tie-in novelisation of *Platoon*) has spoken of a *Platoon II* that would follow the survivors back home – on set each actor had developed a hypothetical future for his character – once the war was over. According to Stone himself, he was 'contracted before *Platoon* was ever released to write a film called *Second Life* to be based on my own experiences in coming back to the States'. As in all such lost projects there is an element of disappointment, but one feels that personal catharsis had been achieved here, and it was better that the momentum for a 'home front' film was carried into *Born on the Fourth of July.*

REEL TIME: War has been described as periods of great boredom contrasted with periods of intense action, and this reflects the shooting of *Platoon*. On a low budget, with little money for fancy camerawork, the style is simple. Long, slow takes during periods of inactivity, with the frenzied battle scenes signified largely by sudden noise and explosions of the special effects. The camera starts cutting rapidly, without time for sequences to settle in the mind and, frequently, in conjunction with the darkness of the night shooting and the anonymity of the uniforms, leaving the viewer in some doubt as to who is doing what. This is the intent, a deliberate move to replicate the chaos and confusion of the battle. When troops run, the camera struggles to catch up, one exceptional sequence following Elias as he silently pads after a contingent of VC, the camera swooping alongside him on a special track, cut and built by the actors with their machetes.

Robert Richardson was given a tough job in photographing the action, and chose to light many of the night ambush scenes by flares, increasing the sense of chaotic action. During the day, they shot between 10 a.m. and 2 p.m., when light was at is hardest and most intense. In daylight, colours are lush and alien, thick dark greens with a coral-pink sky and the deep red of bare earth, while the airbase is a dusty wasteland – there are no environments comparable with Western lands (an attribute the film shares with *Apocalypse Now*, also shot in the Philippines). The North Vietnamese are always presented in silhouette, except when dead, heightening their anonymous menace and linking them all the more with the landscape they seem part of.

MUSIC: The music for *Platoon* is more focussed than *Salvador*, a main theme developed around Samuel Berber's *Adagio for Strings* by Georges Delerue, with that tune hauntingly effective in the periods of calm after the battle. In addition, late 60s acid rock ('White Rabbit' by Jefferson Airplane) and motown ('Tracks of my Tears' by Smokey Robinson) are used to differentiate the radical, progressive 'heads' from the redneck country of the lifers and juicers ('Okie from Muskogee' by Merle Haggard). However, it is not meant as a criticism of the film, rather a tribute, that the best use of sound in the film is in the periods of silence leading up to the ambushes – ambient insect noise broken suddenly by huge explosions to devastating effect.

BOX OFFICE: The film grossed nearly $140 million dollars in the US alone: an amazing achievement in absolute terms, let alone relative to the $6 million budget. It would not be exceeded by any Stone film until *Any Given Sunday*.

CRITICS: Vincent Canby said of *Platoon* that it was 'possibly the best work of any kind about the Vietnam War since . . . *Dispatches*.' The critic for the *Sunday Telegraph* concurred in spirit: 'People came out of *Apocalypse Now* . . . talking about film and acting; they will come out of *Platoon* talking about Vietnam.' Some critics spoke of the gritty perspective taken in the film. In Roger Ebert's opinion, 'Here is a movie that regards combat from ground level, from the infantryman's point of view, and it does not make war look like fun.' This was echoed in the *Times Literary Supplement*: 'The film is explicitly horrible . . . it seems to me to capture very well the confusion, the terror and the idiocy of the war on the ground.' Max Hastings denied any connection to such reality: '*Platoon* has no great truth about war to offer – only about America's perception of itself.' *The Washington Post* described it as 'the first serious youth movie in ages, for at its heart, the war is treated as a rite of passage in its most intense form'.

Some rejected the idea of *Platoon* as presenting any new vision of war through cinema: Philip French wrote of it as 'very close to traditional Hollywood war films' and of a deployment of the usual clichés: 'the sensitive articulate hero . . . the weak second lieutenant . . . the carefully selected range of ethnic melting pot American types'. Alexander Walker agreed but emphasised the film's particularly forceful nature: 'Even if *Platoon* only spells out the ultimate platitude "War is Hell" it has the shock value of obscene graffiti.'

There were negative reviews. Nigel Andrews delivered a lukewarm verdict: 'a thinly conceived film thickened out with quantities of visual and visceral rhetoric and "war is hell" philosophising,' and he finally derided it as 'the war film to go and see with a clear conscience because there is a fashionable liberal moral to the story'. Pauline Kael praised performances and the sense of confusion but had reservations about its intensity: 'Just about everything in *Platoon* is too explicit, and is so heightened that it can numb you and make you feel jaded.' Ultimately she didn't take to Stone, admitting he had talent as a director but disliking his approach, and having no time for his writing, deriding him as a 'hype artist'.

Other critics saw a meteoric rise, notably Paul Attanasia, who described his progress 'from a screen-writer who seemed to bring out the worst in directors . . . to one of the five or six American directors who matter'. Not everyone liked him, but he had indisputably arrived at the big time.

CONTROVERSY: The movie stirred up a storm of media coverage, mostly rooted in the much-proclaimed authenticity of its writer and director. Some scoffed at this; an article in the right-wing *Spectator* proclaimed that 'The film concludes with a sanctimonious dedication [to those who fought]. In fact, it insults their memory.'

Outside the op-ed pages, reports marvelled at the way Stone had connected with contemporary feeling, a *New York Times* article recording that 'There have been reports of incidents at local theatres in which audience members booed or cheered as the film progressed.' It divided opinions between cinemagoers and inflamed passions about the war like no Vietnam film before or since. There remained some question about whether this was partially due to the time of the release – one contemporary article recording opinions of studio heads, that 'had *Platoon* opened a decade ago, it would almost certainly have failed'.

AWARDS: An article in the *New York Times* in 1987 predicted that 'if the Hollywood grapevine is correct . . . *Platoon* will sweep the Oscars two weeks from now.' The grapevine wasn't wrong. The film received ten nominations and picked up four awards – Sound, Editing, Best Director and, the jewel in the crown, Best Film. In addition, Tom Berenger and Willem Dafoe both received nominations for their supporting performances (an appropriate balance for the forces of evil and good), losing out to Paul Newman for his pool hustler comeback *The Color of Money* (Martin Scorsese, 1986). Robert Richardson was also nominated for his cinematography, while Best Screenplay (for which Stone was also nominated) went to Woody Allen for *Hannah and Her Sisters*. Stone made a point of bringing up the issues behind the film in his acceptance speech: 'Thank you for this Cinderella ending . . . what you're saying is that for the first time you really understand what happened over there.'

Earlier that year, Stone had had a prologue to his Oscar success with a BAFTA for Best Director.

TRIVIA: Each soldier's graffiti was personalised, the only outside input being approval from Stone or Dye that it was in keeping with the period. As a result, many of the girls names that can be seen on helmets are those of the actors' own girlfriends of the time.

THE BIG PICTURE: This film secured Stone's reputation, and has maintained it ever since. Whatever the doubts of critics at the time, or polarised decisions over his later work, there are few who would not regard this as a great achievement. Its autobiographical nature also casts light on later decisions – the widening of perspective that *Born on the Fourth of July* would bring to the conflict, *Heaven and Earth* being more a Vietnamese take on American involvement than a truly alternative perspective on the war. It is telling that Stone has never returned to the war itself as a subject – the impression is that something has been laid to rest.

FINAL ANALYSIS: *Platoon* is one of the best films ever made about war – at least, for someone who hasn't been to war. There is something about the tension, the sudden unpredictable action, the weariness and the discomfort that seems timeless, despite the painstaking period detail. The lack of politics just seals the honesty. This is not a film that challenges the war through its ideals or objectives, instead offering comment on how it affected the man in the field.

There is criticism of the Barnes/Elias conflict plot, that it draws attention away from Taylor, the protagonist. This is to miss the point that Taylor makes at the end, that the war between them continues to rage within his soul. Stone has the belief that Barnes and Elias are the two warrior archetypes every soldier chooses as a model (those that are true soldiers, not the O'Neills or the Wolfes). In a war against an apparently invisible enemy, conflict comes from within the ranks, between those who try to remain human and decent despite this intense pressure and those who become bestial machines to defend themselves: physical survival at the expense of the spiritual.

This film strips away any niceties of conduct or justification: this is war in the most brutal terms. A great and powerful work.

Wall Street (1987)

An Edward R Pressman Production
An Oliver Stone Film
Casting: Risa Bramon and Billy Hopkins
Original Music by Stewart Copeland
Costume Designer: Ellen Mirojnick
Editor: Claire Simpson
Production Designer: Stephen Hendrickson
Director of Photography: Robert Richardson
Co-Producer: A Kitman Ho
Written by Stanley Weiser and Oliver Stone

Produced by Edward R Pressman
Directed by Oliver Stone

CAST: Michael Douglas (*Gordon Gekko*), Charlie Sheen (*Bud Fox*), Daryl Hannah (*Darien Taylor*), Martin Sheen (*Carl Fox*), Hal Holbrook (*Lou Mannheim*), Terence Stamp (*Sir Larry Wildman*), Sean Young (*Kate Gekko*), James Spader (*Roger Barnes*), Franklin Cover (*Dan*), John C McGinley (*Marvin*), James Karen (*Lynch*), Saul Rubinek (*Harold Salt* – Gekko's Lawyer)

NOTABLE CREDITS: Dedicated to Louis Stone – Stockbroker 1910–1985 (see **BEING OLIVER STONE**). Chief Technical Adviser – Ken Lipper (see **REAL PEOPLE**).

SUMMARY: *Fly Me to the Moon* plays across a montage of New York street scenes in 1985. Young broker Bud Fox arrives to work at the offices of Jackson-Steinman. He greets co-workers Dan, old, rubicund and desperate, Lou, old, statesmanlike and honest, and Marvin, brash and boisterous. Lynch, their boss, outlines the state of the market and the exchange opens as the clock hits 09.30.

Bud Fox is a junior broker, struggling to scrape together enough business and commission to keep himself afloat. Towards the end of the day he takes a loss when a client refuses to make good on a purchase made on his behalf. Bud must pay the difference. Despite this blow he makes his daily, futile call to the office of financial big shot Gordon Gekko in an attempt to drum up business. Tired and distraught, Bud heads to a bar in Queens to meet his father, Bluestar Airlines union rep Carl Fox. Bud begs some money from Carl, who also tells him of an upcoming Federal Air Authority (FAA) ruling that will exonerate Bluestar of any blame in a recent accident, allowing for expansion.

The next day is Gekko's birthday and Bud goes in person, primed with a present of cigars and a salesman's patter designed to win Gekko's business. He talks his way in, but Gekko sees right through the young broker, dismissing his stock tips as 'dogs with fleas'. Bud – out of ideas – volunteers the information he has learnt about Bluestar. Gekko is impressed and buys some Bluestar stock through Bud. The next morning the FAA announces its decision and the share value rockets. Bud lunches with Gekko who sets him up with a million dollars, instructing him to buy a few shares in the company he originally recommended. But the stock plummets and Gekko convenes another meeting, appearing ready to dismiss Fox. Bud clings on, offering to do anything, and eventually agrees to tail Gekko's archrival, English mogul Sir Larry Wildman. He discovers Wildman's plan to buy up an ailing steel company – Anacott – and Gekko sets about wrecking the Englishman's plans, using Bud as a proxy to push up the share price by tipping off his friends, the *Wall Street Chronicle* and half the financial community. This forces Wildman to buy back the stock at an embarrassingly high price. At the dinner party where this deal is sealed, Bud meets vacuous but attractive interior designer Darien Taylor whom he becomes infatuated with. Gekko offers a Faustian deal to Fox – continue providing him with inside information in exchange for wealth – 'enough money to afford a girl like Darien'.

Bud talks a lawyer friend, Roger Barnes, into acting as a conduit for the purchase of shares for Gekko. He also buys into a cleaning company, which allows him access to office buildings at night and so the secrets contained within their files. Back at the office Dan is fired while Bud is named top trader and given his own office; Darien decorates and moves into his apartment. One of Bud's tasks for Gekko is to buy up swathes of Teldar Paper stock but, under pressure from Roger and Marvin – who feels snubbed by his old friend – he makes one large deal too many and attracts the attention of the SEC (Securities and Exchange Commission). Bud is impressed by Gekko's success with Teldar and puts together a plan for the comprehensive overhaul of Bluestar. Gekko is unsure but agrees to take it on. They meet with union representatives, including Carl Fox, and try to win support. The key is to win funding from the banks (to buy the requisite shares and, eventually, to modernise and expand the company) through a guarantee of union concessions – a wage cut and an increase in working hours. Carl rejects Gekko's advances, much to his son's embarrassment, but his union members, and the other union reps, decide to accept the deal. Bud meets with Roger, who is jumpy because of investigations by the SEC. Coincidentally Roger's firm is involved in the Bluestar deal, and a meeting is in progress. Bud discovers Gekko's real intent: to sell off the hangar land for condos, the planes to Mexico, the routes to a Texas airline and plunder the pension fund, offering the bare minimum to the employees.

Bud confronts Gekko, who excuses his decision on the basis that the firm is 'wreckable'. Darien leaves him – she is loyal only to Gekko. Bud discovers that his father has suffered a heart attack and, with Carl's approval, sets in motion a plan to save Bluestar.

He meets with Larry Wildman, who accepts Bud's offer of union concessions and revenge on Gekko in exchange for keeping Bluestar in business. Bud spreads takeover rumours about Bluestar, causing price rises. Gekko is furious but continues to buy at the inflated price. Suddenly the union reps march into his office, dropping their offer of concessions. Gekko goes to sell but Fox already has his contacts selling off their shares and the price is dropping. Gekko can't dump his stock until Wildman steps in with an offer as insultingly low as the Anacott price was high. Bud returns to his office triumphant, but the SEC have finally arrived with a warrant for arrest. Gekko confronts a taciturn Bud in Central Park. The older man is enraged at the younger's audacity and hurls abuse at him, detailing the opportunities and deals Fox was offered before punching him to the ground. Bud retreats to a nearby washroom where he is revealed to have recorded the conversation – the SEC now have the goods on Gekko.

As the film closes Gekko's fate is left ambiguous, but Fox is phlegmatic. He will do time in jail, and it is Carl's belief that this might not be a bad thing.

ADVANCE PUBLICITY: The poster is a textbook example of mid-1980s bombast – the three principals (Gekko, Bud and Darien) poised over a shot of the Manhattan skyline at night. There were two similar but distinct trailers in the US campaign. The first a fairly straightforward series of extracts, emphasising the visceral dialogue ('when it gets to 18 . . . buy it all') and playing up Stone's previous credentials via the infamous gravely-syrup voice heard on so many trailers of the time – 'From the director of *Platoon*, the next battle is in the greatest jungle of all – Wall Street.' The second trailer dwelled on the more ideological points of the script, making the conflict between greed and poverty key. Both used the pay-off line, 'You can trade everything you believe in for everything you've ever wanted.' Both also used the same backing music, Vivaldi's *L'Inverno* (a piece of music that did not feature in the film), giving a touch of strange classical elegance to this bruiser of a movie. *Wall Street* also received two complimentary full-page advertisements in *Fortune*, in exchange for prominent placement of the finance magazine in the film, where Bud Fox refers to it, at one point, as 'the bible'.

PRODUCTION HISTORY: Stone was unwilling to rest on his laurels after the Oscar triumph of *Platoon*, but did not want to work on any of the lucrative projects offered him, preferring to build an original idea from scratch. He was in contact with a former classmate from NYU,

Stanley Weiser, and together they began work on a screenplay to be
produced by Ed Pressman.

Their first proposal was built around the American quiz-show
scandals of the 1950s, but Stone was uninspired (this idea would reach
the screen in the 1994 Robert Redford film *Quiz Show*). Instead they
turned to the world of business, and wrote a morality play set in the high
finance institutions of Wall Street. Stone has described this as 'a Pilgrim's
Progress of a boy who is seduced, corrupted by the allure of easy money.
And in the third act he sets out to redeem himself.' A simple enough
concept that he himself suggested could take place in many alternative
situations: 'He could have been a cop, he could have been in Vietnam, he
could have been a soldier. Wall Street is background.'

But very significant background. As loose inspiration Stone had taken
the experiences of an old friend (rumoured to be Wall Street broker
Owen Morrisey) who had been a dead-ringer for Bud Fox in the early
1980s – making too much money too easily, he had lost it all. Indeed,
reaching even further back, it relates to the lifetime Lou Stone gave to
the industry with little to show for it, and the career he planned for
Oliver after Yale (see **BEING OLIVER STONE**). *Wall Street* would be a
very personal story, like *Platoon*. As Stone has described it, a suggestion
of what Chris Taylor's life would have been like had he not gone to
Vietnam, made eerily plausible with the casting of Charlie Sheen.

Weiser and Stone completed the script and it was first offered to
Hemdale. John Daly turned it down. The required budget of $15 million
was a big risk for the small company while the subject matter was
complex and seemed unlikely to spark at the box office. For a larger
company, however, this was a mid-level budget, and the risk well worth
taking to secure the follow-up film of an Oscar-winning director.
Producer Ed Pressman took *Wall Street* to Twentieth-Century Fox and
they agreed to make it. Filming began in May 1987.

Research was intensive. While writing the script, Weiser and Stone
had spent a great deal of time in New York, meeting with top executives,
entrepreneurs, officials from the SEC and convicted fraudsters. Now the
production had begun, this was stepped up. In a move reminiscent of
Dale Dye's involvement in *Platoon*, Stone hired Ken Lipper as Technical
Adviser. A former deputy mayor of New York and high-level executive
in the Saloman Brothers investment house, Lipper provided a valuable
link with the financial community. Through him they secured permission
to film on the trading floor of the New York Stock Exchange (the first
film to do so; they also used real traders) as well as the offices of various

firms and the actual restaurants Le Cirque and 21 Club (the site of Gekko and Fox's lunch). The same attention was paid to detail as had been the case in *Platoon*. Ellen Mirojnick ensured that Michael Douglas's suits were hand-tailored after the individualised styles of mid-80s tycoons, eventually costing $28,000 or, as James Riordan reckons, 'about 17 per cent of the film's $165,000 wardrobe budget.' Great care was taken in constructing the custom-built set (representing the offices of Jackson-Steinman) to the specifications of a genuine brokerage firm. This extended to the characters' home lives. Gekko's home and office and Bud's penthouse apartment are stocked with genuine art works (Stone was a keen collector at the time) and the latest electronic appliances. Stone worked with Stephen Hendrickson to develop the deconstructed look of Darien Taylor's home interior design. Product placement had become an important concern. With Oliver Stone now a widely recognised director, many companies were eager to have their goods appear in his latest film. Mineral water companies, car manufacturers and distilleries all made their offers, with *Fortune* magazine being the most prominent to feature. In fact the film is not overly branded, especially not in comparison with contemporary blockbusters, even though one might expect *Wall Street*'s inhabitants to live and die by the brand name.

Filming wrapped on 4 July 1987 after 53 days – 7 days ahead of schedule and $2 million under budget, the rush due to an expected call for a strike by the Directors' Guild. As is often the case with Stone's films, there followed an intense round of editing, as three hours of footage was whittled down to a two-hour film. This was released in America in December 1987, just two months after the largest one-day stock crash since 1929 (see **HISTORY 101**).

CASTING: Charlie Sheen had been cast very early in *Wall Street*'s production. He recalls Stone enigmatically offering him a chance to move from the jungle to the concrete jungle, and instantly accepting. As it happens, the film could have had a much bigger star – Tom Cruise had personally expressed an interest to Stone but the decision had already been made. At 22 Sheen was young for the role of a Wall Street stockbroker, and he was artificially aged by means such as a plush, expensive wardrobe and rounds of expensive dinners. It is quite revealing to compare the sleek, padded businessman of *Wall Street* with the pale, muddied grunt of *Platoon* – roles played within a year of each other. He also took a personal interest in the part, investing a large chunk of his own money into the market to heighten his involvement with the role (his $15,000 portfolio actually bucked the stock market trend, pulling in a four-figure profit).

Jack Lemmon was originally suggested for the part of Carl Fox, but in a casting decision that reaped dividends, the role went to Charlie's real life father Martin Sheen. This grizzled character actor has appeared in many films, including *Badlands* (Terrence Malick, 1973) and *Gandhi* (Richard Attenborough, 1982) but is probably best known for his performance as the dour Captain Willard in *Apocalypse Now*. He has found small-screen fame as President Jed Bartlet in the political drama *The West Wing*. In the film his scenes with Charlie Sheen sparkle, the sickbed reconciliation particularly affecting. It's a small part but important, and Martin Sheen lends the perfect impression of laid-back experience. It would not be the last film on which the father and son would collaborate: their mutual Vietnam film appearances and their performances in *Wall Street* were parodied in *Hot Shots! Part Deux* (Jim Abrahams, 1993).

Another father–son relationship of significance was Kirk and Michael Douglas. Stone originally approached Richard Gere and Warren Beatty with the part of Gordon Gekko, but both turned it down, so he moved on to Michael Douglas. At this stage the younger Douglas had become established as a generic square-jawed hero in TV's *Streets of San Francisco* as well as a range of competent movies such as *Romancing the Stone* (Robert Zemeckis, 1984) and *The China Syndrome* (James Bridges, 1979). Stone thought Michael Douglas could play the villain too, just as his dad had done, for instance in the *noir* thriller *Out of the Past* aka *Build My Gallows High* (Jacques Tourneur, 1947), and it is worth noting that Michael Douglas's other great role – white collar psycho D-Fens in *Falling Down* (Joel Schumacher, 1993) – was also a villainous one. Stone has spoken of Douglas having the look and feel of a sharp businessman, not without foundation given his other life as a successful producer of such films as *One Flew Over the Cuckoo's Nest* (Milos Forman, 1975). Douglas gives a fine performance, another actor who speaks uneasily of Stone's technique of intimidation and his blunt manner of criticism but who probably benefited greatly from this approach.

Things did not go as smoothly for Daryl Hannah. She was cast largely at the insistence of Stone, yet he now believes, and Michael Douglas agrees, that she did not seem happy in the role of the artificial, materialistic spender of 'other people's money'. (Hannah herself has consistently refused to speak about her experiences on the film.) Critics at the time, and many writers since, lambasted her performance. This seems misguided. In a way her hollow, vacuous performance sits perfectly with the superficial empty vessel of the character. When Darien intones her three desires as 'a Turner, a perfect Canary diamond . . . world peace', the last item, added almost as an afterthought, is given the perfect bathetic tone. Were the character given a more hard-nosed feel – for instance, the abrasive estate agent as played by Silvia Miles – she would have had an almost physical unpleasantness that would have brought any audience hostility to bear on the performance rather than what she represents. As Hannah plays it, it is possible to dislike the character for what she is, insubstantial to the point of transparency, rather than for the knee-jerk irritation of grating mannerisms.

OLIVER'S ARMY: In keeping with Stone's hurried effort to get another production going, several of the key crew were brought back from the Philippines and thrown into work on *Wall Street*. Robert Richardson and Claire Simpson were both on their third Stone picture, while A Kitman Ho was on his second as co-producer. John C McGinley again appeared alongside Charlie Sheen. His is another minor turn but memorable, irritating but somehow also engaging. As Bud Fox gets slicker and smoother it is by Marv's occasional loud interjections that the audience can chart the change of his character. Also appearing again was Sean Stone, Oliver's son, now three. He had his first role as Richard Boyle's infant son in *Salvador*, and here played Gekko's spoilt toddler.

CUT SCENES: Originally Lou Mannheim was to be shown making some desperately needed money off an insider deal. This was cut, as it would have tainted one of the only wholly decent characters. Reportedly Ken Lipper was influential here, insisting that the presentation of share dealers couldn't be so unequivocally negative. Quite a few speaking parts were cut, and some footage of street bums. This latter factor is the film's most glaring omission – much of Fox's agonising is blunted by the fairly comfortable life he leads prior to Gekko's corruption.

MEMORABLE QUOTES:
Gekko: 'Wake up, will you, pal? If you're not inside, you are outside, OK? . . . I'm talking about liquid. Rich enough to have your own jet. Rich enough not to waste time. Fifty to a hundred million dollars, Buddy. A player . . . or nothing.'

Gekko: 'Greed, for lack of a better word, is good. Greed is right. Greed works. Greed clarifies, cuts through and captures the essence of the evolutionary spirit.'

Bud: 'What I see is a jealous old machinist who can't stand the fact that his son's become more successful than he has!'

Carl: 'What you see is a guy who never measured a man's success by the size of his WALLET!'

Carl (to Bud): 'I don't go to sleep with no whore, and I don't wake up with no whore, that's how I live with myself. I don't know how you do it.'

GOOD VS EVIL: *Wall Street* is built along a similar moral schematic to *Platoon*. On the one hand there is the good father – though in this case it might be better to say fathers: Carl Fox, the union rep who looks out for his men, who believes in hard productive work and disparages his son's job as being that of a salesman (for Carl Fox 'Money is only something you need in case you don't die tomorrow,' a necessity but nothing more), and Lou Mannheim, the honest broker who believes in the fundamentals, looking out for his clients, not using their money to further his own ends or looking for a shortcut to personal wealth. On the other hand, there is the towering figure of Gekko. His name could be invoked as descriptive of his character (reptilian, oily) but he represents more than just a common shyster. He stands as the embodiment of free-market capitalism, self-interest personified, master of the shortcut, proud of producing nothing. A believer in the law of the jungle, in evolution – survival of the fittest – applied ruthlessly to the financial world, just as Sergeant Barnes applied it to the literal jungle in *Platoon*. Once again good and evil are facets of self-control, this time applied to wealth. Gekko believes there's no such thing as too much, that the aim is to be 'liquid', an aim Bud comes to criticise – 'How many yachts can you water-ski behind?'

Gekko's vision is seductive, and sometimes he does the right thing – albeit unintentionally. The ethics of the film are complicated, as is Stone's own view: 'Half of me likes what [corporate raiders] do because they shake up entrenched management bureaucracies . . . You like what Michael Douglas does – like Sergeant Barnes in *Platoon*.' To an extent, Gekko's keynote speech is not without good points. Greed can be good, the executive looking for personal success might well look to do the best for his company, but this is only half the philosophy. Raw, unmitigated greed will find the easiest route to wealth, whatever the effect on others, as Bud learns in the Bluestar deal.

In the film the moral delineation depends upon ultimate motivation: whether altruism and the greater good is the prime consideration, or whether the self is all that matters.

REDEMPTION OR DAMNATION: The very sort of morality tale that Stone is trying to tell dictates the arc of the story: Bud, comparatively innocent in this world, is corrupted and led to the brink of damnation, realises his error and manages to redeem himself.

The initial naivety of the character has been criticised by some who see it as unrealistic that such a person could get by in a brokerage firm, let alone talk his way into the office of Gordon Gekko. But this is in the nature of the fable. It is necessary that Bud be a corrupted innocent. If he knew what was expected of him when in Gekko's office it would at once present too cynical a view – it would be hard to like Bud or believe his redemptive actions later – and also dramatically hamstring the narrative. The whole point is to watch him slide down into the world of industrial espionage, perks and material greed from an initial belief in hard work, otherwise all the audience would see is a sharp operator get a break from a like-minded figure.

Bud's act of redemption is vital. He sees that Gekko's doctrine of greed is paper-thin, that endless material acquisition is, in itself, pointless and empty, that it is not enough just to own but that self-interest and gain should be tempered by a belief in industry. This is why the film is not anti-business or anti-Wall Street. Carl Fox may believe his son is just a salesman, but Lou Mannheim sees a directly supportive role in stock dealing as part of business, through creation 'of research funding and jobs', not just a way to personal acquisition. Bud can and does do some good. As Gekko points out, Bluestar is a ripe target for any hungry Wall Street shark. It is in Bud's power to deliver the company to a big money financier who will ensure the airline's survival. Through this act it is not just Bud himself who is redeemed, but the institution of Wall Street as a whole.

HISTORY 101: Significant historical links for this film are threefold: those within the script itself, the film as a sketch of mid-80s financial America and the state of Wall Street as an institution on the film's release.

Of the former, the film makes much of its heritage. Lou invokes the image of America under Franklin Roosevelt, a time when free enterprise was forcibly subordinated to a national recovery programme, aimed at bringing the country out of the shadow of the Wall Street Crash of 1929. Over the course of Roosevelt's administration, the economy took a pounding, with devaluation of the dollar and a rise in the national debt, an increase in taxation at high income levels and federal interference in business – all anathema to a committed free-marketer, but necessary for the president's New Deal to boost employment and set the country back on its feet. Lou also speaks disparagingly of Nixon taking America off the gold standard, a move that gave greater flexibility in the setting of interest rates but at the cost of instability elsewhere through increased currency speculation (see **Nixon**). However, these are ultimately cosmetic details and are disposed of rapidly in the opening minutes of the film, to establish both the heritage of the industry and Lou's own distinguished business background as well as his caution – he prefers the slow, steady growth of a gold standard economy to the highs and lows of boom and bust – a status quo he spends the rest of the film decrying.

The real meat of historical significance is in how the film relates to the period of its production. Such is its cultivated detail that it almost comes across as a painstaking period drama. The screen oozes 'contemporary': the blocky mobile phones, the childlike joy over clunky technology, the kitchen appliances spewing out pasta and sushi and the apartment, with its over-designed, expensive yet utterly impractical feel. Everyone looks the part: braces, chunky knitwear, the brash, angled dresses and elaborate hats, slicked down hair and aviator sunglasses, stuffing their faces with steak tartare. Everything is just as one would expect in a pastiche of the period (for comparison see *The Wedding Singer* (Frank Coraci, 1998), which mocks the decade eight years after the event), an impression exacerbated by the crystal-clear photography, which makes the film appear a production of the mid-1990s.

One historical quirk came with the time of release. In October 1987, the New York Stock Exchange suffered Black Monday, a catastrophic one-day collapse with the Dow–Jones index falling by around 500 points, leading to much soul searching over perceptions of runaway greed in the 1980s. It was with this in mind that Stone backdated the events of *Wall Street* to 1985 by overlaying the date on the scenes, so as to avoid accusations that he was cashing in on the crash.

Historians are lukewarm over whether the 80s really were the time of greed and high-spending that Stone, and, indeed, popular opinion, has labelled it. One essay in the collection *Oliver Stone's USA* ('Wall Street' by Martin Fridson) goes to great lengths to establish that the decade was no more greedy or decadent than any other in the twentieth century. This is as open to debate as any other historical opinion (see **JFK**), but it is important to note Stone's main intention: to draw attention to the great drop in age of these rich financiers. The old industrial aristocrats, Rockefeller, Carnegie and Morgan, had been replaced by young whiz-kids in their late 20s and early 30s. *Wall Street* was a deliberate attempt to paint money as a drug akin to cocaine, with similar corruptive effects, and the replacement of wizened philanthropic plutocrats with the gross spectacle of conspicuous consumption.

CONSPIRACY THEORY: The American financial system has had a fair amount of hostility levelled against it by those who see hegemony and controlling power cliques at its head, but this is not what the film is aiming at. One pre-emptive effort to defuse such misreading was to change the heritage of the lead character, who was originally to be Jewish – some crackpots believe American high finance to be controlled by a Zionist conspiracy. The substance of the narrative and the setting are two separate strands, and it is not really fair to read the film as a condemnation of Wall Street. This is no anarchistic anti-capitalist tract: any corruption is on an individual level, not of the system itself. The film was originally to be called *Greed* and that is its true target, not Wall Street itself.

STARS AND STRIPES: The Vietnam War is the antithesis of the American Dream; Wall Street by contrast represents its greatest symbols, the wealth, the power, the dynamism and the entrepreneurial spirit of America. But there is a darker side which is of primary interest to Stone, primarily the unscrupulous avarice of Gekko, but also the complacent incompetence of bureaucratic management, not bad as such but apathetic. Bud gets ahead because he has initiative, but he doesn't (initially) have the integrity to back this up. It is the fine balance between these attributes that represent the idealised American businessman – indeed, the idealised businessman for any Western society built on capitalism.

BEING OLIVER STONE: If *Platoon* was biography, *Wall Street* is tribute, to the life of Stone's father and the life he might himself have led. Stone has drawn directly on his father for the character of Lou Mannheim – a kindly moral voice for Bud. The other paternal influence, Carl, exists solely within the film and it is unlikely he would have had much in common with the thoroughly Republican Lou Stone. There also appears to be an element of Stone Sr in Gekko. 'My father saw the world as a jungle in the Darwinian sense,' Stone has said. 'Nothing works well, but, given the law of nature, capitalism was the best possible compromise.' This comes across in the Teldar Paper speech, the intense belief in a non-interventionist free market. Stone also drew on his experiences at his father's deathbed to write the powerful Bud/Carl Fox hospital scene.

Stone seems to live vicariously through his films, both in feeding his own past and feelings into the story – in this case the idea that this is how things might have turned out had he not gone to Vietnam – and also in his attitude on set. Various accounts speak of him dressing in shirts and braces for the film, and spending a great deal of time in the trendy nightspots frequented by the financial elite. Coupled with the huge amount of research and the vast attention to detail, Stone could be described as a 'method director'. He puts his feelings into the films and absorbs a lot from them in return.

REAL PEOPLE: Of the many people interviewed in research, several had cameo parts. Ken Lipper (see **PRODUCTION HISTORY**) and also Jeff Beck, a trader, are both in the Bluestar boardroom break-up scene. Elements of real traders and financiers were worked into the characters. Wildman was based, in part, on Sir James Goldsmith, later known in British political circles for establishing the ill-fated Referendum Party. Gekko has long been associated with notorious trader Ivan Boesky, and the 'Greed is good' speech is based, in part, on a speech the real Boesky made. Stone insists that this is a simplistic reading, and that influence on Gekko came from an amalgam of Wall Street types, including Donald Trump.

INSPIRATION AND INFLUENCE: The heritage of Hollywood finance films is not particularly rich. The 1950s saw the release of *Executive Suite* (Robert Wise, 1954) and *Sweet Smell of Success* (Alexander Mackendrick, 1957), both cited as influences by Oliver Stone.

If *Platoon* worked a general philosophy of war into a semi-autobiographical tale dominated by specific contemporary details, *Wall Street* applied the morality tale to a specific point in time and space – New York in the 1980s. This does not feature the archetypal movie villainy of monolithic corporations. Entrenched management are the enemy of raiders like Gekko, while the protagonist is not a junior partner, or a mailboy working his way up a company but a trader who buys and sells shares in other companies. The mindset of the film is rooted in the business of its time, close to the greed and hunger that permeates *Scarface*.

Other People's Money (Norman Jewison, 1991) is in turn a response to Stone's film. Danny De Vito plays a Gekko figure who aims to buy and break up a family-owned steel firm; the very ideas of old money and classic Capra-esque business ethics are embodied in Gregory Peck. It is telling that Capra and Stone are the 'competing' styles: One, creator of an idealised Middle America that never existed and the other an arch-exaggerator of Mephistophelian corporate ethics. In Jewison's film, despite the influence of the latter, the former is triumphant. A takeover occurs but the company discovers life after stockholder death: its products being essential for the manufacture of airbags. Though it is the cynical broker whose life changes (very Capra-esque), the importance of *Wall Street* is obvious in providing the mould for the villainous side of the free-market, stocks-and-shares economy.

The Boiler Room (Ben Younger, 2000) acknowledges its debt to Wall Street just as *Scream* (Wes Craven, 1996) recognises its slasher-flick forebears. It takes the cynicism of *Wall Street* to another level. Here the young go-getters are selling shares they know to be valueless to 'customers' who are little more than marks in a huge con trick. When the twenty-something broker team (Vin Diesel, Giovanni Ribisi, Ben Affleck) watch movies together, they worshipfully quote Gekko. Gekko's dubious status as a Darwinian force for corporate evolution has been stripped away by posterity. He survives solely as the embodiment of greed.

One spin-off from Wall Street was a tie-in novel authored by Ken Lipper. Much of it was lifted straight from the script, though a few new elements were added: a brief romance with one of Fox's old girlfriends and an attempt to make more sense of the SEC investigation (they track suspicious Teldar purchases through Fox's college buddies).

REEL TIME: As Robert Richardson said at the time, 'We are making a movie about sharks, about feeding frenzies, so we wanted the camera to become a predator.' The image of the shark is pertinent not just in reference to the insatiable corporate animal Gekko, but also to the camera. It swoops and pans with little rest – representing the idea that money, like the shark, never sleeps. There is some hectic cutting, most notably in the elevator conversation between father and son Fox, and it takes on a crazed hyperactivity during the trading sequences, with a number of split screen effects invoking the frenzied group mentality of the market. This is a success, bringing movement and life to the complicated exposition, and lending a great dramatic significance to times of quiet – for instance, Gekko's Teldar Paper speech.

There are two moments when style intrudes to greater effect. Just after Bud is given power of attorney over Gekko's money, the screen is washed out in a bright flare of light, with its counterpoint coming after Gekko tells Fox to dump the plummeting Bluestar stock – the image darkens to silhouette.

As with *Platoon*, the cinematography shows chaotic activity giving way to welcome stillness.

MUSIC: Georges Delerue was not called upon for *Wall Street*. Instead, in keeping with the tone of the film, Stewart Copeland composed the score. Formerly a drummer for The Police, Copeland provided a relentless, pounding soundtrack, very much a product of its time. It was punctuated by tracks from David Byrne and Brian Eno – playing at a subdued background level and heightening the period detail (also opening somewhat anachronistically with Frank Sinatra's *Fly me to the Moon*). The soundtrack rarely gets the credit that it deserves.

Copeland has gone on to provide music for a disparate range of TV shows and movies. He is also the touring drummer for a recent revival of The Doors, a group now featuring Ian Astbury of The Cult on vocals with original members Ray Manzarek and Robby Krieger (see **The Doors**).

BOX OFFICE: *Wall Street* scored a gross of almost $44 million, pulling in over $4 million on its opening weekend. It easily ended up in the black, but was comparatively disappointing when matched against *Platoon*'s earnings.

CRITICS: Reviews were unanimous in their praise for Michael Douglas's portrayal of Gordon Gekko. 'In a gripping performance Douglas is a magnificent predator, rippling with rapacious purpose' (Richard Barkley, *Sunday Express*). 'Seldom since Orson Welles's day has there been a firework display of such power and gusto. Douglas doesn't steal the film because Gekko *is* the film' (Shaun Usher, *Daily Mail*). 'Such is the power of Douglas's Oscar-winning performance that the entire movie revolves around him' (Sue Heal, *Today*).

Richard Corliss in *Time* mentions a similar theme to that which dominates *Platoon*: 'The entire film is, in fact, a meditation on the dilemma of a son choosing his father.' A piece in the *Times Literary Supplement* wryly suggested that the problem with this reading was the sheer preponderance of choice, naming Gekko, Carl Fox, Lou Mannheim and Larry Wildman before commenting, '*Wall Street* is inclined to see every older male character as a potential role-model.' While an article in the *Independent* pointed out, more worryingly given the message of the movie, that Gekko came out as the most popular choice, talking of 'a bull market in red braces fuelled by all those thrusting young bloods who want to be just like Gordon Gekko'.

This celebration of Gekko is linked with the second most common opinion, that Stone's morality tale was ultimately flawed. In the *Washington Post*, Rita Kempley opined that the film 'is at its weakest when it preaches visually or verbally. Stone doesn't trust the time-honored story line, supplementing the obvious moral with plenty of soapboxery.' Vincent Canby was slightly kinder in the *New York Times*: 'Mr Stone's heart is in the right place but, ultimately, his wit fails him.' *The Face* suggested that the problem was similar to that of the seductive portrayal of Gekko: 'ultimately [the film] gives the impression of being too turned on by the world it should be slicing up'. As the *New Socialist* simply put it, '[Stone] can't decide whether it's better to reign in Hell than serve in Heaven.'

At least the simple plot seems not to have been hindered by the complex technical terminology. 'The movie can be followed by anybody, because the details of stock manipulation are all filtered through transparent layers of greed,' said Roger Ebert. Hilary Mantel agreed: 'The film has such pace and style that it grips and entertains even when you don't have a clue what the characters are talking about.'

Robert Richardson's photography was largely praised: 'The camera stalks through the film like a panther,' said Philip French, and the *TLS* concurred, talking of the 'constantly moving, thrusting camera'.

David Edalstan made two comments on Stone, referring to his timing (see **HISTORY 101**), 'Oliver Stone has a knack for swimming against a tide just as it's about to turn' and also to his political standing, 'Stone is what the liberals have needed all along – a macho blowhard they can call their own.' However, he also had an important criticism, naming Stone as 'the least sensitive director of women I can think of'. Adam Mars Jones was in agreement: 'The setting of *Wall Street* is hardly less male than the setting of *Platoon* but this time the weakness of Stone's imagination for women can hardly escape notice.'

CONTROVERSY: There was a degree of grumbling in the press at the time of release, primarily because of the coincidental timing with the '87 crash. Far from being a handicap, this economic hiccup provided an unbeatable degree of free publicity, enhanced by the spirit of the time, and articles were written on the film's popularity among young workers in the financial sector.

AWARDS: The award to Michael Douglas in the Academy Awards Best Actor category for 1987 demonstrates the disparity between what is written on paper and how it appears on screen – Douglas creates an oleaginous villain of awesome screen presence, and Sheen flounders as a decent guy who – when all's said and done – is a loser. Admittedly he keeps his soul, but how much is a soul worth in the context of Wall Street? Gekko struts away from the Central Park confrontation carrying the film with him, returning to snatch the Academy Award. Douglas dedicated the award to his father and paid tribute to 'Oliver Stone, not only as the director, but for having the courage to cast me in a part that not many people thought I could play'. In September 1987, several months before *Wall Street*'s release, Stone picked up a personal award: the Torch of Liberty award from the American Civil Liberties Union.

TRIVIA: Some of Teldar Paper's vice-presidents are named after people linked to the production. Two names that can briefly be seen as the camera pans across are Stanley Weiser (co-writer of the film), Sean Stone (Oliver's son), Richard Dooley (assistant location manager) and Travis Wright (worker in the props department).

The mention of Davidoff cigars is a particularly egregious example of product placement. This particular brand is made in the Dominican Republic, not Cuba, and one can only surmise that the company made a persuasive offer to the filmmakers to secure mention.

THE BIG PICTURE: Despite the references to real events, firms and use of actual people as bases for characters, *Wall Street* represents the first fictional Stone film since *The Hand* and the first since *Scarface* to be neither autobiographical nor adapted from pre-existing material. It shares much in common with *Scarface*, some heavy-handed symbolism at the expense of materialist eighties culture and a strong sense of meaning – it is difficult for Stone just to tell a story, it has to have some deeper significance. Having said this, *Wall Street* calls for a similar instinctive, individual moral compass to *Scarface*. The relativism of a film where an incestuous psychopath can be seriously written as a twisted hero is absent. But attraction to darker impulses is still evident: in a narrative sense, Gekko is a villain, but he is the star of the film. Though it would take *Nixon* to convincingly combine the two elements, Stone would try to invest a fundamentally unpleasant but charismatic protagonist with a glint of righteousness in *Talk Radio*. There are also links with *Salvador*; *Wall Street* shows what's going on at home while Reagan promotes bloodshed and poverty abroad.

Wall Street is a further example of Stone's films as a 'boys' club' with precious little feminine presence. As the director has said himself, 'I have not done movies about women. I have always picked areas that involve extremist ideas that to date have involved men mostly.' Despite the odd exception (Cathy Moore in *Salvador*, Mallory Knox in *Natural Born Killers*), Stone's treatment of women is undeniably weak, and this is a particularly prominent example.

FINAL ANALYSIS: *Wall Street* makes a fascinating companion piece to *Platoon*, a jab at the audience who recoiled from the horrors committed by Barnes and Bunny, as if Stone is accusing them of similar moral lapses and hypocrisy in their daily working lives. In its other life, as a document on yuppie existence, *Wall Street* ranks as one of the best films of its decade. Of course there has always been a wealthy class, but Stone sets out to capture what he sees as their unprecedented youth and almost naive ostentation – the latest gadgets, latest fashions, even latest art – the opposite to the early American robber barons who would wring the last drop of sweat from their workers but use the money to create New York's most exquisite art collections and best loved buildings. The moralising is a turn-off for many, but is sparingly applied and eased on its way by a great performance from both Sheens. Only *The Boiler Room* challenges the film's status as a financial thriller. And it is a thriller, building to a pounding climax: it is a tribute to Stone that he can build and film a gripping scene from a largely nonsensical and borderline incomprehensible share-dealing scheme. Then, of course, there is Gekko, a genuinely great cinematic creation and Michael Douglas's finest screen appearance to date. Pure cinema alchemy, great fun garnered from unpromising base material.

Talk Radio (1988)

An Edward R Pressman Production
An Oliver Stone Film
Casting: Risa Bramon and Billy Hopkins
Executive Producers: Greg Strangis and Sam Strangis
Music by Stewart Copeland
Film Editor: David Brenner
Co-Editor: Joe Hutshing
Costumes designed by Ellen Mirojnick
Production Designer: Bruno Rubeo
Director of Photography: Robert Richardson
Based on the play *Talk Radio* created by Eric Bogosian and
Ted Savinar and written by Eric Bogosian and the book
***Talked to Death: The Life and Murder of Alan Berg* by**
Stephen Singular
Screenplay by Eric Bogosian and Oliver Stone
Produced by Edward R Pressman and A Kitman Ho
Directed by Oliver Stone

CAST: Eric Bogosian (*Barry Champlain*), Ellen Greene (*Ellen*), Leslie Hope (*Laura*), John C McGinley (*Stu*), Alec Baldwin (*Dan*), Jon Pankow (*Dietz*), Michael Wincott (*Kent*)

NOTABLE CREDITS: This is the first film to feature the credit 'Naijo No Ko' for Elizabeth Stone. A Japanese term applied to the wives of prominent men, it literally means 'success from inside help'.

SUMMARY: Barry Champlain is the brash, opinionated presenter of Night Talk – Dallas's top-rated radio show. He arrives for work on a Friday, greeting his producer girlfriend Laura and long-suffering assistant Stu. He fields a range of calls – racists, rednecks, hoaxers and ordinary folk. Halfway through his show the executive producer of his station KGAB – Dan – informs Barry that his show is to be syndicated and broadcast nationwide by radio company Metrowave from Monday. Metrowave executive Dietz is on hand to confirm the final details. Barry is surprised and a little startled but warms to the idea.

Dietz is pleased to meet Barry but is spooked by the extremist, threatening nature of some of the callers (one sends a package to the station claiming it is a bomb) and by the DJ's uncompromising, confrontational nature.

He later calls ex-wife Ellen in Chicago, begging her to come to Dallas and give him support. Over the weekend Barry, as a local celebrity, attends the confirmation of a new sports coach at a basketball game. There are a few fans present but the majority of the crowd boo him and one woman douses him with soda. On Sunday Ellen arrives in town and Barry goes to meet her (breaking an appointment with Dietz to discuss ground rules for the show) and they reminisce about Barry's early days as a suit salesman, his big break when invited on the show of another talk radio DJ, and the big break-up of his marriage caused by the strain of work and his own infidelity.

The show begins on Monday as usual, but there is no live feed, Dietz claims a scheduling problem but it is clear he has doubts. Barry is furious at this, and sets about laying into his audience more fiercely than ever. He invites the hoaxer from Friday's show to appear in person and Kent, a teenager who claimed his girlfriend had overdosed, arrives – a mop of heavy metal hair on top of a mindless grin. Barry becomes disgusted by Kent, not only for his stupidity but his mindless insincerity. Ellen calls in as Sheryl-Ann, a pseudonym she used to adopt to pad out Barry's earlier shows. She attempts reconciliation but Barry spurns her, using her to vent more abuse. Shocked by the apathy, stupidity and narrow-mindedness of his callers and by his own hypocrisy and lack of empathy, Barry launches into a tirade against the callers, the system he works for and himself, finishing with a full minute of dead air.

Impressed by this forceful display, Dietz confirms that the deal is back on and that national broadcasting will begin as soon as possible. Dan is also impressed, but Barry seems deflated. He walks Laura out to her car, and they part as he prepares to drive out to Ellen to try to talk with her. A middle-aged man appears from the shadows – perhaps one of the enraged callers – and shoots Barry dead. The camera pans across the Dallas skyline as a number of voices, some recognisable callers, some new voices and those of Stu, Dan and Laura offer their epitaphs on Barry Champlain.

ADVANCE PUBLICITY: This was a quick and dirty release and there was little time or motivation for a marketing campaign. The poster was a dingy affair, showing Eric Bogosian's head peering out of the gloom and carrying an ominous tagline, 'The last neighbourhood in town.'

PRODUCTION HISTORY: *Talk Radio* went through several incarnations before reaching the big screen. It began life as a performance piece, a collaboration between actor Eric Bogosian and video artist Ted Savinar. The initial concept, a monologue spoken against a backdrop of video projections, was developed into a one-act play first performed at the New York Shakespeare Festival in May 1987. A proper cast of supporting characters – Stu, Laura and Dan – were later developed and the character of Barry Champlain was given more depth.

Ed Pressman acquired the film rights to the play and began scouting around for a director to helm the piece, with Bogosian to reprise his stage role. Names such as William Friedkin and Alan Parker were bandied around but no concrete deals signed. No film script had been written and the play was rather limited in its initial form (see **INSPIRATION AND INFLUENCE**), so Ed Pressman asked Oliver Stone to take a role as producer of the film, and to work with Bogosian on a cinematic adaptation. Stone was putting the finishing touches to *Wall Street* and planned to start on *Born on the Fourth of July*, but had to wait for Tom Cruise to finish *Rain Man*. Pressman presented *Talk Radio* as a stopgap project – the swift turnaround from *Salvador* to *Platoon* and then to *Wall Street* shows how keen Stone was to keep working at this point. Stone had also taken a bad loss on an investment and, as he put it, 'Ed was there at the right moment and said he'd give me the money back right away if I came in as a producer on *Talk Radio*.'

Stone was still looking at other projects. One was called *Contra*, a spy story involving two CIA agents: an experienced old-hand whose service dates back to Vietnam (Paul Newman was said to be interested) and his younger protégé. Though the project eventually fizzled out (filming in Nicaragua proved impossible), it is interesting to note the similarity of this central conceit with the Tony Scott film *Spy Game* (2001).

Pressman had also optioned the rights to *Talked to Death: The Life and Murder of Alan Berg* and this was used to fill out the character of Champlain. The first draft of the Bogosian-adapted screenplay was finished by December 1987, but Stone pitched it straight back at Bogosian, asking for a comprehensive rewrite. Bogosian's Christmas holiday in Australia went ahead, but he ended up taking along the first draft of *Talk Radio* with copious notes provided by Stone. He returned in January 1988 with a second draft, which underwent a further rewrite by Stone.

By this time pre-production was under way and Stone had gone from producer to director – as had almost certainly been Pressman's intent. There were three main reasons for this decision on Stone's part. As well as a chance to return to directorial work, this more hands-on involvement gave him the opportunity to establish a beachhead in Dallas – to build relationships with crewmembers, studio facilities and the local community that could be employed for *Born on the Fourth of July*. A final reason was financial. Garth Drabinski, the owner of Cineplex Odeon, bought the rights to distribute the movie for $10 million. The film itself would cost $4 million to make (even less than *Salvador*). Stone and Pressman split the $6 million between them. Though far from Gordon Gekko's opinions on what constituted being 'liquid', this reserve would mean that Stone would not have to 'waste time' on projects that did not interest him.

The shoot started in spring 1988 and was finished in 25 days. The film was released in December that same year.

CASTING: *Talk Radio* drew three substantial players from its stage debut, Eric Bogosian, Michael Wincott and John C McGinley (see **OLIVER'S ARMY**). Bogosian specialised in dramatic monologues but had appeared in a number of smaller independent films before *Talk Radio*. Subsequently he has remained low-key, his most prominent film roles being in the Stephen King melodrama *Dolores Claiborne* (Taylor Hackford, 1995) and as the computer-programmer villain in the awful Steven Seagal vehicle *Under Siege 2: Dark Territory* (Geoff Murphy, 1995). He drives this film with paranoid intensity by his looks and an unbelievably rich voice. This is perhaps unsurprising, given his role in the story's birth, but even he, despite being the original Barry Champlain and having co-screenwriter credit, wasn't immune to Stone's psychology of pressure. As he had done with Michael Douglas, Stone pushed Bogosian to the limit, demanding a totally concentrated performance. Bogosian provides an actor's-eye view of work under Stone: 'I just remember a blur of very long days, and being tired, very tired, too tired on Sunday to even get out of bed.' Bogosian recalled, '[Stone] saying don't ask me how you did after a take. If I don't say anything, it means you were good.'

Michael Wincott had an undistinguished career before *Talk Radio* but would appear in several subsequent Stone pictures (see **Born on the Fourth of July** and **The Doors**). Kent is moronic, pathetic, but also creepy and deeply unsettling. Wincott seems miscast despite having originally played the role. Indeed he gives too much depth and menace to a character meant to represent the simplicity of Champlain's majority audience.

Alec Baldwin took the role of Dan, the station's executive producer. As senior member of the prolific Baldwin clan (other members Stephen,

Adam, William and Daniel), he has enjoyed success on stage, screen and TV. His best performance reprised the slick, businessman persona employed in *Talk Radio* for a memorable cameo in another stage adaptation *Glengarry Glen Ross* (James Foley, 1992).

The screenplay added an estranged wife for Barry Champlain. Ellen remains a rather clumsy bolt-on character, not helped by a thin performance from Ellen Greene, who had played Audrey in *Little Shop of Horrors* (Frank Oz, 1986). Producer Laura is somewhat more interesting, primarily because Leslie Hope gives a knowing quality to a character who might otherwise have come across as a dim girl of little significance beyond being a bedroom companion for Barry. Instead she is clearly ambitious in her own right, and has an enigmatic relationship with Barry – tolerant, but with full awareness of his childlike capriciousness. Hope's career had been mainly in TV prior to *Talk Radio* and, after a period of work in obscure B-movies, it would be TV where she would find a degree of contemporary fame, as Teri Bauer in the first season of real-time action serial *24*.

OLIVER'S ARMY: Bruno Rubeo returned as production designer for *Talk Radio*, having missed *Wall Street* while working for Alex Cox on *Walker* (1987), an adventure tale set in Nicaragua. Cox had also tried to secure the services of Robert Richardson as Director of Photography, but Richardson had refused. Rubeo put together a dark, claustrophobic set, heavily influenced by research into real radio stations and advice from technicians. One concession was the incorporation of a radio headset for Champlain, not real but bringing some mobility into the long scenes of radio dialogue.

Ellen Mirojnick was on her second Stone movie and developed a similarly contemporary style to *Wall Street*, though more muted.

One new face on set was that of David Brenner as editor, Claire Simpson having left to further her career (a pattern that would become familiar among Stone's editors). Brenner's name would become more familiar over his editorial stint on three of Stone's future films.

John C McGinley was the only veteran of Stone's previous casts to appear (see **Platoon** and **Wall Street**). This was his third appearance in the role of hyperactive, hysterical sidekick, though this time the character had been constructed for the initial stage run of the story and not in a Stone script.

CUT SCENES: A greater imperative than cutting the film down was fleshing it out, taking it beyond its theatrical roots. This included the addition of Barry's ex-wife and the extended flashback sequence that replaced three monologues in the original play, delivered by Barry's colleagues, that filled in some of the back-story.

Several scenes were added from the life of Alan Berg, including that set in the basketball court. Nonetheless, this comes across as somewhat clumsy and contrived – a rather heavy-handed attempt to highlight the popular attitude to Champlain, which clashes with attempts to portray him as a broadly sympathetic lost soul.

MEMORABLE QUOTES: Most memorable dialogue from the film comes from Champlain's motormouth radio conversations:

Caller: 'A lot of problems with the country today have a lot to do with the continued exploitation of third-world countries.'
Barry [blows raspberry]: 'Wait. Third-world countries? Where'd you learn that phrase, in college? Do you know what it means?'
Caller: 'You're getting off track.'
Barry: 'We're not getting off track, we're getting on. Josh, go back to college; when you graduate, give me a call. A prime example of that uniquely American institution: the concerned bleeding-heart liberal looking for people with problems he can call his own.'

Barry (to caller obsessed with his cat): 'Glenn, take my advice. Stop hangin' around with the pussy . . . and go find some.'

Barry (to neo-Nazi racist): 'Chet, so nice to hear from you again; shouldn't you be out burning crosses or molesting children?'

GOOD VS EVIL: Despite its minimalist nature, *Talk Radio* is a surprisingly complex film, primarily due to the ambiguity of the central character. It is also the least clearly delineated of Stone's early films; there is little sense of a right versus wrong. The film is a spectrum of evil, from the racists who send Barry boxes filled with dead rats and Nazi flags under the guise of bomb threats, to the cheery-voiced white supremacist eager to discuss the holocaust, to religious extremists through to the materially lesser evils of apathy, small-mindedness and stupidity. On this level the film is pessimistic indeed, suggesting that America is doomed by hatred, superficiality and laziness. Champlain berates a country:

where culture means pornography and slasher films, where ethics mean pay-offs, grafts and insider trading, where integrity means lying, whoring and intoxication. This country is in deep trouble, people, this country is rotten to the core and somebody better do something about it.

Barry thinks he is the somebody who knows what that something is, and believes that a nightly trawling of the moral depths through his radio show will bring enlightenment to his audience, awareness of this decay. He is, from his own perspective, a force for good. It's a gloomy vision indeed, where the good is represented by an angry, lying, fickle madman, manipulated for profit by an unscrupulous businessman.

REDEMPTION OR DAMNATION: As with previous films, the eventual judgement on the protagonist is important and here it comes in relation to the character's perception of himself. Barry really believes that he has a role as a guardian of society. He rails against the small-minded, the petty and the bigoted in the belief that this is his purpose and that his words reach out and affect his audience. Towards the end of the show this belief is shattered by his tirade against 'Sheryl-Ann' and the presence of Kent. One shows off his own insincerity, as he vents his fury against an olive branch proffered by his ex-wife, the other destroys any notion that he is an effective force.

Barry exhibits total self-centredness. He sacrifices his marriage for his career. It is implied that he womanises, treating Laura as an obstacle to his work and a house-cleaner in private – all because of his commitment to his work.

Kent reveals how hollow Barry's work is. People don't look up to Barry, they laugh at him. Kent talks of the 'cool things' Barry gets to say, and gets off on the chance to hurl random abuse at one of the callers. The woman who throws soda over Barry says that she hates his show, but cannot explain why she listens to it. Nor can several callers who say they love the show. Even when Barry tries to help, his success is debatable. Kent is correctly judged as a hoaxer on his first call; none of the racist bigots show any sign of changing their ways; a self-proclaimed rapist who calls is neither diverted from his purpose nor can the call be traced; and even Barry's attempts to comfort a 23-year-old who sees no purpose in her existence come out as lukewarm platitudes ('You got two arms, two legs? You blind? You got a bellybutton? You'll be fine'). As station head Dan points out, there are a range of DJs who offer advice on psychological problems and financial problems but Barry's sole job is to 'hang up on people'.

This is the realisation behind his final tirade. He hates the people who call with banal comments and opinions, those who call with hateful, intransigent views, those for whom the show is inconsequential audio wallpaper, and himself for being the ringmaster of all this. Ironically it is this last cry of despair that wins over both the sponsor and Barry's boss. Barry has made himself the subject; it ceases to be a talk show (there is no dialogue, just a monologue and dead air) and becomes a listen show.

There is twin satire on both the personality-driven media, where a celebrity can be completely unaware that listeners are unconcerned with his views and interested only in him, and on corporate sponsors, who like to have just such a meaningless figure as a salesman for their products (in fact, a man who started out peddling suits). But what of Barry? He leaves this show deflated, suggesting to Dan that he would not come in tomorrow – though Dan knows that he will because what else would Champlain do? 'The show's a washout' he says to Stu, and seems to mean *Night Talk* as a whole. Stu suggests that it's not all that important. For Barry, this is the point: 'if it's not important, why am I doing it?' Stu has no answer, referring him to Kent's ultimate response to Barry's attempts to find a set of beliefs at the teenager's core – 'It's your show.' If Barry can't see a purpose to it, no one can.

But there is redemption, in a particularly bleak form, as Barry did get through to one listener. He made such an impression that that person decided to kill him. It might have been crueller to leave Barry alive, going back to his pointless profession day after day, whether nationwide or not. As he himself describes one of his own callers, 'another lost soul going into the Dallas night'.

STARS AND STRIPES: American radio differs greatly in presentation from its British counterpart. Diversity and variety seem to exist in inverse proportion to geographical size and population, a trend perhaps attributable to the concept of syndication. This is applicable to several media – television, radio, newspaper columnists and cartoons (for instance in *The Hand*) – and entails selling a particular product to local distributors (television and radio stations or newspapers). Metrowave, the fictional company in *Talk Radio,* goes one better, owning the radio stations in question and then trawling the country for shows to run on them.

The very title of the film refers to an American institution, the phone-in discussion show. Examples can be found all over America, and some presenters have gone on to become nationally, even internationally, famous. Talk-show hosts are perennially identified as a revolutionary force in British radio, though they have far to go before they reach the influence they have in the US.

BEING OLIVER STONE: It is difficult to assess Stone's personal relation to Barry Champlain without becoming embroiled in speculative psychology. It is possible to read a link in the frenzied attempts of Barry to reach out and affect the lives and thoughts of his audience for the better and in his fear that they do not care about what he says beyond its status as entertainment. Of course, this largely ignores the fact that the character was well developed before Stone was even offered the project. In addition, the director has seemed less than enthused with the psychological connotations of the film in retrospect: 'It's my least favourite movie, possibly because I don't care for the underlying material as much; I was using it as a laboratory.'

Nonetheless it is difficult to imagine that the director of *Salvador* and the creator of *Platoon* would find no sympathy with Champlain, a man who lives and dies through a refusal to dilute the twisted integrity of his opinions and ideas. At the very least it is possible to place Barry Champlain in a pantheon of iconoclastic non-conformists presented by Stone as protagonists – Richard Boyle, Ron Kovic and Jim Garrison are all examples of those who love their country but not what they see happening to it.

REAL PEOPLE: As mentioned above (see **STARS AND STRIPES**), many talk radio presenters have reached heights of fame. Two particular examples are Howard Stern and Rush Limbaugh. Stern is an anarchic buffoon and, despite being an obvious influence on the early representations of Champlain, with his trademark poodle haircut, he is more reminiscent of Kent. Stern, if not the first 'shock jock', is the most famous, basically the model for all radio specialists in humiliation, gross comedy and causing outrage. He even appeared in an autobiographical movie, *Private Parts* (Betty Thomas, 1997).

Conversely, there is Limbaugh, whose chat is political in nature, closer in some respects to Champlain, but different in its ideological basis. Limbaugh is an extreme right-wing Republican and his opinions are appropriately limited, without the anarchy and irreverence in Bogosian's character.

Alan Berg was the disc jockey to have the greatest influence through the story of his life and death – see below.

INSPIRATION AND INFLUENCE: *Talk Radio* the play bears the greatest resemblance to its cinematic namesake during Champlain's on-air rants. Outside of these the two stories diverge. On stage a loose back-story is filled in through three brief monologues, just enough to develop Champlain beyond a mere voice. In the film, Champlain's voice is interrupted by a considerably greater degree of exposition.

It takes a certain sort of play to function on film without significant alteration. Some of the very best (*Glengarry Glen Ross* for instance or Kenneth Branagh's 1995 *Hamlet*) still have a static 'stagey' feel, while the reverse is true of films transferred to stage, which can become dull and lifeless. A director such as Stone (and a cinematographer such as Richardson) have a need for motion in their work, and some of the additional scenes feel very artificial, added just to give a bit of variety to the set-up. In particular, the whole Ellen subplot rings a little false, giving an ambiguity to Barry that further muddles the question of his true nature and motivation. It is difficult to know exactly what to read into his attitudes towards his ex-wife.

That a lot of this additional material comes from *Talked to Death: The Life and Murder of Alan Berg* is little help. Berg had become famous as a bombastic and charismatic talk-show host, a liberal in the style of Champlain and Stern rather than the conservative Limbaugh. Stone and Bogosian liberally borrowed from his colourful career: Berg had started out as a lowly shop assistant; some of Barry's lines (such as asking an elderly caller what she thinks of lesbians) were taken straight from Berg's mouth; the sequence in which Champlain is booed at a basketball game was a direct lift from Berg's life; while his death, at the hand of crazed racists, also provided inspiration for the filmmakers.

But this cut-and-paste addition of scenes is clumsy and flawed. They feel deliberately tacked on, and in the case of the flashbacks a little too forceful in their presentation of the past, with the deliberately wacky 1970s clothes, music and hairstyles. The one element that does work is Barry's death, and it is appropriate that his comes from a lone madman, not a right-wing conspiracy as in the case of Berg. The film does drop references to this conspiracy through mention of *The Turner Diaries*, a right-wing novel from which Berg's murderers took their name – The Order. Champlain's death gives a punctuation mark to the story, a full stop as opposed to the depressing limbo that is the fate of the play's Champlain, and an ironic comment on Barry's fears for his lack of consequence.

REEL TIME: The technical ways in which the story was given a more cinematic feel were more successful than the narrative. For some scenes Bogosian wore a headset to talk to listeners. This allowed mobility at the cost of some credibility – real-life DJs do not generally use them. But even when he is seated the camera creates a feeling of movement and avoids stagnation. It adds to the spoken words of the script – for instance, when Barry speaks of treasuring a Star of David collected from the ruins of a Nazi concentration camp, of holding it when dealing with his most bigoted callers, the camera pans down to reveal only a coffee cup in his hands. It is somewhat contradictory that this works in conjunction with Rubeo's dark, minimalist interior sets, but the combination of the two produces an effect akin to a void – the only contact is with Stu and Laura through thick glass panels.

The best sequence of the film is Barry's closing rant. It involved some intricate camerawork. A heavy frame was attached to the desk facing Bogosian, which held the camera while desk, frame and actor were slowly swivelled, giving a moving backdrop to the static, seated Barry. It is diverting and disturbing and amplifies the feeling of disorientation contained within the DJ's angry, jumbled sentences.

MUSIC: Stewart Copeland returned to provide the original music, but often it is difficult to tell that there is any score at all. 'Bad to the Bone' is Barry's theme tune and it marks the start and end of his shows. Beyond this, and a brief snatch of 'Disco Inferno' (incorrectly attributed to the Bee Gees by Champlain – it is actually performed by The Trammps), there is little obvious music. The score itself is a subtle, minimalist electronic track that runs through some of the more dramatic moments. The sudden orchestral chord can be a rather corny device, normally reserved for horror movies. Here it is quite effective, lending a musical shiver to scenes of Barry opening his hate mail, and a sudden shock to Barry's dismissal of his marriage in flashback. A commendably restrained effort, with the sublime incorporation of 'Telephone and Rubber Band' by Penguin Café Orchestra over the closing credits, an effect reduced in the UK only by this tune's ubiquity in recent years as soundtrack to a mobile phone advert.

BOX OFFICE: The film took a weak $3.5 million at the US box office, not enough to make back the budget by itself, even though this was a very low $4 million. Disappointing, even allowing that this was never intended as a release on the scale of the previous two Stone films.

CRITICS: Many critics singled out Eric Bogosian's Champlain for special praise: 'Bogosian gives an outstanding performance sitting on a time bomb of his own making.' The *Village Voice* compared his role with a character from an earlier Stone film: 'His Barry Champlain isn't just a showbiz opportunist, he's a heroic creep (a sedentary cousin to James Woods's character in *Salvador*).' Ian Penman gave a backhanded compliment to the film, saying that it 'is probably [Stone's] best work to date, but . . . you get the impression that the best bits were already written by Eric Bogosian,' adding that 'the only bits of the film that don't work – a maladroit flashback and a mawkish "love interest" bit – were Stone's main contribution.'

Richard Corliss expressed admiration for a camera that 'crawls with a purpose: the movie gleams like Formica lighted by witchcraft.' The *Guardian* critic also appreciated the cinematography – 'As in *Platoon*, Stone's camera circles and paces and prowls around the onscreen protagonists.' This was not universal. The *Washington Post* critic started approvingly: 'Stone and cinematographer Robert Richardson give the movie a swirling, claustrophobic feel' but went on to suggest that this was an artificial manipulation of the audience, adding that 'even the most lurid spectacles are compelling on one level or another, even if the hold they exert is a dubious one.' He concluded on a view that could be levelled at most of Stone's films: 'What he wants most of all is a reaction, and he's not picky about how he gets it.'

Broadly, opinions were split on the film itself. Some were positive: '*Talk Radio* may be one of the most lacerating American movies of the year. It is also one of the best' (Derek Malcolm, *Midweek*); 'Stone's most thoughtful film since *Salvador*, and the most honest and apocalyptic cinematic view of the media since Paddy Chayevsky's *Network*' (Christopher Tookey, *Sunday Telegraph*). Some were less positive: 'A confused and flashy picture that, like Stone's *Platoon* and *Wall Street*, raises fundamental issues, then proceeds to sensationalise them' (Philip French, *Observer*); 'For all the energy of Bogosian's writing and performance and Stone's assured direction this . . . seems more a harangue than entertainment' (Geoff Brown, *The Times*).

AWARDS: Though ignored at the Oscars, *Talk Radio* did well at the 1989 Berlin Film Festival. Stone was nominated for a Golden Berlin Bear while Bogosian won the Silver Berlin Bear for 'outstanding single achievement'. In addition, the film picked up a bundle of nominations at the Independent Spirit Awards for cinematography, direction and best male lead.

THE BIG PICTURE: There are a lot of reasons to label *Talk Radio* as a cinematic sabbatical. It's a small movie in budget, cast and sets and seems shorter than its 115 minutes. It was not a pet project of Stone's and, to an extent, only exists because of a gap in his schedule, as a warm-up to *Born on the Fourth of July*. In a way it feels like a TV movie in its subdued style and somewhat limited ambitions. It is identifiable more with early screenplays where the narrative priorities are psychological or personal rather than the social or historical concerns of his later work. *U Turn* might be an exception, as there is a similarity in their downbeat, dark stories. However, the latter is a bloated noir epic, with an oddly distinguished cast. *Talk Radio* remains an oddity, an art-house-style film, of polished quality but ultimately the product of sheer opportunism.

A big name director will have films famous to a wide audience, but will probably also have one or two that have fallen into obscurity. Spielberg has his *Duel* (1971) and George Lucas his *THX 1138* (1970). Oliver Stone has *Talk Radio*, which, while not flawless, delivers a powerful message with a low budget and minimalist flair that one might not expect from him.

FINAL ANALYSIS: There are problems with *Talk Radio* that become apparent with successive viewings. In parts it feels like a play that has been deliberately padded out. The additional scenes make a coherent reading of the main character difficult, and there is a meekness to the performance of Ellen that makes it hard to believe she is the great lost love of Barry's life. But when it works, when the lights dim, leaving a pool of light around Barry's desk, when the set, the photography, the script and the acting all come together, the film packs an electrical dramatic punch: the abuse and retorts flowing beautifully, accompanied by unobtrusive but active camerawork that focuses attention on this one man, alone facing off against an army of disembodied anger, hate and pettiness.

A minor gem, not flawless, but still an engaging and underappreciated study in the superficiality of celebrity and of contemporary society.

Born on the Fourth of July (1989)

Universal Pictures presents
An A Kitman Ho and Ixtlan Production
An Oliver Stone Film
Casting by Risa Bramon and Billy Hopkins
Associate Producers: Clayton Townsend and Joseph Reidy
Costumes designed by Judy Ruskin
Music by John Williams
Edited by David Brenner
Co-Editor: Joe Hutshing
Production Designer: Bruno Rubeo
Director of Photography: Robert Richardson
Based on the book by Ron Kovic
Screenplay by Oliver Stone and Ron Kovic
Produced by A Kitman Ho and Oliver Stone
Directed by Oliver Stone

CAST: Tom Cruise (*Ron Kovic*), Kyra Sedgwick (*Donna*), Raymond J Barry (*Ron's Father*), Jerry Levine (*Steve Boyer*), Frank Whaley (*Timmy*), Caroline Kava (*Ron's Mother*), Willem Dafoe (*Charlie*), Cordelia Gonzalez (*Maria Elena*), Ed Lauter (*Legion Commander*), John Getz (*Marine Major*), Michael Wincott (*Vet No. 3*), Edith Diaz (*Madame*), Stephen Baldwin (*Billy Vorsovich*), Bob Gunton (*Doctor No. 1*), Jason Gedrick (*Martinez*), Richard Panebianco (*Joey Walsh*), Anne Bobby (*Susanne Kovic*), David Warshofsky (*Lieutenant*), Reg E Cathey (*Speaker*), Josh Evans (*Tommy Kovic*), Bruce MacVittie (*Patient No. 2*), Lili Taylor (*Jamie Wilson*), David Herman (*Patient No. 1*), Andrew Lauer (*Vet No. 2*), Tom Sizemore (*Vet No. 1*), Corkey Ford (*Marvin*), Rocky Carroll (*Willie*), Tom Berenger (*Recruiting Sergeant*)

NOTABLE CREDITS: As with *Platoon*, the credit sequence featured a montage of the main performances.

Abbie Hoffman (see **Conspiracy Theory**) died shortly after filming was completed. A credit makes note of this – 'In memoriam Abbie Hoffman, November 30 1936–April 12 1989'.

SUMMARY: Massapequa, Long Island, 1956. A group of small boys, including the young Ron Kovic, play 'war' with toy guns. There is a montage of an idealised American childhood: the Fourth of July Parade with war veterans proudly marching; a kiss from Ron's childhood sweetheart Donna as the fireworks burst; a little-league baseball game where Kovic hits a home run; the family gathered round the television for the 1960 inauguration speech of John Kennedy ('ask not what your country can do for you but ask what you can do for your country') and then Ron's mother saying, 'I had a dream, Ronnie, the other night, and you were speaking to a large crowd, just like him . . . and you were saying great things.'

Jump forward about six years to another montage sequence: an older Ron trains with the high school wrestling team (the coach urges the necessity of 'sacrifice') before battling at a wrestling meet. He is eventually defeated – to the audible disappointment of the crowd. Marine recruiters visit the school and Ron decides to join up with his friend Timmy – another friend, Stevie, is sceptical. Ron finds that Donna is being taken to the prom by another boy but on the actual night makes a last-minute decision, running in his socks to the school for one dance with Donna.

Near Cua Viet River, 1967. Vietnam is red, dry and dusty, Sergeant Kovic reassures Private Wilson, from Georgia, as a lieutenant orders them to form a perimeter around a village. Someone gets nervous, starts firing and the whole platoon empty their guns into the huts. A recon team led by Ron discover many dead villagers and children – no soldiers. As medical attention is called in an enemy counterattack is launched. In the confusion Ron pumps bullets into a charging figure – it emerges that he has killed Wilson. Ron informs his commanding officer who tells Kovic to forget it.

Further inland Ron's patrol stalk across a grassy plain. Gunfire from a nearby village cuts them to pieces, killing the radio operator and the lieutenant. Ron fires wildly at the treeline and is shot in the heel, but refuses to stay down. He pulls himself up, firing from a crouch, but is shot again and drops to the ground, his spine severed. A black soldier scoops him up and drags him to safety. He is moved to a hellish field hospital full of dying and badly wounded – a priest administers the last rites.

Bronx Veterans Hospital, 1968, filthy and bleak and another montage: Ron receiving an enema; training in the physiotherapy ward; shouting abuse at the anti-war demonstrators on TV. He is told that he will never walk again, nor be able to have children, but he refuses to accept this and drags himself around on crutches, in a grotesque parody of walking. A bad fall lands him in an iron cast – a desperate attempt to save his leg from amputation. Covered with vomit, he demands 'to be treated like a human being . . . I fought for my country.' But Vietnam means little to the American population.

Massapequa, 1969. He is back home with his nervous parents and the fake smiles of neighbours. He visits Stevie, now the successful owner of a chain of burger bars who patronises Ron with a low-level job ('You've got to walk before you can run') and ridicules the claims made by the government over the need for war in Vietnam. At the dinner table it is clear that Ron's brother shares these beliefs. Nevertheless, Ron proudly sports his uniform for the Fourth of July Parade but sees a crowd mostly silent, some actively hostile, a changed high street with hippie shops instead of drugstores. After a robust introduction to a speech, Ron tries to sound positive but his voice fades away. As he leaves the stage he sees Timmy, also a veteran with a steel plate from a head wound and they talk about their other friends who had gone to war and been killed in action.

Ron visits Donna at Syracuse, but she is a prominent student activist, and somewhat embarrassed by Ron's recollections of their school prom, more concerned with the potential he has to help their movement, and utterly insensitive to his shy declaration of love. At a protest the next day a black veteran hurls away his medals before the police charge, gassing and bludgeoning the students.

Back in Massapequa Ron drinks heavily at a bar, riling two burly WW II vets and making passes at a young girl, barely able to hide her contempt. Dragged back to his house, he rows with his mother – 'Thou shalt not kill, mom. Isn't that what they taught us?' His father advises that he spend some time away.

Ron travels to a veteran recuperation centre in Mexico, actually a centre of drink, drugs and prostitution. The other vets welcome him ('just what we need, another limp dick') and one, Charlie, suggests he visits the local prostitutes. He does, and gets as close as he will to sex, but is dismayed the next day to see her servicing another client. Haunted by his memories of the Cua Viet River, he tries to write to the parents of the soldier he killed. After an argument during a taxi ride he scuffles with Charlie in the dust over who killed more babies, both men hauling their useless legs across the ground and grappling ineffectually. As they lie exhausted, Ron rejects the lotus-eater existence of the Mexican vets: 'Do you remember when things made sense, when there were things you could care about? Before we all got so lost?' Ron travels to Georgia and meets with Wilson's parents and widow. He manages to confess, and gets some release from the young widow: 'I can't ever forgive you, but maybe the lord can.'

Republican National Convention, Miami, 1972. Ron, now a key figure in Vietnam Veterans Against the War (VVAW) leads a march on the convention hall. He talks his way on to the floor, where Nixon is giving his acceptance speech. He is shouted down and eventually muscled out. It emerges that the 'vet' pushing his chair is an undercover cop and an attempt is made to arrest Ron, but a party of other vets rescue him.

Democratic National Convention, Atlanta, 1976. After the publication of his book, Ron goes to make a speech, pushed through a throng of people. The film ends with his mother's words from 1960 echoing in his ears.

ADVANCE PUBLICITY: Stone personally raised awareness with an escalation of his headline-grabbing outrageousness in his comments to reporters. He received a lot of coverage for his assertion that 'we have a fascist security state running the country . . . If I were [President] George [HW] Bush, I'd shoot myself. Existentially there's no hope. His soul is dead.'

PRODUCTION HISTORY: Ron Kovic's book *Born on the Fourth of July* was published in 1976. After the author's appearance at the Democratic Convention in the same year, it was featured in a *New York Times* review and in early 1977 Marty Bregman (see **Scarface** and **Platoon**) acquired the film rights. Al Pacino (star of Bregman's earlier productions, *Serpico* and *Dog Day Afternoon*) and William Friedkin as director were attached to the project. The first draft of the screenplay was unsatisfactory and Bregman turned to Stone, who had recently returned to the west coast after finishing *Midnight Express*. On 4 July 1978, in a small café on California's Venice Beach, Ron Kovic was dining with friends (including journalist Richard Boyle – see **Salvador**) when he first met Oliver Stone. Stone speaks emotionally of the encounter: 'It was as if we had been linked by destiny. Chosen as God's instruments to get a message, a memory out about the war.'

Later that year Bregman put together a deal to film Stone's screenplay. Al Pacino was still on as Kovic but Friedkin had quit, to be replaced by Dan Petrie. However, four days before the scheduled start of shooting, the European end of the US–West German funding fell through and the film was left $8 million short. With the project stuck in limbo, Al Pacino dropped out to make . . . *And Justice for All* (Norman Jewison, 1979) while the release later that year of the similarly themed *Coming Home* left *Born on the Fourth of July* redundant.

The script lay dormant for ten years, despite Stone's best efforts to get it made. *Platoon* raised his profile and, in 1987, Paula Wagner, Stone's agent at Creative Artists Agency (CAA), showed it to Tom Cruise, also a CAA client, who had expressed an interest in working with the director. Cruise liked it. Stone had been looking at earlier 'home front' projects he had written (entitled *Once too Much* and *Second Life*) but shelved them when he heard of Cruise's interest and the possibility of funding from Universal. Stone got back in touch with Kovic, who remembers a promise Stone had made in 1978 – 'If I ever get the opportunity to direct, if I ever break through, I'll come back for you.' Together they revised the script, adding Kovic's appearance at the 1976 Democratic Convention, and took it to Universal where Tom Pollock expressed an interest: 'I realised that it was one of the great unmade screenplays of the past fifteen years.' He offered to put up money to the tune of $14 million. Cruise was billed as the star.

With the same approach that had characterised his previous films, Stone coupled a broad narrative that loosely interpreted Kovic's book with an obsessive attention to detail. The crew, under production designer Bruno Rubeo, turned a Dallas suburb into Kovic's Massapequa childhood neighbourhood. Stone once again called in Dale Dye to provide technical advice (for instance, Marines of the time were not issued with M-16s, but the Korean War vintage M-14). Cruise met with many wheelchair users and Stone consulted with veterans of the 1960s protest movement in an attempt to replicate the feel of the marches.

The film was shot in sequence, apart from the Vietnam and Mexico segments for which the crew decamped to the Philippines, and was finished in 65 days, bang on schedule. The final cost was $17.8 million (a $3.8 million increase was negotiated part way through filming). It premiered in America in December 1989.

CASTING: One of Universal's conditions for backing the movie was that a big name star be attached. Sean Penn, Charlie Sheen and Nicolas Cage were considered for the role but none of them could really match the box office draw of the star of *Top Gun* (Tony Scott, 1986). The film was targeted by Stone as representative of the '*Rambo*isation' of Reagan-era cinema: 'it was essentially a fascist movie. It sold the idea that war is clean, war can be won.' Stone had memorably commented,

'Get the girl at the end if you blow up the Mig. The music comes up. And nobody in the fuckin' movie ever mentions that he just started World War Three!'

Cruise's performance is good, though is measurably better once he adopts the droopy moustache and long hair of the older Kovic, obscuring his recognisable features. He is convincing in a wheelchair and there can be no faulting the research and work he put into the role.

This was a one-man film, something exaggerated through the many locations – Massapequa, Vietnam, the Bronx, Syracuse, Mexico, Miami, Atlanta – leading to a huge turnover from scene to scene. This was not the tight ensemble piece of *Platoon*, nor did its large cast include recurring characters as *Any Given Sunday* would. In fact only Ron's father, his mother, Timmy, Stevie and Donna appear in more than one act, and this had an impact on the tone of the piece (see **GOOD VS EVIL**).

There were several cameos: Ron Kovic featured in the first Massapequa parade as a veteran of earlier wars, while Abbie Hoffman, a major participant in the Yippie movement, an extremist offshoot of Students for a Democratic Society, appeared as a speaker at the Syracuse protest, an appearance that caused some disproportionate criticism (see **Conspiracy Theory**).

OLIVER'S ARMY: Stone relied on several actors from his past films. Raymond Barry and Caroline Kava had both worked on *Year of the Dragon*, and enjoyed the most important parts after that of Ron himself. John C McGinley returned for a very brief appearance in his fourth Stone film (in the Democrat conference). Many other members of *Platoon* would crop up: Corkey Ford (Manny), Chris Pederson (Crawford) as hospital workers, David Neidorf (Tex) as a patient, and Mark Moses (Lieutenant Wolfe) as the doctor who repairs Kovic's leg-pump. In addition, Willem Dafoe and Tom Berenger both played significant parts, in effect reprising Elias and Barnes in a civilian situation – Barnes's animal fury retreating behind the martial courtesy of a recruiting agent, Elias as a disillusioned hedonist, surviving the war but with nothing to shape his life, gathering a new band of heads around him. Michael Wincott also makes a very brief appearance in Mexico, muttering a couple of words of advice to the newly arrived Kovic. *Wall Street*'s Chuck Pfeiffer played one of the Secret Service Agents at the Republican Convention.

Broadly speaking, the crew is the same as that assembled for *Talk Radio*. There was one important addition: a stirring score was provided by John Williams, probably the most famous composer in Hollywood and responsible for some of its best-known themes, such as those for the *Star Wars* films and *ET: The Extra-Terrestrial*.

CUT SCENES: In the original cut of the film the Democratic Convention was much longer, including Kovic's speech in its entirety. This cut was a wise move as it is rare for such speeches to maintain their impact on film. As it stands, the character of Ron Kovic has a definite journey, from unquestioning acceptance to constructive criticism of the government, as well as fulfilling the prophecy his mother makes over the opening credits.

MEMORABLE QUOTES:

Ron: 'There's no God, there's no country. It's nothing; it's just me and this wheelchair for the rest of my life for nothing. Me and this . . . this . . . this dead penis, Mom.'

Charlie: 'Don't shit me, Kovic, you never killed a baby. You never had to. You never put your soul into that war, never put your soul on the line.'

Ron: 'How the fuck do you know? Maybe I killed more babies than you did! Maybe I did, but I don't have to talk about it! Why not? Why the fuck not?'

Charlie: 'What are you hiding? What are you, better than anybody else? You a hero maybe? Got a bunch of medals, but deep down you're full of shit! You never fought, you weren't even there.'

GOOD VS EVIL: This is the story of one man, more so even than *The Doors*, whose Jim Morrison remains an enigma. Few characters make it through more than one act, let alone the majority of the film, there is no single embodiment of evil. This role is instead taken by a recurring bugbear of Stone's – the American establishment.

Born on the Fourth of July goes beyond *Platoon*, which limited its scope to the field of combat, to examine the post-war consequences on the home front. What is more, the perspective is not that of Chris Taylor's idiosyncratic notions of testing oneself, but the red, white and blue-tinted spectacles of Ron Kovic. It becomes clear in the film that blind acceptance of America's policy is wrong. Nor, it is suggested, do the actions of the Mexican veterans represent the right course. There is a middle way between blind loyalty and cynical rejection: the good American questions his government and the actions of his country.

The great 1950s fear of Communism was of an alien force that would remove individuality and leave a grey mass of identical beings. Ironically, this was the consensus that Stone, and Stone's interpretation of Kovic, see as the goal of the American government – unquestioning acceptance of the patriotic end. This is the evil. The converse good is the will of the individual who questions this consensus. The closest the film gets to an embodiment of this is in the Miami convention sequence – the radicalised veterans against the Republican establishment.

REDEMPTION OR DAMNATION: In *Platoon* a choice was presented between a selfish struggle for survival or an attempt to survive while maintaining humanity – a choice that all soldiers made. Here Ron Kovic faces a specific, individual physical challenge – acceptance of the wounds he received in war. This is the story of one person's attempts to reconcile what he was with what he has become and to understand how this change came about. Stone tells it in such a way as to relate Ron's struggle with that of the country as a whole. Physical rehabilitation is but one facet of his recovery; he must also take the blows dealt by his preconceived notions of country, patriotism and service being disproved (see **STARS AND STRIPES**) – to find that sacrifice goes unrewarded except for the guilt-payment of the government disability pension.

Ron's own journey is from the former position of conformity and wholly uncompromising loyalty to one of constructive criticism – challenging those people who have appointed themselves leaders of America and guardians of its values but have corrupted them and soiled the name of the country.

This view holds together, with one important emphasis – the apathy and decadence of Mexico is as unacceptable as the conformity of Massapequa. Like Boyle in *Salvador*, Kovic loves his country, and final redemption comes with involvement in reforming, or attempting to reform, the nation, not with unconstructive self-obsession. Kovic discovers true patriotism – not blind acceptance but a vocal challenge to complacency.

HISTORY 101: *Born on the Fourth of July* unfolds against the backdrop of radical protest politics of the 1960s. While in the Bronx hospital, Kovic watches footage of the riots at the 1968 Democrat Convention in Chicago, where police were ordered to aggressively break up anti-war protests. The violent and shocking scenes relayed to TV viewers across the country, on a scale unseen in any previous protest, contributed to an underlying unrest and dissatisfaction among the young.

There was a wave of intense protest on American campuses in the wake of Nixon's decision to bomb Cambodia in the spring of 1970. These increased dramatically after the death of several students at the hands of the National Guard at Kent State University in Ohio (see **Nixon**). The violence at Syracuse is presented in the context of these protests. The 1972 Republican Convention was also a focus for protest, including a march of Vietnam Veterans Against the War.

In American politics the Conventions are important as national meetings of the two American political parties at which the respective presidential candidates are chosen. At such monumental political gatherings protests are common, and Stone uses them to suggest a changing dynamic. In 1968 the protesters are against the war, in 1972 the protesters have themselves fought in the war and by 1976, embodied in Kovic, they are invited to the Convention itself.

CONSPIRACY THEORY: Despite the attention to historical detail in a broad sense, the facts are massaged to accommodate the narrative. This went beyond divergence from the text of Kovic's book with one significant scene on radical politics written specifically for the film: the Syracuse protest. The police at this small east coast university town made clear to the filmmakers that there had been no violence at the protest held there – Stone had elaborated for dramatic effect. However, the protest scene itself does not come across as manipulation of the truth for nefarious purposes, rather use of licence. All Stone really did was relocate events that were actually taking place across the country to another venue.

One criticism, which is hard to take seriously, was of the presence of Abbie Hoffman. Some made sport of pointing out that Hoffman had not been in Syracuse at the time, but they appear to miss the point: he had also been considerably younger in the 1960s, and was playing an unnamed character in a film.

STARS AND STRIPES: The film shows the woodland war games, the Fourth of July Parade, the baseball playing, the devout Christianity, the wholesome girls, the part-time job – all shorthand for an idyllic small-town American life. Ron is called on by his president to do what he can for his country and sees service as best done through the Marines, thanks to the sharp uniform and parade-ground ethics espoused by the recruiting officer.

Stone's technique is to show these ideals for the fallacies they are. The small-town mindset is backward and narrow-minded, the Christianity hollow and inflexible, the girls don't care for cripples, the job is wage-slavery imposed by cynical entrepreneurs, the fear of Communist conquest is misplaced, real war is devoid of both fancy uniforms and highfalutin codes of honour and the president doesn't want to listen to criticism from his people. Stone and Kovic want their audience to question all the things they take for granted about their country, to deconstruct the ideal of America and rebuild it with a greater connection to reality. The film is a journey of discovery, both physically and intellectually, a journey marked by Kovic's assertion at the end that 'just lately I've felt like I'm home . . . like maybe we're home.'

BEING OLIVER STONE: Stone had invested a lot of himself into the inception of *Born on the Fourth of July* back in the 1970s and the project had never really gone away. Bob Richardson has said, 'We talked about the story while we were working on other pictures, so it had been in the works for some time.' Stone is the kind of director who can nurse the germ of an idea for years, keeping it in stasis until the opportunity arises and, like much of his work (*Platoon, Any Given Sunday, The Doors, Alexander*), this film was the product of a long gestation period.

Kovic and Stone had oddly parallel experiences on their return from service in Vietnam. Both had periods of crisis, and both had to force their way through to a better state of being, both are sceptical towards their government and eventually achieved prominence through their criticism. But while Stone adopts Kovic's personal struggle as a metaphor for the state of the nation, the protagonist remains distinct from the director – perhaps because, like Richard Boyle, Kovic had been present on set as an adviser and co-screenwriter and there had been no need for Stone to overempathise with the lead character. Even without reference to his own post-war experiences, this film would satisfy Stone's desire for a home-front counterpart to *Platoon*.

REAL PEOPLE: Ron Kovic is the one wholly realised character, everyone else is just a bystander or an external force personified – even his parents are little more than manifestations of the conflicting reactions that greeted Kovic on his return home. There is little sense of them as developed characters beyond impulses of liberal well meaning on the part of his father and blind denial on the part of his mother.

The autobiography leaves an impression very close to that created in the film. It tells of a deeply religious patriot who blundered into the war through a belief in his country and what the leaders of that country told him, whose belief soured as he perceived lies that had been told to him, who did terrible things in Vietnam in the name of his country, and who was sent back home a broken man. When presented with his twilight existence, he turned to protest politics in which sphere he has been active ever since. In November 2003 he was present in London for the state visit of President George W Bush, and delivered a petition protesting against ongoing military action in Iraq to Tony Blair, the Prime Minister.

INSPIRATION AND INFLUENCE: The book of *Born on the Fourth of July* was published in 1976. Unlike the film it does not progress in a linear fashion but starts with the moment Ron was shot and then jumps backwards and forwards through time; transfer to a field hospital, his stay in the Bronx Veterans Hospital, his childhood and Marine training, the parade on his return, the estrangements from his parents, the time in Mexico, his growing politicisation. The book finishes with three big scenes – the confrontation at the Miami convention, the death of the soldier from Georgia and the patrol that ended with his paralysis.

The style is bold and confessional, accomplished, moving and very personal. At times it drops into stream of consciousness, while the point of view shifts from first to third person and back, making it difficult to imagine as a film. The changes are partly cosmetic, driven by the need of transposing the emotions expressed in the book on to the screen.

There are also fabrications, episodes created to present the changes that Kovic underwent as part of a cinematic narrative. The Kyra Sedgwick character was created to embody the loss of any chance of a normal sexual relationship – the archetypal high school sweetheart who becomes unobtainable on Kovic's return. Similarly, but more problematical, the scene in which Kovic confesses to the family of the dead soldier was a fabrication. Stone has justified this scene many times: 'My point was that . . . in writing about it, in confessing it, he was making it public, and admitting guilt and going and asking for confession.' In the film, admission of guilt and confession of responsibility takes on a symbolic meaning – the last barrier to Kovic's final reintegration. In the book the death is constantly invoked in an agonised howl, a burden from which Kovic the writer feels he can never be truly released.

Two parts in the book that are skipped over in the film are the period of Marine training (presented compellingly in stream of consciousness) and the account of Kovic's association with the anti-war movement. Some episodes are taken from the text and placed in different contexts – Kovic nearly had a leg amputated long after discharge from hospital, his arrest at the hands of an undercover cop, disguised as a veteran, actually took place in Los Angeles, his invasion of the conference floor in 1972 was successful, and despite intimidation he was able to make a speech. One flaw of the movie is its failure to fully show Kovic's move towards protest politics – part of this is incorporated into the Syracuse sequence, when Ron sees the black veteran discard his medals. The rest is left as a conclusion for the audience to draw, from Kovic's gradual rejection of the internal life, as Stone puts it, 'he passes from the private to the public sphere – that was the concept of his growth.'

Having said this, one sequence is reproduced with special attention to detail – the Veterans Hospital. Every horror and indignity described in the book is shown in the film. There have not been many films made about the severely disabled and Born on the Fourth of July happened to be released at the same time as the only other notable mainstream example of recent years, My Left Foot (Jim Sheridan, 1989) – see **AWARDS**. There had been a number of earlier movies on the subject of wounded veterans. John Savage had appeared as a wheelchair-bound vet in The Deer Hunter, while Coming Home featured Jon Voight in a similar role. This latter film had not only helped sink the first production of Born on the Fourth of July but also employed Ron Kovic as a technical adviser.

REEL TIME: The look of this film was a big departure from Stone's previous pictures. This would be the first to be shot in a wider anamorphic format, complementing an increase in scale across the board with bigger crowds, a greater historical sweep and more locations, distinguished by a variety of filters and lighting techniques.

The opening Massapequa segment is richly evocative of a certain type of mid-twentieth-century American style. Says Robert Richardson, 'We chose a dream-like interpretation of LIFE magazine photography. Atmosphere prevailed. We used an abundance of smoke, rain and pollen in the air.' This lends rich warmth to the nostalgic imagery; the parade especially has a golden hue that contrasts with that held on Kovic's return, presented in a starker light.

According to an American Cinematographer article, 'Stone originally planned to shoot the sequences in Vietnam with a gritty, black and white newsreel look.' But wanting to avoid cliché, this was changed to colour footage, dry, dusty, tinged with vivid yellow, reminiscent of the base-camp scenes of *Platoon*, but devoid of the lush vegetation that marked that film's combat sequences. The camera shoots from the perspective of the American troops, showing the difficulty of reading the situation that led to the massacre of the villagers. Later the Americans are strung out across a barren plain and when Ron is shot, it feels like action taking place in a vast coliseum – there is no doubt about the importance of this wound or its centrality to the film.

Lighting comes into play again in the Veterans Hospital, an optimistic warmth (contrasting with the sordid conditions) giving out to cold gloom as Kovic's hope fades, culminating in the nightmarish sequence where he is strapped into the archaic full body-brace in an attempt to save his injured leg.

After Kovic's return to Massapequa, the emphasis is on camera effects. The point-of-view is low, as opposed to the high angle of the opening war game. The audience is placed in the same position as Ron in his wheelchair. The Kovic house was built to scale (whereas normally sets are constructed slightly wider), creating cramped claustrophobia in the internal scenes. Around 50 per cent of the film was shot using a Steadicam, a specially balanced rig that allows for smooth tracking shots without the need to run a camera along a track. This is especially evident in the later scenes, as the camera follows the increasingly isolated Kovic, most notably during the Syracuse riot, where a long tracking shot captures the melee unfolding around the veteran's wheelchair. This contrasts with the VVAW march in 1972: the shot follows Kovic, this time marching *with* his comrades in an organised movement.

Technically, *Born on the Fourth of July* was somewhat more sophisticated than *Platoon* or *Wall Street*, and marked a move towards the experimentalism of *Talk Radio* but away from a studio set; Richardson and Stone would continue to follow this path in *The Doors*.

MUSIC: Music had been used constructively in *Platoon* to delineate differences between the two groups of US soldiers. It would be used in a similar, if more conventional and heavy-handed way, here to mark cultural and historical differences. The patriotic pomp of 'You're a Grand Old Flag' powers the Fourth of July Parade sequences and is brought in again to run over the credits – though with an ironic edge given the events of the film. The safe, pasteurised American childhood of Ron is represented in rock 'n' roll standards such as 'Rock Around the

Clock' and cloying prom music courtesy of Henry Mancini playing 'Moon River'. The transition to a more radical political stance is prefigured, with a startling lack of subtlety, in the scene of Tommy Kovic strumming 'The Times they are A-Changin' and rammed home by the use of Don MacLean's 'American Pie' in the Veteran's Hospital. Bob Dylan makes another appearance in Syracuse, with 'A Hard Rain's A-Gonna Fall'. The sequence in Mexico was marked out by a hefty slice of Latin music.

The soundtrack was held together with a typically sweeping score from John Williams. Williams is a great composer, but Stone's visuals rarely need any of the powering up that his music normally imbues. Though the partnership can work (see **JFK**), the result here is syrupy, over-sentimental and off-puttingly blunt, hammering home points that the images already make clear. As with *Platoon*, the best use of music can be found in its absence – the ominous silence of the Veterans Hospital at night, or the unaccompanied slanging match in the Mexican desert.

BOX OFFICE: A smashing return to commercial success, with a US gross of $70 million, off a budget of $14 million. After a couple of relative disappointments, this showed that Stone could still rake in the money given the right sort of film.

CRITICS: Oliver Stone attracted a lot of personal flak in reviews of *Born on the Fourth of July*. Alexander Walker drew comparisons with the many writers who suffered from failed attempts to write the 'great American novel', writing that Stone's 'self-advertising flamboyance shows what a superficial talent he has when he addresses himself to the "great American film" '. He goes on to suggest that the director was personally responsible for undercutting Cruise's performance: 'Stone will hardly allow him or his film a moment's pause for reflection,' concluding that 'the film's political points are palpably felt but peurilely [sic] delivered. They are just but they are also banal.' Others, such as Hilary Mantel in the *Spectator*, expanded on a perceived lack of subtlety: 'If in doubt, Stone brings in a big crowd; his ironies are heavy footed and he reaches too often for the expected, the push button image.' Nigel Andrews concurred: 'As in *Platoon*, Oliver Stone seems unable to craft a wartime morality drama except in crudest colours,' and, producing an elaborate metaphor, 'Stone believes in the bank hold-up method of getting an audience response. Never expect the audience to volunteer an emotion . . . because you have earned it,' instead, 'Just wave the weapons of menace and overstatement and you will get the loot.' There were more positive opinions, building on the same foundations: 'Stone may not be the most rigorous of American filmmakers nor the most subtle,' wrote Derek Malcolm, 'but he's like a rhino, charging at his chosen subjects and the visceral power of his filmmaking is often extraordinary.' *NME* was less reserved in its praise: '[Stone's] contempt is made flesh with forceful, blistering visuals. He captures the momentum of his subject matter with an attacking camera.' The review ended, '*Born on the Fourth of July* is an irrefutable tribute to the strength and endurance of the human spirit.'

Points of the film where critics expressed approval included its presentation of Vietnam. *Time* lauded a rejection of the *Rambo* aesthetic: 'everything that was terrific in *Top Gun* – the war, the sex, the male bonding – is found to be toxic here.' Hugo Davenport put the film over Stone's own *Platoon*, praising the director for his effort: 'arguably . . . it comes the closest yet to being the ultimate Vietnam picture . . . Stone moves easily from the intimate to the panoramic.'

There were plaudits for Tom Cruise. Derek Malcolm wrote in *Midweek* that 'what Cruise achieves, given his previous lack of depth, is extraordinary.' But there was no consensus here either. The critic for the *Washington Post* opined that 'Willem Dafoe . . . puts more fireworks into one cameo than Cruise does all movie.'

Pauline Kael did not like the film. She criticised the central actor: 'Cruise has the right All-American-boy look . . . but you wait for something to emerge and realise the look goes all the way.' And the director: 'Kovic's book is simple and explicit . . . Stone's movie yells at you for two hours and twenty-five minutes.' And even the subject: 'It's inconceivable that Ron Kovic was as innocent as the movie and the 1976 autobiography on which it's based make him out to be.'

CONTROVERSY: Right-wing commentators attacked what Pat Buchanan (speechwriter to Richard Nixon and Director of Communications to Ronald Reagan) described as 'at worst a pack of lies written to deceive the young who have no memory of what America was like during Vietnam'. The attacks were prompted by a specific event, Kovic's declared intention to run for Congress as a Democratic opponent to Californian Republican Robert Dornan, and focussed on a specific aspect to the film, its fictionalised elements. Though some had criticised *Platoon*'s vision of the Vietnam War, and *Wall Street* had come under fire for its presentation of the financial world, both these films had been protected by their nature as works of fiction, while *Salvador* had been too obscure to raise any fuss at the time of its release. As a biographical work, with its high-profile release and given Kovic's political ambitions, *Born on the Fourth of July* became the first Stone film to come under sustained attack in the media. As a paraplegic veteran, Kovic was too sensitive a target for political attacks personally, so Robert Dornan and his allies focussed on the film. As Stone has said of Kovic's candidature, 'That politicised everything. It became instant news ... [Dornan] immediately attacked the movie everywhere he could ... Then all the conservatives attacked it ... and that hurt the movie a lot.' Ultimately, either because of the attacks or because his intention had never been entirely serious, Kovic did not run for election. The attacks may have raised questions about the honesty of the film but did not adversely affect box-office receipts, nor prevent a respectable haul of awards.

AWARDS: As well as its Vietnam theme and high box-office earnings, *Born on the Fourth of July* also replicated *Platoon*'s award scoop. David Brenner and Joe Hutshing received an Oscar for their editing, while Stone picked up his second award for Best Director, though Best Film went to *Driving Miss Daisy* (Bruce Beresford, 1989). In his acceptance speech, Stone interpreted the award as 'your acknowledgement that the Vietnam War is not over'. He went on to give it wider symbolic importance, maintaining that it was 'a state of mind that continues all over the world for as long as man ... interferes in the affairs of other men'. There were several other nominations. As well as Best Picture, it was up for Best Cinematography, Best Sound, Best Music, Best Adapted Screenplay and Best Lead Actor, for Tom Cruise. This last nomination was entirely deserved, but it was also right that Cruise lost out to Daniel Day-Lewis for his astounding portrayal of the cerebral palsy-stricken Christy Brown in *My Left Foot* (Jim Sheridan, 1989).

The Golden Globes increased the haul, adding Best Director, Best Motion Picture Drama, Best Actor (Cruise) and Best Screenplay. John Williams had another nomination for his score. Cruise received a nomination from BAFTA for his performance, as did Kovic and Stone for their screenplay.

Professional societies also recognised the film. The American societies of Editors, Cinematographers, Sound Editors and Casting nominated it for their respective awards, while the Directors Guild of America gave it a DGA Award for Outstanding Directorial Achievement. The Writers Guild nominated it for their equivalent.

Stone was nominated for the Golden Berlin Bear at the city's film festival for the second film in a row.

THE BIG PICTURE: As noted above, the many obvious similarities with *Platoon*, and *Heaven and Earth* (1993), would complete a Vietnam trilogy. Stone also continued a biographical trend begun with *Salvador*, and this movie can be identified too as part of a trilogy of biographies of 1960s personalities (see also **The Doors** and **Nixon**).

Stylistically it carried the emotional bluntness and power of *Platoon* and the earlier screenplays to a much larger scale. This spirit of material excess in filmmaking would be called upon in most of his subsequent films – *The Doors*, *JFK*, *Heaven and Earth*, *Natural Born Killers* and *Any Given Sunday*. The trend began here.

The film also exists as a response to *Talk Radio*. Barry Champlain misinterpreted his radio show as attempting to engage with society's problems. The real solution comes with direct action. This raises an interesting paradox: Stone would go on trying to resolve problems with his entertainment. In some ways *JFK*, with its real impact on American politics, might be said to have solved this riddle.

FINAL ANALYSIS: This movie best conveys the sledgehammer aesthetic for which Stone has become renowned. Minimum ambiguity, maximum impact – as the man himself has said, 'I think it's better to be wrong on the side of clarification than of obscurity.' Compare this film with the mystifying plot of *Seizure*, where, as threatened by the evil trio, nothing makes sense. Here there is no possibility of missing Stone's meaning but this does not equate to a lack of quality.

The film is a delivery system for raw emotion, not calculating reason. The basic argument is developed from *Platoon* – war murders and makes monsters out of men, at the behest of a detached government with no idea of the consequences of its decisions. Stone chooses to argue on a basic level, the destruction wrought on and by one man in a futile cause, rather than a dissertation on the politics of the time (this would come in *JFK*). For this to work he captures pain, physical, emotional, mental and spiritual, in unrelenting close-up, with none of the ambiguity that would detract from the message – look at what has happened to this man. It is a work of raw power in intent and that dictates its execution. Brash, sentimental, almost totally devoid of subtlety, but *Born on the Fourth of July* works.

In Production

On top of his screenplays, directorial efforts and cameo appearances in films such as *Dave* (see *JFK*), Stone has put his name to many films as producer or executive producer.

Some of these represent credit for intervention in the creative process – for instance, Bosnian war thriller *Saviour* (Peter Antonijevic, 1998) and, more famously, the Oscar-winning Jeremy Irons thriller *Reversal of Fortune* (Barbet Schroeder, 1990).

Stone also aspired to the status of directors such as Francis Ford Coppola and Steven Spielberg, directors who had stakes in their own production companies. The first manifestation of this was Ixtlan. Initially formed as the corporate representation of Stone's interest in *The Hand*, the title came from *Journey to Ixtlan: Lessons of Don Juan*, a work of 1960s mysticism by Carlos Castaneda. In the early 1990s, Stone looked to expand Ixtlan's remit to the development of outside productions. As vice president of production, he appointed Janet Yang, who had screen-tested for the part of Ariane in *Year of the Dragon*.

As well as involvement with Stone's own projects, Ixtlan had a hand in churning out an eclectic range of films: *South Central* (Steve Anderson, 1992), a tale of gang warfare in LA; *The New Age* (Michael Tolkin, 1994), a black yuppie comedy; *The Day Reagan was Shot* (Cyrus Nowrasteh, 2001), a TV movie dramatising the assassination attempt on Ronald Reagan; and two crime dramas starring James Woods – *Indictment: The MacMartin Trial* (Mick Jackson, 1995) and *Killer: A Journal of Murder* (Tim Metcalfe, 1995). Most prominent in its catalogue are *The People versus Larry Flynt* (Milos Forman, 1996), a hymn to freedom of expression with the unlikely hero of crippled pornographer Larry Flynt (played by Woody Harrelson), and *The Joy Luck Club* (1993), a sentimental drama directed by Wayne Wang, who had been a vocal critic of *Year of the Dragon*'s depiction of the Sino-American community. Ixtlan had also been the driving force behind *Wild Palms*.

After *Natural Born Killers*, a second production house was set up, Illusion Entertainment, through which *Nixon* and *U Turn* were made. Illusion's other works were less prestigious, including the abduction potboiler *Freeway* (Matthew Bright, 1996) and the execrable *The Corrupter* (James Foley, 1999). Its most well known product to date is the brain-dead action flick *SWAT* (Clark Johnson, 2003).

> Stone's production career remains somewhat uninspiring, though few directors in recent years have managed to combine the two careers with consistent success. In theory, Ixtlan and Illusion provide a way for Stone to get his brand of controversial movies made. In practice, though, this has only come to pass once, with *The People versus Larry Flynt*.

The Doors (1991)

Mario Kassar presents
An Oliver Stone Film
A Sasha Harari/Bill Graham Films/Imagine Entertainment Production
Casting: Risa Bramon and Billy Hopkins
Music produced by Paul A Rothchild
Executive Music Producer: Budd Carr
Costume Designer: Marlene Stewart
Edited by David Brenner and Joe Hutshing
Production Designer: Barbara Ling
Director of Photography: Robert Richardson
Associate Producers: Clayton Townsend and Joseph Reidy
Executive Producers: Mario Kassar, Nicholas Clains and Brian Grazer
Produced by Bill Graham, Sasha Harari and A Kitman Ho
Written by J Randal Johnson and Oliver Stone
Directed by Oliver Stone

CAST: Val Kilmer (*Jim Morrison*), Meg Ryan (*Pam Courson*), Kyle MacLachlan (*Ray Manzarek*), Frank Whaley (*Robby Krieger*), Kevin Dillon (*John Densmore*), Kathleen Quinlan (*Patricia Kennealy*), Michael Wincott (*Paul Rothchild*), Michael Madsen (*Tom Baker*), Josh Evans (*Bill Siddons*), Costas Mandylor (*Italian Count*), Dennis Burkley (*Dog*), John Capodice (*Jerry*), Mark Moses (*Jac Holzman*), Will Jordon (*Ed Sullivan*), Robert Lupone (*Music Manager*), Floyd Red Crow Westerman (*Shaman*), Billy Idol (*Cat*), Kristina Fulton (*Nico*)

NOTABLE CREDITS: A closing credit offered 'Special thanks to The Doors for their assistance in making this film, and to John Densmore's book, *Riders on the Storm*'.

This was the third Stone film (with *Platoon* and *Born on the Fourth of July*) to feature a closing sequence, showing the major characters with the names of the actors who played them. The credits include a re-creation of the recording session for *LA Woman*, The Doors' last studio album, with Val Kilmer as Morrison singing the title track. The film is dedicated 'In memory of Rocco Viglietta' – he was an associate of executive producer Mario Kassar at Carolco (see **PRODUCTION HISTORY**).

SUMMARY: A recording studio, 1970. A bearded figure lights a cigarette and slurps on a bottle of whisky: Jim Morrison, preparing to record his poem *An American Prayer*.

New Mexico. A clean-cut family cross the desert. They pass the scene of an accident; a truck of Indians has overturned, scattering the wounded and dying over the road. The young boy in the back looks awestruck. His mother tells him not to worry: 'Jimmy, it's just a dream.' The camera cuts to the boy, now in his early twenties, standing by a roadsign in the desert, hitching to Los Angeles.

Venice Beach, 1965. The young man, Jim Morrison, crosses the beach and spots a pretty redhead girl, Pam Courson, walking her dog. He follows her home and, later that night, climbs to her balcony. She asks why he followed her and he answers that she was 'the one' and departs.

At UCLA film school, Morrison presents his student movie, a non-linear mess of Nazism, dancing women and Frederick Nietzsche. The students and teacher hate it. Morrison quits. Later he returns to Courson's house, asks her to come on a walk and they stroll through the moonlit streets. Jim reads her his poetry and tells her of the shaman, the medicine man who travels beyond his own consciousness to heal the ills of the tribe. They make love on an LA rooftop. Daytime, and Morrison sees an old film school friend, Ray Manzarek, on the beach. Ray is having little luck breaking into the film business but asks to hear the song lyrics Jim has been writing. Blown away by a verse from 'Midnight Drive', he is convinced that they should set up a rock band, 'and make a million dollars'. They agree on a name, The Doors, and gather for practice in Manzarek's beach house with Robby Krieger (guitar) and John Densmore (bass).

Six months later. 'Light My Fire' plays as the camera pans down Sunset Boulevard, ending up outside a small club, the London Fog. Morrison sings 'Break on Through' to an enthusiastic audience including a sleazy executive who offers to sign them up, though the band insist on a unanimous decision. He unsuccessfully tries to split Morrison away from the group, seeing his voice and presence as the real draw. Jim persuades the rest of the band to travel to the desert for a peyote trip, a druggy, barely real scene closing with Morrison following a mysterious figure to a cave where he sees a vision of his own death. The camera zooms into the Indian's eye, cutting to the prestigious club Whiskey à Go Go in 1966. Another Doors gig, and here the band play 'The End'. Jim launches into an obscene improvisation and the club owner flies into a rage. He throws the band out but Jac Holzman of Elektra Records loved the performance; he signs the band up to record with Paul Rothchild as their producer.

In the studio the band race through their first album. A swift montage of Super 8 footage follows the band's 1967 visit to San Francisco, a gig at famous venue the Filmore and a flight to New York.

At the *Ed Sullivan Show*, The Doors are asked to censor 'Light My Fire' to remove the word 'higher', but Jim plays the original version. Later, the band go to a party thrown by Andy Warhol, full of the pretentious and self-consciously trendy New York art crowd. Manzarek, Densmore and Krieger are unhappy but Morrison stays, meeting American actor Tom Baker, Velvet Underground performer Nico and Warhol himself, a vacant, dreamy figure. He experiences a night of drunken excess.

At a press conference the next day, Morrison responds to hostile questions and tells one reporter, Patricia Kennealy, that his parents are dead. At Patricia's apartment they lie together but Jim is unable to have sex, until aroused by bloodletting and copious cocaine. The scene cuts to Jim in bed, this time with Pam but impotent once again. They argue and Jim dangles out of a window; Pam pleads with him to come back inside and they embrace on the carpet.

New Haven, Connecticut, 1968. Jim meets Patricia in a shower stall backstage. As he frantically disrobes, she tells him not to lie to her again: she knows his parents are alive and that his father is an admiral. He tells her of his parents' lack of love. Patricia points out that it is Jim the audience want. Jim claims that it is not him they want, but his death. As they talk, a policeman bursts in and tries to throw them out. Jim is maced before staggering on stage. Morrison prowls the stage angry and resentful. He tells the story of his backstage encounter. As he grows increasingly abusive, a gang of police come on stage and arrest him.

The decline starts with: Jim drunk with Baker and other friends Cat and Dog, Pam trying to nag Jim into domesticity and Pam and Jim fighting at a Thanksgiving dinner. A concert in San Francisco, 1968, plays over Jim's discovery of Pam with an Italian Count last seen at Warhol's party. They are high on heroin and a crazed Morrison hurls Pam into a closet, setting it on fire. Stoned and drunk, he marries Patricia in a pagan ceremony. Back in the studio, work is stalled on the latest album, *Soft Parade*. Too drunk to sing, Jim staggers aggressively through the studio, despite Rothchild's attempts to halt the session. He sees an advertisement on television that uses 'Light My Fire', something he did not authorise. Just as violence looks certain, Pam appears. The session continues.

Miami Beach 1969. Jim is not at the venue. Still on the plane, he loads up on drugs and booze, a bloated, bearded parody of his former self. Rothchild, on the plane with him, thinks his aim is an early death. Finally, Morrison arrives but is barely able to perform coherently, drunkenly lays into the crowd, taunting and insulting them, eventually appearing to show them his penis. The police leap at him but start a riot instead, the stage collapses and Morrison leads a conga line to the tune of 'Break on Through'. He is summoned to court, charged with indecent exposure, profanity and drunkenness. Patricia tells him that she is pregnant, but Morrison urges her to have an abortion, saying that their wedding 'seemed like a bit of fun at the time'. As the trial crashes to a guilty verdict, concert promoters across the country cancel their bookings, other women come forward with demands and a TV plays a montage of late 1960s nightmare images. Jim reckons he is on the edge of a nervous breakdown.

A final reconciliation with the band and Jim leaves for Paris with Pam. Paris, 1971. Pam walks down a corridor, glimpsing the bald figure that appeared to Jim in the desert and has dogged his steps ever since, always glimpsed in the background. Jim is in the bath, peaceful, silent. As Pam realises that he is dead, the camera cuts to Pere Lachaise cemetery, drifting past the tombs of famous writers and poets, ending up at the flower-strewn, graffiti-covered monument to Jim Morrison.

ADVANCE PUBLICITY: The film's concentration on Morrison was evident from the poster campaign – a portrait of Val Kilmer in character, face white with black features and hair coloured with psychedelic flames.

The terse trailers were similarly orientated. A teaser featured Kilmer's Morrison, in silhouette, walking towards a white doorway to 'Break on Through', with a roaring crowd audible in the background. The trailer itself was only slightly longer, showing a rapid montage of scenes. Both things unknown, and between are The Doors.' The second ended with the tagline, 'The ceremony is about to begin.'

PRODUCTION HISTORY: If the history of a film such as *Wall Street* is simple, *The Doors* is an example of how convoluted big-budget filmmaking (especially of a controversial subject featuring characters based on living people) can get. Effectively the story goes back to 1980 and the publication of *No One Here Gets Out Alive* by *Rolling Stone* journalist Jerry Hopkins and former Doors publicist Danny Sugerman. This kick-started a revival of interest in the band, Elektra records released a greatest hits package, *Rolling Stone* magazine put Morrison on their cover and Hollywood started sniffing around for a film deal.

In 1981 producer Sasha Harari paid $50,000 for movie options to the book – the remit was strictly limited and did not include music. John Travolta had expressed an interest in starring and brought in Brian De Palma as writer and potential director. Separately and simultaneously Harari secured the tentative agreement of the band and brought in William Friedkin who declared an intention to make 'the *Raging Bull* of rock movies'. Neither director was aware of the other's involvement.

De Palma ducked out once he heard of another director's interest, but Friedkin hung in until late 1982. The Doors eventually sank the project by demanding an excessive degree of creative control, scaring off potential backers. Harari's option expired about this point, but he convinced the band to sign over their story rights ($750,000 was later paid for the music rights).

To further complicate matters the estate of Jim Morrison had been split five ways after his death. The three remaining Doors had agreed, but it was necessary to get approval from Morrison and Courson's respective families who owned the other two fifths. This was secured through the involvement of Bill Graham, 1960s rock promoter. He and business partner Nicholas Clainos, as comparatively neutral participants with no prior connection to this complex movie deal, obtained the families' permission. One condition was the exclusion of the book *No One Here Gets Out Alive*, which both families disliked. The filmmakers sidestepped this restriction by purchasing the right to Jerry Hopkins's notes for the book.

In 1985 Harari made an attempt to get Oliver Stone as screenwriter, but failed (Stone has claimed that he never received the phone call). Instead, Randall Johnson was hired to write the first of several scripts – his was the only work eventually judged significant enough to merit co-credit with Stone.

The project trundled along at Columbia, but a sudden change of leadership in 1986 put it in limbo. This prompted a brief struggle as other studios tried to grab the film, a struggle won by Tony Ludwig, responsible for Bill Graham's involvement in 1984 (see **PRODUCTION HISTORY**), and now head of development at Imagine Films Entertainment. Stone was again mooted, but The Doors rejected him as too dark.

By 1988, with no deal in sight, Harari's renewed option was again in danger of expiry. Brian Grazer, head of Imagine, tried to put together a deal, which was finally set up by Mario Kassar of Carolco, a studio with which Oliver Stone had a two-picture deal (see **Heaven and Earth**). The Doors had changed their opinions on the director (Robby Krieger was a fan of *Salvador*) and they dropped any objections to Stone, who agreed to direct after work had finished on *Evita* (see **The Ones that Got Away**). The last hurdle to overcome was to clear rights to Morrison's poetry, vital to his concept of the film. Initially, Courson's parents refused unless all references to their daughter's drug habit were removed (just one scene of heroin use was kept in the final cut). Stone eventually got approval from the Morrisons, who were fed up with the whole process and just wanted the picture finished.

By the time pre-production began *The Doors* had already cost around $2 million in rights and for the various drafts of the script, a final version of which was overseen by Stone. Biographies, videos, music and interviews were all consulted, in the usual show of intense physical research. Stone commented about the various interviews conducted and transcripts consulted, that: 'It's like *Citizen Kane*. I could have made a movie just talking to the witnesses.' The movie he actually made was a single highly subjective vision.

It was Stone's biggest production to date, with a shooting schedule of three months and a projected budget of $38 million, including allowances for 30,000 extras for the Miami concert, location shooting in Los Angeles, San Francisco, New York, Paris and the Mojave Desert (the cost of filming on Sunset Boulevard for three nights alone was $60,000) and some expensive post-production digital work at Industrial Light and Magic (see **REEL TIME**). Production design was once again painstaking with a period re-creation of Sunset Boulevard and Venice Beach, which was not a problem for the extras, many of them ageing hippies only too happy to bring their old clothes and beads. The realistic re-creation extended to Patricia Kennealy's New York apartment. Though relocated to a loft in Los Angeles, she discovered prop letters on her desk bearing the correct address for the flat in 1968.

With this appropriate level of Dionysian excess, it is unsurprising to find that Stone uncharacteristically went $6 million over budget. Filming started in March and finished in the summer of 1990, encompassing Oscar night on 26 March, where Stone picked up his third Academy Award (see **Born on the Fourth of July**). The film was released in the USA in March 1991.

CASTING: The whole project, as conceived by Oliver Stone, revolved around the casting of Jim Morrison. At various stages in the past John Travolta, Ian Astbury, Michael Hutchence (of INXS), Bono (of U2) and Christopher Lambert had all been mooted for the part but, after 200 auditions, Val Kilmer was the final choice. He was an early favourite; Stone was impressed by the actor's performance in *Willow* (Ron Howard, 1988). He had also auditioned for Elias in *Platoon*. Kilmer benefited from a superficial visual resemblance and, crucially, a fine singing voice: he ended up singing on many of the tracks used in the film, including all the concert scenes. He took the part seriously, smoking harsh cigarettes throughout the shoot to get a husky edge to his voice. It's an admirable effort that works brilliantly in the isolated context of the film, but appears lacking when compared with real concert footage, where Morrison comes across as a mischievous, prowling, predatory figure. Kilmer plays him as a naïf, dreamily wandering from crisis to crisis, meaning little harm and only dimly aware of his surroundings. Of course, it is impossible for any actor to perfectly replicate such a prominent figure, but in this case the impression is of the manifestation of Stone's agenda for the character.

Though once again a story about just one man, secondary characters were slightly more prominent here than in *Born on the Fourth of July*. Most significant among these was Pam Courson, played by Meg Ryan. This was an odd piece of casting, as Ryan has usually appeared as a kooky female lead in such lightweight entertainment as *Innerspace* (Joe Dante, 1987), *When Harry Met Sally* (Rob Reiner, 1989) and *Sleepless in Seattle* (Nora Ephron, 1993). She does not seem right for a hippie 1960s drug-addict radical, and is visibly uncomfortable in some scenes. Stone puts the choice down to his interpretation of Pam as an 'all-American' girl, though the lasting impression of the film is of Pam as an obstruction to Jim's free spirit. Perhaps this is due to the casting of Ryan, just as the casting of Daryl Hannah in *Wall Street* moved Darien Taylor away from a hardened cynic to a flakier, more superficial character. The nature of the woman herself remains enigmatic.

►▼ Charlie Sheen (below) did his best as Bud Fox, but *Wall Street* belongs to Gordon Gekko, played to Oscar-winning perfection by Michael Douglas (right)

(20th Century Fox/The Ronald Grant Archive)

► Barry Champlain (Eric Bogosian) tells it like he sees it in the cynical, brash and dark world of *Talk Radio*

(Universal Pictures/The Ronald Grant Archive)

◀ In the jungles of South East Asia Willem Dafoe's Elias strikes full-blown Christ pose for his death scene in the powerful, and semi-autobiographical, *Platoon*
(Hemdale Film Corp/The Ronald Grant Archive)

▶ Back on the home front, an unkempt Tom Cruise, as Ron Kovic, carries the flag for anti-war veterans in the second of Stone's Vietnam trilogy, *Born on the Fourth of July*
(Universal Pictures/The Ronald Grant Archive)

▲ Le Ly hides from foreign invaders in Stone's last Vietnam foray *Heaven and Earth*
(Warner Bros/The Ronald Grant Archive)

▼ 'Back and to the left.' Kevin Costner's Jim Garrison gives the jury something to think about in *JFK*
(Warner Bros/The Ronald Grant Archive)

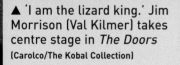

▲ 'I am the lizard king.' Jim Morrison (Val Kilmer) takes centre stage in *The Doors*
(Carolco/The Kobal Collection)

▶ Anthony Hopkins lends a battered and tragic humanity to the disgraced former President *Nixon*
(Hollywood Pictures/The Ronald Grant Archive)

▶▼ Mickey and Mallory Knox (Woody Harrelson and Juliette Lewis, below) spread mayhem across the midwest in *Natural Born Killers*. However, the poster (right) was as close as many in the UK would get to seeing the film for some time

(Warner Bros/The Ronald Grant Archive)

WOODY HARRELSON   JULIETTE LEWIS
ROBERT DOWNEY JR. and TOMMY LEE JONES

THE MEDIA MADE THEM SUPERSTARS.
NATURAL BORN KILLERS

◀ Despite the presence of Jennifer Lopez, *U Turn* proved a wrong turn for Oliver Stone
(Warner Bros/The Ronald Grant Archive)

▼ Jamie Foxx, Al Pacino and Dennis Quaid take a time-out in the breathlessly brutal and unrelentingly macho *Any Given Sunday*
(Warner Bros/The Ronald Grant Archive)

▲ Colin Farrell stars in Stone's most ambitious project to date – *Alexander*

(Warner Bros/Everett/Rex Features)

▼ Oliver Stone steps out from behind the camera for his extended cameo performance in *Any Given Sunday*

(Warner Bros/The Kobal Collection/Zukerman, Robert)

Kyle MacLachlan brought a touch of crisp coldness to the role of Ray Manzarek, a style he had perfected as Agent Dale Cooper in David Lynch's *Twin Peaks*. His performance is good, but after initial enthusiasm seems limited to cramping Jim's style; Stone says, 'The more I studied it, the more I realized [Manzarek] and Morrison had less of a bond as time wore on.' Ultimately, Manzarek is not of great consequence to the intentions of the film, so is sidelined.

There was an impressive host of cameos. Michael Madsen was cast as Morrison's drinking buddy Tom Baker in the same year that he would win wider fame for his performance as Mr Blonde in Quentin Tarantino's *Reservoir Dogs*. Another member of Morrison's drunken posse was British rock star Billy Idol, who had been badly injured in a motorcycle accident and so appeared lying down or on crutches whenever on screen. One of the film's producers, Bill Graham, played the Miami promoter concussed by a microphone. In court, Morrison's attorney was played by William Kustler – in reality a famous lawyer who had defended legendary comedian Lenny Bruce from obscenity charges (with somewhat more success than Morrison's own lawyer enjoyed at this trial). There were appearances from several of those close to Jim Morrison. The engineer overseeing the poetry recording session was John Densmore; Robby Krieger can briefly be glimpsed on Sunset Boulevard (as well as having coached Frank Whaley in playing the guitar); former music producer Paul Rothchild played the bald man in the red glasses, hanging out at the London Fog; and the real Patricia Kennealy oversaw the film's wedding scene.

OLIVER'S ARMY: The other Doors came from previous Stone casts. Kevin Dillon played John Densmore, his first time with Stone since *Platoon*, while Frank Whaley returned from *Born on the Fourth of July* to play Robby Krieger. As with Ray Manzarek, these members of the group are necessary, but they are given little room to develop, seen as a stifling force whose only aim was conventional success.

Michael Wincott (Paul Rothchild) was given a slightly larger role than his couple of lines in *Born on the Fourth of July*. This was his third and last Stone appearance, and his performance is muted but effective, acting as a kind of good father to Jim, appreciative of his talents, genuine in his encouragement but despairing at his self-destructive tendencies. Josh Evans (*Born on the Fourth of July*) played Doors manager Bill Siddons, though this character was largely cosmetic, as was Mark Moses' (*Platoon*, *Born on the Fourth of July*) appearance as Elektra Records boss Jac Holzman.

There are cameos by friends and family, young Sean Stone having quite a prominent role as the young Jim Morrison (reappearing at the birthday party towards the end of the film), while Oliver Stone played the pedantic film professor, poking fun at his own film lecturer, Martin Scorsese. In addition, Richard Rutowski – who had known Morrison – worked on the film's production, and appeared throughout as a mysterious bald figure whom Stone has since categorically identified as Death.

David Brenner had edited *Born on the Fourth of July* and stayed on for *The Doors*, aided again by Joe Hutshing. Robert Richardson continued his regular stint as Director of Photography. Barbara Ling was responsible for the production design – highly evocative of the hippie excess of the period.

CUT SCENES: Nearly 45 minutes of additional scenes were cut from the theatrical release of *The Doors*. Near the beginning Jim visits a small bar – the Turkey Joint – with some buddies. Inside Manzarek, Densmore and Krieger are playing a cover of 'Gloria'. Jim makes a pass at the girlfriend of another college student, grabs one of his beers and jumps on stage to sing along. Ultimately this is a superfluous scene, but quite fun and gives a reason in the film for Krieger and Densmore to be in the finished band (though the real reason was their acquaintance with Ray Manzarek from a meditation class). In fact Manzarek performed in a bar band for whom Morrison occasionally provided vocals.

There is an alternative version of the scene outside the Whiskey à Go Go (just before the trip to the desert), which shows Jim urging the others to go out and take peyote with the Indians. Jim, John and Robbie chat up girls in the queue.

On the flight to New York, Jim and Pam jokily talk about death, Jim saying he'd like to die in a plane crash, or at least die quickly, while Pam talks about slitting her wrists in a warm bath, while an extended press conference sees Jim talking at greater length about the 'death' of his parents, going into grisly details. Another song was originally marked for the New Haven concert, a version of The Doors protest song 'The Unknown Soldier', which starts with Jim being 'shot' by Robby's guitar.

After New Haven, there was a sequence set in a police cell, where Morrison is ridiculed by the cops, before he turns their insults back on them and is beaten for his troubles. He emerges from the station to a messianic reception by adoring fans. This scarcely seems necessary – the audience already knows the police don't like Morrison. There is an extended scene set at his final recording session, with more poetry and an appearance by 'Death' as the janitor, ending with Morrison's drinking buddies crashing into the recording booth.

One absent scene that affects the tone of the film is that of Ray's wedding to his girlfriend Dorothy – the reason for the meal at which Pam threatens Jim with a knife. There is a full hippy wedding, with the bride and groom exchanging vows to the background of a Malibu fog bank. Jim, as best man, arrives late, and Ray is upset. This cuts to a supermarket scene, with Pam urging Jim to collect groceries. An LA free newspaper hammers home the irony with the headline 'Rock's bad boys go soft'. This scene leads on to the footage of Jim and Pam in the park. (Incidentally, for the UK, when Pam wonders about 'the Gravy Train' in that park scene, she is talking about a product for their golden retriever, Sage.)

Jim reacts to the sight of Pam injecting heroin with the Italian Count by sleeping with two teenage girls in a Venice motel. A bang on the door turns out to be Pam, come to find him, and the couple briefly fight.

The decadence of the flight out to Miami was originally greatly enhanced, with a sequence set in a departure lounge. Jim knocks back drinks with Cat, Dog and Baker and they abuse Bill Siddons. When finally on the plane, they harangue the stewardess at length, before being reprimanded by the captain (played by William G Knight, union rep Duncan Willmore from *Wall Street*) who arranges for their arrest at Miami. This was based on an actual flight that Jim Morrison took, resulting in an abortive court case that ran parallel with the Miami indecency trial. Additionally there is a long conversation between Jim and Baker, who insists that Jim's influence will be ephemeral, that no one will remember him.

The Miami trial was originally longer and included footage of protesters against indecency outside the courthouse. There was indeed a 'decency' movement that grew up in the wake of the Miami concert, and led to widespread changes in the booking of bands – causing many in the rock establishment to take a hostile attitude to Morrison and his excess.

One loss to the film was a rather touching farewell scene between Ray and Jim, taking place outside Ray's Venice Beach apartment, after his son's birthday, that refers back to their conversation on Venice Beach in 1965. They talk about Pam – Jim says he likes her because she is flaky but vulnerable and has an image of him as a poet – and Ray gets him to recite one last piece of poetry before he drives off for the airport.

The original ending was a little different, starting with Morrison's grave in Pere Lachaise and then panning back past the other famous poets. It ended with a concert performance of 'Roadhouse Blues' as opposed to the studio version of 'LA Woman'.

MEMORABLE QUOTES:
Pam: 'What's a shaman?'
Jim: 'He's a medicine man, the Indians sent him into a peyote trance and he gets deeper and deeper and has a vision and the whole tribe is healed . . . They even say the first shaman invented sex. They called him "the one who makes you crazy".'

Jim: 'I am the Lizard King! I can do anything!'

Jim: 'Me, they see exactly what they want to see . . . I think of myself as a sensitive intelligent human being, but with the soul of a clown that always forces me to blow it at the most crucial moment.'

GOOD VS EVIL: This is a meanderingly amoral movie, the implication being that Morrison, as a shaman, is beyond any conventional moral judgement – it is difficult to impose traditional concepts of good and evil on a life of Dionysian decadence.

Instead, there is internal struggle, between the idea of Jim as a poet and Jim as a rock god. The struggle between the shy figure seen on stage at the London Fog and the anarchic showman, defying the law and the audience in Miami. The lithe artist who seduces Pam on a Venice rooftop with poetry and the jealous beast who locks her in a closet which he then sets fire to. The drug freak who leaps on to a car on Sunset Strip, declaring that he is the lizard king, and the shambolic drunk, getting pissed in bars and, bearded and big-bellied, sucking on a whisky bottle in a recording studio.

But, either because of legal restraints or Stone's own view of the man, these remain two separate aspects, a split personality, the sense of actual conflict never truly realised. In one scene Morrison will be a sensitive artist, in the next a raging inebriate. Ultimately, one could extrapolate from the film that the dark side took over and led to self-destruction, but this is at odds with the curious sense of peace that is imbued in Morrison's corpse and the reconciliation within the band – there is no real intimation of a final, fatal collapse.

This leaves the film hollow at the core.

REDEMPTION OR DAMNATION: How fares Morrison at the end of the film? Dead, certainly, but there is no suggestion that this premature end could have been any different. It is a fatalistic story – Morrison is predestined to burn brightly but briefly and, despite Pam's efforts at domestication, no alternative existence is ever suggested. This blunts any edge of tragedy. The film's Morrison is a one-dimensional singing, drinking and shagging machine, he never convinces as a prophet, or as a poet. He drifts from scene to scene, rarely making a conscious choice and sliding towards inevitable death in a Paris bathtub.

This partly explains why the film falls so flat; there is nothing to the story, no great struggle or dilemma, just a man destined to record memorable music, but also to die young – there is no suggestion of greater depth, it is simply Jim's fate.

HISTORY 101: The film cobbles together a biography of Morrison from broad truths presented in a selective way. Much is basically true, in the same way that *Salvador* is basically true – history restructured for cinema.

Unlike *Salvador* there is little reference to the world outside Jim's immediate circle. He is hermetically separated from reality – when this brutally intrudes in the form of an arbitrary montage of 1960s death and misery it seems out of place. Stone is so involved with the subject that he loses any sense of perspective, of anything important outside the band. The movie is arrogant in its dismissal of history: excepting a reference to William Blake (from whose writings the band took their name); Morrison is presented as a spontaneous rock star without predecessor while the impact of his music after death is never commented on, save the questionable comparison made between Morrison and other occupants of Pere Lachaise. The story may well be based on a series of facts but apart from the period settings there is nothing historical about it.

CONSPIRACY THEORY: Given the speculation that still surrounds Morrison's untimely death, it is at first surprising that Stone introduced no theories on his demise. This surprise quickly evaporates when the number of external parties with some form of creative control becomes apparent. Sue Heal suggested in *Today* that the director 'was bound up in so much legal red tape that the rock icon's story cannot properly be told'. For instance, Pam Courson's parents had forbidden any suggestion that their daughter was involved in Jim's death, ruling out one popular theory that Jim had snorted Pam's heroin stash. Another theory, one applied to pretty much any high-profile celebrity death, was that Jim did not die, and that the coffin was weighed down artificially. As well as being completely unprovable, this would not have fitted the whole fatalistic obsession with death that Morrison is credited with. As Stone has said, 'I do think that if you live fast and have a good-looking corpse, die after the first act, it does make things more dramatic.'

There is one sequence where some manipulation undoubtedly took place, stretching the truth for dramatic ends. In the studio, Morrison sees an advert for a car company using 'Light My Fire' as a backing track. That this music was employed for such purposes against Jim's will is taken as a sign of the divisions in the band, while the other Doors retort that he was not there to veto their proposal. Notoriously The Doors have a policy of unanimity in these matters and, while the advertisement was filmed, it was never screened, at Morrison's request. Densmore says, 'It never happened. We *were* shown the ad out of town, and dollar signs flashed across our eye-sockets . . . but Jim resisted.'

BEING OLIVER STONE: The project came to Oliver Stone second hand, but it was very much of personal interest to him. He had been introduced to the music of the Doors while in Vietnam, and it frequently crops up as a major influence in his life. 'It was in a hooch. I remember some guy bringing me in, some black guy putting on the tape . . . It was breakthrough music, a great moment.' In another context he said, 'The times in the field deadened me, but hanging out with them in the bunkers, doing dope and listening to that kind of music, restored me.'

Ray Manzarek rather sniffily said of Stone that he 'was over there in Vietnam and the Hippies were back here smoking dope and practicing free love, and he was jealous . . . Oliver Stone is using The Doors to get revenge.' This is a bitter sentiment, springing from the midst of acrimonious debate, and seems completely misguided. Every growing person has their formative heroes, for Stone it was Morrison, a man of whom he said, 'When Morrison died in 1971, it was like the day Kennedy died.' Strong words from the eventual director of *JFK*.

The fascination with The Doors stayed with Stone through his return to America. His first screenplay, *Break*, a surreal hallucination, part *Platoon* (it features prototype versions of Barnes and Elias, called here Lee and Isaac) and part twisted autobiography in the vein of *A Child's Night Dream*, had music from The Doors at its core, featuring lyrics and imagery from many of their songs (for instance, a literal manifestation of 'The End's blue bus, and a physically realised Lizard King). In 1990, while *The Doors* was in production, Stone received a visit from the ex-wife of Bill Siddons and she handed him a manuscript that had been found in Jim Morrison's Paris apartment – the final draft of the script of *Break* that Stone had sent to Morrison.

One of Stone's prominent attributes is to become completely immersed in the experiences of his subject and at least one critic noted a sense of over-identification between the director and his protagonist, 'clearly . . . Stone wanted to *be* Jim Morrison . . . And it is in this tone of subjective narcissism that the film is conducted.' At the very least, this was a deeply personal work for the director.

REAL PEOPLE: Unlike Ron Kovic, Stone could never have the backing of his protagonist's real-life counterpart. Instead, he chose a very personal take on Morrison, avoiding the self-deprecating humour that some mention (with the exception of a brief aside, where the character speaks of himself as a 'clown') and focussing on what Morrison meant to Stone – a spiritual awakening, and imbued with elements of dichotomy – the shy poet combined with the outgoing showman. Just as Nixon would become a mirror for the director, so Jim Morrison was partly a composite of researched material, and partly a very personal interpretation. As the director said, 'There are so many different perspectives. We have presented a reflection of him. I don't think you can ever quite know the man. There's an enigma, a mystery, and that's good.'

There were similar problems with Pam Courson. Meg Ryan has pointed out the contradictions that made the creation of a cinematic Pam so difficult: 'Some said she was a monster . . . and others said, no, she was the sweetest little girl you could come across.' She went on, 'I had to mediate all these contradictory things that I had been told.' The film viewed Pam as a woman who wanted to anchor Jim with both connotations of providing a secure mooring and of restricting his anarchic tendencies.

John Densmore was among many who had known Morrison and who criticised the version that appeared on screen when he said, 'It fails to show Morrison's humour or compassion. It takes a lot of liberties.' Having said that, Densmore crucially added, 'I like it.' In the same article, for *Independent on Sunday*, Jerry Hopkins said, 'He's got it all down pat and the visual scope is amazing,' but, 'it doesn't explain any of the relationships adequately.'

Several people had to be persuaded to approve use of their likenesses. Bill Siddons was hesitant but eventually agreed, though he had similar reservations to John Densmore, fearing that Stone had focussed 'on the more sensational side of Jim's personality and not on the man I knew – a bright, warm human being'. Patricia Kennealy provided inspiration for the Kathleen Quinlan character of the same name, gave her input, and even appeared in the movie (see **CASTING**). However, she was upset at the presentation of the abortion scene, saying that '[Oliver Stone] had the making of a scene that was pure Greek tragedy, and for reasons of his own he turned it into cheap farce.' Stone himself has admitted that, were he to make the film today, the Kennealy character would be given a different name, to indicate that it was not a screen representation of just one person.

Most severe was the fallout with Ray Manzarek, who pretty much disagreed with the script from the start (both Robby Krieger and John Densmore were quite closely involved with the production). He frequently spoke out against the script and he and Stone developed an enmity. It's possible to see a root of this in Stone's primary interest in Jim Morrison. Manzarek (and Densmore and Krieger) are not just relegated to the background, but are pretty much lumped in with police and other authority figures as obstructing Jim and his art.

INSPIRATION AND INFLUENCE: As well as the notes of Jerry Hopkins for his book and a whole slew of original interviews, Stone drew inspiration from two books by Doors intimates: John Densmore's *Riders on the Storm* and Danny Sugerman's *Illustrated History of the Doors* (little more than a collection of contemporary press reports and glossy reprints of photographs).

The film was not based on one definitive account (see **Born on the Fourth of July**), nor on a range of sources whose individual contributions could be identified (see **JFK**); instead, Stone filtered a broadly factual account of Jim's career (and more peripherally the band's), peppered with anecdotes (the scene where Jim traps Pam in a burning cupboard is disputed by some), through his individual vision.

It would be wrong to say that he owes a debt to any previous rock biopic: by their very nature, films in this genre share certain similarities. Stone's concentration on a rock individual of great sexual magnetism, a victim of an enigmatic and ignominious death, perhaps brings his work closest to John Carpenter's *Elvis* (1979) a two-part miniseries starring Kurt Russell.

The individual influence of *The Doors* has been more pervasive than other rock biopics, thanks mainly to the production design. Subsequent films exploring this particular milieu in this particular period cannot help but refer to the film's vision. Two especially prominent examples are *Fear and Loathing in Las Vegas* (Terry Gilliam, 1998) and *Almost Famous* (Cameron Crowe, 2000). The latter, a partly biographical work based on the director's teenage years, bears a particular resemblance to Stone's accounts of chaotic concerts, debauched hotel stays and hazardous plane journeys but views them with a bland nostalgia – removing the negative connotations with which Stone packs his work.

However, the most prominent example of *The Doors'* direct influence is a parody: *Waynes World 2* (Stephen Surjik, 1993). The subject is the organisation of a Woodstock-style event, inspired by a dream experienced by rock dork Wayne Campbell. In a combination of *The Doors* and *Field of Dreams* (Phil Alden Robinson, 1989) he encounters Jim Morrison in a desert environment, not dissimilar to Stone's setting for the peyote trip, and is told, in relation to bands, 'If you book them, they will come.' More amusingly, Wayne is constantly stalked by a 'weird naked Indian,' a reference to this film's omnipresent Richard Rutowski.

REEL TIME: There are some nice examples of camerawork at other points, the Steadicam pursuit through the corridors of the New York hotel or the Super-8 footage that lends period authenticity to the band's early tour, for instance, but the true moments of glory in this film are the concert scenes.

The concert scenes are some of the most impressive ever filmed. Around eight cameras were used to capture every angle, including a Steadicam taken right down into the crowd. A huge piece of kit called a Technocrane was brought over to the US from the UK. *The Doors* was the first American film to make use of this device, able to telescope out from around two to six metres and move nearly five metres in any direction allowing for swooping shots across the stage. The venues were packed with extras (up to 32,000 at points, as well as fake dummy hippies – actually more expensive in practice than live actors) and synchronised action was ensured through a low-frequency 'thumper' track that ran throughout the filming, providing a steady rhythm. The scenes played out like real concerts and the stage was lit so as to allow Val Kilmer the maximum freedom of movement.

Also noteworthy was the first use of digital optical effects in Stone's movies. Industrial Light and Magic, George Lucas's pioneering special effects company provided some impressive moments. The storm clouds with which the film opens were digitally added, as were some of the hallucinatory drug visuals.

MUSIC: The film did not so much have its own score as an ongoing soundtrack of Doors music – 24 songs, including Morrison's own spoken-word work, 'The Movie'. The film was built around the varied range of music produced by The Doors. This construction works almost perfectly. 'Riders on the Storm' opens the ominous desert road scene, developing into 'Love Street' for the sequence in which Morrison pursues Pam. 'Break on Through' and 'Light My Fire' mark the first scenes of the band in session and 'The End' is used for their breakthrough, then switching to the druggy dizziness of 'Alabama Song' and 'People are Strange'. Later 'Touch Me' is used to signal a decline – while a great pop song it is rather regressive – and the abortive performance of 'Five to One' has real rage and frustration to it. The film ends on an upbeat note with the cheery blues stomp of 'LA Woman'.

These songs are integral to the movie, so the fact that Val Kilmer actually sang some of them, allows for an emotional input that wouldn't be available with simple miming. These were: 'Break on Through', 'Light My Fire', 'Crystal Ship', 'The End', 'When the Music's Over', 'Not to Touch the Earth', 'Touch Me', 'Soft Parade', 'The Severed Garden' and 'Five to One'. He does a terrific job – his vocals are literally indistinguishable from Morrison's.

As in *Born on the Fourth of July*, a batch of other music was brought in to mark the tone of certain scenes. In comparison with the smooth integration of Doors music these tunes seem rather heavy-handed in their message: 'California Sun' to indicate Morrison is in sunny Venice Beach, the east coast portentousness of Velvet Underground ('Heroin' and 'Venus in Furs') for Warhol's party and, cringingly, 'Primo Vere' from *Carmin Baruma*, for the rather silly blood ritual scenes between Kennealy and Morrison.

BOX OFFICE: *The Doors* pulled an insufficient $35 million gross from the US box office alone to cover the inflated budget of $44 million. The movie ended up in the black, picking up respectable sums from video sales and international receipts, but was another sign of Stone's commercial inconsistency – a tendency to yo-yo between success and disappointing mediocrity.

CRITICS: The overriding majority of reviews were unimpressed with *The Doors*. Hal Hinson wrote in the *Washington Post*, 'The film is an absurdity – muddled, self-serious, alienating, a Stone drag.' Roger Ebert described it as 'like being stuck in a bar with an obnoxious drunk when you're not drinking'. The *Telegraph* critic opined, 'Visually and structurally the film has the ramshackle air of an extended rock video . . . unpardonable surely in a seasoned filmmaker of Stone's caliber.' Even those with encouraging words qualified their statements: 'Stone . . . loads the film with too much sub-Freudian baggage . . . but the magic, the excess, the frenzy and the *excitement* come across well' (*Time Out*).

As with *Wall Street* and *Born on the Fourth of July*, there was more praise for the main actor. The *Sun*'s critic reckoned that Val Kilmer 'captured the snarling provocative nature of the singer and the sheer energy of his live performances, revealing a surprisingly good voice'. Philip French was of a similar mind: 'Val Kilmer has studied the records, photographs and documentary footage and sustains an uncannily accurate impersonation.' *Rolling Stone* pointed out the film's overemphasis on Morrison: 'Stone's movie isn't really about The Doors. It's a one man show.' Hugo Davenport echoed this: 'The spotlight is so firmly on Morrison . . . that Manzarek . . . guitarist Robby Krieger and drummer John Densmore fade to one dimensional ciphers.' Some even saw this in the characterisation of Morrison. Derek Malcolm reckoned that 'Try as Val Kilmer does . . . you can't see what makes the man tick, though you can appreciate what made him a star.'

Stone came in for some personal stick. Cathy Dillon listed two perennial criticisms in her *Scotsman* review: '[Stone's] sense of humour is not exactly his strongest asset, nor is his understanding of women.' On the latter point she added, 'you can sense the director's tacit sympathy for Morrison's Neanderthal attitude to women.'

A rather inconclusive set of reviews, but Sheila Johnston saw the film itself as inconclusive: 'There's the film about the rock idol . . . the film about the band . . . the film about Morrison and his girlfriend: about cock-rock at its most priapic.' She concluded that it was also a film about a man who claimed that he spoke 'for the spirit of his age'. But these never came to pass, and the viewer is left 'seeing glimpses of the films that might have been but are never fully developed'.

CONTROVERSY: The whole complex story of *The Doors* development was played out in the film trade press, developing over the course of ten years. More specific to Stone's work was pre-emptive criticism of his representation of Morrison that appeared in music and film magazines, as well as mainstream newspapers. This only heightened on release of the film.

AWARDS: A bare trophy cupboard in comparison with previous works. Even nominations were thin on the ground: one for a Golden St George at the Moscow Film Festival and one for Kilmer's performance at the MTV music awards.

TRIVIA: Val Kilmer's choreographer on set was pop songstress Paula Abdul.

THE BIG PICTURE: There is a nice symmetry between this and *Born on the Fourth of July*. Both individual tales, both set in the sixties, in one the protagonist connects with the political counterculture, in the other he is at its musical core. There are differences: Kovic escapes decadent inertia; Morrison embraces it. Later, *Nixon* would show contempt towards this counterculture, and would end in catastrophic collapse rather than either rise to glory or slow corruption.

Visually, *Born on the Fourth of July* has a carefully constructed visual order. The same was probably true of *The Doors* at inception and during production, but on screen there is a sense of anarchy, of the camera as a man stumbling forward, always looking though he might fall over but never quite doing so. This style would recur in *Natural Born Killers* and to a lesser extent in *JFK*, which cloaks its forceful polemic in the guise of visual chaos. *Any Given Sunday* would brilliantly apply the in-your-face immediacy of the concert scenes to American sporting events.

FINAL ANALYSIS: This film amounts to the hagiography of a man who was far from a saint. A highly subjective celebration of a personal hero of Oliver Stone that, as a result of this subjectivity, and the nature of the subject himself, appears to the casual viewer as rather adolescent.

This is meant in the sense of the film's central thesis, which celebrates the most dubious aspects of 1960s culture, presenting flakiness and superficiality as mystical and world changing. It is tricky, if not a devoted fan, to see the collection of decent songs and questionable poetry assembled by Jim Morrison and his band as the deeply significant watershed that Stone does.

In addition, it is pertinent to ask what, of substance, this movie says about the man. The story is familiar from anyone with a passing acquaintance with the sixties or with rock and roll/Hollywood hubris. Get famous, live fast and loose, die young – add some half-baked quotations from Blake and a smattering of poetic angst and you have the fundamentals of Morrison in the film. There really is nothing more to it, certainly not enough to justify the reverential prowl through Pere Lachaise cemetery, past poets and artists of legendary status – in such company Morrison is just a pretty pop star with ideas above his station.

Ron Kovic, Richard Nixon and even Oliver Stone had lives rich enough to easily transfer to cinema. In the context of the film's opening poem, it is difficult to believe there was enough here 'to base a movie on'.

JFK (1991)

Warner Bros presents
In association with Le Studio Canal+, Regency Enterprises and Alcor Films
An Ixtlan Corporation and an A Kitman Ho Production
An Oliver Stone Film
Casting: Risa Bramon Garcia, Billy Hopkins and Heidi Levitt
Costume Designer: Marlene Stewart
Music by John Williams
Co-Producer: Clayton Townsend
Edited by Joe Hutshing and Pietro Scalia
Production Designer: Victor Kempster
Director of Photography: Robert Richardson
Executive Producer: Arnon Milchan
Based on the books *On the Trail of the Assassins* by Jim Garrison and *Crossfire: the Plot that Killed Kennedy* by Jim Marrs
Screenplay by Oliver Stone and Zachary Sklar
Produced by A Kitman Ho and Oliver Stone
Directed by Oliver Stone

CAST: Kevin Costner (*Jim Garrison*), Kevin Bacon (*Willie O'Keefe*), Tommy Lee Jones (*Clay Shaw/Clay Bertrand*), Laurie Metcalf (*Susie Cox*), Gary Oldman (*Lee Harvey Oswald*), Beata Pozniak (*Marina Oswald*), Michael Rooker (*Bill Broussard*), Jay O Sanders (*Lou Ivon*), Sissy Spacek (*Elizabeth Garrison*), Brian Doyle-Murphy (*Jack Ruby*), Gary Grubbs (*Al Oser*), Wayne Knight (*Numa Bertel*), Jo Anderson (*Julia Anne Mercer*), Vincent D'Onofrio (*Bill Newman*), Pruitt Taylor Vince (*Lee Bowers*), Joe Pesci (*David Ferrie*), John Candy (*Dean Andrews*), Jack Lemmon (*Jack Martin*), Walther Matthau (*Senator Russell Long*), Ed Asner (*Guy Bannister*), Donald Sutherland (*X*), Sally Kirkland (*Rose Cheramie*), Tony Plana (*Carlos Bringuier*)

SUMMARY: Caption: 'To sin by silence when we should protest makes cowards out of men.' Ella Wheeler Wilcox.

The film opens with a Martin Sheen voice-over about major historical events such as Eisenhower's warning on the military-industrial complex, Kennedy's election, the Bay of Pigs and disarmament talks with Russia. Archive footage appears of 22 November, the day of Kennedy's visit to Dallas. As the open limo cruises towards the freeway the shot cuts to black, a shot rings out and a flock of pigeons take off from a rooftop.

New Orleans District Attorney (DA) Jim Garrison is told of the shooting by assistant DA Lou Ivon; at a nearby bar they watch the report of Kennedy's death. At a different bar private investigator Guy Bannister drinks heavily with buddy Jack Martin. He celebrates the death of the man who abandoned Cuba and together they walk back to Bannister's office. Martin jokes about writing a book on activity in the office and a drunk Bannister pistol-whips him.

Garrison orders one of his employees to follow up Oswald's time in New Orleans. At the office the one name connected with Oswald is that of David Ferrie, a former airline pilot. An anonymous caller places Ferrie in Dallas around the time of the shooting, claiming that he was to fly Oswald's getaway plane. Garrison questions Ferrie, shortly after Oswald is himself shot by nightclub owner Jack Ruby. Ferrie is shifty and evasive, constantly changing his story. Garrison sends him to the FBI for further questioning but they release him without charge. The New Orleans investigation is apparently wrapped up as the appointment of the Warren Commission is announced.

Three years later. Garrison is flying over Washington with Senator Russell Long of Lousiana. They discuss President Johnson's escalation of the war in Vietnam and Long talks of his scepticism for the Warren Commission's lone gunman theory, citing the mediocrity of Oswald's marksmanship and suggesting that he was just a decoy. Garrison investigates all 26 volumes of the Warren Report and is shocked by what he finds – questions unanswered, leads not followed up, absurdities unchallenged in a shoddily arranged, haphazard document. He takes his two deputies Ivon and Bill Broussard, a pugnacious street lawyer, to New Orleans, retracing Oswald's steps from the summer of 1963. The HQ of Oswald's pro-Castro group was in the same building as PI Guy Bannister. Nearby are the New Orleans offices for several intelligence agencies. Garrison decides to reopen the case.

They investigate the anonymous caller who linked Ferrie and Oswald – Jack Martin, furious after his beating. Martin speaks of Bannister as a political operative on the far right – infiltrating student meetings and especially involved in the organisation of anti-Castro Cubans. He had a hand in training camps in the Louisiana bayou, until Kennedy's administration ordered them shut down. Martin had handled Bannister's regular PI work, and had seen the procession of strange individuals and paramilitaries to pass through the office, including Ferrie, Oswald and a mysterious white-haired figure he identifies as Clay Bertrand.

Over lunch, Garrison questions law-school buddy Dean Andrews, a greasy hack lawyer. In the Warren Commission report Andrews said he was contracted by Bertrand to be Oswald's lawyer. Now he denies ever meeting him. Garrison puts pressure on Andrews to identify Bertrand, but Dean refuses. He, like Martin, is afraid for his life.

Broussard has dug up another informant who claims to know Bertrand. Willie O'Keefe, a male prostitute, currently serving time. Garrison visits him in jail and O'Keefe tells of attending parties with Bertrand, Ferrie, Oswald and a group of Cuban exiles, where they raged against Kennedy and spoke of assassination through 'triangulation of crossfire'.

The investigation team meet at a restaurant where it emerges that several key witnesses are dead. Few details on Oswald's life have been released by the CIA/FBI but what is available is bizarre. Oswald joined the Marines and worked as a radar operator at a Japanese airbase, from which U2 spy planes were flown. He obtained a discharge and travelled to Russia, where he took Russian citizenship and promised to hand over all he knew (shortly afterwards a top secret spy plane was shot down, sabotaging a peace conference). Oswald married and returned to the States, with the help of the State Department – suggesting that he might have been an American agent with the intention of stopping the conference. On his return Oswald is set up with his job in the book depository.

In Dallas, Garrison and Ivon talk to witnesses, many of whom point out a white picket fence behind a grassy knoll as the source of the shots. Others speak of strange behaviour by police and official investigators. A showgirl remembers seeing Ruby, Ferrie and Oswald together, but refuses to testify – she doesn't want to become 'a statistic'.

In the book depository, Garrison and Ivon re-create the shooting. There are many unanswered questions. It takes too long for the number of shots to be fired and it made no sense for Oswald to fire at the time he is alleged to. Ivon reckons on three teams of professional shooters being likelier – a triangulation of crossfire, one team in the depository, another in an adjacent building, the final team behind the grassy knoll.

At a conference in Garrison's house new evidence is presented. There are sightings that suggest to Garrison a group of decoy Oswalds who consolidate a reputation for hatred of Kennedy, support for Castro and skill with guns. He even suggests that Oswald never pulled a trigger (nitrate tests suggest he had not fired a gun and no prints were found on the rifle until days after the shooting), that he was there solely as a fall guy, a patsy. Broussard has been talking to his underworld contacts and identifies Clay Bertrand as an alias for respected local businessman Clay Shaw.

Shaw is brought in for interrogation and denies links with Ferrie, O'Keefe or Oswald but Garrison is convinced of his guilt.

Next day, the news of the investigation is all over the papers. Ivon fields a call from a furious David Ferrie, his name implicated in the reports. At a meeting, Ferrie confirms a lot of what they have heard. Oswald and he were friends, Ferrie and Shaw are both CIA, the agency was involved with the exiled Cubans and Operation Mongoose. However, no one really knows who killed the president – 'The fuckin' shooters don't even know.'

A few days later Ferrie is dead – a suspicious suicide.

Garrison travels to Washington to meet with anonymous informer X, a former colonel involved in destabilisation of foreign regimes. He weaves a tale of embittered CIA officers, worried Pentagon generals, an ambitious vice president, and an informal chain of agreement (thus allowing 'plausible deniability'). He insists that the key questions are not how Kennedy was killed or who killed him but why, and suggests a reason: Kennedy's attempts to massively cut overblown defence and intelligence spending, partially through a pledge to withdraw from Vietnam and partially through commitment to peace with Russia. X refuses to testify and doubts Garrison's chances but wishes him luck and insists that the investigation go ahead.

Clay Shaw is arrested, photographed and, in shock, gives his alias as Clay Bertrand. As trial preparations progress, there is conflict. Bill Broussard cannot believe the involvement of every branch of government, and walks out. Garrison wants him back but Ivon refuses to work with Broussard so Garrison fires Ivon. However, Jim Garrison is abortively interviewed on TV and Broussard makes an attempt to frame him in a homosexual tryst. After a tearful reunion with his family, Jim witnesses Robert Kennedy's murder on television. He also learns that Broussard has turned all their trial information over to the feds.

Garrison's case has two stages. First, he must prove that a conspiracy existed in the assassination of John Kennedy and, second, that Clay

Shaw was involved in this conspiracy. His witnesses to identify Shaw and Bertrand as the same person are ridiculed. Shaw's own identification of the alias Bertrand is ruled inadmissible – no attorney was present. Shaw denies it all.

Garrison moves on to proving a conspiracy. The autopsy is a chaotic joke, and Kennedy's brain is missing from the national archives. He ridicules the magic bullet theory – that one bullet caused seven wounds in two people – and calls witnesses to identify several points of origin for the gunfire. He moves on to speculate on what might have happened on 22 November. An epileptic fit distracts police and the three teams of shooters move in. Oswald is eating lunch when Kennedy is killed. As the assassins calmly break down their guns and leave, the depository team dump the rifle Oswald is supposed to have used and the shell casings. Oswald himself leaves the building. Garrison casts doubt on Oswald as the lone killer of Tippet, a policeman whose murder led to Oswald's arrest and the incredible intuition that drew officers to the cinema in which Oswald was hiding out.

The assassination was part of a coup d'état, he claims, with President Lyndon Johnson an accessory after the fact. In an emotional closing speech, he calls for the release of files, suppressed until 2038, and pleads that the jury do not forget Kennedy, a 'dying king'. The verdict – not guilty – is delivered, but a juryman is interviewed, expressing agreement that a conspiracy existed, merely doubting that Shaw was involved. Garrison vows to fight on for the truth.

ADVANCE PUBLICITY: The poster campaign played on the same theme as *Born on the Fourth of July* – a prominent American flag and the figure of Kevin Costner suggests patriotism, but questioning rather than blind acceptance. The trailer described *JFK* as 'the story that won't go away'. A montage of some of the racier and more suggestive dialogue is played against an urgent extract from the John Williams score and a backdrop of Kennedy's signature appearing on a piece of paper – paper then blown in half by a bullet.

JFK was the first of two films (with *Nixon*) to be backed with the release of a comprehensively annotated screenplay, an attempt to answer those who criticised the film as a work of fiction or fantasy. The script is dense with footnotes and it is difficult to fault the intention. In addition, the book of the screenplay is bulked out substantially by the reprinting of 97 articles written about the film – both negative views of journalists such as George Lardner and justification from Stone himself and other supporters.

One of the less admirable marketing moves came among the standard practice of choosing favourable quotes for the promotional posters. David Ansen, film critic for *Newsweek* (incidentally, a publication in the vanguard of intense criticism of Stone) is quoted on this poster as saying, 'Don't trust anyone who claims that this movie is hogwash.' In the printed review Ansen had importantly added, 'And don't trust Stone either.'

PRODUCTION HISTORY: In 1988 Stone attended the Latin American Film Festival in Cuba. While there he encountered Ellen Ray, publisher of the radical journal *Covert Action Information Bulletin*. Among the recent books to come from her Sheridan Square Press was *On the Trail of the Assassins*, an account of Jim Garrison's 1969 trial of Clay Shaw for conspiracy in the murder of President Kennedy – the only charge to be prosecuted in relation to the assassination. One day the two found themselves stuck in the faulty lift of a Havana hotel, and she started talking to him about the assassination. Stone recalls, 'Eventually I read the book and thought it was a great detective story. Purely on that level I thought it would make an exciting movie.' Stone bought up the movie options for $250,000.

As he read more books on the subject, particularly the burgeoning quantity of independent research, Stone became interested in filming a wider alternative to the Warren Report. While *Born on the Fourth of July* was still in post-production, and before a deal had been finalised for *The Doors*, Stone began laying the groundwork for *JFK*. He met with Jim Garrison and L Fletcher Prouty (the inspiration for X), optioned Jim Marrs's compendium of alternate theories and assassination information, *Crossfire: the Plot that Killed Kennedy*, and hired a recent Yale graduate, Jane Rusconi, to head up his research team. Before starting on the screenplay, he and his researchers ploughed through reams of documents and spoke with many assassination witnesses.

In 1989, with a rough outline prepared, Stone set out to obtain studio support. He had been in discussions with Warner Brothers about directing a film on the life of Howard Hughes but progress had stalled. Instead, Stone presented *JFK*, in this early stage, a more balanced presentation of various different theories on the interpretation akin to the Japanese film *Rashomon* (Akira Kurosawa, 1951). One of the Warner executives who met with Stone to discuss the project was Terry Semel, who had played a major part on other similarly controversial political films such as *All the President's Men* and *The Parallax View*. Warner Brothers agreed to fund the project to the tune of $20 million.

Stone set to work on the script, hiring Zachary Sklar, Garrison's editor for *On the Trail of the Assassins*, as co-writer. He provided access to a wide range of material that had not ended up in the finished book. To this was added the sum of the research carried out by Jane Rusconi's team on other aspects of the assassination, and the overarching military-political vision supplied by Fletcher Prouty. Also crucial was the work of John Newman, who asked not to be credited so as not to affect reviews of his forthcoming book, *JFK and Vietnam*.

On the Trail of the Assassins became just one of several plotlines, and the film took on a more complex structure described by Stone as 'four DNA threads ... The Garrison story ... about a man following a local lead to its natural conclusion'. The 'fascination of the Oswald legend' made up the second storyline while 'the third idea was to go to Dealey Plaza and recreate the murder, and then see it again and again throughout the movie.' Fletcher Prouty 'became the fourth story. It became the means by which we were able to move between New Orleans, local, into the wider national story of Dealey Plaza.' This broader sweep necessitated some changes: 'For example, I don't believe that at the trial Jim Garrison ever went through an exhibition of Dealey Plaza like we did.'

With this new, epic structure and a casting policy that filled the films' 200 + speaking parts with a huge range of well-known Hollywood faces, Stone needed to double the budget proposed by Warner Bros. To this end he courted Israeli producer Arnon Milchan. Milchan had a shady past in the arms trade (specifically the enhancement of Israel's nuclear weapons programme), but had also bankrolled a number of respected movies including *King of Comedy* (Martin Scorsese, 1983), *Once Upon a Time in America* (Sergio Leone, 1984) and *Brazil* (Terry Gilliam, 1985). Now he brought the weight of his newly established film company Regency Enterprises, in partnership with French pay-per-view channel Canal+, giving Stone the financial backing he needed.

Even with confirmation of the budget, there were plenty of challenges ahead, with 156 pages of script to shoot in a 79-day schedule. It was here that Stone reaped the benefits of an established presence in Dallas (see **Born on the Fourth of July**), though his intentions for Dealey Plaza were to push this relationship to the limit. Displaying his customary attention to detail, Stone spent $4 million on restoring the Plaza to how it looked in November 1963, including the construction of appropriate advertising hoardings, the pruning of trees, the repainting of window frames on the book depository building, and $50,000 to the Dallas Historical Society for permission to use the sixth floor window that Oswald is alleged to have perched at (and only the window – a museum had been set up on that floor, so the sniper's nest itself had to be reconstructed elsewhere in the building). The film followed the path that Oswald is supposed to have taken after shooting Officer Tippett, and Stone contributed another chunk of money to the restoration of the cinema he hid out in; $40,000 was paid out to gain access to the Zapruder footage.

With the exception of an ongoing media barrage (see **CONTROVERSY**), filming proceeded according to the plan, with the last scene (Garrison and X meeting near the Washington monument) in the can by the end of July 1991. This left 5 months for editing before the Christmas release date. This was a mammoth undertaking with thousands of optical effects to be inserted, as well as the 220-odd speaking parts to be mixed and around 95 scenes using 15 different film stocks. That the film was completed at all is amazing, and even more amazing that it came in on time and within budget. *JFK* was released in the USA in December 1991.

CASTING: The casting model for *JFK* was the star-packed war film *The Longest Day* (Andrew Marton, Ken Annakin, Bernhard Wicki, 1962). In Stone's own words, 'Since *JFK* is a very cerebral movie, I thought it would help to offset the facts and the dryness of it to have familiar signposts along the way who you felt comfortable with.'

This cast was built around the lynchpin of Jim Garrison. In real life a colourful figure, Stone deliberately chose to tone him down, presenting Garrison as a modern day Jimmy Stewart. This seemed to be the only thing about the character he could decide on – around twenty actors were under consideration for the role of Garrison, from the intriguing (Alec Baldwin, Kyle MacLachlan) to the somewhat more esoteric (Marlon Brando, John Malkovich). The two favourites were Harrison Ford, who turned the part down, and a sceptical Kevin Costner. After coming under pressure from his agent, Mike Ovitz, his wife Cindy and Stone himself, Costner eventually agreed to take the part. His rather bland acting style is no bad thing as the character of Garrison is effectively a cipher, solely there to represent the search for truth, to inspire trust and suggest a certain worthiness. Costner's performance is perfectly adequate but it is debatable whether he is even the star of the film, or whether the real star is the film's grand theory and its supporting evidence. The rest of the cast have comparable roles, as vessels of theory and evidence.

The best performances are from those who have been given something to get their teeth into. Gary Oldman's eerie Oswald, Kevin Bacon's sly O'Keefe or Joe Pesci's manic Ferrie. Ed Asner and Jack Lemmon are a great double act as Guy Bannister and Jack Martin, the latter delivering a whiny, wheedling performance, which he would perfect as Shelley Levine in *Glengarry Glen Ross*. John Candy (Dean Andrews) is effective in pretty much the only straight dramatic performance of his career while Tommy Lee Jones is generally good as Clay Shaw (he looks a lot like him) but delivers a mannered performance that occasionally comes across more like a pastiche of a Bond villain. Donald Sutherland is little more than an exposition delivery system, though is note perfect with his calm, authoritative voice and stately bearing. In the office, Costner has ample support from Michael Rooker, Laurie Metcalf and Jay Sanders. Once again, however, these characters are little more than mouthpieces to relay evidence, recite facts or suggest alternative analysis.

This is probably the reason why Sissy Spacek's Elizabeth Garrison is so sidelined. Neither a manifestation of misogyny on Stone's part, nor a poor casting choice; rather, there is little for her to do in the context of the film. There is a half-hearted attempt to have her represent the average American, bemused as to why anyone would want to re-investigate the assassination, but this does not really work – one gets the impression that it was difficult for Stone to write a part so removed from his own feelings on the subject.

There were noteworthy cameos. Perry Russo, the main basis for the character of Willie O'Keefe, played the man at the bar who cheers Kennedy's death while Jim Garrison himself played the role of Earl Warren. Production designer Victor Kempster briefly appears as the man involved in the attempt to frame Garrison at the airport.

OLIVER'S ARMY: Frank Whaley (Timmy in *Born on the Fourth of July* and Robbie Krieger in *The Doors*) briefly appears as one of Oswald's doubles, Tony Plana (*Salvador*'s Major Max) played anti-Castro agitator Carlos Bringuier, Dale Dye took the role of evil General Y (in addition to providing technical advice on firearms and ballistics) and Richard Rutowski cameos as the white picket fence gunman. Stone's personal doctor, Chris Renna, also appears as a doctor during Kennedy's autopsy at Bethesda while Sean Stone played Jim Garrison's son.

David Brenner had left Stone's employ, and his assistants Joe Hutshing and Pietro Scalia shared the editing credit – both had been working on

Stone's films since *Wall Street*. Barbara Ling would be replaced by Victor Kempster on production design, the sober offices, middle-class houses and cluttered apartments a far cry from the hedonism and excess that she created for *The Doors*. Robert Richardson remained as Stone's right hand for this huge project, continuing the trend for experimentation and mixed film stocks.

CUT SCENES: The initial UK home release cut of *JFK* was 181 minutes. A few years later a director's cut was released, with a running time of 205 minutes. These extra minutes are split between material that adds to the bulk of evidence in the film, but does not in itself constitute any new argument, and several scenes pertaining to Garrison's personal struggle.

The former category is the larger. The DVD cut of the film introduces the character of George De Mohrenschildt into Suzie's report on Oswald's early life. De Mohrenschildt was a White Russian (anti-Communist) oilman who befriended Oswald after his return from Russia; he had links to the CIA and drew connections between Oswald and the rifle for the Warren Commission. Garrison suggests that De Mohrenschildt was Oswald's 'handler' – assuming that Oswald was an intelligence agent.

Jack Martin's scenes are extended to suggest Guy Bannister's complicity in Oswald's Fair Play for Cuba Committee. The scene in the book depository is extended to include discussion of changes to the motorcade route. A later scene in Garrison's house expands on the 'fake Oswalds', adding footage of Frank Whaley's 'Oswald' recklessly test-driving a car and another Oswald sighting is built in, this time linking him with David Ferrie and Clay Shaw, alleging that the trio drove out to Clinton, Alabama, to take place in a voter registration drive. Most of this evidence is superfluous, when not actively confusing, and its absence does not harm the film.

Other restored scenes for the Director's Cut bulked out the personal involvement of Garrison, an area that had been consciously trimmed down. When the story of Garrison's reopened investigation breaks, there is a heavily dramatised section where the DA gives his staff the opportunity to quit the case, a total fabrication but a way of affirming the basic decency of the principal's action. The major additional sequence follows the resignation of Bill Broussard, with Garrison's talk-show appearance and the airport incident. It's all garnered from the book (though Broussard is a composite of several 'traitors' on Garrison's team). The final sequence to be restored featured a witness at Shaw's trial, who undermines the entire prosecution through delusion and paranoia. He is revealed to fingerprint his daughter regularly to make sure she is his daughter and has not been replaced by a double. It is also mentioned that he was 'Broussard's witness'.

There were a number of scenes not to appear even in the director's cut. A longer version of the discussion between Garrison and Dean Andrews suggests that the lawyer became acquainted with Clay Bertrand through the legal help Andrews provided for Bertrand's gay friends.

Garrison told in his book of the offer of a Louisiana judgeship in exchange for dropping the case. This, along with Garrison's sanctimonious rejection, is added to a sequence that dramatises the number of eccentrics who clogged the DA's offices at the time of the investigation. There is also talk of myriad small donations from regular Americans – a direct reference to *Mr Smith Goes to Washington* (Frank Capra, 1939).

There was even more footage of evidence and theories that failed to make the director's cut. Missing movie film, reports of a dry run for the motorcade, suggestions that Ruby was injected with cancer, Oswald being interviewed in Russia and at home in Dallas – for which Gary Oldman learnt some Russian.

Probably the most questionable of these additional scenes gives extra screen-time to the stand-in for Lyndon Johnson. This was previously confined to a brief scene with his war cabinet, where he is given the line, 'Get me elected, then I'll give you your damned war,' a line actually attributed to him in different circumstances (see **Index of Quotations**). A piece of pure invention, it posits a phone call from Johnson, demanding that someone be arrested just to calm the nation.

One curio from *JFK* is a piece of improvisation that Oldman asked Stone to film, even though it was too odd to include in the finished film. Edited into scenes from the respective funerals of Kennedy and Oswald it had Oldman, playing the ghost of the alleged assassin, giving hypothetical testimony to an empty courtroom and declaring his innocence. It's an eerie monologue but doesn't work. In the film, Oswald is a blank slate, a puppet endlessly manipulated. He exists not as a personality but as an absence of personality, and this development of the character as the ghost would ultimately have been harmful.

MEMORABLE QUOTES:

Garrison: 'We gotta think like the CIA, black is white and white is black. We're through the looking-glass people.'

Garrison: 'The sixth and fatal shot, frame 313 . . . is the key shot. The President going back and to his left, shot from the front and right. Totally inconsistent with a shot from the depository. Again, back and to the left. Back and to the left . . . So what happens then? Pandemonium.'

Garrison: ' "Treason doth never prosper," the poet said. "What's the reason? For if it prosper, none dare call it treason." '

GOOD VS EVIL: There are similarities between the moral schema of this film and of *Born on the Fourth of July*. In both cases the main protagonist must overcome a complacent trust in country to question his government. But whereas the earlier film told a personal story, this is film used to convey information, on what the authors (Stone, Garrison, Marrs and a slew of other assassination researchers) perceive as a specific American injustice and their evidence of why this is the case.

As a result, the morality is 'black and white'. Garrison, as soon as he realises the flaws in the Warren Report, becomes a fighter for truth against the shadowy forces who arranged the assassination of a president. Effectively, in Stone's anti-establishment eyes, the courtroom battle is a rematch where good may not win but can at least reveal evil's existence.

Evil is not found in the smug media or the bureaucratic law agencies, the mid-level organisers (Bannister, Ferrie) or even the shooters (as Ferrie points out, even they don't know who originally ordered the shooting). They are the forces X speaks of, nameless, faceless but, out of cinematic necessity, given limited physical form in the body of Clay Shaw.

REDEMPTION OR DAMNATION: The character of Garrison makes a promise at the end of the film to continue pursuing the truth, even if it takes 30 years. Despite this, viewers know that, if such 'truth' exists, Garrison did not find it – the Warren Commission report, amended in part by the verdict of the House Select Committee on Assassinations (HSCA), remains the official view on the JFK assassination. However, the film ends in triumph despite the courtroom defeat, and this is rooted in the struggle more than any achievement. Like Ron Kovic, Garrison has opened his eyes and begun to question the government of a country, in the name of protecting that country and its people and has brought this criticism into the public eye.

Perhaps the real world is the sphere that matters most in terms of redemption or damnation. The question is ultimately being asked of the jury, a proxy for the audience: Will you take action or remain complacent? For a film that is an alternative history lesson more than a fictional drama, its effect on and implications for its audience are more important than judgement on its characters.

HISTORY 101: History is important in the majority of Oliver Stone's films, history as backdrop, as stage for the actions of characters representing real people. *JFK* is about history, but not in some loose dramatic way – it is history as polemic. What is especially interesting is that the film is not assembled as a blunt piece of propaganda (though it comes close at times) but rather as an argument. This argument comprehensively rejects the Warren Commission report, by calling on the mass of literature produced by independent researchers and leaning heavily on the findings of the House Select Committee on Assassinations. Convened in the late 1970s in the face of mass scepticism over JFK, the committee was set to deliver a verdict in support of Warren's investigation. At the last minute, some controversial acoustic evidence led the committee to conclude that more than one gunman was involved. Though occurring after the events of the movies and therefore not represented in them, this conclusion is key to Stone's ongoing justification.

'I do not think of myself as a cinematic historian now or ever and, to the best of my knowledge, have not made that claim,' said Stone, instead describing his intention thus: 'I'm presenting what I call the countermyth to the myth of the Warren Commission report because, honestly, I don't have all the facts.' No truth has been incontrovertibly established here, the questions of why and who are still unanswered satisfactorily, so why not at least accept Stone's well-researched view as a contribution to the attempt to understand? It is not rigid history but nor is it complete fabrication.

But in any study of the past, new research will emerge to supplant the old. On 22 November 2003 the BBC broadcast a documentary to commemmorate the fortieth anniversary of JFK's assassination. As part of its remit, the show comprehensively rubbished the claims of Stone's *JFK*. Without drifting into speculation, it destroyed the basic principles of the argument: 'Magic Bullet' *is* feasible – JFK and Governor Connally were sitting at an odd angle – the shot was not difficult for a trained, albeit mediocre, marksman, the bullets used could have chopped through two bodies without losing mass and the HSCA's acoustic evidence of a third gunman is highly suspect. So, in making *JFK*, Stone entered into the sort of dialogue which is never definitive.

CONSPIRACY THEORY: Though the film itself takes the form of a vast conspiracy theory, comparatively little is direct manipulation by Stone himself. Pretty much every alternative theory as presented here has been taken from the vast body of independent assassination research accumulating since the 1960s.

This is not to say that these sources are infallible or incorrect in their entirety, but rather to deflect accusations of those who view the film as a product solely of Stone's fevered brain – even the idea that the assassination occurred so as to prevent a retreat from Vietnam, a conclusion wholly sympathetic with Stone's own opinions on that war, can be traced back to the sources.

The only real way in which Stone might be personally accused of manipulation or weaving a fictional account, beyond his own credulity in believing the literature (and it is notable that he rejected some of the more extreme suggestions), is in his presentation – powerful, forceful filmmaking. In this the director can make few claims to objectivity. While he makes some effort to highlight areas of conjecture – 'Let's just for a moment speculate' (in the courtroom scene), or 'This is just speculation people' (in a staff meeting) – these are far from adequate; such throwaway lines are quickly forgotten in the following sweeping hypotheses. Visual cues are also inconsistent – filters and stocks change frequently but there is no one visual effect that denotes a theoretical scene clearly.

It is this failure to make his film responsibly, to appreciate the need for a consistent cinematic grammar within such a complex movie that leads to the fairest accusations of manipulation.

BEING OLIVER STONE: Stone had not been a supporter of JFK and had campaigned for Republican Barry Goldwater in the 1964 election. This film played into his anti-establishment instincts and, on a personal level, it marked a turning point in his public image. *JFK* created a popular reputation that has not really faded: Stone as the wild-eyed paranoid conspiracist, detached from reason or reality. He played to this perception in the comedy *Dave* (Ivan Reitman, 1993), in which Kevin Kline plays the titular presidential look-alike called in to impersonate a comatose Commander-in-Chief. In one sequence, a TV interview shows an adamant Stone insisting that the President has been replaced. In the long term this image of Stone has been detrimental as people preferred to look for wacky theories in *Nixon* than appreciate the film.

The controversy surrounding *JFK* heightened Stone's reflexive anti-establishment instincts to paranoid levels and turned this press perception of Stone into a self-fulfilling prophecy. The thin-skinned director saw a conspiracy in those writing against him and this has hardened into an active scepticism and hostility (see **Natural Born Killers**).

REAL PEOPLE: The Jim Garrison who appears in the movie is very much a sanitised version of the real-life Garrison, who has been accused of playing to the media, twisting the facts, arresting a suspect for no good reason, using hypnosis and truth drugs to conduct interrogations and even collusion with the mafia.

Most of these accusations are unproven, though the exception is the most bizarre: Garrison readily admitted using hypnosis and sodium pentothal on key witness Perry Russo.

His career is a matter of clearer record. Garrison served as New Orleans District Attorney from 1962 to 1974. In 1974 he was acquitted after accusations of mafia connections but went on to lose the election. In 1977 he was elected to the Louisiana Court of Appeals, eventually retiring in 1991.

His trial of Clay Shaw ended in collapse, the jury reaching a not-guilty verdict after less than an hour's deliberation, as shown in the film. A further trial against Clay Shaw on charges of perjury was thrown out before reaching trial.

Stone sidesteps the problems of representation in this movie. His Garrison, like many other characters, is a composite: 'I've taken the license of using Garrison as a metaphor for all credible researchers.' On another occasion, the writer-director freely admitted, 'There are many flaws in the real Garrison, but we decided not to deal with them in the film, because you either had to make Garrison the issue or make Kennedy the issue. I chose Kennedy.' Just as the Garrison case forms a dramatic skeleton on which other theories and facts can be arranged, so Garrison himself is secondary to the conspiracy unravelled in the narrative.

Garrison's assistants were composites of the many staffers to have helped in the investigation. This technique extended to Willie O'Keefe, a fictional version of the key eyewitness Perry Russo and several homosexual prostitutes called by Garrison as witnesses.

Other characters tended to be based on individuals and outlined mainly through careful casting. An exception was X, aka Fletcher Prouty, a former army colonel who provided the information and opinions that shape the film's view of high-level involvement. In reality

Garrison never met Prouty, at least not during the trial. Clay Shaw was a real man, but his role remains enigmatic. Suffice to say that Stone clearly believes his involvement. Several superficial details are retained: his distinctive hair, his cigarette holder and a taste for antiques. He was a homosexual, and Garrison writes of sado-masochistic tendencies, so while Stone's presentation of this might lack restraint it is in keeping with the source material. This did not present protest from various gay-rights groups that perceived prejudice in the suggestion of a 'gay mafia' based in New Orleans and responsible for Kennedy's murder.

INSPIRATION AND INFLUENCE: The direct aftermath of the assassinations of JFK (1963), Robert Kennedy and Martin Luther King (both 1968), and the revelations of Watergate, resulted in a golden age of paranoid conspiracy movies. *Day of the Jackal* (Fred Zinnemann, 1973) used Frederick Forsyth's novel to hypothesise a near-successful attempt on the life of Charles de Gaulle, *The Parallax View* was a dark vision of corporate conspiracy while *All the President's Men* (Alan J Pakula, 1976) is comparable to *JFK* in its revelation of a huge conspiracy from a seemingly minor incident. One film often referred to by Stone in interviews was *Z* (Constantin Costa Gavras, 1968) and its influence is immediately apparent. A left-wing political candidate is killed at a rally and what is thought to have been an accident is revealed to be murder, arranged by shady right-wing groups and senior officers in the army.

Stone also looked for inspiration to the social and political melodrama of Frank Capra, leavening the sinister conspiracy with what Stone called 'good corn', old-fashioned sentimentality. Of particular note is *Mr Smith Goes to Washington* with Jimmy Stewart as a naive young senator, struggling against the establishment. Along with other decent men such as Gary Cooper and Gregory Peck, Stewart is an explicit model for the cinematic Garrison.

The Kennedy assassination had been invoked before, but never in such a prominent film. *Executive Action* (David Miller, 1973) had made a similar attempt to unravel a conspiracy, placing the blame at the door of big business and the military, but with a messier case than that constructed by Stone. In the novel *Libra*, Don Delillo hypothesised a plot to force Kennedy back into Cuba by a staged assassination attempt, hijacked by a rogue agent intent on killing the president – Oswald remained a patsy. A film of this book was in production at the same time as *JFK*, but collapsed amid unproven accusations that Stone had used his influence to nobble the project.

Scores of books were consulted to provide the factual basis and any bibliography of these sources would take up pages (as it does in the published screenplay). The two biggest influences were credited in the film: *On the Trail of the Assassins* and *Crossfire: the Plot that Killed Kennedy*. The former is Garrison's own account of the investigation and the trial, and provides the basic narrative structure, the chain of events, and the climactic trial. *Crossfire* is an encyclopaedia of conspiracy theories, a condensed history of the assassination research scene, and pretty much the most comprehensive single work available on alternate theories. It is from this that many of the details are taken, details that are built into the ultimate theory of the movie. One uncredited influence was John Newman's *JFK and Vietnam*, which contained a theory central to the film: that Kennedy intended to withdraw from the war in the Far East, while Johnson increased the number of troops.

It is difficult to rate the impact of *JFK* on popular culture. The frenzied editing has become ubiquitous, as have certain phrases, for example, 'back, and to the left', 'we're through the looking glass people'. It has, unintentionally, become shorthand for paranoid mania. *The Simpsons* take *JFK* as inspiration for an episode of *The Itchy and Scratchy Show* 'with guest director Oliver Stone'. Beyond these scraps, there is little of substance. In the final analysis, it was a specific film, on a specific event and with a specific agenda, not a trendsetter for future films.

For its true impact, one must turn from Los Angeles to Washington. Congressman Lee Hamilton had been badgered by his aide Eric Hamburg (see **Nixon**) into investigating declassification for the HSCA's restricted files. Hamburg and Hamilton met with Stone and his people and the film was yoked in to boost momentum. The movie's release led to huge publicity and the JFK Assassination Records Collection Act was passed by both houses of Congress and signed into law by George HW Bush Snr, just a few weeks before the election of 1992. It should be noted that after ten years and the release of thousands of documents, no single, credible alternative to the Warren Commission has emerged (see **HISTORY 101**).

REEL TIME: There is a real contrast between light and dark in this film. The best example is during the lunch conversation between Garrison and Dean Andrews where Garrison is brightly lit and Andrews mired in shadow. The gloom matches the shady aspects of the conspiracy: the murky Pentagon scenes, the sepulchral down-lighting of the Bethesda autopsy, the low-lights of the party at which O'Keefe hears Ferrie and Shaw discussing assassination and the creepy dim atmosphere of Ferrie's apartment. In comparison, Garrison and his crew carry light where they go, interviewing Martin at the racetrack, O'Keefe in the open air prison, stalking Dealey Plaza.

JFK is at its most technically impressive in its assembly, the chopping together of footage of all stocks and types into a coherent visual narrative. For instance, staged re-creations, documentary and home-movie footage are combined to create the opening montage. The aim was simple, in Richardson's words, 'we created a strong documentary feel for the first two sections of the film.' For purpose of emphasis, Stone employed what he referred to as vertical editing: cutting images and footage into a sequence to support, or contrast with, the spoken sentiments – the fictionalised theory of Ferrie's death or the snippets of Shaw and Andrews played while the attorney denies ever meeting the businessman.

The result is a powerful cinematic essay, replete with visual footnotes. But the most effective moment in the film is nothing to do with skilled lighting, virtuoso directing or sharp editing. It is the simple replay of a piece of Super-8 movie footage filmed by Abraham Zapruder in Dealey Plaza, 22 November 1963.

MUSIC: This is John Williams's second score for Oliver Stone, and also his best for him. Having said that, none of his work for the director has the same instantly recognisable spark of his greatest tunes such as *Jaws*, *Star Wars* or *Indiana Jones*. Technically admirable, the music veers from the incessant drum-beat of Kennedy's arrival in Dallas to the accompanying string section (a mournful anthem) to the faintly sinister music that emphasises the conspiratorial elements of the rest of the film, building to a finale with the courtroom scenes: here is the moment when music, film and dialogue come together at their most unified and persuasive, specifically the crescendo of sound and visuals that make up the Zapruder film sequence, underpinned by Costner's hypnotic 'back, and to the left' mantra.

The music is subordinated to the film, powerful, loud but less distinct as a tune than as a driving theme. This might be because Williams composed the score before the movie had been completed – writing to general specifications rather than intimate knowledge of the finished movie. Yet it works well.

BOX OFFICE: *JFK* enjoyed an opening weekend of $50 million, and went on to take $70 million at the American box office. What made this doubly impressive was its immense length. Exhibitors don't tend to like films of more than 2 hours – great length limits the number of showings per day. *JFK* was over three hours, and still turned in one of the best gross earnings of any of Stone's films, an impressive achievement particularly at that time.

CRITICS: Some critics celebrated the filmmaking even as they expressed doubt over the history. 'The verdicts in *JFK* may convince few people of the truth of its proposition. But no one will be able to say that its QED hasn't been entertainingly argued' (Alexander Walker, *Evening Standard*); 'Yes, *JFK* is propaganda packed as high voltage tension, intrigue and human drama . . . it's also the year's first unmissable film' (Shaun Usher, *Daily Mail*).

Others qualified their doubt over factual elements, welcoming an attempt to reopen debate on the assassination. 'At least, he sets the stage for a good argument. And that's where *JFK*'s real power lies – in stirring the national debate' (Marjorie Baumgarten, *Austin Chronicle*); 'It's more complex and intelligent and less flashy than his earlier work . . . one can't deny the force and sincerity of Stone's call for more debate' (Geoff Andrew, *Time Out*). However, Nigel Andrews criticised a subjective selection of facts, writing that Stone 'treats the riddles of history, not as a jigsaw to be pieced together . . . but as a rag-bag of surmises to be forced into rhetorical harmony.'

Kevin Costner attracted some fairly scathing reviews. Some were straightforwardly negative: 'Costner is simply not a layered enough actor to carry the movie's entire emotional baggage . . . in short he comes out as a sickly boy scout' (Sue Heal, *Today*); 'many of Stone's dramatic efforts are dulled by Costner' (Desson Howe, *Washington Post*). But there was some mitigation to this criticism: 'Perhaps the milquetoast casting is ironically appropriate: the real story's about Kennedy. Someone with a personality would only get in the way.'

Rolling Stone praised one area of filmmaking: 'The camera work of Robert Richardson and the editing of Joe Hutshing and Pietro Scalia are outstanding,' elaborating that it creates 'a vast cyclorama that sets the mind reeling with possibilities and provocations.' The homophobia of which Stone was accused was placed in a wider context. Anne Billson wrote, 'in my view the writer-director is far harder on women than on the gay characters, who are at least interesting to watch.' Mark Amory highlighted the fact that 'Sissy Spacek is virtually the only woman as a one-note whining wife.' An aspect that Christopher Tookey also picked up on: 'The domestic side of Garrison's life is a compendium of clichés . . . they are further embarrassing proof that Stone can't write for women.'

CONTROVERSY: An unannounced visit to the set by George Lardner, a correspondent from the *Washington Post*, led to a heavily critical article based largely on a version of the script that had been leaked to him by Harold Weisberg – an assassination researcher unhappy with the director's approach. 'On the Set: Dallas in Wonderland' (*Washington Post*, 2 June 1991) sparked a blaze of controversy in the American press. Stone immediately launched a counter-offensive through op-ed retorts and letters pages (comparable to Garrison's own demands for equal coverage in the wake of a one-sided NBC report in the late 1960s).

Attacks tended to concentrate on Garrison, on new interpretations of Kennedy's Vietnam policy, on the integrity of other contributors (especially L Fletcher Prouty, member of several right-wing organisations) and on Stone's own motives and approach. They varied from factual nitpicking to personal attacks ('the director of *JFK* is not, as he claims, an artist. He is a polemicist'). The best criticism was in defence of the Warren Report, paraphrasing the opinion of criminal lawyer Edward Bennett Williams, 'Considered by itself, the commission report might be picked apart by its critics; but what . . . did they present in its place?' Another intelligent overview of the world of JFK research compared the dogmatism of assassination buffs versus Warren apologists with the intractability of medieval religious disputes ('The sum of all fears', David Klinghoffer, *Washington Times*, 23 December 1991). Defenders were thinner on the ground, but numbered some big names including novelist Norman Mailer and critic Roger Ebert. Regular reporters and commentators were pretty much universally hostile. The British press took a similarly adversarial stance. *The Times* and *Sunday Times* printed several critical articles, though in mitigation the latter also printed a lengthy defensive piece from Stone.

This categorised the director's reaction. He submitted retorts to any major publication that would print them and appeared on any TV show that would have him, refusing to just accept criticism. There was an ulterior motive here. Despite the generally negative consensus, the coverage represented fantastic publicity and boosted the films takings. As Garry Trudeau put it, at the end of a lengthy piece detailing the various media attacks in a pastiche of written reports on the assassination, 'Laughing all the way, Stone roars off to the bank.'

AWARDS: *JFK*'s nomination tally harkened back to *Born on the Fourth of July*, but most awards were for technical achievement rather than in recognition of artistic merit. After several nominations, Robert Richardson finally picked up his Oscar for cinematography. An Oscar also went to the editing team of Joe Hutshing and Pietro Scalia. *JFK* failed to score for any of its six other nominations, Best Music, Best Sound, Best Director, Best Screenplay, Best Picture and Best Supporting Actor for Tommy Lee Jones – a surprising nomination in the first place.

After the ceremony, Jack Valenti, head of the MPAA (Motion Picture Association of America) and former aide to President Johnson, launched a scathing attack on the film, comparing Oliver Stone to Nazi propagandist Leni Riefenstahl, making reference to the mesmerising power of her 1936 work *Triumph of the Will* and concluding, 'many young people, gripped by the movie, leave the theatre convinced they have been witness to the truth.'

Stone had won the Golden Globe for Best Director. Technical categories had also done well at the BAFTAs. Sound and editing won their respective categories while nominations were received for the screenplay and, again, Tommy Lee Jones. On a personal level, in 1990 Stone was presented with the Upton Sinclair Award, presented by the Liberty Hill Foundation, in recognition of Stone's grass-roots activism through his controversial and confrontational movies.

THE BIG PICTURE: As a subjective work of political history, the first instinct is to compare this film with *Nixon*. It also ties in with Stone's concerns about Vietnam, giving a villainous rationale to the war that tormented Chris Taylor and crippled Ron Kovic in *Platoon* and *Born on the Fourth of July*.

With *JFK* the editing builds the story, in contrast with the long, steady shots of *Born on the Fourth of July* or even the frenetic cuts of *Salvador*. These earlier films are purely linear in structure, while *JFK* leaps all over the place, deliberately using its camera to mark a change in location or re-creation of an earlier event. Frenzied camerawork of this style would be applied to *Natural Born Killers*, but with less rational method. Stone extends his investigation into the rot he sees at America's heart. If *Born on the Fourth of July* questions the state's attitudes to its citizens, *JFK* suggests that even the president is not safe. *Nixon* would go further, asking whether the president is even relevant.

FINAL ANALYSIS: Of all the nominally historical films to come out of Hollywood, *JFK* should be the last to be taken at face value. It is the boldest and most visually inventive political or historical film to be made in the last 30 years. It is also uncompromising in its agenda and its argument. Pretty much every line of its dialogue, every character and every shot requires careful analysis and thorough background research. There is documentary evidence to support much of what it says, but how much credence can be put in this evidence is more or less a matter of individual judgement. Stone has constructed a persuasive counter-myth, one with many flaws, just like the Warren Report 'myth' it refutes. But it is greatly to the film's credit that it publicly raised questions about the report, and demanded they be answered. How many other movies can list an act of Congress as a direct result of their release?

This is the one Oliver Stone film to have transcended aesthetic concerns, becoming a political document. That it was also a stylistically significant piece of cinema and a profitable box office draw ranks *JFK* with *Platoon* as Oliver Stone's most successful films.

Heaven and Earth (1993)

Warner Bros Presents
In association with Regency Enterprises, Le Studio Canal+
and Alcor Films
An Ixtlan, New Regency, Todd-Ao/Tae Production
An Oliver Stone Film
Casting: Risa Bramon Garcia, Billy Hopkins and Heidi Levitt
Costume Designer: Ha Nguyen
Music Composed by Kitaro
Edited by David Brenner and Sally Menke
Production Designer: Victor Kempster
Director of Photography: Robert Richardson ASC
Executive Producer: Mario Kassar
Co-Producer: Clayton Townsend
Based on the books *When Heaven and Earth Changed*
Places* by Le Ly Hayslip with Jay Wurts and *Child of War,
***Woman of Peace* by Le Ly Hayslip with James Hayslip**

OLIVER STONE Heaven and Earth

Screenplay by Oliver Stone
Produced by Oliver Stone, Arnon Milchan, Robert Kline and
A Kitman Ho
Directed by Oliver Stone

CAST: Hiep Thi Le (*Le Ly*), Tommy Lee Jones (*Sgt Steve Butler*), Joan Chen (*Mama*), Haing S Ngor (*Papa*), Debbie Reynolds (*Eugenia*), Conchata Ferrell (*Bernice*), Dustin Nguyen (*Sau*), Vivian Wu (*Madame Lien*), Robert John Burke (*G.I. Paul*), Timothy Carhart (*Big Mike*)

NOTABLE CREDITS: A dedication runs 'For my mother, Jacqueline Stone'.

SUMMARY: The small village of Ky La in Vietnam has existed for an age in sync with the rhythms of the rice harvest and through Buddhist devotion. Hiep Thi Le's voice-over tells of the arrival of French Colonial forces in 1953, with accompanying images of destruction of the lush agricultural scenes and aggression. After independence and partition, Ky La enjoys a few short years of peace, in which Le Ly grows from a small child to a young woman, working in the fields with her mother and praying with her father.

The war brings two opposing forces to the village. By day the South Vietnamese, and Americans, lecture the villagers on the need for vigilance, train a militia, bring in teachers to indoctrinate the young and fly the flag of the South. At night the Vietcong arrive, preaching the rightness of their cause, raising guerrilla forces in the shadows, killing officials and teachers sent from the South and flying their own flag. Le Ly's mother sends her two sons to war and Le Ly is later afflicted by nightmares about their fate (a local wizard assures her mother that one is safe, though the other's fate is unsure). Le Ly acts as a scout for the VC, is identified, imprisoned and tortured – only her family's influence in government gains her release. This causes more problems, arousing the suspicions of the local VC cadre, which orders her execution. Instead of killing her, the two young VC entrusted with this task rape Le Ly, and threaten her into silence.

Life is too difficult to stay at Ky La, so Le Ly and her mother travel to Saigon where they find work in the household of wealthy Ahn. But Ahn and Le Ly find themselves mutually attracted, and she comes to bear his child. Despite attempts at abortion, Ahn's wife finds out and, furious, insists that Le Ly and her mother leave the house, thwarting Ahn's efforts to provide for his bastard child.

Le Ly takes to selling whisky, cigarettes and marijuana to American GI's on the streets of Danang. She stays with her sister, who is provided for by her GI lover, but who grows jealous of their father's greater affection for the younger Le Ly and throws her out. One day a friendly Military Policeman offers her a chance to make a large sum of money, by sleeping with two soldiers about to return to the States. Le Ly has steadfastly avoided prostitution, but the cash would feed her family for a year. Eventually she agrees.

Le Ly returns to her village. Her home is devastated and her father is ruined, gradually drinking himself to death. She cannot stay long, there is still ill-feeling against her, but he is sad to see her go. Soon after he dies.

Le Ly secures a more respectable job in a nightclub and rides through Danang on a scooter. A friend asks her to help rip-off Sergeant Steve Butler, who is looking for a prostitute. She reluctantly agrees and dashes off once money has changed hands, but he pursues her. They talk, and she sees him as tender and loving. He is looking for a wife to take back to the States. Despite her mother's protests, she marries him and has children. After an attack on their military base home, they travel to the United States.

In California Le Ly meets her in-laws. Steve's chubby sister, and his elderly mother welcome her and her sons into an apparent paradise of food and consumer goods, but Steve is not wealthy. He has a former wife to support and is counting heavily on being offered a job back in the Far East. After an awkward Thanksgiving dinner, he reveals this job to Le Ly: selling arms. She is shocked and their relationship begins to deteriorate. Le Ly opens her own delicatessen, without telling Steve, who is furious when he finds out. She is unhappy that her sons refuse to speak Vietnamese and that Steve spends money on guns. One night he breaks down, almost shooting her, before sobbing of his nightmare in Vietnam, where he fought as a black-ops killer, murdering suspected VC. She tries to forgive him but the marriage breaks down and she files for divorce.

Steve continues to stalk her and one Sunday kidnaps their sons after church. Le Ly is grief stricken. Then she gets a call from her sister, who had moved to the States and married one of Steve's comrades, to say that her ex-husband and her sons have stopped there on their way to Canada. She rushes to her sister's house to discover that Steve has killed himself.

Eighteen years after leaving Vietnam, Le Ly returns with her sons. She sees Ahn, greatly reduced in status after the Communist victory, but delighted to see their son. She travels out to Ky La to meet with her family and to discover that her eldest brother survived the war. There is tension, and her brother sees Le Ly's return as more trouble for a beleaguered family. Le Ly prays at the local shrine: she has returned home, but it can never be the place she once knew.

ADVANCE PUBLICITY: The film came from a true story and Le Ly Hayslip and Hiep Thi Le were wheeled out for the obligatory press junket, but the film failed to arouse the same level of interest as *JFK* or *The Doors.*

Interestingly Tommy Lee Jones received prominence in the billing and on the rather bland poster, despite only featuring in about 50 per cent of the film. The trailer was similarly nondescript. A potted synopsis of the film runs through Le Ly's village origin, her meeting with Steve and her departure for the United States. Oliver Stone's name was mentioned in the context of *Platoon* and *Born on the Fourth of July*, with *Heaven and Earth* billed as 'the third film in an extraordinary trilogy'.

PRODUCTION HISTORY: Le Ly Hayslip's first book, *When Heaven and Earth Changed Places* became a source of interest to Hollywood producers soon after its release in 1989. One of the interested parties was Robert Kline, president of Todd-Ao at the time and he began negotiations to pick up the rights. Kline suggested the project to Oliver Stone, a subject in the documentary series *Profiles of Excellence* with which Kline was involved. After meeting Le Ly, Stone agreed to take on the film.

He began writing a script, working without collaboration for the first time since *Platoon*. One problem he encountered early on with working from *When Heaven and Earth Changed Places* was the lack of a true ending. The Vietnam section of the narrative ends with Le Ly whisked off to America by 'Ed', one of the men who would be incorporated into Steve Butler (see **REAL PEOPLE**), while the return to Vietnam which closes the book makes little mention of her experiences in the USA. A solution was found on an expedition of location scouting. Le Ly was marking up a manuscript on the flight to Ho Chi Minh City, a manuscript that turned out to be the second volume of her memoirs: *Child of War, Woman of Peace*. From this, Stone was able to take details of her experiences in America and weave them into the film, employing a similarly non-linear fragmentary approach to that of the books. The film would cut from a significant Vietnam scene to one in America and back again, building to the climax of her return to Vietnam, counterpointed with the death of Steve in the US.

JFK had been a huge success, one on which Stone could capitalise. He was able to renew the relationship with Arnon Milchan and Warner Brothers, as well as receiving support from Carolco's Mario Kassar (who was still owed a movie from Stone – see **The Doors**), enabling a Hollywood film with a uniquely Vietnamese point of view, and a sceptical take on American materialism, religion and society, to be budgeted at an impressive $33 million.

The director, with Le Ly Hayslip, Joan Chen and Hiep Thi Le, travelled to Le Ly's home village of Ky La, where Chen and Hiep were put through a two-week 'boot camp' in the everyday life of the Vietnamese peasant. They lived with local families, carried water and worked the fields – an experience in enforced method acting familiar to the re-cruits in *Platoon* and a reminder of Stone's autocratic perfectionist approach. Meanwhile, after the government objected to any anti-Vietcong messages in the film, Robert Richardson, Victor Kempster, Le Ly and a camera assistant travelled Vietnam under the guise of a documentary crew filming a story on Le Ly. In fact they were shooting some of the amazing landscapes and lush verdant foliage that make up part of the opening montage – the most purely beautiful photography in any of Stone's films.

Principal filming took place in Thailand with Phang Nga standing in for the Vietnamese countryside. Victor Kempster was charged with the mammoth task of re-creating Le Ly's childhood village. To this end 34 hard buildings were constructed of stone and concrete in the style of the originals, as well as dozens of soft bamboo and wood structures, all linked together with roads and moats, while over 900 acres of fallow paddy-fields were sown with rice, in the style of Vietnamese paddies. The appearance of the solid, permanent buildings is somewhat different from the rickety wood huts seen in many films set in Vietnam (including *Platoon*). Le Ly was so taken with the new 'village' that for a time she took up residence in the building that represented her old home. The population was filled out by several hundred extras, many culled from the expatriate Vietnamese community of Thailand. Costume designer Ha Nguyen was a native of Vietnam, and put together some 2500 hand-made outfits in 8 weeks. At the end of the time in Phang Nga, the village was gutted to simulate the effects of war.

For the urban scenes of Danang and Saigon, the crew used the architecture of Bangkok and Phuket. Shop fronts in the older quarters of the two cities were re-dressed with signs contemporary to late 1960s Vietnam, and a mansion constructed in 1915 for a Chinese businessman acted as Ahn's luxurious town-house; period European furniture and a library of Vietnamese books were flown in. So great was the concentration of military traffic during the chaotic scenes around the American embassy, where Le Ly searches for Steve, that rumours spread of a coup against the Thai government. The film's commitment to military details was not insignificant: Dale Dye drilled actors to play the representatives of four armed forces (French, Vietcong, South Vietnamese ARVN and the US Army).

Back in the USA, location filming in California was hampered by torrential rain. Filming began on 19 October 1992 and the shoot lasted 64 days. The movie was edited electronically – a first for Oliver Stone – on a British Lightworks system. It was here that flaws with the non-linear structure of the film became apparent. As Stone laconically puts it, 'It didn't work.' The scenes were put back into chronological order, with several major cuts to push the running time down to the agreed 2 hours and 20 minutes. Though adding a degree of suspense, especially with the character of Steve, this was not a wise decision. The result is stodgy linearity, which clashes with the film's spiritual aspirations, any tension is an artificial result of the editing, rather than inherent in the narrative.

Heaven and Earth was released in the USA at the end of December 1993.

CASTING: The freedom that Stone enjoyed as a result of *JFK*'s success extended to casting decisions. He wanted to cast a complete unknown in the key role of Le Ly and an open casting call went to all major communities of *Viet Kieu* (expatriate Vietnamese) in the United States and Canada. Auditions were advertised and held in San Francisco, Santa Fe, Houston, Washington, Dallas, New Orleans, Virginia, Washington, Orange County and Vancouver throughout the autumn of 1991; 16,000 people responded. One of these was Hiep Thi Le, a 22-year-old physiology student from the University of California's institution at Davis. She ended up auditioning largely by accident, having travelled to the audition with her sister: 'Obviously, I couldn't sit in the car and wait all those hours, so I went in.' Something in her performance grabbed Stone's attention, he describes it as 'a light around Hiep and a purity of character that's astonishing. She is exactly what she appears to be, a totally spontaneous person.' Hiep had herself fled Vietnam in 1979, with her family, and spent time in the administrative and national limbo of the boat-person.

It was a brave move for Stone, a brave effort by Hiep (her character appears in every scene) and it almost works. Le Ly's book is curiously emotionless in that it is free of rage or vengeance and this translates to the story – to an extent there is little for the actor to do, the character is buffeted by forces beyond her control, buoyed by the tenets of her faith. The whole approach of the film is alien to the Western mindset, which led to some overly harsh criticism. Nevertheless, if one were looking for a great example of acting on a debut, one could do worse than point to the moment on the Danang bridge when Le Ly decides to sleep with the young soldiers for their money.

Hiep Thi Le is the fulcrum for the film. In a comparable way to *Born on the Fourth of July* her character is the one constant, with complete changes of supporting cast between scenes. At home in Ky La, Le Ly spends time with her father, played by Haing S Ngor, a Cambodian actor who had won repute, and an Academy Award, for his performance in *The Killing Fields*, which dealt with Khmer Rouge atrocities in that country, atrocities of which he had personal experience. He has little to do here, but is quietly effective, managing some touching emotion when Le Ly leaves him for the last time. Ngor died in 1996. Mama was played by Joan Chen, a Chinese actress who had risen to prominence in *The Last Emperor* (Bernardo Bertolucci, 1987), the story of China's last imperial ruler. She was also famous on American TV screens for her regular appearances on David Lynch's *Twin Peaks* and was in *The Joy Luck Club*. Chen was initially uncertain about the role: she was required to mute her beauty behind ageing make-up and teeth blackened by Betel nut.

Tommy Lee Jones takes over for most of the Danang and America sequences. He provides solid support as Steve, and handles the gradual change from heroic John Wayne rescuer to paranoid, suicidal breakdown with aplomb. There is good support at the American end too. Conchata Ferrell plays Steve's sister, a large gregarious blunt American woman, a creation that comes across as eerie and monstrous in the garish lighting of the California sequences and after the subtle delicacy of Vietnam. She totally overwhelms the low-key performance of Debbie Reynolds as Eugenia. Reynolds had found fame as a star of light entertainment and musicals – notably the awesome *Singin' in the Rain* (Gene Kelly, 1952) – and through her singing career. *Heaven and Earth* represented a return to cinema after a 19-year absence. There are also two noteworthy cameos. Jeffrey Jones, an ogre-like actor of menacing presence, as the Christian minister and Le Ly Hayslip herself, who appears as the jewellery dealer to whom the screen Le Ly sells some gold.

OLIVER'S ARMY: With the major exception of Tommy Lee Jones, this was a departure for Oliver Stone in terms of casting, with no other actors taken from his usual pool of talent. There were a few cameos from family and friends; Sean Stone and personal doctor Chris Renna appear as a recalcitrant schoolboy and a Jesuit schoolmaster. Dale Dye also made an appearance, playing Larry, a friend of Steve's, in the VC attack on Steve's base.

Regular assistant director Joe Reidy (a crew member since *Talk Radio*) was unable to work on the film, he had a newborn baby, and was replaced by Herb Gains. The move away from America applied to the crew too, with a Vietnamese costume designer and a Japanese composer. There was a consistency to the core members of the crew with involvement from Victor Kempster, David Brenner (taking over from Joe Hutshing and Pietro Scalia) and Robert Richardson – recently elevated to the ranks of the American Society of Cinematographers and so adding ASC to his credit. Associate producer credits went to long-time casting guru Risa Bramon Garcia and Stone's sidekick Richard Rutowski.

CUT SCENES: One of the biggest cuts to the film, aside from the comprehensive restructuring that took place at the editing stage, was a reworking of the opening scene, the introduction to Vietnam. It starts with an extended version of the black-and-white dream sequence that Le Ly now experiences in Ahn's household, relating to a story told in Le Ly Hayslip's book of a maiden who returns home after twenty years to her village, finds it desolate but brings it back to life through prayer. In the film, as she prays, colour bleeds back into the picture, and the audience sees the whole gamut of village experiences. A great deal of care and attention went into the sequence, which is almost documentary in places, and the richness of the production design really is shown to the full. There is a loose underpinning narrative: the birth of Le Ly, her growth, the relative wealth of her family and a sermon on the importance of rice, the arrival of the French (expanded upon and including the brutal murder of Le Ly's neighbours, told in the form of a ghost story) and the eventual rebuilding of the village. It is fascinating stuff in itself, but runs a little too long.

There are several other, shorter cuts, most of them to the American scenes. The hostility of the Christian Butler family to Buddhism is revealed, with Steve talking of Le Ly's Buddha statue as a golden calf. He also asks Le Ly to dissolve her business (something that one of Le Ly's real husbands – Dennis Hayslip – actually did). There is also a glimmer of real enmity between Eugenia, Bernice and Le Ly – something that never becomes apparent in the film as released.

This scene ends with Le Ly's promise to talk with a local priest, Father Bob. This gives an extended role to Jeffrey Jones, and allows for some rather heavy-handed comment, as Le Ly's dreamy, poetic championing of Buddhism is matched against Bob's cold attempts to 'sell' her on Christianity, like a used-car dealer. Stone cut this as he was nervous of its robust criticism of Christianity in the wake of *JFK*'s controversy, and it was probably the right move. As the American section of the film is short, and almost wholly satirical, this extra scene might have proved too much.

It has its counterpart in Le Ly's later encounter with a Buddhist monk, presumably prior to her decision on a divorce. The monk recommends that she be thankful for what she has, and postulates that Steve's violence and aggression is from having served his life's purpose, by leading her from Vietnam. This was cut for reasons of time, as was a brief scene with Le Ly's divorce lawyer, played by Kathleen Quinlan from *The Doors*: another satirical scene that demonstrates the contrast between marriage as an expression of love and the cold legality with which it is terminated. There might also be a link with the businesslike basis of marriage in Vietnam – the discomfort of a divorce is presented as the unhappy consequence of not having shown sense in the marriage alliance.

There are two other American scenes. At Steve's funeral, the repressed formality of a Western burial is deliberately compared with the overt emotion of the same ritual in the East. It might have been interesting in a comparative sense had a third funeral been included, in which a local VC leader gives a eulogy to the two girls seen blowing themselves up with a grenade. He talks of the honour of sacrifice and of death before capture. As it is, both scenes were cut, leaving only the funeral of Le Ly's father.

An aftermath of the funeral is Bernice and Eugenia's final appearance. Ultimately little more than an excuse to present them as gruesome harpies (though based on material from the book), they bully Le Ly over money, her shrine and her children. In all cases she presents no argument until they ask for pictures of Steve back, when she suddenly refuses. This causes them to scurry out, threatening legal action. Most of these American scenes rub in a point that is already obvious.

One last sequence expands on Le Ly's return to Vietnam to tell a story that was in the book. Le Ly's mama was upset that the body of her son, killed fighting in the war, was never recovered. One day she spotted a huge snake, sluggish and ill, and, convinced that it was a manifestation of her son's spirit, she pushed it into a tube and buried it in their graveyard. This is relayed in full and is a nice emotional touch, but no great loss to the film.

MEMORABLE QUOTES: The script is not strong for this film, with no particularly memorable lines.

GOOD VS EVIL: As noted at the time of release, this is a story of survival. In this it is a straightforward adaptation of the biographical source, as opposed to *Born on the Fourth of July*, where the material was shaped into an ideological message. As a result, ideas of struggle and conflict are largely removed from the mystical or the metaphorical (ironic given the Buddhist bent of the story, and the preponderance of gnomic peasant lore) and are instead manifested in largely straightforward physical terms: Le Ly's survival in the turmoil of events following the shattering of her peasant lifestyle.

The film gets closest to ideological conflict in America. As Le Ly is faced with a gradual diminution of her national origins, she is urged to take on Western ways and chastises herself for becoming greedy and selfish as an American while bemoaning her sons' refusal to speak Vietnamese. But she remains steadfast in her beliefs and this battle never seems more than superficial: behaviour, habits, language, not fundamental thinking or values.

Le Ly is supported in her struggle by Buddhist notions of karma – a fixed purpose in life. This drains a lot of the dramatic tension from a film that becomes a carnival of tribulations, a succession of problems that Le Ly must overcome. She never really develops as a character, beyond a brief lapse into Western nagging, but stays constant, maintaining principles and standards in the face of troubles. She experiences pain and strife, but there is never any question of her inherent goodness, nor that of the traditional ways. It makes sense in the context of the character (see **BEING OLIVER STONE**) but is rather dull in a dramatic sense. Her father and sister are much more interesting with their human failings, alcoholic despair in the former, and a self-centred moral decay in the latter. The same is true of Tommy Lee Jones, an inherent decency concealing a great pain, a man who changes completely when back in the beige world of lower-middle-class America as opposed to his status as skilled warrior in Vietnam.

REDEMPTION OR DAMNATION: This one-dimensional moral schema renders questions of damnation irrelevant. Le Ly suffers, but never flirts with darkness, as earlier Stone protagonists had done. Nor does she reach a point where she is ready to give up, consigning herself to oblivion as her father does and as Ron Kovic came close to doing in *Born on the Fourth of July*.

Having said that, the movie does have a somewhat downbeat ending, with what appears to be a permanent divide between Le Ly and her old village way of life – there is no intimation of the links she would forge between her old home and her adopted country (see **INSPIRATION AND INFLUENCE**). There is a fatalistic inevitability to this: Le Ly rarely makes a choice but clutches at the best chance for her survival. She is alienated from her home, but this seems arbitrary, not a price exacted for a decision she made but simply another hardship she must stoically bear.

HISTORY 101: Stone returns to his favoured venue of Vietnam here, encompassing, for the first time, experience of the French war (albeit only briefly) as well as the American. Politically, the representation never gets more specific, beyond a brief mention of the government's pro-Catholic, anti-Buddhist policies. This is in keeping with Stone's previous films, where in-country politics are less important than the brutal realities of war. This time, however, the lack of political detail is carried back across the Pacific to the USA. There is period detail in the clothes, hair and the music, and exaggerated psychedelia of the art design, but no specifically historical touchstones.

The largely a-historical feel of the book has been kept in, the overriding theme being the general suffering of ordinary Vietnamese whether at the hands of Americans or Vietcong. The details are less important than the end result.

STARS AND STRIPES: Le Ly is an immigrant to America, just like Tony Montana in *Scarface* or Joey Tai in *Year of the Dragon*. But here Stone investigates from the perspective of ordinary immigrants, the urge to conform with Western society and the overindulgence and material obsession that go hand in hand with the land of plenty but without descent into criminal corruption. It is a scary, noisy disorienting ordeal, and the cleverest achievement of the film is to make the audience feel this at a personal level through an abrupt change from the smooth, naturalistic style that had prevailed up to that point.

BEING OLIVER STONE: Despite its largely forgotten and unfairly derided status, *Heaven and Earth* was a highly significant film for Oliver Stone. This would be the first (and, to date, only) of his films to feature a woman as the protagonist. Some have criticised the manner in which the character was constructed, specifically that certain attributes were minimised: 'heroic action in war, entrepreneurial success and social action – which so intriguingly co-exist with her romantic and spiritual philosophy – are played down,' said critic Margaret O'Brian, concluding that, 'unlike the heroes of *Platoon* and *Born on the Fourth of July* Le Ly is a heroine who does not articulate her pain.' This is unfair to Stone, it ignores the tenderness that is imbued in Le Ly: the pain she has to endure does not need articulation, it is up on the screen, in her rape, her childbirth, her family struggles, her displacement, her abuse, her divorce and her return to a family not her own. Moreover, this misses the influence of Eastern philosophy on the film; Stone converted to Buddhism during the shoot (partly due to his contact with Le Ly) and applies some of the tenets of this religion to the plot. The film functions on one level as a Buddhist tract to preach acceptance and forbearance. Le Ly is not Chris Taylor or Ron Kovic, she did not choose to become involved in the war, and suffers due to events over which she has no control.

Lost in the snide put downs of a 'dull' film with a 'flat' lead character is appreciation of the spiritual centre of this film, not in Western concepts of admitting or venting frustration, but in Eastern ideas of karma and tolerance.

Mention of Taylor and Kovic are important. Stone has capital invested in Le Ly, as he did with the earlier characters. All three are narrators of the war in Vietnam. This time not the story of his own experiences, nor those of another vet, injured and alienated back home, not even to redress the balance with a film based on the Vietcong. He wanted to refer to the civilian casualties, 'hundreds of nameless, faceless Vietnamese are blithely and casually shot, stabbed and blown to smithereens.' Stone's concluding question is this: 'Entire villages are laid to waste, with not one microsecond of thought or care given to those inside the little bamboo hamlets being napalmed. Who were they?'

Finally, it is not pleasant, but it is relevant, to note that this was a time of great upheaval for Stone, with the slow, inexorable collapse of his marriage to Elizabeth. It seems likely that this time of personal change, coupled with the great spiritual shift in his life, found an outlet, a mirror or a counterpoint in *Heaven and Earth*'s elegy to family, to faith and to country.

REAL PEOPLE: Le Ly Hayslip appears very much in the film as in the books, but there is an important coda that is never properly represented: the books incorporate her journey to reintegrate with her homeland, specifically the establishment of various clinics under the auspices of the East Meets West Foundation. This is the opportunity that Stone misses, the sense of a healing circle, a life altered almost to the point of destruction by the intervention of the West, converted into salvation through American support for her Foundation.

The other characters within the film are based closely on accounts from within Le Ly's book. Steve is a composite of several other men, of whom a few are drawn upon heavily. The man whose first name is used was a passing acquaintance. The initial encounter with Steve is drawn from her first meeting with Ed, an elderly civilian contractor. Likewise his opinion of Oriental women: 'I want . . . a good Oriental wife who knows how to take care of her men.' Ed briefly took her back to the United States before they returned to Vietnam, living on an army base deep in the countryside. It was here that she met Dante, a young major, who ensured the evacuation of Le Ly and her children, as shown in the film. She returned to the States and was introduced to Dennis Hayslip (from whom she takes her surname) by friends of Ed, who had died of emphysema. The American scenes are composite of Dennis and Ed, religious Middle Americans who, the latter especially, wanted to convert Le Ly from her Buddhism. It was while with Dennis, a gun collector, that Le Ly worked as a circuit board solderer. Dennis died after their messy divorce (see above). She met up again with Dante, who promised her a decent life after obtaining a lucrative contract, as the film's Steve did. She discovered that this was in the arms trade and that Dante was living off his parents. They broke up. Finally came Cliff, who provided the colour for Steve's psychosis. Cliff was, basically, a con man, adept in convincing others of his status as a high-rolling property developer (he knew Le Ly after she herself had become a prominent real estate dealer). His excuse, once his tricks had been discovered, was that he had been a veteran, involved in 'Psy-ops', the murders that so haunt Steve in the film.

Whether this was true, or a lie, it is material that appears in Le Ly's autobiography and which is used in the film.

INSPIRATION AND INFLUENCE: *Heaven and Earth* is one of the few entries into the packed genre of Hollywood Vietnam movies to be truly unique – no other film has presented a villager's eye view of the conflict.

The script is drawn from a faithful adaptation of a single source – the collected autobiography of Le Ly Hayslip, *When Heaven and Earth Changed Places* and *Child of War: Woman of Peace*. A comparable work to the bestselling *Wild Swans* (a story of three generations of Chinese women encompassing the civil war of the 1940s and the Cultural Revolution), these follow the experiences of Le Ly, almost identical to those she suffered in the film. In a sense the film finishes too soon and there is no acknowledgement of the later work she was to do in establishing public health centres in Vietnam, part of the output of the East Meets West Foundation.

There was condensing of the material. Two arrests by Republican South Vietnamese became one interrogation and, the biggest single alteration, Le Ly's experiences with eight American men are compressed into the character of Steve – see **REAL PEOPLE**.

There was also a degree of simplification. The village and routine of Ky La was re-created under the watchful eye of Le Ly herself, but as an isolated community. There is an uncomfortable hint of the new age primitivism that influenced liberal thinking in the 1990s – the idea of an idyllic simple peasant life. In reality, transport by bus and internal flight was common, and Le Ly was a member of a well-off family. Perhaps this is unjustified criticism – only so much can be shown in one film – but it does conform to Western stereotyping. This extends to Ahn, who by the end is portrayed as little more than a manual worker. In fact, though the Communist victory led to him losing much of his estate, he still maintained important contacts and stayed in regular correspondence with Le Ly (confusingly this correspondence is referred to just once in the film) and was vital to the establishment of the East Meets West Foundation.

But apart from this, even the most unlikely or apparently contrived events have their roots in the book: the ominous arrival of the American helicopter, the early conversation about Le Ly coming from her mother's 'belly-button', the changing of the flag to South Vietnamese, North Vietnamese and back to South Vietnamese on an almost daily basis, the struggle over religion when in America, an attempted rape in an employment office and the pursuit of Le Ly across Saigon by a smitten American. The one notable exception is Steve's suicide. Though this instability is based on Dennis Hayslip, who also suffered a mysterious death, the book reports it as accidental. While staking out a school attended by his and Le Ly's children he lit a fire in the back of his van to keep warm and asphyxiated.

REEL TIME: *Heaven and Earth* is beautiful in a way that is alien to every other of Stone's films. The first hour is framed landscapes, perfectly composed village photography and lush colours: travel brochure sequences. Even the arrival of foreign soldiers is conducted with artistic flair, destruction is wrought with a burnished orange flame, and the arrival of the helicopter is conducted with grand magnificence – a hat fluttering off in the breeze, which becomes a downward gale, washing across the rice paddies. It's a beautiful moment, and the air of ominous mystery is perfectly conveyed. The helicopter remains an object of dread throughout, involved in the black-and-white dream sequence where she imagines the death of her brother. This lasts until her eventual salvation through one of these machines.

The first act of the film, in Vietnam, invokes a documentary style of photography akin to *Salvador*, action and passivity caught through the lens of an objective reporter. Everything is conveyed from the perspective of truth. More accurately, through the use of light, filters and stock that suggest reality.

This contrasts with the second act, America, where artificiality is the watchword. Here a whole bag of tricks is opened. The production design steps up several notches, with earthy warmth replaced by the bright hues of synthetic clothing, a harsh lighting scheme and a larger-than-life set that suffocates the tiny figure of Hiep Thi Le. The culmination comes in the supermarket, a brash statement of American opulence, endless shelves stacked with produce and a sublime moment where Le Ly's stunned figure is enveloped in a fisheye lens, the shelves folding around her for a metaphor of American materialism embracing its newest communicant.

MUSIC: The Japanese composer Kitaro puts together a soaring score, reminiscent of John Williams but with a distinct Oriental edge, though the music is unexceptional, apart from the majestic opening sequence. It chatters along nicely enough, but fails to really hit the buttons. The exception comes in one fine shot in the midst of the introductory scene: a wandering conjurer releases a dove in slow motion, and the orchestra kicks in. It is shamelessly manipulative and, for a moment, sublime.

As with previous soundtracks, there is an invocation of period spirit through songs. In this case, middle-of-the-road saccharine tunes such as 'Mellow Yellow' by Donovan, 'Can't Take My Eyes off You' by Frankie Valli or 'Sugar, Sugar' by the Archies. Entirely appropriate tunes, suggesting middle-of-the-road, lower-middle-class America.

BOX OFFICE: A huge box office failure, *Heaven and Earth* was budgeted at $33 million but took only $5.9 million in US receipts. This is not that surprising in hindsight, the film received bad notices and was on a subject that would never be a hit at the multiplexes, especially with its underlying anti-Americanism. Nonetheless, this huge failure was somewhat of a shock.

CRITICS: Many reviewers were scathing in their criticism. 'It's that unusual combination of a film that is both gruelling to watch and unbelievably fatuous' (Anne Billson, *Sunday Telegraph*); '*Heaven and Earth* is a very brave film – and a very bad one' (Quentin Curtis, *Independent on Sunday*); 'Cry? I could have wept with boredom.' (Alexander Walker, *Evening Standard*).

Others were slightly more specific, a common complaint being the bludgeoning direction and superficiality. Hugo Davenport opined that 'the problem is not the story but Stone's relentless overstatement. He approaches the subject as though it was an emotional carpet-bombing mission.' Martin Woolacott commented on the emotional impact of the visceral imagery: 'when you give in to the intensity of his efforts . . . it is sometimes with a sense, not of being convinced, but of being subdued.' Angie Errigo wrote in *Today* that 'Humourless Stone makes a fiercely expert job of the action sequences . . . but he hams up the emotional moments into cringe-making melodrama.'

Others, however, were more positive. Nigel Andrews praised the scenes between Le Ly and Steve: 'Stone films these domestic corridor scenes with an intensity so fierce that they almost work,' going on to suggest that he 'might find more power – as any good artist finally does – in splitting the atom of personal encounter.' Roger Ebert was much more enthusiastic: 'In a time when few American directors are drawn toward political controversy, Stone seeks it out. He loves big subjects and approaches them fearlessly.'

Derek Malcolm thought the film composed of 'such thunderous brush-strokes that you don't always feel that they add up to much,' but added that 'Stone's sincerity, and filmmaking ability, is palpable throughout.' He was also positive on the main role: 'There is no doubt that the inexperienced Hiep Thi Le, required to age 30 years and act her socks off, gives a holding performance at its centre.'

Others took a different view on the young actress. 'Although Hiep Thi Le is a beauty and performs adequately, she does not have the power really needed to carry a film of this scope' (Angie Errigo, *Today*). The *Independent*'s critic saw Le Ly as secondary in Stone's eyes: 'the newcomer who plays Le Ly is radiant and sweet, but she can't hold her own opposite [Tommy Lee Jones] . . . Stone is more interested in him.' This was echoed in some critics' reprise of the theme of women in Stone's films. Geoff Brown observed that 'Stone has scarcely turned into a caring feminist,' suggesting – in answer to the question 'What went wrong?' – 'Maybe the effect of penetrating a woman's experiences over 30 years proved too much for him.'

On the subject of the film and Vietnam, there was enthusiasm: 'I reckon Oliver Stone's *Heaven and Earth* is the best of his Vietnam trilogy' (Sheridan Morley, *Sunday Express*). But there was also criticism. 'Stone isn't able to say much about Vietnam except that it's not America, or much about Hayslip that isn't about his own fantasies of otherness and oriental "wholeness"' (Jonathan Romney, *New Statesman*).

Sheila Johnston added an interesting comment on the film, '*Heaven and Earth* isn't a tragedy . . . The film is simply about the will to survive: it's a chain of travails without the psychological growth that would give the story structure and meaning.'

CONTROVERSY: One story on the film, reported at the time of release, seems bathetic in comparison with the furore surrounding *JFK*'s, but it adds a touch of irony. US immigration officials refused Le Ly's mother and sister entry to the country for the purpose of watching the film's premiere.

AWARDS: *Heaven and Earth* could not even take consolation from success at awards ceremonies to offset critical and financial failure. Kitaro won a Golden Globe for his score. Apart from that, there was nothing.

THE BIG PICTURE: There is something to be said for this film as a reaction to America, a response to the overwhelming hostility that greeted *JFK*, a conscious decision to move away from the US, both in mentality and subject.

Apart from this, there is the notion of a Vietnam trilogy. *Heaven and Earth*, *Platoon* and *Born on the Fourth of July* are biographies of people involved in the Vietnam conflict, each in sharp contrast to the others. They make for a powerful triptych.

FINAL ANALYSIS: In some ways a weaker cousin of *Born on the Fourth of July*, in others a bombastic variation on the theme of war's civilian casualties, *Heaven and Earth* actually comes across as a surprisingly delicate and engaging movie. The lack of a grand moral struggle takes a little getting used to within the context of other Oliver Stone movies, but is not entirely unwelcome.

In the opening scenes a visual spectacular unfolds through vignettes of village life lovingly re-created and photographed. There is a dip when the film moves to Saigon – dusty streets familiar from *Apocalypse Now* and *Full Metal Jacket*, undeserving of the attention lavished here (were it not for the imperative of the source material). Things pick up again with the introduction of Tommy Lee Jones, who powers the remainder of the film. Hiep Thi Le keeps things ticking over, and invests enough emotion to maintain momentum, but is unable to carry the film on her own. She is weighed down by a questionable script and the character is never as fully realised as Chris Taylor or Ron Kovic.

Lack of feminine empathy is a charge that dogs Stone's steps, and not without cause. If nothing else, however, this film proves that he is not an irredeemable misogynist in his filmmaking. However, his Le Ly is thin, especially given the material available. Part of this can be excused given the spiritual aspiration, but good intentions are not enough to make good cinema. Enchanting though *Heaven and Earth* may be visually, a nagging feeling is that Stone's most enjoyable work is with his brash, brassy, much-criticised but full-flavoured male-oriented movies.

Wild Palms

Stone was following in the footsteps of fellow director David Lynch when he became involved in the production of *Wild Palms*. Lynch had been the driving force behind *Twin Peaks*, a deliberately surreal, twisted tale revolving around the death of local girl Laura Palmer in the eponymous logging community. In late 1992, through Ixtlan, Stone signed on as executive producer to the six-hour mini-series *Wild Palms*.

Bruce Wagner had written the comic strip on which this was based for *Details* magazine, weaving a confusing story of kidnap, shady conspiracy and the borders between illusion and reality, set in contemporary Hollywood society. Harry Wyckoff is pulled into a nightmarish world through the Wild Palms Agency, its head Senator Anton Kreutzer, and its scheme to dominate the masses through a consciousness-altering drug Mimezine.

The TV series took these basic elements, but shifted the plot to 2007. The Wild Palms Agency was changed to Mimetech, a company tinkering with reality through holograms made interactive through Mimezine, an 'empathogen'. The story was more clearly defined, for instance, sketchy references in the comic were expanded into a war between the Fathers, an authoritarian group headed by Kreutzer and originating in his New Realism movement (at least partially inspired by Scientology), and the Friends, a resistance movement all but crushed by the Fathers' links with the government. The comic's dense web of family relations (everyone seems to be related through a variety of marriages and the substitution of newborn babies) added an element of soap opera, and perhaps pandered to Stone's own obsession with parent–child relationships.

As well as a regular cast, which included *Salvador*'s Jim Belushi, Kim Cattrall, Ernie Hudson and Robert Loggia, the series was sprinkled with cameos – Brad Dourif appears in several episodes and cyberpunk author William Gibson plays himself, as does Oliver Stone. In one rather self-indulgent moment the camera lingers on a chat show, where a grey-haired Stone is being interviewed about the supposed release of the files to do with the assassination of JFK fifteen years after Stone's own film and that the conspiracy turned out to be even larger than his film envisaged.

Wild Palms was broadcast in America in 1993 but failed to attract much attention, save that generated by the name of the executive producer. It is rather ponderous, and the soap elements sometimes melodramatic, but it is enthralling in places, even if its predictions for *JFK*'s validity in 2007 seem unlikely to be realised. Its questioning of the boundary between perception and reality has grown in popularity as a subject for movie sci-fi, for instance, in *eXistenZ* (David Cronenberg, 1999) and most famously in the *Matrix* trilogy (Andy and Larry Wachowski, 1999–2003).

Natural Born Killers (1994)

Warner Bros presents
In association with Regency Enterprises and Alcor Films
An Ixtlan/New Regency Production
In association with JD Productions
An Oliver Stone Film
Casting: Risa Bramon Garcia, Billy Hopkins and Heidi Levitt
Costume Designer: Richard Hornung
Edited by Hank Corwin, Brian Berdan
Production Designer: Victor Kempster
Director of Photographer: Robert Richardson ASC
Co-Producer: Rand Vassler
Executive Producers: Arnon Milchan, Thom Mount
Story by Quentin Tarantino
Screenplay by David Veloz, Richard Rutowski and Oliver Stone
Produced by Jane Hamsher, Dan Murphy and Clayton Townsend
Directed by Oliver Stone

CAST: Woody Harrelson (*Mickey Knox*), Juliette Lewis (*Mallory Knox*), Robert Downey Junior (*Wayne Gale*), Tommy Lee Jones (*Warden Dwight McClusky*), Tom Sizemore (*Detective Jack Scagnetti*), Rodney Dangerfield (*Mallory's Dad*), Russell Means (*Old Indian*), Pruitt Taylor Vance (*Kavanaugh*), Joe Grifasi (*Duncan Homolka*), Edie McClurg (*Mallory's Mom*), Kirk Baltz (*Roger*), Marshall Bell (*Deputy No. 1*), Everett Quinton (*Wurlitzer*), Balthazar Getty (*Gas Station Attendant*), O-Lan Jones (*Mabel the short-order chef*), Steven Wright (*Dr Emil Reingold*)

SUMMARY: A swift montage of mid-western American imagery (an eagle, a transcontinental freight train) gives way to a pre-credit sequence set in a sleazy roadside diner. A young man in sunglasses eats key lime pie while his girlfriend dances to the jukebox. A trio of rednecks walk in and one makes a move on the girl, sparking a bloodbath of guns, knives and brutal beatings. The young couple are Mickey and Mallory Knox and they have killed their way down dusty Highway 666.

A flashback reveals the details of their first meeting in the style of a cheap sitcom *I Love Mallory* – but the canned laughter is a response to Mallory's father's verbal abuse of his family and sexual abuse of his

193

daughter. Mickey, a meat delivery boy, arrives and it's love at first sight. He whisks Mallory off on a date in her father's new car, but the police chase him down. He takes advantage of a dust storm to escape from an outdoor prison detail, and gallops back to Mallory's house. They kill her abusive father and her mother, who did nothing to help her daughter, but let Mallory's brother go.

Their killing spree is related in a tawdry true-crime show: *American Maniacs*. The host, rabid Australian Wayne Gale, tells how the couple always leave one survivor as witness to their crimes. Mickey and Mallory marry in an impromptu ceremony on a bridge, conducted by Mickey. They drive into town and to a cheap motel where they make love, but are interrupted by Mickey's constant lascivious glances at a female hostage tied in the corner. Mallory runs off disgusted and seduces a local garage attendant, only to kill him because he was 'too eager'.

The next day super-cop Jack Scagnetti arrives at the garage crime scene. He has a barely hidden lust for Mallory and declares his intention to track the couple down. Later he murders a prostitute, as if attempting to commune with Mickey.

The Knoxes are lost in the desert, high on mushrooms. They stumble across an old Indian and are invited into his home. He has foreseen the arrival of these demons (whose inner thoughts and turmoil are, to him, literally written across their chests) and conducts some sort of ceremony over their bodies. But Mickey has vivid nightmares of his miserable childhood, and, semi-conscious, shoots the Indian dead. The pair are shocked that they have killed someone who genuinely reached out to them. They flee but the surrounding fields are full of rattlesnakes and both are badly bit. Mickey and Mallory arrive in a nearby town with its 'Drug Zone' – a lurid green pharmacy where they try to buy antivenin, an alarm is set off and Scagnetti is on the scene. Mallory is grabbed and cuffed and Mickey is savagely beaten.

One year later. Jack Scagnetti arrives at Batonga Penitentiary and meets with Warden Dwight McClusky to discuss Mickey and Mallory's incarceration. They are nominally to be transferred to a psychiatric institute, but all McClusky wants is to get them on the road where Scagnetti can find an excuse to kill them. However, before they can be shipped out, Wayne Gale asks to interview Mickey as a Superbowl special edition of *American Maniacs* and McClusky agrees, excited by the promise of celebrity.

The interview goes live, with the whole prison watching on TV. Mickey says violence is inherited and the audience sees his father commit suicide. He denies anyone is truly innocent, saying that murder is natural, that everyone has a secret sin in their past and that many people walk around 'already dead'. In killing them he is only acting as fate's messenger. His only real regret is killing the old Indian. He talks of his demon being slain by love of and for Mallory. The prisoners are excited by his delirious, semi-messianic ramblings. During the advert break, Scagnetti visits Mallory, who appears to seduce him but actually breaks his nose with a headbutt – the guards rescue him and hold her at gunpoint.

Mickey talks of the 'purity' of murder, of being evolved from Wayne – described as 'not even an ape . . . a media person' who, in selling murder makes it impure. He talks of being a 'natural born killer'. Wayne is ecstatic at the interview, but it has sparked a riot. McClusky leaves to coordinate the response and Mickey grabs a gun, shoots some of the guards and herds the survivors out of the room. He fights his way to Mallory's cell and kills Scagnetti. Together they shoot their way out, Wayne joins in, caught in the moment, while McClusky is torn apart by the mob – all of this caught on camera.

Somewhere out in the woods, Wayne finishes the interview: Mickey and Mallory are to stop killing and settle down, after taking Wayne's life – their last victim. When he argues that they need to leave a witness, they point to the camera that is still running. Wayne is gunned down.

A closing montage of killers, violence and famous media trials ends with a last shot of Mickey, a pregnant Mallory and their children in a mobile home on an unidentified highway.

ADVANCE PUBLICITY: The poster campaign emphasised the menacing image of Woody Harrelson, shaven-headed in pink John Lennon sunglasses, wielding a shotgun. The American theatrical trailer played off Oliver Stone's previous films, saying that they had examined America's past while this film would look at the present and the future – basically advertising it as a comment on contemporary society. It finished on a note that came close to capturing the spirit of the finished film. 'In the media circus of life, they were the main attraction.'

PRODUCTION HISTORY: In the late 1980s, Roger Avary wrote a lengthy synopsis for a potential movie entitled *End of the Road*, which he showed to friend Quentin Tarantino. Tarantino, still several years away from the breakthrough of *Reservoir Dogs* (1991), took the concept and created two screenplays, *True Romance*, which would be filmed by

Tony Scott in 1993, and *Natural Born Killers*. This latter screenplay he
developed with a friend, Rand Vassler. During the process (at about the
stage that weightlifting twins the Hun brothers offered $300,000 of
funding, see **CUT SCENES**) Tarantino got the greenlight to film
Reservoir Dogs. The facts are still in contention today, but Vassler was
left with the *Natural Born Killers* script on the vague condition that he
shoot 20 minutes on 16mm film as a 'guerrilla' project – independent,
ultra-low budget, effectively a home-made show reel to entice further
funding.

Vassler then met with Jane Hamsher and Don Murphy, co-founders of
JD Productions. Vassler had archaic paperwork establishing a claim to
the whole of *Natural Born Killers* and, presented with a live offer from a
production company and the potential funding that went with this,
signed over these rights on a two-year option. Shortly afterwards the
producers ditched Vassler as the nominal director of the project. He
launched a lawsuit but failed to make any progress, eventually agreeing
to take a co-producer credit.

The couple took the script around Hollywood, where it eventually
reached the hands of producer Thom Mount, with Sean Penn expressing
an interest in directing. Here the waters are muddied further, but Stone's
account places him at a dinner party with Mount and Penn: 'Thom told
me about the script at the table, but he didn't tell me that Sean Penn was
supposed to direct it . . . Days later I read it and told Thom it was a great
idea . . . Then I went back and found there was a whole devil's nest
involved.' Don Murphy recalls the next stage of development: '[Stone]
wanted to know if Sean Penn was really interested . . . [Mount] says,
"Well, why?" and Oliver says, "Well I might want to direct it," and in
the blink of an eye, Sean's out and Oliver can do it.'

Jane Hamsher and Dan Murphy met with Stone and eventually
pressed him to make *Natural Born Killers* as soon as *Heaven and Earth*
was finished, a speedy resolution being good for them too – their
two-year option was fast expiring.

Stone's own professed aims for the film were inconsistent. In a *New
York Times* article, written shortly before its release, he declared, 'I
really wanted to do a combination of a road movie, like *Bonnie and
Clyde*, and a prison film, like *The Great Escape* and *Papillon*.' In a
documentary on the making of the film, he stated his thoughts as 'let's
just lighten up and go for a summer action movie . . . something that
Arnold Schwarzenegger would be proud of.' An interview with Gregg
Kilday for *Entertainment Weekly* suggested he wanted to make 'a fast

road movie about mass-murder, the criminal-justice system, and the American media, and have wicked fun. A nasty-boy kind of thing.' The various contributors to the film would ensure the film touched these eclectic themes. Shortly before leaving for Thailand, Stone requested that Hamsher and Murphy arrange for a rewrite. David Veloz, a friend from USC and later a writer on *Behind Enemy Lines* (John Moore, 2001), did this for $5000 – providing much of the first act introduction of Mickey and Mallory (including *I Love Mallory*) and fleshing out their characters. On return from the Far East, Stone went through the script again with Richard Rutowski, weaving in the spiritual, shamanistic and demonist elements, developing themes and concerns expressed in *The Doors* and *Heaven and Earth*. Tarantino was unhappy to find what had happened with his script and declined screenwriter credit, instead appearing under the heading 'story by' (see **INSPIRATION AND INFLUENCE**).

Stone was halfway through a six-picture deal with Arnon Milchan, who agreed to provide backing. But there was still a need for the involvement of a major studio with their marketing and distribution muscle, and for this Stone turned to Warner Brothers. Their one condition was a bankable star in the lead role, requiring Stone to seek out a bigger name than the original proposition of Michael Madsen (*The Doors*) – Woody Harrelson was eventually chosen and Madsen had to be rather awkwardly 'un-cast'. What had been posited to Hamsher and Murphy as a 'quick, inexpensive project similar to *Talk Radio*' was now on the release schedule of a major studio, with a budget of $33 million.

The locations, like the story, would be split into two distinct parts. The road movie would take place in the dusty wastelands of the southern states, mainly New Mexico, with some work being done on a soundstage at Albuquerque. The style of the movie was anarchic and experimental and while much of this took the form of stocks, filters and lighting, some would be physically manifested on set. Rear-projection was used in the soundstage, but the cameras were also taken out on location, for instance to project footage on to the side of buildings. Additionally in the Indian's hut, words were projected directly on to the chests of Mickey and Mallory, while the vivid green tint in the Gallup drugstore was not the result of gels or filters, but had been created by the purchase and installation of several thousand green light bulbs, costing about $20,000.

Despite being mainly interiors, the second half, the jailbreak sequences, would be shot on location too: at Stateville maximum-security prison in Illinois. For the donation of a $50,000 cable

TV system and a daily wage of $25 for prisoner extras, the crew were allowed a remarkable degree of freedom, to the extent of shooting the riot with real prisoners.

The atmosphere on set matched the look of the film – chaotic in the extreme. Stone seemed to live up to his emotional involvement with whatever project is current. Robert Downey Jr said to a *Telegraph* journalist that 'a Saturday night with Oliver Stone after a long week is basically pagan Rome 26 AD.' Stone threw himself into frenzied partying and kept the anarchic rock and roll aesthetic of the soundtrack a key influence on set (see **MUSIC**). This excess extended to demands on the cast and crew. In two celebrated incidents, both Robert Richardson and a cameraman were injured in attempting to get the shot of Mallory running into the prison door (for which they used the simple technique of physically rushing the camera into the door). In the fight between Mallory and Scagnetti, Lewis physically smashed Sizemore's nose into the wall. Stone kept the camera's rolling – it is real blood oozing down Tom Sizemore's face.

Shooting was completed in 53 days, and the monumental editing process began. The movie was cut with stock footage culled from old horror movies, nature documentaries and newsreels, with many optical effects and plate projections (for instance the windows of Mickey and Mallory's motel room) were added. Eventually the film was complete, cut down to a summer-film friendly 2 hours in length. It was released in America in August 1994.

CASTING: Stone chose Woody Harrelson, from a list that included Kevin Costner and Mel Gibson, on the grounds that he saw a sickness in Harrelson, a hidden violence. He makes the part of Mickey his own, the physically powerful frame, offset by a deceptively sleepy farm boy look – a contradiction that reaches its zenith in the interview with Wayne Gale where Mickey takes on an almost predatory slyness, the look of a big-cat toying with his quarry. He also has great chemistry with Juliette Lewis, who does a comparable job with Mallory.

To an extent the film is an inversion of *Heaven and Earth* and Mallory a negative of Le Ly – a similarly powerful female character but aggressive rather than passively defensive. There were some problems with Lewis on set; she didn't, or wouldn't, respond to Oliver's demand for a muscled hardbody Mallory (the desired look was Linda Hamilton in *Terminator* 2) but ultimately she delivers a wild, witty and enjoyable performance.

Wild would perfectly describe the three other key players – Tommy Lee Jones, Tom Sizemore and Robert Downey Jr. Jones, with the theatrical mania of Warden McClusky, was saved from self-parody only by the universally weird tone of the film and Sizemore's Scagnetti is a mirror of Mickey, with a badge and a mission. Robert Downey Jr does great things with Wayne Gale, putting all the sleaze of the tabloid TV journalist up on the screen. The character is rather blunt satire and such a joke has been done before, for instance the obsequious Dick Thornberg in *Die Hard* (John McTiernan, 1988), but the idea is made fresh by Downey Junior's performance.

One other actor who calls for special mention is Rodney Dangerfield, who enjoyed an extended cameo as Mallory's disgusting debased father. A stand-up actor of Vaudevillian style, his normal approach is built around the one-liner, and his performance in a dramatic part occasionally seems awkward, but taken in the context of the sit-com pastiche it adds to the surreal and haunting quality of that sequence.

OLIVER'S ARMY: Alex Ho was not involved as producer on *Natural Born Killers*, his role being taken by Clayton Townsend. Like several editors before him (and like Robert Richardson after *U Turn*), Ho's relationship with Stone had run its course. Interviews on the subject of divisions tend to cite vague petty reasons for the splits, though when it comes to editors, Stone tends to speak of a programme of rolling apprenticeships, giving experience to editors who go on to do major work for Hollywood, a theory that holds some water when one looks at the subsequent career of colleagues such as Pietro Scalia (*Gladiator*, an Oscar for *Black Hawk Down*) and David Brenner (*Independence Day*). Ho and Stone had worked together since before the latter even became prominent as a director (see **Year of the Dragon**), and had directly collaborated on seven movies since 1986. This in itself is amazing, especially when given Stone's rather tempestuous reputation.

Stone was still surrounded by many familiar faces. The bond with his DOP seemed stronger than ever, despite some concern of the latter over the film's subject matter. Richardson contributed much to Stone's most visually inventive film, putting impressive experimental camerawork together under intense pressure. In Stone's words, 'I'm not the kind of director who likes to stop working; I like to keep the energy going. Bob has been terrific in that respect: he's flexible enough to keep shooting and find a way to do it no matter what the circumstances.'

Hank Corwin and Brian Berdan filled the gap left by David Brenner's departure, carrying out the demanding editorial task. There was also a more prominent position for Stone's friend Richard Rutowski, who assisted him on the screenplay, specifically adding the demonic influences that haunt Mickey and Mallory. Dale Dye was again credited as technical adviser. On screen he has a comical cameo as the partner of a police officer killed by Mickey and Mallory. Sean Stone played Mallory's brother.

Tommy Lee Jones provided, as he had done for *Heaven and Earth*, the main touchstone to previous films, this being his third performance in a Stone picture, drawing level with John C McGinley.

CUT SCENES: The violence of *Natural Born Killers* was an issue for the MPAA when it came to certification, and Stone had promised Warner Bros a rating of NC-17, rather than the more restrictive R, which would have limited potential box office. Stone says that their main problem was with the anarchism of the film, the chaos, non-linearity and fast, confusing cuts. Some of the more excessive scenes were trimmed, most notably the prison breakout sequence where images such as Warden McClusky's severed head impaled on a spike were removed. The gradual shaving away of the odd second of footage is best illustrated in the fact that 150 cuts removed only three minutes of screen time.

Five lengthier scenes were cut for reasons of time and pacing. Stone filmed a different introduction for the Indian, who initially finds Mickey and Mallory (rather than vice versa) while wandering the desert with his flock. Preceding this, the couple's argument turns nasty, with Mallory pulling a gun on Mickey when he comments that a man in the 1990s needs 'choice'. She makes him take off his trousers, when the Indian's sheep appear. One, a ram (fitted with a head mounted camera), charges Mickey, representing, according to Stone, a 'purity' that detects the demon in Mickey. He and Mallory eventually follow the Indian back to his hut.

A particularly unpleasant scene was at the trial of Mickey and Mallory, and is preceded by a lengthier sequence set outside the courtroom, including a cameo by Richard Rutowski, described as a 'weird man' by Wayne Gale. Mickey is defending himself and Mallory, and cross-examines the lone survivor of an attack on a teenager's slumber party. Played by Ashley Judd, the witness, Grace Mulberry, quakes in the box as Mallory graphically describes the death of her brother, arguing that as a nine-year student of the martial arts he should

OLIVER STONE Natural Born Killers

have been able to fight Mickey off. Grace calls Mickey a vampire and he makes a cryptic comment about fate, before saying that it is her time to die and stabbing her to death with a pencil. This is out of place in the context of the revised movie, when the Indian's death is supposed to begin their move away from violence. It is also quite harrowing to watch.

One brief cut-scene features a visit to a drive-in cinema en route to the Drug Zone and some apparently improvised dialogue on the meaning of death.

Two rather gratuitously indulgent scenes feature the comedians Steven Wright and Denis Leary. Wright remains in the film as a psychologist, but an extended take of his interview with Gale was filmed and then edited down. He describes the appeal of Mickey and Mallory to the young, and how the couple 'shocked a country numbed by violence'. Denis Leary's scene is totally irrelevant, featuring one of the sometime actor's trademark rants to camera. It's dull, ultimately meaningless and was thankfully cut.

Another scene cut to speed up the final act was an interview between Wayne and the Hun brothers, a pair of bodybuilding twins of moderate fame in America. They talk of having had their legs amputated by Mickey and Mallory (who stopped to apologise when they realised who the twins were) and how this has inspired them to do their best. It's pretty clunky stuff, featuring one great line: 'Never is a long time, Wayne.' The brothers had been early backers of the film, and the scene was filmed as part of a promise to include them in the movie.

As *Heaven and Earth* had an alternative beginning, so *Natural Born Killers* has an alternate ending. This downbeat variant reprises the role of the 'guardian angel', played by Arliss Howard, who appears briefly in the opening diner scene, reading a *New York Post*, and turns up at the end to lend a hand in Mickey and Mallory's escape. After Wayne's death he is in the back of Gale's TV van, with Mickey and Mallory in the front. He is disappointed when they tell him he has to get out and asks, if he cannot stay with them, could he just 'have a taste' of Mallory. Mickey gets angry and, just as they are about to throw him out of the van, he raises a shotgun and kills them both. This would have been a nihilistic step too far, and have further confused the film's verdict on its protagonists.

MEMORABLE QUOTES:

Mickey: 'You just got to hold that shotgun in your hand and it becomes clear like it did for me the first time. That's when I realised my one true calling in life.'

Gale: 'What's that, Mickey?'
Mickey: 'Shit, man. I'm a natural born killer.'

Gale: 'I'm alive for the first fucking time! Thanks to Mickey! Let's kill all these mother-fuckers!'
Mickey: 'Give me that [takes gun]. You're not centred, Wayne.'

GOOD VS EVIL: There are a number of relevant concepts in the film. The idea of Mickey as a force of nature and murder as natural, as opposed to the artificial restraints of society, expresses Stone's perennial argument against the establishment and conventional thinking. There is also the conflict between 'love' and 'the demon', perhaps best interpreted as compassion versus aggression. The most pertinent conflict within the film, however, is the one that includes the viewers of the film themselves.

The notion of 'audience' is omnipresent in the film be it in the form of TV viewers, the criminals in the jail or simply the survivors left at the scene of Mickey and Mallory's crimes. In a sense, if the film is guilty for showing violence then the viewer is accessory after the fact for lapping it up. The film asks the question, what does it mean to be watching a violent film, which suggests that the use of violence for purposes of entertainment is a great evil.

Mickey's description of murder as 'pure' is not the same as saying it is a positive thing to do on a regular basis. He means that murder, or killing, is a natural act, and only when repackaged in the name of popular entertainment does it become unnatural. The act of violence is wrong; so is the act of selling it.

The film is effectively saying, don't shoot the messenger (admittedly a questionable choice of cliché). There are films, TV shows, comics and books that have no compulsions about the use of violence as entertainment, and that choose to present this in such a way as to minimise discomfort to the viewer or reader.

Natural Born Killers may not be subtle, but it does leave the audience in an ambiguous position. If the audience can accept that Mickey and Mallory have moved beyond murder, through their realisation that their actions were a result of over-immersion in a violent popular culture, where does that leave the cinema audience?

REDEMPTION OR DAMNATION: At the end of the film, Mickey and Mallory choose to leave behind the media, literally walking out the frame of the camera. They have also chosen to leave behind their history of violence. A natural response would be to demand they do penance for their crimes, but this would be inconsistent within the context of the film, given that the pair redeem themselves through mutual love and a rejection of the media. The conventional method for punishment, imprisonment, is as much a target for criticism in this film as the media, though the blows Stone aims are less effective and less complex – it does not count as biting satire to paint a prison warden as a leering buffoon. Ultimately the prison exists as a contained setting in which Stone can unleash anarchic savagery, perhaps suggesting the consequences of a repressive penal system.

Stone views true penance and redemption in a more abstract, spiritual sense. The relationship of Mickey and Mallory is born in violence and aggression, but Stone argues for the development of love as a healing and a redeeming force.

In his interview with Wayne, Mickey speaks of love beating the demon. 'The demon' is ill-defined, but perhaps best seen as a combination of a heritage of violence (passed on by parents) and a culture of violence (as the Indian sees it, 'Too much TV'). This is the spark of optimism in a fairly black film: that true human compassion and care for another can overcome the veneer of violence that is part of human nature and exaggerated by an exploitative media. Mickey draws on his love for Mallory to overcome violent impulses, and they both choose to abandon the pervading culture of film and TV violence that literally 'demonised' them.

HISTORY 101: The end of *Natural Born Killers* includes a nightmare channel hop past coverage of the great media-hyped crimes of the mid-1990s; Stone calls it 'the demon gallery'. It includes the OJ Simpson highway pursuit, The Bobbett case, where a severed penis caught the attention of the whole country, the televised beating of black LA motorist Rodney King and the ice-skating scandal of Tonya Harding.

It's trash culture: history through the worst excesses of the media and *Natural Born Killers* came out at the perfect time to capitalise on it. With a similar degree of luck experienced with *Wall Street*, the OJ Simpson story broke in July 1994, just as work was being completed on the film.

STARS AND STRIPES: *Natural Born Killers* does for tabloid news shows what *Talk Radio* did for its titular medium. These are the preserve of 'journalists' such as Geraldo Rivera and Australian Steve Dunleavy and talk-show host Maury Povitch, whose watchwords are sensation, polemic and condescension. *American Maniacs* actually comes rather close to the bone, reminiscent of 'good guys always win' vulture shows such as *America's Dumbest Criminals*. In defence of Stone's bulldozer style, it's difficult to satirise a genre that's already so far over the top.

BEING OLIVER STONE: One way to view *Natural Born Killers* is as the raging storm that followed the calm eye of *Heaven and Earth*. If the Vietnam picture was a deep, cleansing breath then this is the raging exhalation, expressing the turmoil that surrounded his personal life at the time. Stone's second marriage was in the process of collapse – as filming progressed he and Elizabeth went through a trial separation in April, a brief reconciliation and an abortive request for divorce on her part in May. The couple finally broke up in August 1994.

Part of the fury was also rooted in another uneasy relationship – that with the media. Since *JFK* Stone had come to see himself as persecuted by the press. In interviews with mainstream publications (less so with specialist film magazines) his attitude is quite often hostile and occasionally verges on the paranoid. Given the barrage of criticism levelled at him for the assassination epic, this attitude is easy to understand. In *Natural Born Killers* he presents his reply: the press as manipulative and hypocritical in the relation between their subjects and their audience.

INSPIRATION AND INFLUENCE: As mentioned above (see **PRODUCTION HISTORY**), Stone saw *Natural Born Killers* as his road movie, specifically naming *Bonnie and Clyde* (Arthur Penn, 1967). This was one of the films to usher in the brief Hollywood New Wave of the 1970s: deliberately technical and self-consciously cinematic, adopting the point of view of nominal bad guys and glamorising their actions, laying on the bloody violence and finishing with a downbeat ending. It's possible to spot the influence of *Bonnie and Clyde* in general tone as well as specific details – in both cases the male half of the couple is arrested for car theft, and both feature a relentless police officer, operating on the very edge of the law.

A greater specific influence was Quentin Tarantino's original screenplay, eventually published in 1995, despite opposition from Oliver Stone. Tarantino jumps from the diner scene straight to Batonga penitentiary. *American Maniacs* takes up a greater portion of the script (some 38 pages out of a total 117) and deals with their career in comprehensive flashback, running through numerous hold-ups (briefly hinted at in Stone's version), cop murders and the trial itself, including the brutal murder of Grace Mulberry (see **CUT SCENES**). There is also a film-within-a-film, *Thrill Killers*, presented as a movie of their exploits and echoed in the restaging of Patrolman Gerald Nash's murder in Stone's *American Maniacs*, as well as references to a rock band releasing a record about the couple. There is greater investigation into the special sentence they received (life without parole and without any form of contact, explaining Mickey's unsent letters) and the reasons for the transfer to Nystrom Psychiatric Hospital.

It also dwells longer on Wayne and his crew, who are given specific personalities and the usual Tarantino pop-culture debate over which of Spielberg's films is the best and a conversation about doughnuts. The interview is much slacker, and the riot breaks out for no particular reason – Mickey and Mallory are able to use it as cover for escape, when they kill Wayne – for personal reasons rather than the scathing hatred of the media in general present in the film.

There are a few changes to other characters. Scagnetti is not the wannabe Mickey of the film, and has few distinguishing characteristics. He's a 'supercop', and an author, but is recruited solely to assassinate the couple. He makes no attempt to seduce Mallory, but does mace her, in revenge for which she later kills him. McClusky is a high-level bureaucrat who quickly leaves the story – it is Wurlitzer who leads the guards against the riot, which is never manifested in the scale it has on film. Indeed, it is only referred to, never actually portrayed.

Heavy-handed Stone may be, but there is a purpose to the film that is difficult to spot in this rather thin screenplay, in which the violence, more intense and focussed, has even less point. Mickey and Mallory still escape, using an 'underground railroad' of their adoring fans, whom the couple plan to visit and presumably kill – there is little indication of a change to their lifestyle. Ultimately there is no purpose to Tarantino's script, beyond an elaborate joke around the couple's habit of leaving a witness behind, building to the punchline of Wayne's camera being the final witness.

REEL TIME: One of Stone's most frequently repeated quotes is from William Blake: 'The road of excess leads to the palace of wisdom.' If this maxim applies to any of his films it applies to *Natural Born Killers*. The hallucinatory styling of *The Doors* is brought together with the frantically chopped editing of *JFK* to create a film that greatly exceeds the sum of its parts. The list of source material is impressive: standard 35mm film (colour and black and white), 16mm, Super-8 footage (the wedding scene on the bridge), Beta (the format used for TV shows, employed for *I Love Mallory*) and front and rear projection (the driving sequences, and sometimes used to shoot footage directly on to the side of buildings) while hardcore animation, stock footage and movie-clips were cut directly into the film. The angles used are many, varied and often strange, the editing is violent and the lighting is far from natural, frequently sickly and virulently intrusive. Says Stone, 'I didn't want to portray realistic murder because it's been well done ... in *In Cold Blood* [Richard Brooks, 1967] and ... *Henry, Portrait of a Serial Killer* [John McNaughton, 1990].' Instead, he deliberately rejected reality: 'The style we chose was perfect for this particular film: it reflects that hallucinogenic quality that is in the killers' minds.'

There are frequently two layers to the visual images, the foreground action of the scene and a further layer of images indicating a seething undercurrent of anger and violence – for instance in the motel scene, the windows are filled with images of sickness, historical violence and brutal images from contemporary action movies, or in the Indian's hut, where Mickey and Mallory's inner natures are projected on to their bodies. Another ongoing theme is green as the colour of sickness: in the Drug Zone pharmacy, or the key lime pie in the diner.

Robert Richardson speaks of a change in the second act: 'we went to a very conservative approach in the prison to settle the film back down.' This is not to say things turn conventional, there is still a sudden close-up here, a cut to stock footage there, and the overall effect is quite disconcerting and underlines a gradual build up of pressure released in the riot sequence. Just before the violence kicks off there is the visually impressive interview between Mickey and Gale, distinctive tints to the lights for each participant and one of Robertson's distinctive techniques – a harsh downlight producing a glowing corona, a halo around the subject's head, here focussed on Mickey.

Ultimately, there is no overall 'look' to a film so frantically experimental that the director himself has said, 'There are things in the movie that are still beyond my fingertips, beyond comprehension.' It is uniquely distinctive, not only among Stone's own films but in the context of American cinema. Perhaps the closest any other filmmaker has got is Quentin Tarantino with *Kill Bill* (2003/4), on which Bob Richardson was cinematographer, and which ironically owes a great debt to *Natural Born Killer*'s groundbreaking style.

MUSIC: On the subject of the editing, one writer asserted that 'under the knife of Brian Berdan and Hank Corwin, *Natural Born Killers* becomes the ultimate music video.' The soundtrack certainly reads like a roster for a music video channel, albeit a particularly eclectic one, partially due to Jane Hamsher who suggested tracks from left-field contemporary artists. From the hard rock of L7 and Nine Inch Nails (front man Trent Reznor was involved in the compilation), through 50s rockabilly (The Shangri-La's 'Leader of the Pack'), to the punk of Patti Smith, Bob Dylan's crooning (his song 'You Belong to Me' was included by his special permission), rap from Dr Dre and ska from the Specials, topped and tailed with the resonant gloomy voice of Leonard Cohen on 'The Future'.

Its mish-mash of styles, with little regard for continuity or sensibility, is perfect for this confrontational film. Indeed, confrontation was the order of the day while filming. As Jane Hamsher puts it, when it came to the shoot, 'Oliver would frequently have a song already in mind that he wanted to use as playback on the set to create a strong ambience.' Actual filming would be accompanied by ear-splitting rock music and other random noise.

BOX OFFICE: The sizeable $50 million budget was (just) cleared by US box office takings of $50.3 million. The movie picked up sizeable receipts in other territories and in video takings, eventually making a decent profit.

CRITICS: The *Daily Mail* led the charge against *Natural Born Killers*, in its reviews as well as the comment. Its critic, Christopher Tookey, said that it 'amounts to a feature length advert for mass killing'. Others riffed on the wave of notoriety the film had attracted, raising its profile above a level that the content justified. The critic for *Time Out* summed this up: 'Trailing hype and ludicrous tabloid hysteria in its wake, Oliver Stone's film is at once a phenomenon (you should see it) and unremarkable (you'll probably be disappointed).' Nigel Andrews was of a similar opinion: '*Natural Born Killers* is a passionately mad, frequently bad, passably interesting, probably unmissable movie.' He concluded on a negative note: 'We sense an artist who has become enmeshed in – nay, who has leapt to embrace – the very crassness and crudity he seeks to discredit.' Others echoed this qualification: 'It's an impressive spectacle, but behind the pyrotechnics is a trite pseudo-admonishment about America's couch-potato conspiracy,' wrote Desson Howe in the *Washington Post*.

Many writers condemned the film for glorifying violence. Hal Hinson wrote that 'The main problem with *Killers* . . . is that it degenerates into the very thing it criticises.' *Rolling Stone* concurred, suggesting a longer history to Stone's production of cheap entertainment, 'Though Stone holds up a mirror to a dark world, he's too chickenshit to hold it up to himself . . . Stone has been in the exploitation game as far back as *Seizure*.' Quentin Curtis contended that 'by muffing his point about the dehumanising force of television, Stone actually invites his audience to glory in his glamorous killers.'

Some focussed on the lack of subtlety. The *Telegraph* said, 'it's a sustained assault on the senses, shot in MTV style, with all the pinpoint accuracy of an elephant gun in the hands of an enraged chimpanzee.' The critic for the *Village Voice* brought a nice turn of phrase: 'Stone never fences with a rapier when he can wrap his hands around a Louisville Slugger.' Roger Ebert put the lack of subtlety in a positive light: 'Stone has never been a director known for understatement or subtlety. He'll do anything to get his effect, and that's one of the things I value about him.'

Time built on the idea of a visual assault: '*Natural Born Killers* plunders every visual trick of *avant garde* and mainstream cinema,' concluding, '*Natural Born Killers* is the most excessive, exasperating, most . . . let's just say it's the *most* movie in quite some time.' *New Statesman* presented things a little more negatively: 'it certainly represents some breakthrough in terms of the speed and intensity with which it marshals its images, but it does so without any sense of rhetorical complexity.' Alexander Walker was of a similar opinion: 'by pushing an on-off button on an editing table you actually demote human creativity. You end up with an overload of mechanically induced sensations.'

There was derision at Stone's claims for his film as satire. 'Mr Stone could well turn out to be the most influential American filmmaker of his generation. But as a satirist, he's an elephant ballerina' (Janet Maslin, *New York Times*); '*Natural Born Killers*, alas, is satire on the media made by someone with absolutely no sense of humour' (Anne Billson, *Sunday Telegraph*).

CONTROVERSY: While *JFK* came under sustained attack for its historical assertions, *Natural Born Killers* was hit at from pretty much every angle. The initial stages of the film's release were overshadowed by a very public spat between Stone and Tarantino, blown out of proportion by a media obsessed with conflict between two generations of radical filmmakers. The actual 'fight' was mundane: it amounted to a refusal on Tarantino's part to go and see the film, while Stone attempted to block publication of the original screenplay (see **INSPIRATION AND INFLUENCE**). More brutal was the feud that built up between Tarantino and Jane Hamsher and Don Murphy, the young co-founders of JD Productions, whom Tarantino accused of stealing the script.

It took several months for the film to achieve the level of infamy it carries with it today. In England, the film had the misfortune to be released in the wake of the Jamie Bulger child murder case, when tabloid newspapers were calling for harsh restrictions on the distribution of what they saw as violent, exploitative movies. While being assessed by the British Board of Film Classification (BBFC) a campaign, headed by the *Daily Mail*, called for the film to be banned. The BBFC fudged the issue, refusing to set a troublesome precedent that would result from banning the film, but also refusing to allow its release. For months the film sat in limbo – at the one authorised screening (for the 1994 London Film Festival) tickets changed hands for around £100 each. Eventually it was approved for release towards the end of February 1995. Warner Brothers became ultra-sensitive about the film, and, in the wake of the 1996 Dunblane school massacre, the studio indefinitely suspended the film's release on video; it was not until 2001 that *Natural Born Killers* was finally released on to the UK domestic market on video and DVD.

The majority of the 'copycat' killings for which *Natural Born Killers* was blamed took place in the US and its name was linked with a number of violent murders in Georgia, Utah, Louisiana and even Paris. In Louisiana in March 1995, a friend of lawyer-turned-novelist John Grisham – Cotton Gin owner Bill Savage – was murdered by killers who said in their statement that they took LSD before watching *Natural Born Killers* 20 times. Arguing that the makers of a film should have the same responsibilities as the makers of any other product, and should be liable for any illegal acts caused by that product, Grisham suggested that there were grounds for a lawsuit against the director and the studio. The family of another victim of the pair, Patsy Ann Byers, took this advice and launched a lawsuit against Oliver Stone. In March 1999, the Supreme Court ruled that Stone was not protected against such a lawsuit by the right to free expression. A verdict with huge implications for the future of the film industry was averted when the Louisiana court finally threw out the case in March 2001.

AWARDS: Stone received a nomination as Best Director at the Golden Globes but aside from that the slate of major awards was clear. The film was luckier at the Venice Film Festival where Juliette Lewis was named best actress, and the film itself received a special jury award. Lewis was also nominated, with Woody Harrelson, in the best couple and best screen kiss categories at the MTV music awards.

THE BIG PICTURE: Stone returns with great vigour to a diagnosis of an American sickness he first began in *Talk Radio*, having just presented the malady through the eyes of an outsider (*Heaven and Earth*). If *Talk Radio* had shown a man desperate to make a difference to a radio audience interested only in cheap titillation, *Natural Born Killers* exaggerates the theme of entertainment, pointing the blame at a cinema audience who, in the earlier film, had been permitted to sneer at Barry Champlain's moronic callers. In both *Heaven and Earth* and *Talk Radio* the travails of the protagonist, one finding eventual peace and the other succumbing to perpetual turmoil released only by death, take centre stage. Here the priority is the message (as with *JFK*). Mickey and Mallory's personal development is ultimately secondary and it is important that their eventual salvation comes when they literally walk out of the shot (an effect marred by the coda in the mobile home).

At least part of this message is the condemnation of Hollywood exploitation films and it seems, from the video montage in Mickey's motel room, that he counts *Scarface* and *Midnight Express* among these films. As an attempt to defuse cries of 'hypocrite', this is an astute move.

FINAL ANALYSIS: As satire, *Natural Born Killers* is neither the deft scalpel of Jonathan Swift nor the schoolboy sneering of *Private Eye*. Rather, it is a Technicolor bulldozer, powering out of the screen with a complete absence of subtlety or ambiguity. This is little surprise from Oliver Stone.

In a primitive sense, Stone's distasteful view on murder is right. What Mickey and Mallory did, and what murderers and rapists the world over do, harkens back to mankind's dark primeval nature, which is more powerful and much older than the news stories or action films that glorify or lasciviously condemn such actions. Stone is calling for greater care and less frivolity in exploring these darker regions of the mind, while at the same time asking the audience, if you abhor violence such as this, why keep watching it on the TV and in sanitised action films? In an inverted echo of Stone's desire to make a 'Summer blockbuster' (probably never serious in the first place), screenwriter Larry Gross wrote of the film's relevance to the usual batch of flash-bang machine-gun operas churned out by the major studios, '*Natural Born Killers*'s secret Utopian ambition is to put Hollywood Action Cinema out of business. It can't be purified. It can only be razed to the ground.'

It's not an easy film to like. It lays itself open to misinterpretation, is wilfully populated with a collection of thoroughly unlikeable characters and, even if watched sympathetically, presents a great challenge to the audience. However, it startles with its visual technique and features a strong core of performances. Powerful and ugly but thought-provoking.

Nixon (1995)

From Hollywood Pictures
Andrew G Vajna presents
An Illusion Entertainment Group/Cinergi production
An Oliver Stone Film
Casting: Billy Hopkins, Heidi Levitt, Mary Vernieu
Production Consultants: Robert Scheer, Christopher Weilles Scheer
Costumes designed by Richard Hornung
Music by John Williams
Co-Producers: Eric Hamburg, Dan Halsted
Edited by Brian Berdan and Hank Corwin
Production Designer: Victor Kempster
Director of Photography: Robert Richardson ASC
Produced by Clayton Townsend, Oliver Stone, Andrew G Vajna
Written by Stephen J Rivele, Christopher Wilkinson and Oliver Stone
Directed by Oliver Stone

CAST: Anthony Hopkins (*Richard Nixon*), Joan Allen (*Pat Nixon*), Powers Boothe (*General Alexander Haig*), Ed Harris (*E Howard Hunt*), Bob Hoskins (*J Edgar Hoover*), EG Marshall (*John Mitchell*), David Paymer (*Ron Ziegler*), David Hyde Pierce (*John Dean*), Paul Sorvino (*Henry Kissinger*), Mary Steenburgen (*Hannah Nixon*), JT Walsh (*John Ehrlichman*), James Woods (*HR 'Bob' Haldeman*), Brian Bedford (*Clyde Tolson*), Kevin Dunn (*Charles Colson*), Fyvush Finkel (*Murray Chotiner*), Annabeth Gish (*Julie Nixon*), Tony Goldwyn (*Harold Nixon*), Larry Hagman ('*Jack Jones*'), Ed Herrman (*Nelson Rockefeller*), Madeline Kahn (*Martha Mitchell*), Saul Rubinek (*Herb Klein*), Tony Lo

Bianco (*Johnny Roselli*), Robert Beltran (*Frank Sturgis*), John Diehl (*G Gordon Liddy*), John Cunningham (*Bob – Dept. of Labor Film*), John C McGinley (*Earl – Dept. of Labor Film*), Michael Chiklis (*TV Director*), Joanna Going (*Young Student*), David Barry Gray (*Richard Nixon – Aged 19*), George Plimpton (*President's Lawyer*), Corey Carrier (*Richard Nixon – Aged 12*), Tom Bower (*Frank Nixon*), John Bedford Lloyd (*Cuban Man*), James Pickens (*Black Orator*), Bridgitte Wilson (*Sandy*), Ric Young (*Mao Tse Tung*), Tony Plana (*Manolo Sanchez*)

NOTABLE CREDITS: Giving the impression that even the film thinks itself to be too long, the credits run over Hopkins's version of Nixon's rambling resignation speech. As the actor leaves the White House, the film cuts to footage of the real man on his departure. Then comes Stone's own closing narration and a montage of significant members of the cast – for the first time since *The Doors*.

SUMMARY: (The following is taken from the director's cut of the film.) Opening caption cards:

This film is a dramatic interpretation of events and characters based on public sources and an incomplete historical record. Some scenes and events are presented as composites or have been hypothesized or condensed.

For what is a man profited if he shall gain the whole world and lose his soul? Matthew 16:26

The Watergate burglars prepare for their operation. The film cuts to police mug shots taken after their capture.

1972 – 18 months later. General Alexander Haig pads through a darkened White House. Over the soundtrack are extracts from news reports of the time – reference to John Dean's testimony and to Alexander Butterfield's revelation of a hidden taping system. Haig walks into a sombre, fire-lit room where President Richard Nixon is sitting in the darkness. Haig hands over a selection of tapes and, after threading them on to the spools of the player, leaves Nixon alone.

The tapes take the audience back to a discussion in the Oval Office following the Watergate break-in between Nixon, Bob Haldeman (his chief of staff at the time), John Ehrlichman (his domestic policy adviser) and John Dean (legal counsel to the president). There is little to link the burglars to the White House, except the revelation that one burglar – E

Howard Hunt – is still registered as a White House consultant. Nixon wants Hunt paid off, and the FBI investigation into the burglary derailed – Haldeman is ordered to warn Helms of 'the whole Bay of Pigs thing'.

Eighteen months into the future: Nixon reflects back to the 1960 election. The film focuses on a key point in that election – the TV debate between Nixon and John F Kennedy. Nixon, sweaty, flustered and ill is confronted by Kennedy's promise of complete support for Cuban attempts to overthrow Fidel Castro. Nixon cannot bring himself to breach national security in answering (plans are already afoot to effect an invasion). On election night, defeated, Nixon reflects on his father, who was a failure too.

There is a black-and-white flashback to Whittier, California, in 1925, and Frank Nixon's grocery store. The audience sees Richard's brothers, older rambunctious Harold, younger Arthur and Donald, Richard's own subservient relationship with his mother, a demanding, highly religious woman, and the austere, tough nature of his father.

1930–4: Richard's failed attempts to play football for Whittier College.

1962, and another defeat for Nixon in the race for Governor of California.

There is conflict between Pat and Richard, and threat of divorce. Nixon promises not to campaign again, and he delivers a rambling concession speech, promising the reporters that they won't have Dick Nixon 'to kick around any more'.

Nixon's apparent political obituary is told through a pseudo-newsreel commentary. His early victories and election to the House of Representatives as an anti-Communist and his rise to the Senate are shown; also his seat on the House Un-American Affairs Committee, his ruthless prosecution of suspected spy Alger Hiss (convicted of perjury) and his eventual two terms as vice president including the famous 'Chequers speech' in which he successfully defended himself against accusations of corruption.

At a cocktail party in 1963, Nixon meets with prospective Republican candidate for 1964 Nelson Rockefeller and old friend John Mitchell. Nixon complains of missing the thrill of politics and feeling mentally deadened. Mitchell advises he makes some money.

22 November that year and Nixon is a spokesman for Studebaker at an exhibition in Dallas. One of the rich Texans present invites Nixon to a private party, where he and his friends urge the politician to run in 1964, citing his strong anti-Castro and anti-Communist credentials, and brushing aside any objections Nixon has regarding John Kennedy and

Lyndon Johnson. The ominous discussion reaches a conclusion and an uneasy Nixon flies out from the very airport at which JFK is about to arrive.

A television reports Kennedy's upcoming funeral. As Nixon's mind wanders, he recalls the death of his own brother, the younger Arthur, from meningitis.

Lyndon Johnson declines to run in 1968, encouraging Nixon, who announces his candidacy over Pat's objections. He attends a public debate and comes over as charismatic and confident.

J Edgar Hoover is impressed by the debate and is looking for an alternative to Bobby Kennedy for President. He meets with Nixon at a racetrack, and steers him away from embarrassment in the form of Johnny Roselli, a gangster. Hoover promises support to Nixon, as long as Nixon supports him.

Back in 1972, Nixon discusses this meeting with Haldeman. The gangster, it emerges, was involved in Track 2 – a swingeing CIA programme to promote covert assassinations in Africa, the Far East, Latin America and Cuba. The mafia were involved because of a common hatred of anti-gambling Castro and Nixon was the White House liaison. CIA man Howard Hunt also worked on Track 2, as did many of the Cubans later involved at Watergate. Kennedy wasn't told about Track 2 when he took office, and didn't find out until after the Bay of Pigs.

Nixon recalls the deaths of John and Bobby Kennedy as clearing his way into the White House, but expresses his victory as over four bodies, the third being Arthur and the fourth Harold. Another flashback to the early 1930s and the audience see Harold in the advanced stages of tuberculosis. It was this death that meant Richard would be the Nixon son to attend college, and which set him on his political path.

The film snaps back to the Republican Convention of 1968. Nixon's victory speech immediately cuts to footage from the secret bombing missions Nixon was to launch into Cambodia, in an attempt to flatten VC training camps, and install a government subservient to US interests.

The bombings lead to protests and the protests result in the shooting of four students at Kent State University. At a dinner on the presidential yacht, Nixon is hard on the protesters but in private he admits that he cares, insisting that the public figure of Nixon cannot be seen to care.

Protests intensify and Nixon travels to an inconclusive meeting with Richard Helms of the CIA. He demands greater involvement of the agency in domestic surveillance of radical student groups (he is convinced that they are in the pay of Russia) and the return of controversial private papers – the documents that link him with Track 2.

Late one night he questions his Cuban valet Manolo over the people's love for Kennedy. He is upset at the ongoing student protest and drives out to the Lincoln Memorial at the dead of night to meet with some of the protesters. There is little agreement, but just before Nixon is hustled away by his Secret Service agents, he hears a young female student describe the huge military-industrial-espionage complex as 'the beast' and all but admits his lack of control over it.

The story jumps forward to the wedding of his daughter, Tricia Nixon, held at the White House. Nixon confers with Hoover, complaining of an epidemic of leaks. Hoover recommends that Lyndon Johnson's bugging equipment be reinstalled – he informs the President that Kissinger is already recording all phone calls. Later, at the wedding, Nixon is pulled to one side and informed of the Pentagon papers leak.

A meeting is quickly convened. Nixon and Kissinger rage against State Department official Daniel Ellsberg, the man behind the leaks. Charles Colson, special counsel to the President, recommends the formation of 'the Plumbers' – a White House investigation team to plug leaks.

Nixon meets with his cabinet, laying into them and promising no mercy for any leakers. The audience are then taken to China, and the historic 1972 meeting with Mao Tse Tung. On Air Force One, the press congratulate Nixon over the success of his mission.

He meets again with the Texans who are displeased by the lack of action over Cuba and the continuation of Lyndon Johnson's civil rights programme. But Nixon holds firm, if the men want to take their money elsewhere they could give it to segregationist candidate George Wallace, a move that would lead to the election of left-wing Democrat George McGovern. Nixon crushes McGovern in the 1972 election.

Again the camera follows Nixon and his team aboard Air Force One. He hears a report that the Vietnamese have accepted the Paris Peace Plan, but also that Kissinger is the source of many of the leaks. He talks of the harsh sentences passed on the Watergate burglars, nearly 40 years in some cases, in an attempt to force testimony. The plane hits a knot of turbulence, as if to signify the beginning of the administration's end.

Things unravel quickly – Dean, Ehrlichman and Haldeman all resign, and Nixon tries to present this as an end to the controversy but, after a frosty dinner scene between Pat and Richard (the former pointing out the latter's increasing isolation), Dean is seen testifying against the White House. A visit from Russian premiere Brezhnev is a shambles, with Nixon more concerned about the growing fragility of his presidency.

The audience hear Alex Butterfield's revelation of the White House taping system and see Nixon erase the infamous 18.5 minutes of tape. A brief snatch of the tape is suggestive: 'whoever killed Kennedy came from this thing we created, this beast . . .'

Nixon is weakened after an attack of phlebitis, but he refuses to give in. He orders the sacking of Archibald Cox, assigned to prosecute the case by the Justice Department, which leads to a constitutional crisis. Impeachment hearings are imminent and Kissinger and Haig press him into resignation. Weeping and cursing, he is led off into the shadows by his wife. However, the end credits frame a triumphal coda, with an emotional farewell speech, and the presence of five presidents at his funeral in 1994.

ADVANCE PUBLICITY: As with *JFK*, an early draft of the script was leaked to the press (specifically the magazines *Time* and *Newsweek*), who promptly presented it as a crazy conspiracy film (see **CONTROVERSY**). There was a concerted effort at a pre-emptive defence. An annotated screenplay was published before the film had even been released. This featured the original script (though quite different from the finished film – see **INSPIRATION AND INFLUENCE**) complete with 168 footnotes to historical works and original sources, a collection of essays written for the publication, including works by Nixon associates John Dean and Alexander Butterfield, Watergate burglars Eugenio Martinez and E Howard Hunt and screenwriters Stephen Rivele and Chris Wilkinson and a substantial slice of original sources: memos, letters and transcripts of Nixon's tapes. This was supplemented by a CD-ROM release which featured many more original documents as well as documentary video footage.

The American theatrical trailer entirely sidelined Oliver Stone's involvement, focussing on Hopkins's performance as Nixon. It's a clumsy effort, though to be fair the film does not lend itself to soundbite summary. Most of the best lines are in there, but it was ultimately impossible to cut the slow thoughtful film into trailer format. It was similarly difficult to capture the film's spirit on poster: the result a gloomy effort with Hopkins's Nixon peering out of the shadows. In an attempt to jazz it up, the original tagline, 'He knew everything about power – except its price,' was changed to 'The president can bomb whoever he wants.'

PRODUCTION HISTORY: With *Natural Born Killers* in the editing suite, Oliver Stone began searching for his next project. A number of titles were under consideration, most on the theme of political biography. *Hoover* was one suggestion, based on a book by Curt Gentry about the infamous FBI director. *The Mayor of Castro Street* was another, a biopic of San Francisco politician Harvey Milk – the first openly gay man to secure significant political office only to be murdered in 1978 by an anti-gay conservative. The story of Martin Luther King and his assassination was almost filmed as *Memphis* – though this clashed with another project on the civil-rights activist under development by Jerry Weintraub, and was eventually dropped. *Noriega* seemed the firm favourite for a while. Al Pacino had been cast as the disgraced Panamanian dictator, and pre-production was under way. However, there were doubts over the script. As Stone puts it, 'The tone of the piece was never clear . . . He was sometimes a buffoon and sometimes this horrific figure. It was varying all over the place.' When the decision to cancel the project finally came, Pacino's contract had reached its 'pay or play' stage – even without a film, he had become entitled to a $10 million payoff. Instead, an agreement was reached to cast the actor in a future film (see **Any Given Sunday**).

Eric Hamburg (see **JFK**), now employed at Ixtlan, had suggested Richard Nixon as a subject and commissioned a script from JFK researcher Stephen J Rivele (who had postulated the involvement of the Corsican mafia in the assassination) and his writing partner Chris Wilkinson. They worked on the idea of Nixon as a self-contradictory personality and developed the concept of 'the beast'. Stone carried out rewriting work on the script, assisted by creative input from *Los Angeles Times* columnist and author Bob Scheer, and his son Christopher.

Despite a brief revival of interest in *Evita* (see **The Ones That Got Away**, p. 47), the first drafts of the script of *Nixon* had been completed and it became Stone's next film.

But the production hit a snag when it came to funding. Warner Brothers and Arnon Milchan were unwilling to back *Nixon* to the degree required by Stone, who asked for over $40 million for what amounted to a 3.5 hour period piece revolving around a pack of middle-aged men in suits. Eventually, Stone turned to Andy Vajna at Cinergi, who used his company's affiliation with Disney to raise the $42 million budget. Stone's end of the project was not managed through Ixtlan, but rather the Illusion Entertainment Group, a separate production company run for Stone by Dan Halsted.

This deal was completed only five weeks before the start of the shoot – up to then Stone had personally financed some four weeks of pre-production and rehearsals. Filming began on 1 May 1995. For the first time since *Talk Radio* location shoots would not play a major part in a Stone film. Instead, the film was shot almost entirely on a Los Angeles sound stage, with a small amount of filming, primarily establishing shots, in Long Beach and Washington DC. One piece of luck for the crew was the recent completion of the Rob Reiner film *The American President* (1995), from which *Nixon* borrowed the Oval Office set, having made a few minor changes to establish 1970s period detail. As usual authenticity was important, and Stone had support from a range of well-connected technical advisers – most of the living participants in the Watergate saga were involved, consulted with or contacted and people such as John Dean (who appeared in the *March of Time* sequence), Howard Hunt, John Ehrlichman and Alexander Butterfield lent on-set advice (the latter putting together a re-creation of the White House taping apparatus).

After a 61-day shoot editing began. In a 1996 interview Stone described the combination of team and individual effort: 'We had Brian [Berdan] in one room, Hank [Corwin] in another and Tom Nordberg [Associate Editor] in a third.' Each editor would assemble a sequence and then 'The scenes would revolve from one room to another depending on how successful they were' until Stone judged them complete. Indeed, the consistently complex nature of editing in Stone's films led the same interviewer to suggest that the director had 'taken the possibilities for improvisation and rewriting in the post-production/ editing process to a new level'.

Nixon had its US release in December 1995.

CASTING: The most surprising piece of casting in *Nixon* was that of the title role. Stone was originally after Warren Beatty, but Beatty declined. Stone then asked Tom Hanks and Jack Nicholson, but neither expressed interest. Though the idea of Hanks in the role is odd, the final choice was no less surprising.

Stone traces the decision back to one of Hopkins's most celebrated films: 'When I saw him in *The Remains of the Day* [James Ivory, 1993] I saw that sense of depression and isolation which I felt about Nixon.' He later expanded upon this: '[Hopkins] had that necessary roughness, gruffness. At the same time he had enough sensitivity to really allow us to see into his window, his eyes.'

Some criticised the lack of a physical resemblance, and this was accentuated by a decision to minimise the use of prosthetics; a false nose was experimented with – see the newsreel footage of Nixon's early campaigns – but ultimately abandoned, and Hopkins's only physical aids were a sculpted widow's peak wig, a set of false teeth and brown contact lenses. Hopkins was initially reluctant to take the role, and it took several visits to London by Stone, and a threat to offer the part to Gary Oldman, before he finally agreed. In interview, Hopkins has put the case from his perspective: 'I sensed that this wasn't just an opportunity to play a great part . . . it would be a personal challenge – a chance . . . to do something truly risky.'

The voice fluctuates, sometimes verging on a Welsh lilt, and the lack of resemblance is occasionally distracting – though there are brief moments where Hopkins comes scarily close to the hunched shape of Nixon. It is in the mannerisms that he is most successful, the joyless salesman's smile, the neck turtled into perpetually hunched shoulders, the contrived V-sign gesture of triumph. It is possible to interpret the snarling, pacing performance as verging on pantomime, though it might be more instructive to think of Hopkins's exaggerated gestures as conveying Nixon's exaggerated attributes: his great tenacity, insatiable hunger for power and looming paranoia.

While still in contention for the part, Warren Beatty had conducted a reading for Stone, with Joan Allen standing in for Pat Nixon. Afterwards, Beatty reportedly turned to the director and said, 'But, Oliver, look no further. You've got your Pat right here.' Allen was a successful stage actress, who had enjoyed a quiet but distinguished movie career. She puts in a solid supporting performance as Pat Nixon, aided by a startling physical resemblance, and manages to use the character's comparatively brief screen time to really bring home one of the film's key points: the barriers Nixon built up, isolating himself even from family.

Another great supporting performance, aided by uncanny similarity in appearance, was Paul Sorvino's Henry Kissinger. He captures the academic's chubby swarthiness and monotone grumble. It was somewhat of a departure from Sorvino's previous most prominent role, gang boss Paulie in *Goodfellas* (Martin Scorsese, 1990). *Nixon* is a gangster film of sorts, but Kissinger was always an outsider to the Anglo-Saxon inner circle of Haldeman, Ehrlichman, Mitchell and Dean.

The latter three of these are all well represented, Ehrlichman by JT Walsh, a stock character actor, ubiquitous in the 1990s until his untimely death in 1998, Mitchell by EG Marshall, who plays the former attorney-general as a grandfather figure, and the part of Dean going to nasal, nervy David Hyde Pierce. Cameos went to Larry Hagman, playing an unscrupulous Texas oilman in the style of JR Ewing, his character from *Dallas*, and George Plimpton, a prominent east coast literary figure and editor of the *Paris Review* (he died in 2003).

British actors were well represented in the movie. As well as Hopkins, cockney actor Bob Hoskins was given the role of J Edgar Hoover, playing him with pantomime-intensity as a revolting toad, greasy but with great influence. A big theme of the film is Nixon's obsession with his mother and one final piece of notable casting was Mary Steenburgen. Steenburgen treads a careful line here, trying to capture both a compassionate but deeply religious mother, and the domineering shadow she cast over the rest of Nixon's life. The script gives little opportunity for softness in Hannah, but Steenburgen lends a degree of warmth to what could have been a cold, loveless character.

OLIVER'S ARMY: James Woods returned to the cast of an Oliver Stone film for the first time in nearly ten years. Bob Haldeman was a strait-laced conservative, and Woods does a good job in reigning in his more extreme tendencies. He had done little of great interest since *Salvador*, save his wriggly performance as a feckless con-man in *Casino* (Martin Scorsese, 1995).

Tony Plana made his third appearance as Nixon's valet. Chuck Pfeiffer reprised his role as a Teutonic Secret Service agent from *Born on the Fourth of July* (another Secret Service agent at the racecourse was played by Stanley White, see **Year of the Dragon**) while John C McGinley clocked up his fourth Stone film. Saul Rubinek had appeared in *Wall Street* as Gekko's lawyer.

Three Stone family members featured too: Sean as Richard's brother Donald, though not referred to by name in the film; youngest Stone brother Michael as youngest Nixon brother Edward (in the scene following Harold's funeral); and Oliver himself as the unseen interviewer of Nixon's mother. He also provided voice-over for the epilogue at Nixon's funeral.

There was *almost* complete continuity of major crewmembers. Risa Bramon Garcia left casting in the hands of Billy Hopkins and Heidi Levitt, who were joined by Mary Vernieu (formerly a casting associate on Stone's films since *The Doors*). Garcia has since moved into directing with quirky indie film *200 Cigarettes* (1999). John Williams returned to provide his third score for a Stone film (see **MUSIC**).

CUT SCENES: A recent director's cut restored some 28 minutes of footage to the original three-hour cut of *Nixon*. The main beneficiary of these changes was Sam Waterston's refined, urbane and slightly deranged performance as CIA Director Richard Helms. The original script postulated an intricate subplot on the subject of secret papers implicating Nixon in a covert action programme in various African, Asian and South American states (see **SUMMARY**). In one lengthy sequence, the president and Helms clash over the fate of these papers. Later, Dean's call that Mitchell be sacrificed to the Watergate investigators is padded out by Haldeman's report on Helms's rage over mentions of the 'Bay of Pigs thing' – linked to these documents. These scenes end up as dead weight, undercutting some of the film's more serious concerns with tiresome speculation. Other sequences include a cabinet meeting held shortly after Nixon's return from China where he rages against leaks and a brief scene set before Tricia's wedding where Hoover inspires the installation of a recording system.

In addition, there were a number of scenes that crop up in the published screenplay and were filmed, but never made it into the extended special edition. An extended version of Nelson Rockefeller's reception featured additional dialogue between Rockefeller and Nixon, emphasising how far the latter had fallen since his defeat in California, and predicting the Republican defeat of 1964. It also allowed a more formal introduction for Nixon and Kissinger and expressions of mutual admiration. Dropped for length, it stayed out of the director's cut, and rightly so. The Kissinger introduction is superfluous, and awkward. There is plenty of opportunity in later scenes to view the odd love/hate relationship posited between the two men.

A brief addition to the first Jack Jones meeting provides a needless barbeque introduction for Sandy (the prostitute) and Nixon, while a second Jack Jones scene features a bull-riding sequence, hinting unsubtly at 'the beast'. The scene is pointless and detracts from one of Nixon's few screen triumphs, suggesting that he went to the ranch to beg for campaign funds and so undercutting the scene where Nixon threatens the tycoon. A final addition comes after the China summit where Nixon talks of the electoral consequences of recognising communist China – of voting blocs won and lost. It's a rare presentation of Nixon's political acumen but meaningless in the context of the film.

MEMORABLE QUOTES:

Nixon: 'I'm not powerless. Because . . . because I understand the system, I believe I can control it. Maybe not control it totally. But . . . tame it enough to make it do some good.'

Young Woman: 'It sounds like you're talking about some wild animal.'

Nixon: 'Yeah . . . well maybe I am.'

Nixon (to Kennedy's portrait): 'When they look at you they see what they want to be. When they look at me they see what they are.'

GOOD VS EVIL: In building the screenplay for *Nixon*, Stephen Rivele and Christopher Wilkinson invented a concept they called 'the Beast', a self-sustaining entity of pure conservative, reactionary instinct simultaneously unaware of its existence. A twisted gestalt of military-industrial complex, ultra-rich Wall Street financiers, the intelligent community and every extremist special-interest group extant within the American body politic, Wilkinson described 'the Beast' as 'a headless monster lurching through post-war American History, instinctively seeking figureheads to wear its public face . . . destroying them when they no longer serve its purpose'. Wilkinson goes on to say, 'The Beast also became a metaphor for the dark side of Nixon himself. The monster within that relentlessly drove him.' The ongoing battle of *Nixon* is both external and internal. External against those forces that perpetuated the Vietnam War and continued their own agenda against his wishes, internal against his base political instincts: the hatred, jealousy and paranoia that drove him, that took him to such extremes in defeating his domestic 'enemies'.

The good is a less tangible force in this film. There is a sense of it in Nixon's strict Quaker upbringing, in his belief in the inherent goodness of the conservative silent majority and in his foreign policy, reopening relations with Russia and China. But the film is primarily interested in decline, in, as Kissinger says towards the end, 'the defects of his qualities'. A parabolic career where the same tenacity and uncompromising aggression that took him to the presidency would eventually seal the end of his administration.

Struggle is at the very heart of this film but, as a tragedy, this dark side is both more interesting and inevitably victorious.

REDEMPTION OR DAMNATION: Oliver Stone described Richard Nixon as 'a giant of a tragic figure in the classical Greek or

Shakespearean tradition. Humble origins, rising to the top, then crashing down in a heap of hubris.' With this in mind, it is scarcely a surprise that Nixon ends up damned, a victim of those darker impulses that win the moral conflict at this film's centre.

As presented by Stone it is the paranoid obsession with bugging his opponents, plugging leaks by any means necessary and lying so as not to show weakness that leads eventually to this downfall. So convinced is he that the leaks he sees as damaging to the administration come from inside the White House that he even bugs himself, and thus records the evidence that destroys him.

HISTORY 101: It is important to distinguish, as far as possible, between established fact and speculation. By and large, fact forms a skeleton on which the speculation and subjective representation of Nixon are built. The film explains this basic history well, especially in the *March of Time* newsreel. Nixon climbed rapidly through the House of Representatives and the Senate, partially through his hard-right persona of the time. He had a rocky period as Eisenhower's vice president, yet survived and was only narrowly defeated in 1960.

After election in 1968 he enjoyed a golden period of foreign policy (excepting the sizeable matter of increased bombing programmes in South East Asia). Nixon's early days are also accurate in broad terms, though the family dynamic shown on screen is very much a subjective psychological interpretation.

There are several specific events which, while not necessarily fiction, are still very dubious assertions given unwarranted credibility by the context. Track 2 is far from fully established, as is the idea that Nixon was in charge of any such policy while serving as vice president – this was justified by Stone largely on the basis that someone in government must have approved Track 2 as initiated by Dulles, CIA chief in the 1950s – see **CONSPIRACY THEORY**. Having said that, this is not fictional alternative history in the style of *Fatherland* (Christopher Menaul, 1994), which posits a German victory in World War II. It is rather a highly subjective interpretation of solid research. As with earlier works, Stone displayed great attention to the smallest details. For instance, at the dinner on the presidential yacht the teetotal Ehrlichman is shown drinking a glass of milk.

Some scenes were the result of compression for reasons of time, as the caption card forewarned. The meeting between Hunt and Dean on a bridge was especially criticised as never taking place, but Stone justifies it as a way of cutting out the Byzantine way by which Hunt's demands for money were conveyed to the White House and by which payment of these demands were met.

CONSPIRACY THEORY: In a sense the highly subjective nature of the film renders the entire movie an elaborate conspiracy theory, with the manipulation of established fact to a particular end. There is one particular thread running through the film that can be linked with the polemical counter-history of *JFK*. Along with the fictional creation of Jack Jones, the embodiment of the wealthy reactionary interest, with an implied willingness to circumvent democracy to achieve its ends, Stone, with his screenwriters, plants a personal theory on the 18.5-minute gap on Nixon's tapes. The film suggests that Nixon believed Kennedy's assassins were a product of Track 2.

Nixon establishes an idea that could be linked to many of Stone's movies: the beast. As a force in the film, it is chilling and powerful. As a theory of history it is almost laughable, but perhaps not entirely without merit; it connects with Stone's avowed intention to get people thinking, to prevent them from mere acceptance of what is reported and taught.

BEING OLIVER STONE: On return from Vietnam Stone was only peripherally involved with student protests against Nixon. This is not to say he was apolitical or opposed to the protesters, more that he rejected their halfway measures. 'I was into more radical violence. When they took over NYU and all the kids trashed the place when Cambodia was invaded I thought they were nuts.' Stone's own suggestion: 'I said, if you want to protest, let's get a sniper scope and *do* Nixon.'

These views have mellowed somewhat in the interceding 25 years, but there still burns a passionate commitment to his country and to serious political commentary.

REAL PEOPLE: Unsurprisingly with a biopic, pretty much every character in *Nixon* is based on and named after a real person in the life of the president, from the Watergate burglars to the man himself.

Henry Kissinger worked for failed Republican candidate Nelson Rockefeller before becoming Nixon's National Security Adviser and all-round foreign policy guru, a key player in the diplomatic recognition of China. He became Secretary of State in 1973, holding the position through to 1977. Kissinger remains a highly controversial figure, whose role in the overthrow of Salvador Allende's left-wing Chilean government in 1973 and bombing of Cambodia has come back under the spotlight in more recent times.

Key presidential advisers – Haldeman, Ehrlichman, Mitchell and Dean – remain most famous for their roles in the Watergate cover-up. Haldeman and Ehrlichman were responsible for counsel, while Mitchell was a long-time confidant of the President, appointed Attorney-General until his resignation in 1972, when he became Campaign Manager of CREEP (the Committee to RE-Elect the President). Incidentally, the film is broadly accurate in its representation of his wife Martha – as an individual she caused constant headaches for those trying to engineer the cover-up. Dean handled the legal implications to Nixon.

These people (along with Alexander Butterfield, an aide to Bob Haldeman, Charles Colson, another presidential adviser, G Gordon Liddy, a former aide to Ehrlichman and staffer on CREEP, Howard Hunt, White House Consultant, spy novelist and CIA operative and Ron Ziegler, a former Disneyland tour guide and associate of Haldeman's ad firm turned Press Secretary) made up 'The President's Men' a term referring to the inner-circle of loyal advisers whose ranks thinned out through resignation. For instance, the simultaneous resignation/sacking of Haldeman, Ehrlichman and Dean led to the appointment of General Alexander Haig, formerly an adviser to Henry Kissinger, to the post of Chief of Staff. Hoover was still Director of the FBI, and had been since 1924 with companion Clyde Tolson – though the film's fairly heavy insinuations of homosexuality remain unproven.

Jack Jones is a fabrication, as is Trini Cardoza, though the latter bears a resemblance to Bebe Rebozo, Nixon's closest friend outside politics. At the centre of this film is Nixon himself and a key idea here is that of Nixon as a chameleon: the character separates official, presidential decisions through use of the third person; the screenplay recycles Kennedy's adage about Nixon having to choose who he was going to be on any one day; and the newsreel narrator comments that 'we never knew who Richard Nixon really was'. Given the lack of historical consensus, and given the disclaimer at the start of the film, Stone's particular spin on Nixon, as an ambitious man constantly struggling against evil both internal and external, haunted by religious guilt but mired in the mud of politics, paranoid and angry but incredibly sensitive, is as valid as any other.

INSPIRATION AND INFLUENCE: As mentioned above, many sources of information were consulted to provide the research for *Nixon*. Three biographies formed the foundation: from the left, the psycho-biography of Fawn Brodie, *Richard Nixon: the Shaping of his Character*; Stephen Ambrose's conservative multi-volume work *Nixon: the Education of a Politician 1913–62*, *Nixon: the Triumph of a Politician 1962–72*, *Nixon: Ruin and Recovery 1973–90*; and from the right, *Nixon: a Life* written by former British MP Jonathan Aitken.

The only book to be explicitly mentioned in the credits as an influence was *The Final Days*, a comprehensive examination of the last 100 days of the Nixon administration by Watergate journalists Bob Woodward and Carl Bernstein. This provided many of the incidental details that filled out the latter stages of the film – nothing is a complete fabrication – and some of the lines ('the cowardice of the Eastern establishment' was in reality attributed to Kissinger while Pat had said of the recording system, 'the tapes were like love letters'). While it seems somewhat dramatic to suggest civil war towards the end of the film and the suggestion was never seriously raised in Woodward and Bernstein's work, both Gerald Ford's transition team and Leon Jaworski's investigators raised the question of what to do had Nixon tried to use the military to stay in power.

Stone has mentioned the influence of classic directors such as Sergei Eisenstein and DW Griffith on the style and look of Nixon, but the biggest single cinematic influence was Orson Welles's *Citizen Kane* (1941). On a thematic level, both films dealt with a quest to find the true identity of a great man.

REEL TIME: After *JFK* and *Natural Born Killers*, the look of *Nixon* seems oddly staid and classical. This is strange, as this film is at least as idiosyncratic as Stone's earlier political effort. Stocks are changed rapidly, indeed more effectively and consistently, with black and white employed for Nixon's early years and hand-cranked footage (on both 16mm and 35mm film) used to recreate historical footage, while digital alteration is employed, sparingly, to insert Anthony Hopkins into period film, in the style of *Zelig* (Woody Allen, 1983) and *Forrest Gump* (Robert Zemeckis, 1994). The impression of a less adventurous style is down to a more static camera. A lot of the film consists of men in suits, talking. There was a lot of dialogue to be covered, and simply not enough time to allow for fancy camerawork, though the movie is not devoid of deliberate cinematic art. In places it is comparable to *Wall Street*, in the way the camera darts ahead of or pursues its subject. Cameras placed at high angles are employed to give an overbearing gravity to many of the scenes. The lights are positioned to create striking, expressionist shadows of the scenes where Nixon is alone with his tapes (sometimes the lights required for this effect – and for Robert Richardson's trademark 'halo' of bright light around a subject's head – were so powerful that they set light to tables and even the carpet).

MUSIC: This would be John Williams's last score for Oliver Stone to date. It is perfectly adequate, yet seems less imaginative than *Born on the Fourth of July*'s soaring orchestral style, or *JFK*'s portentous anti-march. There's something derivative about Williams's interpretation, a stridency cheaply reminiscent of the composer's imperial march from *Star Wars* (George Lucas, 1977). This resemblance is perhaps not surprising given Williams's prolific output.

A few songs crop up in the soundtrack too, notably 'Fever', which runs somewhat incongruously over an explanation of Track 2's origins. Probably the finest moment of the score is during the operation on Nixon's phlebitis, a chaotic melange of sound, ending with a delicate piece of ragtime jazz, over some Kennedy home videos – a poignant reminder of presidential mortality.

BOX OFFICE: *Nixon* flopped badly with a $50 million budget yet only $13.5 million receipts at the US box office. *JFK* had offset an intimidating running time with a blazing press controversy, powerful publicity machine and dynamic subject matter – a mystery surrounding the death of a president. Richard Nixon proved a less enticing draw.

CRITICS: There was a broadly positive reaction from critics. Roger Ebert described *Nixon* as 'One of the year's best films.' Desson Howe wrote, 'Oliver Stone's bullying, obsessive style works like a treat in *Nixon* . . . You may disagree . . . But you will not be bored.' Alexander Walker rated the film highest in the context of the director's back catalogue: 'A great film then? Not quite, but Stone's best to date.' Derek Malcolm praised both the movie and its star: 'It is an extraordinary roller-coaster ride, capped by a great actor stretched to the limit by his part.' He had earlier written, 'If this isn't an Oscar-winning performance, made up equally of reticence and bravura, I don't know what is.'

Malcolm's words on Hopkins were far from typical. The *Sunday Telegraph*'s verdict was that 'Anthony Hopkins is miscast. It's not that he gives a bad performance . . . it's just that the actor can't help sounding Welsh.' The *San Francisco Examiner* said that he 'all too often looks more like Ed Sullivan than Nixon'. *Rolling Stone* separated the category of resemblance and performance, saying that it was a 'bum impersonation but a towering performance . . . as the infamous Tricky Dick'. This was as close to a consensus as opinion on Hopkins would get.

The argument on history reached a form of synthesis, best expressed by Alexander Walker – 'Film is not objective. Nor is history. Both are complex constructs that rework individual interpretations to suit the ends of historians or biographers.' Derek Malcolm put it slightly differently: 'That this history is sometimes painted in garish terms is indisputable . . . but . . . the film succeeds in suggesting that the truth can often be stranger than fiction.'

The pounding camerawork, usually cause for congratulation in a Stone picture also came in for criticism. Christopher Tookey believed that 'Stone's technique of intercutting black-and-white with colour footage is even more obtrusive and less illuminating than it was in *Natural Born Killers*.' James Delingpole chipped in: 'There is indeed something nauseating about the busy camera-work, choppy editing and hallucinogenic visuals . . . it leaves you feeling too ill to be bored.'

There was much discussion concerning 'the beast', the most cynical comment coming from the *Sunday Times*, which said that this narrative construct 'would, it seem, consist of everyone minus whoever is the subject of Stone's current film'. One opinion echoed down the line from *Platoon* onwards was repeated in the *Sunday Telegraph*: 'recast each of Stone's movies with Oliver Stone in the lead and you wouldn't go far wrong, especially since they're as much about the director's psyche as about the modern history of America.'

CONTROVERSY: Attacks came thick and fast in the media, but from a much smaller (if no less vociferous) group than the detractors of *JFK*. The target for these attacks was the factual basis, or lack thereof. An opening salvo came from Richard Nixon's own family. *The Times* quotes a statement made by his daughter, Tricia, saying that the filmmakers:

> concocted imaginary scenes of the Nixons' private life, Richard Nixon's family life as a boy and a young man and his public life that are calculated solely and maliciously to defame and degrade President and Mrs Nixon's memories in the mind of the American public.

This criticism had not been based on a viewing of the film, however, but a leaked copy of the script, though it focussed on a central concern in the film – Nixon's alleged involvement in 'Track 2'.

Former Nixon speechwriter and *New York Times* columnist William Safire weighed in, describing the film as a 'hatchet job' by a 'cinematic pseudo-historian' and again identifying the key transgression as an attempt 'to tie Nixon in to murders in the Eisenhower years'.

Those whose works were used as background were also negative: Jonathan Aitken refuted Stone's claims in a lengthy article for the *Daily Telegraph* and Stephen Ambrose criticised his work as referenced in the published screenplay. He had a point – in the screenplay Stone cites page 84 of Ambrose's second Nixon volume as proof of the President's heavy drinking. In fact, the passage reads, 'whatever Nixon's problems in life . . . alcohol was not one of them.' As with *JFK*, however, every accusation has a refutation. In his review for the *Independent on Sunday*, Quentin Curtis quoted a later passage of Ambrose (speaking of the possibility of Nixon having a drink problem): 'There is much conflicting evidence on both sides of the question, enough to make any final judgement impossible.' This quote, taken out of context, might do well to sum up the debate over *Nixon* – many may have grumbled, but no one could conclusively disprove its hypotheses.

AWARDS: Heidi Levitt picked up an award from the Casting Society of America in recognition of the diverse assembly of actors; for similar reasons, the whole cast was nominated by the Screen Actors Guild. Major awards were thin on the ground, though the film picked up four Oscar nominations – male and female actor for Anthony Hopkins and Joan Allen, one for adapted screenplay and one for John Williams's score.

THE BIG PICTURE: *Nixon* at first seems a perfect companion piece to *JFK*. However, it has more in common with *The Doors*, *Born on the Fourth of July* and *Platoon* as a 1960s biography of a protagonist living in the shadow of 'the beast'. There are also strands reaching back to *Salvador* – the state of play in 1980s South America is partly a legacy of Nixon's policies.

To date, Stone has yet to return to the 1960s/70s for inspiration; in fact, he has closed the book on future productions based on American politics and politicians: 'through Kennedy and Nixon, I was able to say everything I had to say. Now I'm finished.'

FINAL ANALYSIS: It's not history, not in the sense of dry tomes, nor is it a simple dramatised life. It is rare to see a cinematic biography whose subject is neither lionised nor damned and Stone is keen to condemn the environment in which Nixon worked more than the man himself, who is presented as a doomed, tragic figure. *Nixon* echoes contemporary study with its portrayal of the subject, an enigmatic character of whom this picture suggests a certain interpretation. Given Stone's reputation for polemic, it is no surprise that there is a determinedly subjective bent to the narrative. This is not an even-handed study, but nor is it smug denunciation. Stone has put together a great work here (despite some weak moments of conjecture), which relies on solid research as much as sensationalism. He makes little attempt to paint Nixon as the archetypal bugbear to liberals. He chooses, instead, to sketch an angry, paranoid, complex man – a fascinating portrait, albeit one that many might disagree with.

But universal agreement is not something that, one imagines, Stone would regard favourably. What is important is to see Nixon as more than the crook of left-wing legend or a staunch conservative hero, immune to any criticism. In this reading, more might have been gained from looking at Nixon's domestic legislation (establishment of the Environmental Protection Agency (EPA), civil rights) or even expansion on his foreign policy (his historical visits to the Middle East) – examining his career through established policies rather than pondering on grey, ill-defined hypotheses.

Stone's extra-American viewers might question the point and the detail of this film. This is to ignore an involving study in obsession with power and its ephemeral nature in the modern world: a man can occupy the pinnacle of political power and still change little. In this sense, at least, *Nixon* is universally relevant.

U Turn (1997)

Phoenix pictures presents
An Illusion Entertainment Group Production
In Association with Clyde is Hungry Films
An Oliver Stone Movie
Casting by Mary Vernieu
Co-Producer: Richard Rutowski
Costumes Design: Beatrix Aruna Pasztor
Music Composed, Orchestrated and Conducted by Ennio Morricone

OLIVER STONE U Turn

Executive Music Producer: Budd Carr
Edited by Hank Corwin, Thomas J Nordberg
Production Designer: Victor Kempster
Director of Photography: Robert Richardson ASC
Executive Producer: John Ridley
Produced by Dan Halsted, Clayton Townsend
Screenplay by John Ridley
Based on the book *Stray Dogs* by John Ridley
Directed by Oliver Stone

CAST: Sean Penn (*Bobby Cooper*), Nick Nolte (*Jake McKenna*), Jennifer Lopez (*Grace McKenna*), Powers Boothe (*Sheriff Potter*), Claire Danes (*Jenny*), Joaquin Phoenix (*Toby N Tucker*), Billy Bob Thornton (*Darrell*), Jon Voight (*Blind Man*), Abrahim Benrubi (*Biker No. 1*), Julie Haggerty (*Flo*), Bo Hopkins (*Ed*), Valery Nikolaev (*Mr Arkady*)

NOTABLE CREDITS: The description in the opening credits of an 'Oliver Stone Movie' suggests *U Turn* is to be more frivolous than its predecessors.

SUMMARY: Drifter Bobby Cooper is racing across the desert with $30,000 cash to pay off a Russian gangster in Las Vegas, a gangster who has already chopped off two of Bobby's fingers. In the middle of Arizona his Ford Mustang blows its radiator hose. The nearest town is Superior and the damaged car limps to its one gas station, run by grease-caked mechanic Darrell. With a long wait for repairs and the temperature rising, Bobby shoulders the bag with the money and heads to a diner.

On the way he meets Grace McKenna, a beautiful, sultry Native American girl. He flirts with her and together they go back to her house. They are kissing when her husband, local real-estate salesman Jake unexpectedly bursts in. He attacks Bobby, who makes a quick exit. As Bobby walks back into town, he is intercepted by Jake, who offers him a lift. During the journey Jake reveals that he is sick of his wife and offers Bobby, whom he pegs as an unscrupulous rogue, a cut of her life insurance (some $50,000) to kill her. Bobby turns this down, and heads to the grocery store to buy a soda. However, he is caught up in an armed robbery, during which the money in the bag is blown to smithereens.

Now desperate, Bobby heads back to the garage in an attempt to retrieve his car. But Darrell is asking $150 for the repairs – money that Bobby doesn't have. Back in town, the drifter calls everyone he can think of, from ex-girlfriends to his mother, all of whom hang up on him. Finally he tries Mr Arkady, the gangster to whom he owes the money. This goes no better, and Arkady dispatches a henchman to Superior.

After an interlude in a diner, where a young thug called Toby 'TNT' Tucker challenges him to a fight for a perceived slight on his girlfriend, Bobby slouches to McKenna's office, where Jake talks of his strange marriage – he was married to Grace's mother after the death of her first husband, Grace's father. Bobby finally agrees to kill Grace for $10,000. He is to make it look like an accident so takes her to local landmark Apache Leap. She speaks of her sad history – her mother died after a strange fall from the cliff – and he cannot bring himself to kill her; instead they make love. Afterwards, Grace tells him of $100,000 hidden in Jake's safe, but he wants nothing to do with it, not quite trusting her. Back in town, Bobby has another run in with TNT, before being picked up by the sheriff, Virgil Potter. Potter is highly suspicious of the man, effectively recommending that he leave town. Bobby tries to do so, first begging Darrell to let him off the $150 (Darrell not only refuses, but raises the price to $200), then scrounging a bus ticket to Juarez, Mexico. On his way out of the depot, he sees Arkady's henchman, who is arrested by the sheriff before he can get to Bobby. Momentarily relieved, Bobby grabs a Coke, but is jumped by TNT who grabs his bus ticket and rips it up in a jealous fury. Bobby beats him senseless then, with little alternative, calls Grace and agrees to kill Jake.

Night falls. Grace leaves the bolt off the door, before retiring with Jake to the bedroom. Bobby, wielding a pipe, quietly lets himself in, but bumps into a shelf. Jake hears a noise and heads downstairs. He surprises Bobby, threatening him with his own gun: it transpires that Jake and Darrell are brothers, that they had been working together to keep Bobby from leaving and that Darrell had broken into the trunk and taken the gun. With this gun to his head Bobby agrees to kill Grace, but now for just the $200 needed to get out of town. However, he conspires with Grace, and together they kill Jake.

Bobby pays off Darrell and retrieves his car, which they pack with the money (now $200,000) and Jake's body. But on the way out of town they encounter the sheriff, who reveals that Grace had been promising to run away with him. In a drunken rage, he reveals that Jake was Grace's real father, as well as being her husband, when Grace suddenly shoots him dead. They travel to Apache Leap to dispose of the bodies – Bobby is shocked by Grace and suggests they split the money and go their separate ways. She has other ideas, and pushes Bobby over the cliff, but

Bobby, wary of Grace, had taken the keys from the ignition, and she is forced to clamber down after him. He seizes the chance to strangle her. Bleeding, broken and shot by Grace in her dying throes, Bobby hauls himself up the cliff and into the Mustang. Just as he begins to pull away, the replacement hose breaks and he is left, stranded in the desert, laughing hysterically as the vultures circle.

ADVANCE PUBLICITY: An interesting note on the poster campaign was recorded in *Empire* magazine. The tagline ran, 'Sex, murder, betrayal. Everything that makes life worth living.' This came awfully close to the line written for the 1963 Billy Wilder movie *Irma La Douce*, which ran, 'A story of bloodshed, passion, desire and death . . . everything in fact that makes life worth living.'

PRODUCTION HISTORY: *Nixon* was a flop. Much of Ixtlan's work in progress was along a similar vein of political cinema (for instance *Memphis*) and thus was similarly becalmed. There was no immediate follow-up, and Stone took time off from filmmaking, returning to *A Child's Night Dream*.

He also kept busy through Ixtlan, with the release of one of its flagship productions, *The People Versus Larry Flynt* (Milos Forman, 1996) that Stone produced, and through hectic battles over *Nixon* and *Natural Born Killers* in the press and, in the latter case, the courts (see **Natural Born Killers**). He continued work on another long-term project, a biography about Alexander the Great with Tom Cruise mooted to star (see **Alexander**).

In this context, the sudden appearance of *U Turn* resembles that of *Talk Radio* nine years earlier. A novel and film rights from author John Ridley, under the working title *Stray Dogs*, came through producer Dan Halsted. *Nixon* had been costly in both dollars and in time, and Stone was conscious of this: '*U Turn* was, in part, an experiment to prove to myself . . . that [movie-making] can still be done in a less hyped and pretentious way.' He seized the script as a quick, easy film, projected at a 37-day schedule (though it eventually ran to 42) and with a budget of $16 million (eventually running to $20million), the lowest since *Born on the Fourth of July*. The picture was not developed through Ixtlan but Illusion, and financing was arranged through Phoenix Pictures, a relatively new company that had also backed *The People Versus Larry Flynt*. Mike Medavoy, chairman and co-founder of Phoenix, had previously worked with Stone while employed at Orion, where he had been involved in the distribution of *The Hand* and *Platoon*. He had gone on from there to work at Tristar, the eventual distributors of *U Turn*.

The script came ready-made, but there is some question over the provenance of the final shooting version. Screenwriting credits are a touchy business in Hollywood, and often go to arbitration by the Writers' Guild of America (WGA), a chaotic process by which various script drafts are analysed for pertinent elements, the presence of which in sufficient quantity necessitates an on-screen credit. The published script of *U Turn* bears a close resemblance to the source novel in terms of settings, characters and dialogue. There was one substantial addition: the elaboration on Grace's heritage and the introduction of incest, but Stone himself pointed out the problem: 'For a film director to receive writing credit, he must have contributed at least 50 per cent . . . our [Stone and Rutowski's] contribution was about 40 per cent.' However, in public at least, Stone was philosophical about the decision: 'It's a rule intended to protect the original author, and I have been on the other side of the fence.'

Irrespective of authorship Stone had a script and funding. Location was found in the Arizona ghost town of Superior, located 60 miles outside Phoenix. In the book the dead-end stop-off point of the protagonist was called Sierra, but the town persuaded the filmmakers to keep its real name in the script. In the old mining town on the frontier of Indian territory, the crew all but took over Main Street for the period of shooting, spreading a layer of dirt over the paving. For effect Victor Kempster aimed to shape the set 'as if architectural development had ceased sometime during the 1960s.' Storefronts were resurrected from period photographs, and the production office was based in a building that had used to be the town's brothel. Outside town, McKenna's house was based in a nearby mansion, the Castle on the Rock, built by a copper baron in the 1920s. The chasm around which Bobby's aborted assassination attempt on Grace and the climactic double-cross occurs was a nearby landmark called, as in the film, Apache Leap, where many Native American warriors had jumped to their deaths rather than be captured alive by the US cavalry.

Though intended to be a quick and easy production, *U Turn* was dogged by difficulty. As well as problems with cast and crew (see below) there was conflict over the name. *Stray Dog* (1949) was a film by renowned Japanese director Akira Kurosawa, and he and his estate did not look kindly on an American film with such a similar title. This was changed to *U Turn*, with its connotations of changes, deception and double-cross. There were also problems with the source material itself. The script had been based on Ridley's unpublished novel, and he seized the chance to arrange a publishing deal, with the novel to be rushed out before the movie so as to ride the expected wave of interest in a new Oliver Stone film. The book was eventually released but the conflict had been acrimonious. Stone's view: 'I don't want to see this writer ever again in my life.' Ridley's response: 'These guys don't know the difference between gratitude and servitude.'

The film was completed, edited and released in the US in October 1997.

CASTING: Relations were tense on set, not least because of the confusion over the film's leading man. Stone wanted Sean Penn to play the role of Bobby Cooper, but Penn was committed to another project and Stone turned to Bill Paxton. Paxton seems a somewhat odd choice for the role of a down-at-heel drifter; he is better known for a string of undemanding tough guy roles in such fare as *Aliens* (James Cameron, 1986), *Apollo 13* (Ron Howard, 1995) and *Twister* (Jan de Bont, 1996). Reports differ as to the exact nature of problems on set; suffice to say that Paxton was not happy with the part. Some say that he was prepared to stay if no replacement could be found but Stone remembers a somewhat less amicable situation: 'It looked like it wouldn't happen . . . It was a very dicey thing.' Fortunately, Penn became free, and Paxton left the film. From his perspective this was probably a wise move, as it left him free to appear in James Cameron's incredibly successful *Titanic* (1997).

Penn and Stone had crossed paths before, just before production began on *Natural Born Killers*. He had also been suggested for the part of Ron Kovic in **Born on the Fourth of July**. One of Stone's reasons for rejecting Penn at the time was his 'bad boy' image and his attitude was little better on set; there was no love lost between actor and crew. He does put in a better performance as the thoroughly unpleasant Bobby than might have been expected from clean-cut Bill Paxton but, having said that, it is unlikely that the character would feature prominently in any portfolio of Penn's best work. He can make unpleasant people sympathetic – for instance in *Dead Man Walking* (Tim Robbins, 1995) – and had played the snivelling weasel card before and to much greater effect as the coke-fuelled lawyer in *Carlito's Way* (Brian De Palma, 1995). Here he is just wasted.

Another more general problem was with the tiny budget. Specifically most of the money was earmarked for equipment, but despite this Stone wanted an A-grade cast. Clayton Townsend was left with the challenging task 'to convince the usual suspects we've worked with . . . that there was no room for stretching beyond the financial constraints.' One early consequence of this frugality was the loss of Sharon Stone as Grace. Unhappy with the low basic rate, and lack of a 'back-end' deal (to collect a share of box office receipts), she left to be replaced by Jennifer Lopez. Now a globally famous pop star, back in 1997 J-Lo was several years from her first record deal, and barely known in the world of cinema. Stone cast her on the basis of her big screen appearance in the Woody Harrelson/Wesley Snipes buddy movie flop *Money Train* (Joseph Ruben, 1995) and her physical appearance: a dusky Latin beauty, Lopez was perfect for the half-Navajo Grace (it is more difficult to imagine Sharon Stone in the same part). She also had experience in contemporary *noir*, a small role in the mediocre *Blood & Wine* (Bob Rafelson, 1996), but her big break would come after *U Turn*, in the laid-back romantic thriller *Out of Sight* (Steven Soderbergh, 1998) – the undisputable highpoint of a disappointing film career. She is given little to do in this movie: Grace is one of the most grotesque manifestations of misogyny in a Stone film, a callous, sadistic, murderous cock-tease, with leaden, sexless dialogue – her allure is pretty much entirely due to lecherous lingering camerawork. Lopez drifts through the film, rarely seeming to care about the character – a feeling it is easy to empathise with.

In keeping with the bad-boy theme, Nick Nolte was cast as Jake McKenna. Nolte had picked up an Oscar nomination for a critically acclaimed performance in *Prince of Tides* (Barbra Streisand, 1991), but his Jake McKenna is little more than a scenery-chewing lunatic, who quickly crosses the line from menacing to self-parody. It comes as a relief when his head is finally stove in.

Billy Bob Thornton, acclaimed for his directorial debut *Sling Blade* (1996), was cast as hick gas station attendant Darrell. Claire Danes, the winsome female lead in *William Shakespeare's Romeo + Juliet* (Baz Luhrmann, 1996), played clueless small-town trash Jenny. Joaquin Phoenix (born Leaf Phoenix and brother of deceased actor River), who would go on to play mad emperor Commodus in *Gladiator* (Ridley Scott, 2000), was her equally clueless but ragingly jealous boyfriend Toby 'TNT' Tucker. Jon Voight had found critical fame in *Midnight Cowboy* (John Schlesinger, 1969) but had since come to specialise in a slew of crazed cameo roles, continuing the trend with a self-consciously eccentric turn as the blind Indian.

On paper, this is an impressive ensemble, but the whole is much less than the sum of its parts: the audience is presented with a cacophony of irritating characters, played with eye-rolling melodrama by everyone concerned – the first marked failure of Stone's belief of excess on set.

OLIVER'S ARMY: The one familiar face in this film is that of Powers Boothe, previously Alexander Haig in *Nixon*. His Sheriff Potter is the most tolerable of a bad lot, until the final reel when he too collapses into a frenzied hysteria. Boothe is an under-appreciated actor, and his performance up to that point is nicely balanced, if unspectacular, as the standard issue suspicious and apparently slow-witted sheriff. This is all thrown away in the laughable final few minutes.

There are two cameos from family and friends. Sean Stone appears briefly in the grocery store, and Richard Rutowski has a small role as the second robber of the same grocery store.

The crew were the usual collection of Oliver Stone regulars. Victor Kempster, Clayton Townsend, Mary Vernieu (who took sole charge of casting chores) and Robert Richardson (though work commitments to Barry Levinson's *Wag the Dog* meant that the last stage of cinematography was left in the charge of Jeff Kimball). There were three significant new arrivals: costume designer Beatrix Aruna Pasztor, producer Dan Halsted (who had worked on *Nixon*) and, most significantly, legendary composer Ennio Morricone (see **MUSIC**).

MEMORABLE QUOTES:
Toby N Tucker: 'Everyone around here call me TNT. You know why?'
Bobby: 'They're . . . not very imaginative?'

GOOD VS EVIL: All of Oliver Stone's other films have featured something that could be described as good. This is not the case with *U Turn*, which boasts a cast of obnoxious irritating characters with not a single attractive attribute among them. All are venal and selfish in their own way. Anything close to a manifestation of love is stripped of any admirable connotation and expressed in the base forms of lustful obsession, manipulative seduction, violent jealousy, fickle flirtatiousness or brutal atavistic sex. Treachery is rampant, and evident in even the most banal level of relationship (near the end the 'blind' Indian inspects a coin and walks off with his 'dead' dog). It is impossible to analyse the film's moral conflict, simply because there is no force for good. Even Bobby's quest, his motivation for escaping the clutches of Superior, is tainted and corrupted – to pay off a gambling debt. From what the audience see of the character, it is nigh on impossible to care a jot for his life and impossible to connect with him in any emotional sense beyond revulsion. He is as bad as any other character, and in such a world of moral (or perhaps immoral) equivocacy there can be no true protagonist, beyond one elected simply by screen time and point of view imposed by the camera and the script. Stone spoke of his theory of *film noir* characters thus: 'At the end of the day you empathise with them because you know that given the worst circumstances in life you might end up like them.' Maybe so, in an abstract sense, but it is one thing to sympathise with the elegant loser, doomed from the very start – for instance Robert Mitchum in the classic *noir Out of the Past*. It is quite another to ask for any meaningful empathy with a selection of characters constructed of worst case scenario upon worst case scenario and guided by worst possible instinct and motivation.

REDEMPTION OR DAMNATION: Given all this, it is unsurprising that the universal verdict in this film is damnation. For Bobby, Grace, Jake and Virgil this comes in the form of an ignominious death. For everyone else, there is a form of damnation in a continued dead-end desert town existence.

Stone described the movie as about 'the karma of six people who all intersect like scorpions in a bucket,' adding 'of course it all leads to the consequences of their behaviour'. In a spiritual sense, perhaps employed as a fable, this might be satisfying enough but in a dramatic narrative it feels rather hollow. Some find fault with the simplicity of the 'pilgrim's progress' of Bud Fox in *Wall Street*, but at least there was some sense of a moral journey undertaken, of redemption earned after spiritual struggle. Here the message, such as it is, is even simpler – these people, unpleasant and bad to the core, get their comeuppance. For such a bitterly cynical film, this 'reap what you sow' message is inadequate.

STARS AND STRIPES: The small desert town, isolated in a wilderness of rocky, inhospitable terrain and often, as in this case, the remnant of an ephemeral mining town is a staple of American filmmaking, especially the Western, though its most recent manifestation has been as the background for road movies from *Easy Rider* (Dennis Hopper, 1969) onwards. Stone takes this basic concept and gives it a spin out of *Blue Velvet* (David Lynch, 1986) – the idea that behind closed doors, no matter how ordinary in appearance, the strangest most twisted affairs might be taking place. Admittedly, there is little ordinary about Superior. It seems to take a cue from the profoundly odd black comedy *Nothing* *but Trouble* (Dan Ackroyd, 1991), a fairly dismal film that features a yuppie couple arrested for a speeding offence and dragged into a bizarre small town in Pennsylvania, ruled over by an insane autocratic judge and populated with a cast of grotesques only a few degrees more excessive than those of *U Turn*. In both cases, and unlike Lynch, the surreal twist on the small town takes the shape of broad farce, and is difficult to warm to or like. Rather than a side of the American Dream this is an American Nightmare, both for the protagonists dragged into this hallucinatory world and the viewer who is subjected to it.

BEING OLIVER STONE: There are no direct links to Oliver Stone in this story – for a start it is fiction, but also adapted from a script and novel with which he had no initial involvement. There are preoccupations and ideas that resonate through some of his work, and which were added to the script later in development – specifically the deeply odd relationship between Jake and Grace – reminiscent of the the incestuous connotations of *Scarface* and the twisted child/parent relations in *Seizure, Born on the Fourth of July* and *Nixon*.

The collapse of *Nixon* hit Stone hard. Since 1995 he has only completed two films, with a third scheduled for 2004. This was also due to changing personal interests. On top of his novel, Stone would expand his production activity and look at work on TV and in the sphere of documentary filmmaking (see **Alexander**).

INSPIRATION AND INFLUENCE: John Ridley is a stand-up comedian with a fascination for *film noir* – an important influence on *U Turn* through Ridley's source novel *Stray Dogs*. The book fleshes out a few of the story's details. The nature of Cooper's debt to the Las Vegas gangster (Italian here rather than Russian) is clarified. Cooper (called John in the book) is a shiftless drifter and sometime professional gambler, who finds himself conned into a rigged poker game incurring a debt of $13,000 – money he obtains by breaking into the safe of a former workplace in Phoenix, Arizona. He drives towards Las Vegas, arriving at Sierra (changed to Superior, see **PRODUCTION HISTORY**) through the same mishap as in the film. From here the story unfolds along similar lines, with mainly cosmetic changes. There is a second meeting with Jake after the failed assassination attempt on Grace (the substance from this meeting is condensed into the film's one meeting in Jake's office). The gangster sends two henchmen into town – one flirts with the waitress at the diner – and both are killed by the sheriff, though the event is not described. There is a slight change to the struggle at Jake's house – it is Cooper who kills Jake, strangling him, rather than Grace butchering him with a hatchet. In the book there is no suggestion that Jake gives Cooper another chance to kill Grace.

The biggest difference comes with the nasty incest subplot, and the intimations of inbreeding that go with it (another addition to the film is the blood relation between Darrell and Jake). Stone and Rutowski write in the idea of Grace sleeping with her father (and eventually killing him), presumably in some sort of connection with the Oedipal themes that Stone highlighted in the work of Jim Morrison in *The Doors*. They also made some changes to the story's climax. In the novel the Sheriff is a corrupt pragmatist, asking merely for a cut of the loot to look the other way. The idea that Grace has seduced the whole town in her efforts to escape is faintly ludicrous, and smacks of the misogyny that seems a major motivation behind the creation of the character. At the end of the book, both characters are doomed but positions are reversed: John lies broken at the bottom of the gully while Grace sits in the Mustang, without the keys to the ignition.

It's not a good book, at best a bog-standard crime thriller and a far from obvious candidate for film treatment. However, there is something more likeable about its protagonist. He has a little more backbone, he does not get arbitrarily punched out by Jake when discovered *in flagrante* with Grace, and is a less whiny figure all round. He is a gambler who takes chances trying to seize control of his destiny, which makes his continual bad luck somewhat ironic. The film's Bobby rarely makes decisions or even takes chances so much as being backed into situations by forces beyond his control (a poor echo of the fatalism in *The Doors* and *Heaven and Earth*).

In the production notes to the film, Stone describes *U Turn* as a form of *film noir*, rooted in gloomy, cynical, fatalistic detective thrillers of the 1940s; the genre has not died out and enjoys frequent revivals. Key to this has been adaptability of the basic themes. Many films have taken a period approach to *noir*, for instance *Chinatown* (Roman Polanski, 1973) or *LA Confidential* (Curtis Hanson, 1997), but others have applied the hard-bitten, cynical style to science fiction, *Blade Runner* (Ridley Scott, 1982), and even horror films, *Near Dark* (Kathryn Bigelow, 1987). This last film is also an example of desert *noir*, a strand that uses small desert towns to isolate drifting strangers like Bobby Cooper, in a self-contained universe. An early example was the Spencer Tracy thriller *Bad Day at Black Rock* (John Sturges, 1955) where a one-eyed wanderer uncovers a dark secret in the archetypal desert town. Indeed, this film was quoted as an influence in the production notes. A film that seems to have the greatest influence on *U Turn* (primarily through the book – it lends much to the basic structure as envisaged by John Ridley, and Robert Richardson has mentioned that Stone 'had never seen it') was *Red Rock West* (John Dahl, 1992), a blackly comic tale of a drifter, Nicolas Cage, who is mistaken for a hit man and hired by a local big shot, Dennis Hopper, to kill his wife, Lara Flynn Boyle, who then offers Cage double the money to kill Hopper.

REEL TIME: The key technical problems of *U Turn* came in the form of the desert location. The sun rose late, 8.30, meaning a comparatively short period of time with ample light for shooting. Additionally, it swiftly became fierce, the intense light washing a lot of colour out of the image as it appeared on film. Initially Richardson suggested shooting in black-and-white, but a colour image was important, to keep the movie financially viable. Instead, Stone and Richardson turned to colour-reversal film stock. Temperamental and difficult to handle and develop, the stock allowed the camera to capture colour that the fierce sun might usually have bleached out, as well as the deep black shadows the same light cast – keeping that intense contrast that marks the *noir* aesthetic.

There is also much of the switching between angles, cameras and film stocks that has become familiar in Stone's films. But what had previously lent a skewed reality to conventional political thrillers, or conveyed the psychedelic intensity of 1960s rock and roll, here appeared unnecessary and self-consciously wacky.

MUSIC: Ennio Morricone is famed, and rightly so, for the instantly recognisable themes he wrote for Spaghetti Western maestro Sergio Leone – including *A Fistful of Dollars* (1964), *The Good, the Bad and the Ugly* (1966) and *Once Upon a Time in the West* (1969). However, as with most cinematic composers, he has also completed a lot of work that is much less distinctive. *U Turn* falls within this category: it is not bad, merely undistinguished – empty, predictable, bog standard.

BOX OFFICE: *U Turn* was another disappointing box-office showing. As of 2 November 1997 – nearly a month after release – the film had grossed only $6.6 million. Of Stone's last four films, three had failed to repay the original budget from theatrical receipts.

CRITICS: Those who hated *U Turn* tended to do so with a passion. The *Village Voice* review began badly: 'It is clear from the first jazzy ominous flourishes that this film is running on empty.' And it got worse: '*U Turn* is an unbelievably clumsy and pretentious attempt to make the sort of mock *noir* that the Coen brothers invented with *Blood Simple*.' While Matthew Sweet, writing in the *Independent on Sunday*, described it as 'a jumpy neurotic thriller with very little method in its madness'.

There were positive reviews, for instance, *Asian Age*'s review opined that 'Under Stone's adept ministrations and a self-restraint he rarely exhibits – *U Turn* truly works.' But most qualified their praise. In the *Observer*, Sam Taylor wrote, 'For nearly two hours it is pure unadulterated pleasure: Stone as a brilliant filmmaker without the baggage of significance and showiness.' He added, 'Only in its final reel does *U Turn* fulfil your worst expectations.' Tom Charity picked on the film's emptiness: 'It's quite watchable, for a while, but strangely passionless and utterly pointless.' Alexander Walker's view was almost identical: 'This caricatural collection of weirdoes . . . is oddly watchable . . . What does it all add up to? Hard to tell.'

The *Telegraph* picked up on Stone's amateur psychological concerns, and took a negative view: 'Unfortunately Stone has seen fit to impose his own Freud-for-beginners back stories on the characters.'

The critic for the *Sunday Times* saw special significance for *U Turn* in the body of Stone's work saying that it 'homes in with unerring accuracy on Stone's one true subject as director. He's finally done it: he's made a picture all about paranoia.'

AWARDS: *U Turn* was Stone's first film since *The Doors* to receive no major awards or nominations. The only mention it did get was at a ceremony of dubious merit – the Golden Raspberry awards, where Stone was nominated as worst director. At the same event, Jon Voight was nominated as worst supporting actor.

TRIVIA: Liv Tyler made a brief cameo as a customer in the bus station. She had been visiting boyfriend of the time Joaquin Phoenix on set.

The exact amount of money owed in the film is unclear. The published screenplay suggests $13,000, the subtitles $30,000 and the dialogue is fuzzy.

THE BIG PICTURE: The desert setting has more than a passing resemblance to the hunting grounds of Mickey and Mallory in *Natural*

Born Killers, and the two films are comparable in other ways. Both are dark tales with unpleasant characters, but the earlier film has a point to it, as well as a tinge of redemptive humanity in Mickey and Mallory's love, whereas this one seems like unrelenting misery for misery's sake. *U Turn* is a step backwards in this sense, presenting the struggles of its cast as sheer voyeuristic entertainment, rather than aiming at some ulterior meaning, and forgetting that unpleasant protagonists, without this purpose, are unpleasant to watch.

FINAL ANALYSIS: *U Turn* is a depressing exercise in tedium. The plot meanders from twist to predictable twist with a languor as if affected by the desert heat. The limited impact of these twists is further reduced by a total lack of interest in the fates of the characters concerned.

The flaws are fundamental: there is a basic subversion of expectations regarding the main plot – in classical narrative terms this should revolve around repayment of the debt owed to the Russian gangster. It is possible to get away with a lot in filmmaking, some might say the whole art-form is about misdirection and sleight of hand, but it's very difficult to leave a plot strand that first appeared significant hanging in the breeze. It takes a master of subtlety to make this work – Hitchcock did it all the time – but Stone is not subtle. It is not just a case of Stone missing his target but highly questionable whether there was any target at all. The film is pointless.

Incest can work in a *noir* plotline, *Chinatown* for instance. But where that movie built to its horrifying conclusion, here the idea is shoehorned into the script with little meaning or motivation save to add darkness. Its actual result is to give a sordid nasty edge to an already unpleasant little film. To crown it all there is, simply, no one to root for.

U Turn is not so much bad as ugly: it's offensive, tedious and better off forgotten.

A Child's Night Dream

After *U Turn*, Robert Weil, an editor at St Martin's Press, got in contact with Stone, having read about his novel *A Child's Night Dream* in an interview. The majority of the novel, completed in 1967 after Stone's return from the Merchant Marine, was rotting on the bed of the East River, but Stone pulled out the 230 remaining pages of the manuscript and polished it up for publication in 1997.

> The result is difficult to credit as anything other than adolescent self-indulgence, the sort of work that probably languishes in many an angst-ridden 19-year-old's desk drawer. It employs a tortuous stream-of-consciousness style, a wholly unsuccessful attempt to ape the work of James Joyce or William Burroughs, to relate the same sort of free-spirited journey of discovery familiar to readers of Jack Kerouac or JD Salinger. The book is rife with unintentional humour and disturbing imagery, disorganised in structure and utterly self-obsessed.
>
> Few screenwriters have gone on to noteworthy literary careers (William Goldman is an exception with *The Princess Bride*) and Stone will not be among them, at least not on the basis of this effort.

Any Given Sunday (1999)

Warner Brothers Presents
An Ixtlan/The Donners' Company Production
An Oliver Stone Film
Casting by Billy Hopkins and Mary Vernieu
Music Score by Robbie Robertson, Paul Kelly and Richard Horowitz
Music Supervisor: Budd Carr
Co-Producers: Eric Hamburg, Jonathan Krauss and Richard Rutowski
Costume Designer: Mary Zophres
Edited by Tom Nordberg, Keith Salmon Stuart Waks and Stuart Levy
Production Designer: Victor Kempster
Director of Photography: Salvatore Totino
Executive Producers: Richard Donner and Oliver Stone
Produced by Lauren Shuler Donner, Dan Halsted and Clayton Townsend
Screen Story by Daniel Pyne and John Logan
Screenplay by John Logan and Oliver Stone
Directed by Oliver Stone

CAST: Al Pacino (*Tony D'Amato*), Cameron Diaz (*Christina Pagniacci*), Dennis Quaid (*Jack 'Cap' Rooney*), James Woods (*Dr Harvey Mandrake*), Jamie Foxx (*Willie Beaman*), LL Cool J (*Julian 'J-man' Washington*), Matthew Modine (*Dr Ollie Powers*), Jim Brown

(*Montezuma Monroe*), Charlton Heston (*AFFA Football Commissioner*), Ann-Margret (*Margaret Pagniacci*), Aaron Eckhart (*Nick Crozier*), John C McGinley (*Jack Rose*), Lauren Holly (*Cindy Rooney*), Lela Rachon (*Vanessa Struthers*), Lawrence Taylor (*Luther 'Shark' Lavay*), Bill Bellamy (*Jimmy Sanderson*), James Karen (*Christina's Adviser*), Elizabeth Berkley (*Mandy Murphy*), Andrew Bryniarski (*Patrick 'Madman' Kelly*), Duane Martin (*Willie's Agent*), Clifton Davies (*Mayor Tyrone Smalls*), John Daniel (*Suitor in Christina's Box*)

SUMMARY: Caption card: 'I firmly believe that any man's finest hour – his greatest fulfilment of all he holds dear – is that moment when he has worked his heart out in a good cause and lies exhausted on the field of battle, victorious.' Vince Lombardi (1913–70).

The Miami Sharks are a major football team in the AFFA (Associated Football Federation of America) that have recently fallen into stagnation. After their ageing veteran quarterback 'Cap' Rooney is injured during a game, a new star is found in third-string substitute Willie Beaman. His rise to fame has its counterpoint in the slow decline of coach Tony D'Amato – in his fourth decade of management for the Sharks. He was hired by the father of current owner Christina Pagniacci, herself struggling with the legacy of a sport that killed her father. Her approach is cold and businesslike, and she is preoccupied with a secret plan to move the team to a more lucrative venue in Los Angeles.

Success changes Willie, who refuses to follow the plays ordered by the coach and falls out with his fellow players, putting his individual ambition ahead of team success. The other players have their own problems: running back Julian Washington is a free agent on a limited contract and needs to increase his playing statistics to guarantee an advertising contract; defensive linebacker 'Shark' Lavay discovers potentially life-threatening injuries but has to continue playing to support his family; Cap Rooney struggles to return to form, at the same time as realising that his career is coming to the end; young team intern Ollie Powers clashes with the pragmatic senior doctor Harvey Mandrake. D'Amato is trying to deal with change as well, reconciling his lifetime devoted to the game with a new scientific corporate approach that is alien to him, and with a non-existent family life – his marriage ended in divorce and he has little emotional contact beyond ephemeral 'relationships' with prostitutes.

These crises come to a head at a crucial play-off. The Sharks unite for Cap Rooney's last game as starting quarterback. He ends his career in triumph, while Willie Beaman learns important lessons about the true nature of leadership and teamwork, and their importance over mere talent and individual flair. 'Shark' is injured making the tackle that earns his bonus, and he leaves the field on a stretcher, safe in the knowledge that he has provided for his family. Julian Washington finds a greater attachment to the team that employs him, dedicating his efforts to winning the game, not just increasing his own profile. Christina undergoes reconciliation with her mother, widowed by American football long before the physical death of Mr Pagniacci, and is thwarted in her attempts to move the team by a wily football commissioner. Tony D'Amato sees his team win the game with a last-minute touchdown, and it renews his fervour.

An epilogue flips the film on its head. It reveals that the Sharks lose their next game, and so are out of the championship. D'Amato resigns, taking up the coaching position at a newly established football club in Albuqueque, having been given a degree of corporate control he lacks in Miami. He takes with him new superstar Willie Beaman, a bond having formed between the old coach and the young player.

PRODUCTION HISTORY: Oliver Stone had been working with the concept of a football movie for some time. He describes one early version as 'about an ageing linebacker, which was a treatment I'd written with Charles Bronson in mind, in the early 80s'. Like many other ideas of this period, it never got beyond the hypothetical stage, and Stone did not return to the subject of pro-football until the late 1990s.

Post *U Turn*, Stone's name had been linked with a number of big projects: the perennially rumoured *Planet of the Apes* remake (eventually completed by Tim Burton in 2001) and another Tom Cruise collaboration in the shape of *Mission: Impossible II* (ultimately directed by John Woo for a 2000 release). He had been slated as director for an adaptation of Bret Easton Ellis's cult novel *American Psycho*. However, Leonardo DiCaprio ducked out of the lead role, causing the budget to be massively cut and Stone to be dropped from the picture as prohibitively expensive. The film was eventually released in 2000, directed by Mary Harron and starring Christian Bale.

The football movie idea had been revived during the making of *Nixon*, via Richard Weiner, a sportswriter and the son of a consultant to Richard Nixon. Weiner had worked with famous quarterback Joe Montana on a book, *The Art and Magic of Quarterbacking*, and was persuaded to work on some ideas for a script, collaborating with another

OLIVER STONE Any Given Sunday

veteran of the sport, retired tight-end Jamie Williams. Together they came up with a story, based around racism in the sport and centring on the struggles of a black quarterback, under the working title of *Monday Night*. Eventually this was discarded (though Weiner and Williams were credited for technical assistance) in favour of a similar story with the title *Any Given Sunday* adapted by Daniel Pyne and John Logan. Stone involved himself in rewrites and would eventually share credit with John Logan for the finished version.

A production deal was tentatively arranged with Turner Pictures, and confirmed by Warner Brothers after the Turner Broadcasting/Time Warner merger of 1995. But Warners already had a football movie in development. Based on the book *You're OK – It's Just a Bruise*, written by Robert Huizenga, former team physician to the Oakland Raiders, their script, *Playing Hurt*, dealt with the dubious practices of team doctors, who use huge amounts of painkillers and other drugs to keep footballers on the field. Richard and Lauren Shuler Donner were working on this film through their production house, The Donners' Company, and an agreement was eventually struck to merge the two productions. However, costs began to rise steeply, and the proposed casting of Robert De Niro took the budget to $55 million – unacceptable at that time. The production was frozen, and Stone went off to make *U Turn*.

By the time he returned to work on *Any Given Sunday* in early 1998, the script had changed again. The location had shifted to Miami (earlier drafts had set the film in San Francisco and Chicago) and a cluster of other characters and subplots had joined the story of a white coach and his black quarterback – Stone's rationale: 'I wanted to tell a story with 10 or 15 characters, like *Ben Hur* did in the old days.' But production was far from smooth. There were several rewrites (problems that Stone attributes to 'getting the black vernacular and all the football jargon right') and there were further budgetary concerns. The original start date of April 1998 was put back to December 1998, and then finally to January 1999. This uncertainty caused flux with cast and crew but also gave Stone the chance to put some work in on another pet project – see **Alexander**. In addition to filmmaking hiccups, there was disagreement with the National Football League (NFL), which disliked some elements of the script (largely negative of the NFL's corporate philosophy) and refused to associate itself with the production. As it owned the rights to all team names and insignia, had considerable clout with the regional offices and could limit access to technical crew (such as cameramen) involved with the sport, this posed a fairly serious problem.

Eventually the budget of $55 million was agreed to, though it was necessary to take on heavy product sponsorship to raise some of the money. Fortunately this was relatively easy in a sports film, an area already rife with product placement (a substantial chunk of funding came from bodybuilding powder Met-Rx). The NFL's intransigence was circumvented through the creation of a fictional league, the AFFA, populated with a whole slew of fictional teams – the Minnesota Americans, the Chicago Rhinos, the Los Angeles Crusaders, the New York Emperors and the Dallas Knights. There was close cooperation with certain individuals and teams. The crew secured the use of several major venues – the Miami Rose Bowl, the Miami Dolphins' Pro-Player Stadium and Texas Stadium, home to the Dallas Cowboys. Shooting was also carried out in a variety of luxurious Miami locales – the scenes set in Rooney's house were filmed at the home of Dan Marino, a renowned quarterback for the Dolphins.

The main challenge came with the five games that take place in the film. Actors, stunt doubles and professional players mingled on the pitch, and an astonishing array of cameras was used to capture the action (see **REEL TIME**). With the intense demands of these scenes, the necessity of wrangling 10,000 extras for some of the crowd scenes and the challenges of dealing with a large cast of fairly major actors, it is small wonder that Stone has said, 'I don't think I've ever worked harder over a whole film over a period of time as I did here.' Amazingly, the film came in on time, completed in 65 days (though the cost had risen to $65 million), and was released in the US at the end of December 1999.

CASTING: The changes to the shooting schedule caused fluidity in the cast. Ving Rhames was originally set to play 'Shark' but was forced to pull out, as was David Duchovny who was up for the role of Ollie Powers. Puff Daddy had been slated to play Willie Beaman, but also left the set, though an additional prompt to his departure came from friction between him and Al Pacino.

In the impressive cast that eventually emerged, Pacino is the jewel, having been offered the role in the wake of abortive attempts to film *Noriega* (see **Nixon**). He is an actor who seems destined to work always in the shadow of Michael Corleone, the tormented demon of Francis Ford Coppola's *Godfather* trilogy (1972, 1974 and 1990). Having said that, he rarely fails to entertain, and he has his moments here, including the obligatory motivational locker room speech, which verges on the melodramatic but just about works – a description that could be extended to the rest of his performance.

His wrinkled demeanour is set in contrast against the smooth, youthful Jamie Foxx. He is excellent as Willie Beaman, all the more so as this represented a demanding first lead role for Foxx, a stand-up comedian, musician and TV star formerly cast in supporting roles in *The Truth About Cats and Dogs* (Michael Lehmann, 1996) and *Toys* (Barry Levinson, 1992). He did have the advantage of quarterback experience, admittedly only on his high school team.

Cameron Diaz was a good choice for a somewhat odd role, the twenty-something daughter who now runs her father's football empire. In the course of filming she really came to prominence through gross-out comedy *There's Something About Mary* (Bobby and Peter Farrelly, 1998) with a kooky, comic turn that has become her regular shtick, but here she delivers a respectable performance as a hard-nosed, cold-blooded businesswoman.

Diaz plays a deeply troubled character, her mother a sodden alcoholic and Rooney's wife (the excellent Lauren Holly) an abusive spouse. The most sympathetic female character is the prostitute who gives affection for money (a recurring character, she can also be seen in *Salvador*, *Wall Street*, *Born on the Fourth of July*, *Heaven and Earth* and *Nixon*). Her incarnation here is played by Elizabeth Berkley of *Showgirls* (Paul Verhoeven, 1996). Some might pick up on the stereotypical Stone dichotomy of 'harpies and whores' as indicative of his usual mishandling of women. However, it is important to note that all of Stone's most interesting and important characters have flaws to overcome, irrespective of their sex. More upsetting is the blandness caused by miscasting, such as Meg Ryan in *The Doors*. Diaz plays a character who, like everyone else in the film, has to learn to adapt. As does Lauren Holly's domineering wife. Perhaps there is an element of sexism, but nothing on a par with the repulsive character of Grace in *U Turn*.

The team is represented by a great ensemble cast. LL Cool J is one of several rap stars to take up movie acting in the 1990s. His Julian Washington is brilliantly brash and egocentric and Cool J's powerful frame works well in the context of American football. The right build was no problem for Lawrence Taylor, an ex-NFL player, who had been accepted to the prestigious Hall of Fame. Despite some tension on-set as to a possible jail sentence for cocaine possession, he turns in a cracking performance. Another former player on the cast was Jim Brown, also a Hall of Fame star, who had retired from pro-football in 1967 to take up a career in acting. Coincidentally he gets a brief mention in *Nixon* as one of the former University of Syracuse footballers the president speaks of at the Lincoln Memorial.

Dennis Quaid has no record of professional football, does have a reputation for solid square-jawed heroes, and does a pretty good job here with a fairly insubstantial role.

The film is littered with footballing cameos. Indeed, many of the extras filling out the ranks of the Sharks and standing in for the other teams are players or former players in the NFL or the Arena League (an indoor football league). Jamie Williams (see **PRODUCTION HISTORY**) did some work on these scenes, as did Terrell Owens, wide receiver for the 49ers at the time. These players took the 'games' seriously – at one point Owens was supposed to be making a break for the end zone and outran the dolly tracking the shot. Other cameos came from much older stars of the game, who stood in for the various opposing coaches: Bob St Clair (San Francisco 49ers) at Minnesota; YA Tittle (New York Giants and the 49ers) and Pat Toomay for the Chicago Rhinos; Dick Butkus (Chicago Bears) for the Los Angeles Crusaders; Warren Moon (Kansas City Chiefs) for the New York Emperors and Johnny Unitas (Baltimore Colts and San Diego Chargers) at Dallas.

One final, and particularly impressive, cameo can be found in the brief appearance of Charlton Heston as the commissioner. Still a craggy and imposing presence, with his deep, rich voice unaffected by age, Heston makes his few minutes on screen count. Early in 2003, Charlton Heston made public his battle with Alzheimer's, and has retired from filmmaking as a result.

OLIVER'S ARMY: Aside from Pacino, who had spoken Stone's lines in *Scarface*, James Woods also returned for this film, in a brief but thoroughly enjoyable performance as the unscrupulous team doctor, Harvey Mandrake. Closer to Richard Boyle than *Nixon*'s stiffly obnoxious Haldeman, Woods appears to have great fun with a role that demands little of him and he leaves a lasting mark with his limited screen time.

John C McGinley enjoys a more substantial role than his previous two appearances for Stone. Even though many of his lines were also cut, he is on top form: as obnoxious as Sergeant O'Neill in the role of cigar-chomping reporter Jack Rose. Stone himself enjoyed a substantial cameo role as a loudmouthed football commentator, though he maintains that he took the part when no suitable actor could be found.

Nevertheless, such prominence seems more self-indulgence than a Hitchcockian signature or trademark. His sons also appear, both as spectators with Michael Stone as a child with an ice cream and Sean somewhat oddly brawling with a man in a gorilla suit.

The most significant change to Stone's regular crew was the absence of Robert Richardson. Reports on the reason differ. Some talk of tension between the director and his DOP, some report a simple scheduling clash – Richardson was already committed to work on Martin Scorsese's *Bringing Out the Dead*. Stone has spoken, independently, of both reasons being factors, of 'scheduling and commitment problems' but also that '[Richardson] was becoming increasingly critical of my work.' He goes on to suggest that Richardson was keener on projects such as *Alexander* than *U Turn* or *Any Given Sunday*. Salvatore Totino was brought in as replacement. This was his first feature after a career working on advertisements and music videos (among them REM's 'What's the Frequency Kenneth?' and Radiohead's 'Fake Plastic Trees') and he does a sound job.

Another new arrival was Mary Zophres, costume designer for the Coen brothers since *Fargo* (1996), who had to design several sets of completely original team uniforms. Victor Kempster remained as production designer.

The usual turnover of editors took place, with Hank Corwin leaving and Tom Nordberg, who had worked on *U Turn*, taking over with a credited team of three others – *Any Given Sunday* was an editing challenge on a par with that of *JFK*.

CUT SCENES: There are several basic cuts in existence. The original cinematic release (2 hours and 40 minutes), an airline and a television version – both cut down for length and content – the DVD cut of 2 hours 36 minutes, and a foreign cinematic release, clocking in at 12 minutes shorter than the American original. This last cut involved dropping some of the more technically complex scenes on the pitch, trimming the dialogue and activity.

There were also a slew of cut scenes, mainly dropped for reasons of length. One riffs on the idea of the pre-game ritual, with huge defensive back Madman praying over his shrine to the rock band Metallica, and chanting a form of mantra to inspire his playing. This is followed by a similar mantra from wide receiver Jimmy Sanderson, and footage of the team marching back on to the pitch for the second half of the Minnesota game, including Madman laying into one of the opposing fans.

Many of the scenes feature more screen time for Woods's Dr Mandrake and Modine's Ollie Powers. In one, Mandrake snaps a dislocated finger back into place, despite Ollie's protest that the player needs an X-ray. Pretty much all their scenes revolve around this conflict – standard ethics versus a perceived gladiatorial glory to the sport and a recognition that players, having only a few years of peak performance, should be allowed to go ahead with their game. At the benefit there is a lengthy discussion as the doctors walk along a promenade; Mandrake sees the role of the doctor as keeping the team going, keeping it together and on course for victory, irrespective of long-term consequences. After the California game the point is rubbed home by their respective bedside manners: Harvey with total optimism, brushing aside any fears, Ollie with a more cautious diagnosis. Ollie retains a scepticism that crops up in an extended take on Shark's party, where he hears that the linebacker had actually suffered a skull fracture. This leads to the revelation of Shark's injury as played out in the final cut. There is a coda to this story arc that was also dropped – Sanderson begs Ollie for drugs to help him in the Dallas game. Ollie refuses, saying that they are not necessary and, in rather predictable movie fashion, Sanderson goes out and scores the points without their help.

The benefit party also includes a chat between the mayor and Jim Brown's Montezuma character, where the latter is assured of a job should he ever need it – this is perhaps in appreciation of long service to the team, but there is also a hint at the racial motivation. Just as the black players do best when they stick together, so this applies outside the sport. The sequence finishes with a rather nasty scene where Shark explains the intricacies of one of his recent plays while masturbating Mandrake's wife under the table. It's a manifestation of the 'work hard, play hard' ethic, but is superfluous (the party at Shark's house conveys the message perfectly) and unpleasant.

One brief sequence gave Dick Butkus the opportunity of an improvised monologue; Stone offered him the choice of subject and Butkus opted to harangue one of the referees in an amusingly abusive scene. Another piece of improvisation, also unfortunately cut, was a lengthy chat between Pacino and Woods on the plane to California. They talk about getting old, and struggle with pill bottles. Though irrelevant it is amusing, and strangely touching.

Two press conferences were filmed but weren't incorporated into the movie. The first takes place after the defeat to the Americans, and features Jack Rose attacking d'Amato for his reliance on running plays.

The second comes after victory over the Crusaders, when Rose continues to attack D'Amato, and D'Amato responds with a hail of invective. Neither scene is essential, they build the antipathy between Rose and D'Amato but do little else – though it is fun to watch McGinley and Pacino.

There are a couple of additional locker room scenes, one where Beaman chastises Washington for perceived faults in his game, and another where he is approached by a white member of the team to join a prayer group – an advance he angrily rejects, pointing out that no one paid him any attention while he was on the bench.

Another cut scene from Shark's party involved a conversation between Willie and the offensive coordinator Crozier. They are interrupted by a crippled man, who turns out to be a former star quarterback, wrecked by painkillers and violent play. This is a heavy-handed message, but adds to the ambiguity of a film that both condemns the chemical crutches that keep badly injured men playing while praising the gladiatorial spirit of the gridiron warriors and their brief but glorious careers. It's a great performance by ravaged former boxer Tex Randall Gibb.

Another actor to be dropped was Jim Caviezel, playing D'Amato's estranged son, who rejects a feeble attempt at reconciliation on a golf course. The wreckage of the coach's family life is evident from the drunken call he makes to his wife, which appears in the film, and this awkward attempt at reconciliation adds little to the story. It should act as a mirror to the relationship between Diaz and Ann-Margret, but there is no happy family for D'Amato beyond his team and the scene plays slow and largely meaningless.

There is extended coverage of the rivalry between Willie and Julian – the criticism in the locker room, as mentioned above, a sequence where Julian is seen at his palatial condo watching Willie's interview with Jack Rose and a scene where the two make up shortly before the Dallas game. This pre-match sequence also includes a short speech from Montezuma, in the vein of Pacino's exhortation to grab every inch. After the game, there is an extended celebration sequence in the locker room, with interviews of the players, a brief cameo by major US sports agent Lee Steinberg and a couple of scenes allowing closure for D'Amato with Pagniacci and Rooney. D'Amato states his intention to resign to Pagniacci, while Rooney informs the coach that this will be his last season.

Several scenes, not shown at the cinema, were cut into the DVD release. Jimmy Sanderson and Julian Washington are seen taking cocaine at the charity ball – ironic as the charity in question is an anti-drugs programme. Later, in the Sharks' communal shower, Willie speaks to Luther about an upcoming dinner with the coach. Luther advises that he take flowers – a practical joke that Willie falls for and explains the bouquet he carries on his visit to D'Amato. Another features the prostitute Mandy Murphy, and D'Amato making an abortive proposal to her in the bathroom of his house. A grim addition to the film's final game shows an opposing player's eye being literally forced out of its socket – a nod, perhaps, to an idea for a similarly disembodied eye to be included in *Platoon*.

MEMORABLE QUOTES: The film builds to one of the best set-piece speeches in Stone's career:

D'Amato: 'In either game, life or football, the margin for error is so small, I mean one half a step too late or too early and you don't quite make it . . . Because we know that when we add up all those inches that's going to make the fucking difference between winning and losing, between living and dying . . . if I'm going to have any life any more it's because I'm still willing to fight and die for that inch. Because that's what living is. The six inches in front of your face.'

GOOD VS EVIL: Unlike any of Stone's other films, this has no one clear protagonist. Instead conflict (both internal and external) is examined from the perspective of the football team, at all levels from management through the team doctors to the players themselves.

The key word here is team. All must work together – as Tony D'Amato puts it in his inspirational speech, 'we can win as a team or lose as individuals'. Bad in this film is synonymous with selfish, for example, Pagniacci trying to cut costs and boost profits, Willie becoming obsessed with his own fame at the expense of his team-mates and Julian blind to anything but securing his lucrative trainer contract. It is only when differences are patched up, and everyone learns to appreciate their place in the greater hierarchy, that the team can find success and avoid ignominious defeat. For the gestalt entity of the team these are the equivalents of good and evil.

The suggestion, perhaps, is that the modern approach to the marketing of sport is to blame. It is the temptation of money and fame that lures players to think themselves above the team. In turn they are expected to make sacrifices – their health and, if necessary, their life.

REDEMPTION OR DAMNATION: The film comes across as the polar opposite of *U Turn*. As Stone puts it, 'everyone's a winner.' If the film is seen as a succession of crises, all the main characters come out not only having survived but also having learned and benefited from them. The coach has rediscovered his love of the game, and has found a new job where he will have managerial control; the young quarterback has learned leadership and teamwork while the elder has ended his career in spectacular style; the owner is reconciled to her mother and has come to terms with the burden assumed from her father; and the linebacker has battled through injury to provide for his family. The one possible exception is Dr Mandrake, who leaves the team with little indication of appreciable change. Having said that, there is little to damn him for either, in keeping with the somewhat ambiguous attitude the film has towards medical treatment of players. Mandrake's philosophy was based on a warped devotion to the team, to winning no matter what, and is somewhat born out by Luther's pleas to be let back on the pitch.

STARS AND STRIPES: Gridiron football is perhaps the most complex of the big four North American pro sports (the others being basketball, ice hockey and baseball). It combines brief snatches of intense, brutal violence with lengthy periods of inaction and fiendishly intricate strategy.

The sport itself is not the subject of any criticism in the film. Stone creates a mythos around it as a modern manifestation of the gladiatorial warrior spirit, an image that is bluntly pressed in the film, notably through the use of footage from *Ben-Hur* (William Wyler, 1959). It is the corporate management of the game that comes under attack, both through the mercenary attitude it encourages in some players – the free-agents who are retained on short-term contracts, as represented by Julian Washington – and the management of the various 'franchises', the somewhat distasteful corporate way through which teams are distributed to various locales, sold to the highest bidder who gains a guaranteed monopoly in a particular area, like an investor paying a fast-food chain for the right to open a local branch. More specifically, the racial make-up of the sport is brought under question.

BEING OLIVER STONE: Stone has been a lifelong fan of the San Francisco 49ers (an enthusiasm referenced in the film – it is revealed that San Francisco beat the Sharks in the play-offs) but beyond this there is little explicit autobiographical reference. Some might read a lot into the divorce of D'Amato, or harassment by the media, but there is nothing here that does not make sense in the context of character or the film. Rather than Stone's effect on the film, it might be productive to speculate on the film's effect on Stone. This, the second-highest-grossing film in his canon, came after two successive box-office flops, a critical gutting over the release of his book and turmoil within his production company. *Any Given Sunday* was a solid and undeniable success.

INSPIRATION AND INFLUENCE: There have been films about baseball – *Major League* (David S War, 1989), *Bull Durham* (Ron Shelton, 1989) and Basketball – *White Men Can't Jump* (Ron Shelton, 1992), but very few about gridiron football. The large-scale, intense action makes re-creation a very demanding enterprise, and the success here is testament to Oliver Stone's skill. One notable exception, *The Longest Yard* (Robert Aldrich, 1974), concentrated on amateur prison-yard football.

When it comes to specific influences, former player Pat Toomay produced a novel following the trials and tests of a pro-football player – *On Any Given Sunday*, from which the film took its title. More esoteric background information came from *You're OK – It's Just a Bruise*. A confessional account of author Rob Huizenga's time as internist for the superbowl-winning LA Raiders side of the 1980s, it mixes boardroom politics, behind-the-scenes anecdotes and wince-inducing accounts of gruesome injuries and drug abuse. This lent much of the colour and incidental details to the medical scenes – dislocated fingers, rapid fluid transfusion and painkiller prescription. In addition, the relationship of Powers and Mandrake is closely modelled on Huizenga's account of his relations with senior Raiders' doctor Robert Rosenfeld, a proponent of the pump them with drugs and let them go on playing school. Huizenga comes across as ethical young Powers, insisting on proper treatment for players. The Shark Lavay subplot is a direct lift from the book's story of LA player Mike Harden (though in reality it was Huizenga who resigned in protest). The story of the crippled quarterback was inspired by the fate of injured player Dave Dalby.

REEL TIME: Stone and Totino's style for the action sequences feeds off a kinetic brutality harkening back to the frenzied handheld camerawork of *Salvador* and *Wall Street*. Key here are the games themselves for which an approach was taken reminiscent of strategy on *The Doors*'s concert sequences: an enclosed venue, centring on one point of action which radiates out through a crowd of extras. The arena was flooded with cameras – the usual fixed positions to capture the big picture and for crowd reactions and an astonishing array of portable equipment, including cameras strapped directly to key players (referred to as 'ratcams'). Another piece of equipment used for these scenes was the 'image shaker' a device that saw wide usage on *Saving Private Ryan* (Steven Spielberg, 1998) to replicate the effects of artillery explosions by creating a shake effect on a focussed image. The close-in camerawork, and the casting of professionals and former professionals to fill out the line of scrimmage, takes the viewer right into the heart of a fast and violent game that can seem somewhat slow and staid when watched on television.

Most of the off-pitch scenes (with the exception of the parties) feature a traditional dramatic style of two or three actors, fixed cameras and steady editing. But so intense is the action that these sequences can feel like little more than breathing room.

The lighting and production design is warm throughout, deep reds and yellows. Totino said of the games themselves, 'Generally I didn't use any stadium light . . . I wanted to stay away from that look because all football movies are shot that way.' The intense Florida sun provided much of the light for the day games. The two night sequences, the second half of game one and the rain-sodden game at New York, were somewhat more experimental, with the action lit entirely from one side, creating what amounts to a silhouette. The main problem came at Texas Stadium, a venue with a huge aperture in the roof (constructed, so local lore goes, so that God can watch his favourite team play). The crew blocked off this hole, a massive task, and the stadium was lit artificially. Imaginative lighting was used in one other scene, the charity ball, where Totino was unable to erect lighting rigs inside the architecturally significant Sky Mansion being used for the set. Instead he floated helium balloons filled with four powerful bulbs around the set, lighting the party from above.

MUSIC: Though *Any Given Sunday* has a score, an effective but largely undistinguished electric guitar composition, it is very rarely heard in the film. This is due to the soundtrack, which has an astonishing 81 separate pieces of music listed in the closing credits. Pretty much every moment of on-pitch action (and off-pitch partying) is accompanied by a snatch of pop music, occasionally no more than a few seconds long. There is representation from pretty much every genre: the electronica of Moby, Fatboy Slim and the Propellerheads, the stadium glam of Queen and Gary Glitter, even the europop house music of Mousse T. One of the most interesting conceits of the film is to mark a separation of the white and black players on the team through the use of music (in a similar way to the division between the heads and the squares in *Platoon*). In the locker room the audience see the black players listening to rap – a genre that features extensively in the soundtrack as a whole – and the white defensive backs listening to the heavy metal of Metallica. This is an interesting curio that serves little overall purpose, as the racial commentary of the film is pitched above the team level.

Several of the songs were compositions specifically for the film, notably the two contributed by Jamie Foxx – 'My Name is Willie' and the title track to the film, 'Any Given Sunday', the latter an enjoyably mellow track, and much better than the former, which exists largely within the context of the film as an indication of Beaman's swollen ego. LL Cool J also wrote a song, 'Shut 'Em Down', a generic, forgettable piece of hip-hop.

BOX OFFICE: *Any Given Sunday* cleared a gross of $75.5 million by March 2000. This was the highest gross since *Platoon*. Having said this, the profit margin was far lower – only $10.5 million after the budget of $65 million is taken into account.

CRITICS: The critical consensus of the film was best summed up in *Empire* magazine: 'Despite the film's multifarious faults . . . there can be no argument that this is one of the most visually exciting experiences you will have this year.' The appeal of the visceral action seemed to depend on the sensibilities of the viewer. Veteran critic Alexander Walker's opinion on the film was, 'a threat to sanity. From start to finish, it's shot like a 162 minute trailer . . . and just as unintelligible.' On the other hand, Nigel Andrews of the *Financial Times* admitted, 'It's a long, loud, grandstanding often barmy movie, of which I enjoyed every second.'

Despite the odd dissident – Lee Pinkerton in the *Voice*: 'all the elements are good but there's still too much football' – most British critics were fairly happy with a film revolving around this American game. An upbeat Philip French described the film as 'exciting and involving' despite the probability that 'many of the underlying strategies on the playing field will be lost on British audiences.' The more savvy American commentators detected a 'dumbing down' of the sport; Roger

Ebert was critical of a film where 'there isn't really a single sequence of sports action in which the strategy of a play can be observed and understood from beginning to end.'

While some critics saw the sport, violent and simplified as it was, at the centre of the film – Peter Bradshaw wrote in the *Guardian*, 'ultimately, Stone is just intoxicated with football for itself, the harsh power and slo-mo poetry of stegosaurus proportioned men and their contest for glory' – others took a wider view, for example, James Christopher in *The Times* suggested that Stone 'compacts an epic vision of the 21st century into an American football stadium'. The *New York Times* critic spoke of this as another instalment in Stone's ongoing 'hyper-macho vision of modern American life as a primitive bread-and-circuses carnival of power, greed, lust, fame and violence' while Nigel Andrews took one further step, saying, 'this is more than a film about America, this is a film that *is* America.' This fitted in fine with Andrew O'Hagan's view that Stone 'is a big director, and a blunt one – the most consistently grand American mythographer since DW Griffith'.

AWARDS: Like *U Turn*, *Any Given Sunday* received no major awards and only two noteworthy nominations – for Stone at the Berlin Film Festival and Jamie Foxx at the MTV movie awards.

THE BIG PICTURE: After war in the field, war on the home front, war in politics, the secret war of intelligence agencies, and war as high finance, war on the sports field was one of the few unexplored areas left for Stone, and this film bears the combat metaphor on its sleeve. The contempt for the media that stretches back to *JFK*, and possibly even *Talk Radio*, is also evident: broadcasters more interested in grabbing ratings through controversy and conflict than meaningful, constructive criticism.

FINAL ANALYSIS: There is also more than a hint of the mid-life crisis to this movie, which occasionally comes across as the cinematic equivalent of a bright red sports car and a blonde trophy wife. The big noises and clashing action is nothing new to Stone's work in itself, but it is more the way that this interacts with the painfully try-hard soundtrack, the desperate attempts to be 'relevant' with regard to youth (especially black youth) culture and a cameo which is uncomfortably prominent. Having said this, it has never been in Stone's nature to be subtle or understated, and if one overlooks this unsettling veneer on the film, its good points come shining through. Technically it is a great achievement, and it is also a brave departure from Stone's usual narrative approach – he has used an ensemble cast on several previous occasions but never with this many separate plot strands. To an extent it also manages to couple the mystical masculine honour and bonding of *Platoon* with the hyperkinetic aesthetic of *Natural Born Killers*: it's a brutally violent spiked bat of a film in its action sequences (including the drinking and partying as much as the football games) while maintaining a mythic tone, gladiators and team-play, which should be laughable, but works within its context.

Interlude: Two Documentaries

'If I hadn't gone to Vietnam, I'd probably be on Wall Street now . . . maybe a journalist, out in foreign places covering wars. I'd have loved that.' In the hiatus following *Any Given Sunday* Oliver Stone would put this dream into practice. These two documentaries were originally intended as parts of a trilogy on revolutionary leaders; the third was to have featured Kim Jong II of North Korea but has never been realised.

Comandante (2003)

In February 2002, Oliver Stone travelled to Havana, Cuba, to interview President Fidel Castro. After three days he had collected 30 hours of footage. At any time Castro had the option to call a halt to proceedings. At no point did he do so.

The interview opens in Castro's office. A warm-up selection of questions about lifestyle and time spent working are interspersed with archive footage of the 1959 revolution, of the triumphal march into Havana, of a younger Castro making various speeches to his people. The camera pans through a department store, prowls along the streets of Havana. Stone rides in Castro's presidential limo, digging a handgun out from behind his seat. They visit a medical college, a school, Castro's private cinema (though he hasn't watched a film there in ten years) and the gallery of contemporary art. Stone dines with Castro's son and grandson and various surviving leaders of the revolution. The film closes with a touching farewell at Havana airport.

The discussion is similarly wide-ranging. There is recollection of milestone events, the revolution, the Bay of Pigs invasion, the missile crisis, the death of Che Guevara . . . but the approach is informal and fairly loose, Stone rarely pressing for an answer beyond Castro's opinion as given.

There are also more personal questions, and personal revelations. Stone tries and fails to get an answer about Castro's love life; the audience learn more about his taste in movies. He is a big fan of Brigitte Bardot, Sophia Loren and Charlie

Chaplin and has seen *Titanic* – but only on video. There is talk about ideology, and answers that go beyond the usual dogmatic platitudes. He presents religion as a matter of personal choice, capable of leading to good or to evil, of the future of humanity in the world – generally optimistic in hoping that reason will prevail. There is even humour – after a conversation about Viagra, Castro jokes that this is another CIA assassination attempt – and a rather incongruous reference to Stone's own interests – Castro's verdict on the Kennedy shooting (no one could fire a rifle that fast and accurately).

The rather predictable final question is whether Castro would change anything. The equally predictable answer – no, he wouldn't.

A somewhat mystifying caption card, perhaps chosen more as Stone's verdict on the contemporary USA and HBO's treatment of his documentary: 'Those who would give up essential liberty to obtain a moment of temporary safety deserve neither liberty nor safety' Ben Franklin.

The interview itself is shallow but wide. This is neither a penetrating investigation of a life nor an attempt to push Castro into a corner (for a classic example of aggressive political interview, see David Frost's televised session with Richard Nixon in the mid 1970s). However, what the audience do get is a discussion that treats a demonised Communist leader as a human being. Stone is quoted as 'having approached Castro the way he would approach an actor. He'd push until he knew he had gotten what he could, then quit.'

A *Film Comment* piece on *Comandante* was scathing – '[Stone] is no kind of journalist at all – left, right or centre.' It went on to demolish the interview at great length: a lack of investigation into political limitations, a failure to probe economic problems (in part untrue – Castro touches on the country's woe since the collapse of the Soviet Union), no questions on the fate of the country following Castro's death and a total lack of follow-up questions, instead a tendency to make jokes.

These are fair points, but views such as *Screen International*'s 'the subject is the only controversial thing about the film' miss the point. Many news reports and contemporary magazine shows often choose to paint the subject in a deliberately sensationalist light in order to attract ratings. Many are the films, documentaries and special reports that focus on Cuba as a repressive regime and Castro as a dictator. For fear of sounding flippant, what is wrong with seeing another side? To see them as self-publicising filmmaker and crafty oppressive dictator at this moment is perhaps overly cynical – one could, for just a brief second, view them as war veterans, each with their own scars.

HBO pulled *Comandante* days before its planned broadcast date. The *Film Comment* piece quoted the network's reason: 'The decision came in the light of recent Cuban government crackdowns on dissidents . . . the network apparently plans to broadcast the documentary if and when Stone returns to Cuba, re-interviews Castro and updates the film's material.' In spring 2004 a sequel,

Looking for Fidel, was screened on US television. Though more searching, many of the real questions behind Castro remain unanswered.

Persona Non Grata (2003)

In November 2001, in the midst of the Palestinian intifada, Oliver Stone travelled to Palestine with the intent of recording an interview with the major forces involved on both sides of the Arab–Israeli conflict. He spent time on the West Bank and witnessed the lifestyle of ordinary Palestinians caught up in the crossfire.

He met with Benjamin Netanyahu and Ehud Barak, and encountered their uncompromising views towards the Palestinians (though Barak comes across as gnomically articulate – 'it is not poverty that creates terror, it is terror that creates poverty'), and Shimon Peres, who took the view that 'history is written in red ink – we shouldn't teach the history of the past, we should teach the history of the future.'

He also met with representatives of Hamas – an extremist Islamic group, whose ambassador refused to shake hands with Stone's female assistant as he was on his way to the mosque – and the Al Aqsa brigade, who claimed their argument was more with the Israeli settlers.

He spent time in the beleaguered compound of Yasser Arafat in the town of Ramallah. All attempts to meet with Arafat were thwarted, until a savage round of suicide bombings led to Israel closing the border.

Stone and his crew escaped in Canadian embassy vehicles. A final interview with Netanyahu was interrupted by another suicide attack, just up the road from the building.

This was filmed before *Comandante,* but it is evident that the final production is a compromise on the original intent. A somewhat shorter, less polished, but still intriguing production, *Persona Non Grata* began life as a film on the ongoing dispute between Israelis and Palestinians, an interview with Yasser Arafat at its centre, but this was hampered by intransigence on the part of Arafat's staff and worsening relations between Palestinians and Israelis. As one watches the film unfold, the goal of a one-on-one between Stone and Arafat becomes more elusive, and the situation of the crew, if never truly perilous, more risky. They are caught up in growing riots, are trapped in hotel rooms and prepare to dash out, if need be, to record the expected razing of Arafat's fortified compound. The shoot ends in panicked flight. The nominal goal has not been achieved, and what remains is, objectively, little more than a snapshot of a geopolitical situation that changes from day to day.

Nonetheless it remains a fascinating and depressing document. It's dark stuff, much more so than warm cuddly Castro. He can evade the questions of his interviewer, can stroll through leafy atria or along sun-kissed streets. In the contested towns of Palestine, the misery, fear and anger of the Arabs and fear, anger and misery of the Israelis render any cosy Q and A largely irrelevant.

OLIVER STONE Alexander

As parts of an abortive trilogy they are very different films. The former rich with nostalgia for the days of Che and a time in which Cuba was hailed as the hope of the Third World rather than pitied by the New World Order. It paints the portraits of a leader who is now a cuddly *Titanic* fan more than rebel firebrand and a country that, reading between the lines, is counting the days to their Comandante's death, for a return to the global status quo of capitalism.

The latter is saturated with despair, irreconcilability and futility. Stone is another righteous reporter to be thwarted by the quagmire of Middle Eastern politics, but the images he brings back are still fascinating.

Neither can claim much long-term significance, but *Persona Non Grata* is the more ephemeral. When Castro eventually does die, *Comandante* will be one of the few English language documents to treat him sympathetically.

Alexander (2004)

Casting by Mark Bennett, Lucinda Syson and Billy Hopkins
Production Design: Jan Roelfs
Art Direction: Jonathan McKinstry and Kevin Phipps
Music composed by Vangelis
Director of Photography: Rodrigo Prieto
Film Editing: Yann Hervé, Alex Marquez and Thomas J Nordberg
Produced by Moritz Borman, Jon Kilik, Thomas Schühly, Iain Smith and Oliver Stone
Executive Producers: Gianni Nunnari and Fernando Sulichan
Written and Directed by Oliver Stone

CAST: Colin Farrell (*Alexander*), Jared Leto (*Hephaistion*), Anthony Hopkins (*Ptolemy*), Rosario Dawson (*Roxanne*), Angelina Jolie (*Olympias*), Gary Stretch (*Cleitus*), Jonathan Rhys-Meyers (*Cassander*), Val Kilmer (*Philip*), Ian Beattie (*Antigonus*), Brian Blessed (*Leonidas*), Francisco Bosch (*Bagoas*), Elliot Cowan (*Young Ptolemy*), Raz Degan (*Darius*), Rory McCann (*Crateros*), Joseph Morgan (*Philotas*), Connor Paolo (*Young Alexander*)

NOTABLE CREDITS: Dale Dye acted as both Second Unit Director and Senior Military Adviser.

SUMMARY: Born in 356 BC, Alexander assumed the leadership of Macedonia in 336 BC on the assassination of his father, Philip, who had himself been on the brink of launching a campaign against Darius III – 'King of Kings' and sovereign of the Persian Empire.

Alexander secured his power base in Greece through a campaign against the recalcitrant Thebes before leaving for the Hellespont (today the Sea of Marmara). Behind he left his mother – the fiery Olympias – as Greece's queen, and Antipater – trusted officer of Philip – as general of a guardian force.

Alexander cut through Asia at a furious pace, defeating the Persians at a number of famous battles – Granicus, Issus, Gaugamela – and forcing Darius into ignominious flight and eventual murder at the hands of mutinous officers. In his stead, Alexander took to the throne of Persia and accepted the mantle 'King of Kings', but was unprepared to set a limit to his kingdom. He led his army into Afghanistan and into India.

His list of victories grew but he became personally unstable, murdering a comrade, Cleitus, after a drunken argument and coming under criticism from others for his adoption of Persian ways. He acquired a wife, Roxanne – daughter of an Iranian baron – and a string of lovers, including Hephaistion, an officer in his army, and Bagoas – a eunuch, taken into his household in the Persian style.

In India, Alexander continued a successful campaign, accepting submission or defeating those who resisted, such as Porus, despite the presence of fearsome war elephants. Alexander's eastward expansion was halted at the river Hyphasis, when his men – who by then had been marching for eight years – refused to go any further. As his army turned, so did Alexander's luck. He suffered a serious chest wound at the siege of Multun and led his forces on a disastrous march through the desert of Makran.

Alexander had executed a number of formerly close compatriots (veteran general Parmenion, personal historian Callisthenes) over fears of various plots to have him killed, and had himself come to the throne as a result of intrigue and political murder. While resting in Babylon in preparation to launch a fresh campaign into Arabia the question of conspiracy rose again. In 323 Alexander died after a week's serious sickness and accusations of a poisoning were swiftly levelled against Cassander, the son of Antipater. Within 70 years Alexander's empire had broken up, though Greek influence would persist for centuries to come.

ADVANCE PUBLICITY: As the first Oliver Stone film in five years, and wielding an impressive budget, *Alexander* has been subject to the usual level of press scrutiny for such an anticipated project. Most attention has been paid to the antics of hell-raising lead Colin Farrell, but a lot has also been paid to the abortive 'rivalry' with the delayed Baz Luhrmann film *Alexander the Great* (see **PRODUCTION HISTORY**).

PRODUCTION HISTORY: The genesis for *Alexander* can be found back in 1990. At this early stage Stone had been in discussions with American novelist Gore Vidal over a script for a film based on Alexander's life. According to Stone, '[Vidal] offered to write Alexander the Great for me . . . at his villa in Rivello, Italy, I turned his ultra-homoerotic suggestions down.' Nineteen ninety was a busy period for the director and, like many other ideas of the time, it was put to the bottom of the pile.

In 1996 the idea was revived, and Stone worked on the script alone, using Robin Lane Fox's biography of the Macedonian king as a basis (see **INSPIRATION AND INFLUENCE**) and spending time in Greece conducting further research. Tom Cruise was mooted for the lead but turned it down, allegedly because of the prominence of Alexander's bisexual tendencies. The project went back into suspended animation.

In 1998 Stone had tried to expand his career into TV with a proposed series for American network ABC entitled *De-Classified*, which dealt with unsolved mysteries of a conspiratorial nature. For instance, one episode was to investigate a 1996 plane crash and allege the involvement of the US military. In justification of cancellation, a spokesman for the channel spoke of Stone's tradition of mixing fact and theory when he said, 'We came to believe that television viewers could find it difficult to distinguish between the two forms.' After the release of *Any Given Sunday* Stone moved back into the sphere of the documentary, with a planned trilogy of interviews with controversial world leaders (see **Two Documentaries**). After meeting Castro and becoming embroiled in Ramallah, Stone returned to filmmaking, announcing a revival of *Alexander* towards the end of 2002. This time Stone was able to put together funding for the massive $150 million budget. Producer Moritz Borman of Intermedia explains Hollywood's change of heart: '*Gladiator* came out and worked really well, and everybody in Hollywood who saw it said, "Whoa, maybe we should go back and make these kind of pictures."' The finance was assembled from a slew of independent sources, with Warner Bros to distribute.

As with previous works, and in keeping with the needs of the genre, location shooting was to play a vital part in Stone's latest film. In

September 2003 Stone began filming in Morocco with the Maghreb standing in for the dusty plains of Persia. Initially it looked as though this would be where *Alexander* would come up against *Alexander the Great*, a similarly themed project produced by Dino De Laurentiis, helmed by the flamboyant Baz Luhrmann with Leonardo DiCaprio in the lead and a script based on a series of novels by Valerio Manfredi (a third project – a mini-series under the auspices of Mel Gibson – had recently folded). However, Stone avoided suggestions of a frantic rivalry: 'The race for me has always been with my script, not with Baz. He has great vision and I liked his *Romeo and Juliet*.' In any case, this confrontation was not to be. In the wake of the Casablanca terrorist bombings of spring 2003, production of *Alexander the Great* in Morocco was cancelled (Australia was chosen as a substitute). Since then it has been subject to ongoing delays, with a tentative release date of 2005 but completion looks increasingly unlikely.

Stone's insistence on continued production in Morocco earned him plaudits at the 2003 Morocco Film Festival, where he received an Etoile d'Or in recognition of his contribution to the country's film industry. He also had the opportunity to dine with the country's king.

Stone shot around Agadir, Marrakech and Essouira in the shadows of the Atlas Mountains, used to give a snowy backdrop to Alexander's march through the mountain ranges of Cappadocia and Afghanistan. England's studio complexes were chosen for the construction of elaborate sets. In the first months of 2004 Stone and his crew set off for Thailand to shoot the film's re-creation of Alexander's Indian campaign, complete with lush vegetation and the massed ranks of war elephants. The film is scheduled for release in the autumn of 2004.

CASTING: Heath Ledger was initially favoured as Alexander, but was replaced early on by Colin Farrell. The young Irish actor, having started out on the small screen in *Ballykissangel* has become ubiquitous, with roles in a number of Hollywood action features including *Minority Report* (Steven Spielberg, 2002), *Daredevil* (Mark Steven Johnson, 2003), *The Recruit* (Roger Donaldson, 2003) and Ixtlan production *SWAT* (Clark Johnson, 2003). He has also displayed some acting ability in World War II POW legal drama *Hart's War* (Gregory Hoblit, 2002). *Alexander* must count as the most demanding job of his career to date – one of the greatest and most successful generals to have lived, a man who changed the world, who was worshipped as a god and possessed an enigmatic personal life rife with alcoholism, shady plots and sexual relationships not just with his three wives but also with his eunuch Bagoas and close friend Hephaistion. Hephaistion is played by Jared Leto and his physical relationship with Alexander looks set to be portrayed graphically on screen.

It is this last aspect that has prompted most on-set gossip (off-set, the media is dominated by stories of Farrell's drinking prowess and breathless talk of romance with his co-star and on-screen mother Angelina Jolie).

Jolie's Olympias looks likely to draw heavily on the actress's eccentric reputation, as the Queen herself was reputed to be an exotic character – a keen follower of Dionysius. Twenty-five-year-old Rosario Dawson plays Alexander's Persian bride, while Brian Blessed, bearded veteran of many disparate films from the respectable (*Hamlet*, Kenneth Branagh, 1996) to the ridiculous (*Flash Gordon*, Mike Hodges, 1980), plays Leonidas one of Alexander's early tutors. Robin Lane Fox has a somewhat unconventional career role – he rides in the front rank of the Macedonian cavalry charges.

OLIVER'S ARMY: Other interesting casting comes in the form of *Nixon*'s Anthony Hopkins as Ptolemy, who in reality was a similar age to Alexander, having been one of the young Macedonian nobles to have grown up with him and to have formed the basis for his early officer corps. This raises the possibility that the film will be told in flashback, from the perspective of the older Ptolemy who seized control of Egypt as Pharaoh in the wake of Alexander's death, and who would supervise the burial of the young general in the Egyptian city of Alexandria.

Val Kilmer (*The Doors*) will be reunited with Stone for the first time in thirteen years, as Philip of Macedon, Alexander's father. This amounts to a cameo appearance – though important in setting the scene for the film, the King died when Alexander was only twenty, and the son swiftly outstripped the achievements of his father.

The five-year gap in Stone's career means that there are few familiar faces in the behind-the-camera line-up for *Alexander*. Casting was overseen by Billy Hopkins and editing by Thomas Nordberg, while the trusty Dale Dye returns for the first time since *Natural Born Killers*. Robert Richardson appears to have moved on completely from work with Stone, collaborating now with Quentin Tarantino on *Kill Bill* and Martin Scorsese on the Howard Hughes biopic *The Aviator*. Similarly Salvatore Totino has left Stone's employ, being replaced by Rodrigo Prieto, a Mexican cinematographer who had worked with Stone on

Comandante and *Persona Non Grata* (see **Two Documentaries**, p. 260) – while Victor Kempster's post has been taken by Jan Roelfs.

GOOD VS EVIL: As well as the element of conspiracy that Stone looks set to inject, the story of Alexander is basically one of glorious victory over external obstacles offset by internal turmoil. Heavy drinking, a refusal to accept limits on his conquests, a fixation on the Homeric values of Achilles and a brutal nervous collapse after the death of Hephaistion. After attempts to deify Jim Morrison, Stone has moved on the story of the true Dionysian hero: a man who lived for excess in all aspects of his life, with the ongoing conflict with himself and others that this implies.

REDEMPTION OR DAMNATION: This will be the fulcrum of the movie – as with *Nixon*, it is unlikely to be a dry balance sheet of successes versus failures but rather one man's achievements viewed in the lights of the forces that drove him. The question remains, will the film celebrate the achievements that are possible with total self-confidence or make a point on the emptiness of worldly gains, of a territorial empire that crumbles within years of death? An ongoing obsession on Stone's part with the archetypal classical hero and aforementioned parallels with Jim Morrison marks the former interpretation as the more likely. Unlike the vacillating, impotent Nixon, Alexander was a man who bent the known world to his ends. There are greater parallels with the plot of *JFK* – it is widely suggested that Alexander was killed to further the self-interest of a small coterie of high-ranking officials.

HISTORY 101 and **CONSPIRACY THEORY:** If incorporated into the film (and Stone's words on the script imply that this will very much be the case), this last point will be a lot more plausible than it is in *JFK*. The story of Alexander seems tailor-made for Stone – a corpus of agreed facts with many grey areas, leaving themselves open to subjective interpretation. The **SUMMARY** above is a brief synopsis of established history. Doubts remain over Philip's assassination, the numerous supposed plots that led to the execution of several of Alexander's friends and the story of his own death. In his biography, Robin Lane Fox puts cases for poisoning or a short, fatal illness, but suggests problems in each case. In an article written in early 2003, he admitted, 'For historians, one of the fascinations about Alexander is the gaps in what we can never know.' Hadding said, 'I leave it to Oliver Stone to fill them out, recognising that they give such scope for the imagination.' Stone looks set to take this as an opportunity to illustrate his belief in the timelessness of conspiracy – 'In Alexander's own untimely death at 33, we have again strong evidence of a conspiracy of family clans.' Stone wrote in 1998, 'Did he die of fever or poisoned wine? I choose to believe the latter.'

REAL PEOPLE: The lack of truly established facts means that the character of Alexander is a blank canvas on which any interpretation, within reason, can be laid out. An earlier script, mooted for production in 1996 in parallel to Stone's effort, focussed on the idea that Alexander was killed for his growing cowardice and decadence. Baz Luhrmann's film intends to concentrate on Alexander's relationship with his mother. Given his draft of the script for *Conan the Barbarian* (see **The Ones that Got Away**, p. 41) Stone looks likely to present Alexander as a great king brought down by lesser men.

INSPIRATION AND INFLUENCE: *Gladiator* (Ridley Scott, 2000) single-handedly revived a moribund genre. As well as *Alexander*, its success has ensured the making of *Troy* (Wolfgang Petersen, 2004) starring Brad Pitt, in addition to productions based on the famous battle of Thermopylae (where 300 Spartans battled thousands of Persian invaders) linked to George Clooney and on the career of Carthaginian general Hannibal with Vin Diesel mooted to star.

The golden age of the classical epic lies far in the past. *Ben-Hur* (William Wyler, 1959) and *Spartacus* (Stanley Kubrick, 1960) are the key works to spring to mind, and the genre was characterised by the huge costs necessitated by the vast scale. It was this expense that made swords-and-sandals pictures unpopular – *Cleopatra* (Joseph L Mankiewicz *et al*, 1963) did little business at gross expense and, with a few exceptions, the classical world was rarely a subject for Hollywood afterwards. The rise in digital technology has reversed this trend – *Gladiator* was able to turn a half-built set with few hundred extras into a howling mob of thousands. This century's viewers can be supplied with grand spectacle at affordable prices and, as Ridley Scott's movie has proven, will flock to see it.

Aside from his personal interest, Stone's academic inspiration came from Robin Lane Fox's 1973 work *Alexander the Great*. It is a colourful and opinionated book, keeping close to its subject with occasional forays into wider areas such as the cultural impact of Macedonian invasion and their tactics in battle. Fox is unafraid to hypothesise when evidence is thin and this is perhaps what drew Stone to his work.

There are huge gaps in the historical record and, in the light of the furore surrounding *JFK* and *Nixon*, it is entirely appropriate that Stone's next historical work deal with a subject where the very sources on which the orthodox view is based are themselves copies of original documents made centuries after the event. In this instance it is not just a case of Stone delving into the shadows of a well-lit past, but of dealing with a time of universal historical twilight, where the best-established facts are still, ultimately, a good guess.

MUSIC: The Greek composer Vangelis is the embodiment of 1980s mood instrumental. He is best known for the memorable score to *Chariots of Fire* (for which he won an Academy Award) and the haunting electronic chords that accompanied *Blade Runner* (Ridley Scott, 1982). It will be very interesting to see what he makes of 4th century BC Asia.

TRIVIA: A perennial problem with any period drama is the issue of accents. Mel Gibson has taken the fiercest line on this – his *Passion of Jesus Christ* (2004) was filmed entirely in the languages Aramaic and Latin. Most other films have taken a more relaxed line and are filmed in English, often casting British actors in the roles of senators or courtiers with grittier Americans portraying the soldiery and protagonist.

Stone is trying a different tack. In an attempt to differ between the various ethnic groupings, while filming entirely in English, the actors will employ different Celtic accents. This means that Alexander will speak in Colin Farrell's own broad Irish accent. Whether this rather bizarre move pays off remains to be seen.

FINAL ANALYSIS – BEING OLIVER STONE: Part of the reason for Stone's long absence from mainstream cinema might be due to his personal problems. In June 1999 he was arrested for possession of hashish and drunk driving. Shortly afterwards he entered rehab. Despite the commercial success of *Any Given Sunday* there are suggestions of a midlife crisis – a lack of direction perhaps enhanced by the box-office failure of *Nixon*. The two films subsequent to this cannot be described as ambitious in the same way as his political work. This might have prompted his move into documentary filmmaking, something more easily identified as 'worthy'.

Of course, this is supposition, made no easier by Stone's lack of public image over the period (the press has no interest in a star or director who lies low). In this context the production of *Alexander* is most heartening. It is a return to filmmaking on the scale of *The Doors* or *Any Given Sunday* with the historical ambition of *Nixon* and *JFK* and the warrior's eye view of battles honed in *Platoon* and *Heaven and Earth*.

It is good to be able to finish a study of Oliver Stone's work on such a note. *Alexander* may be brilliant, it may fail, but there is no faulting the ambition, the vision, the obstinacy (keeping the project alive for over ten years), the excess and the embrace of controversy that have marked the highest points of Stone's career.

Bibliography

Inspiration and Screenplays

JFK: The Book of the Film, screenplay by Oliver Stone and Zachary Sklar, research notes Complied by Jane Rusconi (Applause, New York, 1992)

The Making of Oliver Stone's Heaven and Earth, Michael Singer, from the screenplay by Oliver Stone with additional text by Oliver Stone, Le Ly Hayslip and Hiep Thi Le (Orion, London, 1993)

Nixon: An Oliver Stone Film, ed. Eric Hamburg, screenplay by Stephen J Rivele, Christopher Wilkinson and Oliver Stone (Bloomsbury, London, 1996)

Aitken, Jonathan, *Nixon: a Life* (Weidenfeld & Nicolson, London, 1993)

Ambrose, Stephen E, *Nixon: the Education of a Politician, 1913–62* (Simon & Schuster, London, 1987); *Nixon: the Triumph of a Politician, 1962–72* (Simon & Schuster, London, 1989); *Nixon: Ruin and Recovery, 1973–90* (Simon & Schuster, London, 1991)

Block, Lawrence, *Eight Million Ways to Die* (Robert Hale, London, 1983)

Bogosian, Eric, *Talk Radio* (Faber & Faber, London, 1989)

Bonner, Raymond, *Weakness and Deceit: US Policy and El Salvador* (Hamish Hamilton, London, 1985)

Brandel, Marc, *The Lizard's Tail* (Secker & Warburg, London, 1980)

Brodie, Fawn, *Richard Nixon: the Shaping of his Character* (WW Norton, New York, 1981)

Garrison, Jim, *On the Trail of the Assassins* (Penguin, London, 1992)

Hayes, Billy with William Hoffer, *Midnight Express* (Andre Deutsch, London, 1977)

Hayslip, Le Ly with Jay Warts, *When Heaven and Earth Changed Places* (Pan Macmillan, London, 1994)

Hayslip, Le Ly with James Hayslip *Child of War, Woman of Peace* (Pan Macmillan, 1994)

Hopkins, Jerry and Danny Sugerman, *No One Here Gets Out Alive* (Plexus, London, 1980)

Huizenga, Rob, *'You're OK – It's Just a Bruise': a Doctor's Sideline Secrets about Pro-Football's Most Outrageous Team* (St Martin's Griffin, New York, 1994)

Kovic, Ron, *Born on the Fourth of July* (Corgi, London, 1995)

Marrs, Jim, *Crossfire: The Plot that Killed Kennedy* (Carroll & Graf, New York, 1989)

Ridley, John, *U Turn* (Bloomsbury, London, 1998); *Stray Dogs* (Hodder & Stoughton, London, 1997)

Stone, Oliver and Oliver Stone and Richard Boyle, *Platoon/Salvador: The Screenplays* (Ebury, London, 1987)

Tarantino, Quentin, *Natural Born Killers* (Faber & Faber, London, 1995)

Wagner, Bruce, *Wild Palms*, illustrated by Julian Allen (Arrow, London, 1993)

Woodward, Bob and Carl Bernstein, *The Final Days* (Secker & Warburg, London, 1976)

Oliver Stone

Oliver Stone: Interviews, ed. Charles LP Silet (University Press of Mississippi, Jackson, Mississippi, 2001)

Oliver Stone's USA: Film, History and Controversy, ed. Robert Brent Toplin (University Press of Kansas, Kansas, 2000)

Beaver, Frank, *Oliver Stone: Wakeup Cinema* (Twayne, New York, 1994)

Hamburg, Eric, *JFK, Nixon, Oliver Stone and Me* (Public Affairs, New York, 2002)

Kagan, Norman, *The Cinema of Oliver Stone* (Roundhouse, Oxford, 1995)

Mackay-Kellis, Susan, *Oliver Stone's America: Dreaming the Myth Outward* (Westview Press, New York, 1996)

Riordan, James, *Stone: The Controversies, Excesses, and Exploits of a Radical Filmmaker* (Aurum, London, 1996)

Salewicz, Chris, *Oliver Stone: The Making of his Movies* (Orion, London, 1999)

Films – General

Above the Line: Conversations about the Movies, ed. Lawrence Grobel (Da Capo, London, 2000)

Directors Close Up, moderated and edited by Jeremy Kagan (Focal Press, London, 2000)

Fifty Contemporary Filmmakers, ed. Yvonne Tasker (Routledge, London, 2002)

From Hanoi to Hollywood: The Vietnam War in American Film, ed. Linda Dittmar and Gene Michaud (Rugers University Press, New Brunswick, 1997)

Halliwell's Film and Video Guide (19th Edition), ed. John Walker (HarperCollins, London, 2003)

Inner Views: Filmmakers in Conversation, ed. David Breskin (Faber & Faber, London, 1992)

Me Jane: Masculinity, Movies and Women, ed. Pat Kirkham and Janet Thumin (Lawrence & Wishart, New York, 1995)

Movie Talk from the Front Lines, ed. Jeremy Roberts and Steven Gaydos (McFarland & Company, New York, 1995)

Projections 2: A Forum for Filmmakers, ed. John Boorman and Walter Donohue (Faber & Faber, 1993)

Vietnam: Images, War and Representation, ed. Jeffrey Walsh and James Aulich (MacMillan, London, 1989)

Adair, Gilbert, *Hollywood's Vietnam* (Heinemann, London, 1989)

Auster, Albert and Leonard Quart, *How the War was Remmebered: Hollywood and Vietnam* (Praeger, Westport, 1988)

Biskind, Peter, *Easy Riders, Raging Bulls: How the Sex 'n' Drugs 'n' Rock 'n' Roll Generation Saved Hollywood* (Bloomsbury, London, 1998)

Caine, Michael, *What's it all About?* (Arrow, London, 1992)

Christiensen, Terry, *Reel Politics: American Political Movies from Birth of a Nation to Platoon* (Basil Blackwell, New York, 1987)

Devine, Jeremy, *Vietnam at 24 Frames a Second* (McFarland & Co, Jefferson, NC, 1995)

Fleming, Charles, *High Concept: Don Simpson and the Hollywood Culture of Excess* (Bloomsbury, London, 1998)

Fulwood, Neil, *One Hundred Violent Films that Changed Cinema* (Batsford, London, 2003)

Gehring, Wes, *American Dark Comedy: Beyond Satire* (Greenwood Press, Westport, 1996)

Gianos, Philip, *Politics and Paranoia in American Film* (Praeger, Westport, 1998)

Goodridge, Mike, *Screencraft: Directing* (Rotovision, London, 2002)

Horsley, Jake, *The Blood Poets: A Cinema of Savagery, 1958–1999: Volume II, Millenial Blues* (Scarecrow Press, Maryland, 1999)

Katz, Ephraim, *The Film Encyclopedia* (3rd edition), revised by Fred Klein and Ronald Dean Nolan (HarperCollins, New York, 1998)

Kolker, Robert, *A Cinema of Loneliness* (Oxford University Press, London, 2000)

Lane, Anthony, *Nobody's Perfect: Writings from the New Yorker* (Picador, London, 2002)

Palmer, William, *The Films of the Eighties: A Social History* (Southern Illinois University Press, 1993)

Pratt, Ray, *Projecting Paranoias: Conspiratorial Visions in American Film* (University of Kansas, 2001)

Thompson, David, *The New Biographical Dictionary of Film* (Little, Brown, London, 2002)

Walker, Mark, *Vietnam Veteran Films* (Scarecrow Press, New Jersey, 1991)

Wiley, Mason and Damien Bona, *Inside Oscar: the Unofficial History of the Academy Awards* (Ballantine, New York, 1993)

Worrell, Denise, *Icons: Intimate Portraits* (Altantic Press, New York, 1989)

Miscellaneous

August, John and Jane Hamsher, *Natural Born Killers: A Novel* (Signet, New York, 1994)

Boyle, Richard, *GI Revolts: The Breakdown of the US Army in Vietnam* (United Front Press, New York, 1973)

DeLillo, Don, *Libra* (Penguin, London, 1988)

Greenberg, David, *Nixon's Shadow: The History of an Image* (WW Norton, London, 2003)

Lipper, Ken, *Wall Street: A Novel* (Grafton, London, 1988)

Morgan, Iwan, *Nixon* (Arnold, London, 2002)

Nevis, Allan and Henry Steele Commager with Jeffrey Morris, *A Pocket History of the United States* (Pocket Books, New York, 1992)

Stone, Oliver, *A Child's Night Dream* (St Martin's Press, New York, 1997)

Woodward, Bob and Carl Bernstein, *All the President's Men* (Bloomsbury, London, 1998)

Index of Quotations

Introduction

1   'The standing joke was that . . .' *Stone: the controversies, excesses, and exploits of a radical filmmaker*, James Riordan (Aurum, London, 1996) p. 16

2   'My father taught me how to write . . .' Oliver Stone quoted in 'Oliver Stone takes stock', Alexander Cockburn, *American Film*, December 1987

2   'We could have done it better, Huckleberry', Oliver Stone quoted in *Innerviews: Filmmakers in Conversation*, ed. David Breskin (Faber & Faber, London, 1992) p. 105

2   'everything had been stripped away . . .' *Stone*, Riordan, p. 27

3   'I was a novelist . . .' Oliver Stone quoted in *Above the Line: Conversations About the Movies* (Da Capo, London, 2000) p. 78. Originally published in *Playboy*, August–September 1997

Seizure

10   'We raised about fifty grand . . .' Oliver Stone quoted in *Stone*, Riordan, p. 79

15   'When I get contacts . . .' Oliver Stone quoted in *The Cinema of Oliver Stone*, Norman Kagan (Roundhouse, Oxford, 1995) p. 27

15   'the screenplay includes two or three . . .' Vincent Canby in the *New York Times*, quoted in *Oliver Stone*, Salewicz, p. 27

15   'a sadomasochistic ditty . . .' review of *Seizure*, Jerry Oster, *New York Daily News*, 13 March 1975

15   'stylishly filmed . . .' review of *Seizure*, *Variety*, 20 November 1974

Midnight Express

20   'an exploitative masochistic fantasy of incarceration . . .' *The Blood Poets: A Cinema of Savagery, 1958–1999: Volume II, Millenial Blues*, Jake Hornsley (Scarecrow Press, Maryland, 1999) pp. 48–9

23   'some consolation for all the men and women . . .' Oliver Stone quoted in *Inside Oscar: The Unofficial History of the Academy Awards*, Mason Wiley and Damien Bona (Ballantine, New York, 1993) p. 564

The Hand

26   '[Rimbaldi] worked so hard . . .' Oliver Stone quoted in 'Oliver Stone and *The Hand*', Bob Martin, *Fangoria*, December 1981. Reprinted in *Oliver Stone Interviews*, ed. Charles LP Silet (University Press of Mississippi, Jackson, 2001) p. 7

26   'There was a lot of studio pressure . . .' Oliver Stone quoted in *The Cinema of Oliver Stone*, Kagan, p. 41

27   'one, it was a horror film . . .' *What's it All About?* Michael Caine (Arrow, London, 1992) p. 445

28   'I'd been advised . . .' Oliver Stone quoted in 'Interview with Oliver Stone', Michel Ciment, *Positif*, April 1987. Reprinted in *Interviews*, Silet, p. 46. Trans. Nelle N Hutter-Cottman

30   'because of his desire . . .' *Stone*, Riordan, p. 121

32   'a clever horror tale . . .' 'Review of *The Hand*', Vincent Canby, *New York Times*, 24 April 1981

32   'one of the more intelligent efforts . . .' 'The matrix of movie reviewing', Andrew Sarris, *Village Voice*, 13 May 1981

Scarface

35   'dropped the name of a guy I knew . . .' Oliver Stone quoted in *Stone*, Riordan, p. 127

35   'very pleased with the movie', Oliver Stone quoted in *Stone*, Riordan, p. 130

37   'Tony Montana is a nut . . .' Oliver Stone quoted in 'Point Man', Pat McGilligan, *Film Comment*, January/February 1987

39   'farewell to all drugs', Oliver Stone quoted in 'Point Man', McGilligan

Year of the Dragon

42   'a dissident gangster group . . .' Oliver Stone quoted in 'Point Man' McGilligan

45   'The Chinese are the biggest importers . . .' Oliver Stone quoted in 'Point Man' McGilligan

46   'You want nice dlink [sic] . . .' *Year of the Dragon*, Robert Daley (Hodder & Stoughton, London, 1982) p. 13

The Ones That Got Away

48   'I wanted to shoot it in Germany or Russia . . .' Oliver Stone quoted in *Stone*, Riordan, p. 101

48   'I criticised some changes he had made to my script . . .' Oliver
      Stone quoted in 'Radical Frames of Mind', Nigel Floyd, *Sight and
      Sound*, January 1987. Reprinted in *Interviews*, Silet, p. 10

50   'failed to charm Argentina's president . . .' 'Top director walks out
      of Evita movie', Baz Bamigboye, *Daily Mail*, 8 July 1994

50   'She was too sedate in the first half . . .' Oliver Stone quoted in
      'History, Dramatic License, and Larger Historical Truths: An
      Interview with Oliver Stone', Gary Crowdus, *Cineaste*, vol. 22, no.
      4 (1997) reprinted in *Interviews*, Silet, p. 193

Salvador

53   'On the back seat of his car . . .' Oliver Stone quoted in 'Oliver
      Stone: Salvador', in *My First Movie*, ed. Stephen Lowenstein
      (Pantheon, London, 2001) p. 152

54   'con them into giving us all their tanks . . .' Oliver Stone quoted in
      My First Movie, p. 153

54   'sort of road movie' Oliver Stone quoted in *Stone*, Riordan, p. 170

55   'He's kind of religious isn't he . . .' James Woods quoted in *Stone*,
      Riordan, p. 155

61   'the improbability of Boyle's knack . . .' review of *Salvador*, David
      Robinson, *The Times*, 23 January 1987

62   'I beg you, I ask you, I order you . . .' Archbishop Romero quoted
      in *Weakness and Deceit: US Policy and El Salvador*, Raymond
      Bonner (Hamish Hamilton, London, 1985) p. 178

65   'This is the sort of role James Woods was born to play . . .' review
      of *Salvador*, Roger Ebert, *Chicago Sun-Times*, 25 April 1986

65   'it is that performance which is central to the film . . .' review of
      Salvador, *New Socialist*, December 1986

65   'a radical riposte to the *Rambo* school . . .' review of *Salvador*,
      Nigel Andrews, *Financial Times*, 23 January 1987

65   'a salutary antidote for films like *Top Gun* . . .' review of *Salvador*,
      William Parente, *Scotsman*, 24 January 1987

65   'Stone does a fine job . . .' 'Reporting Some Chilling Truths', Ian
      Bell, *Scotsman*, 22 August 1986

65   'sensational, but not unduly sensationalised', review of *Salvador*,
      Philip French, *Observer*, 25 January 1987

65   'The film does not romanticise . . .' review of *Salvador*, Derek
      Malcolm, *Guardian*, 22 January 1987

65   'viewers . . . will be hard put to tell . . .' review of *Salvador*, Walter
      Goodman, *New York Times*, 5 March 1986

65   'the film is unable to treat . . .' review of *Salvador*, Judith
      Williamson, *New Statesman*, 30 January 1987
66   'By the end of 1987 Oliver Stone . . .' review of *Salvador*, NME, 24
      January 1987
66   'on the ground that it's grim portrayal . . .' *New York Times*, 8 July
      1987

Platoon
70   'the IWT [I Was There] factor . . .' *New York Times* article, David
      Denby, 19 January 1987
71   'I banged on every door in California . . .' Martin Bregman quoted
      in *Stone*, Riordan, p. 96
74   'I just thought it would be enough to document exactly what
      happened . . .' Oliver Stone quoted in 'Oliver Stone' by Chuck
      Pfeiffer, *Interview*, February 1987
75   'We didn't really *see* the North Vietnamese . . .' Oliver Stone
      quoted in 'Personal Struggles and Political Issues: An Interview
      with Oliver Stone', Gary Crowdus, *Cineaste*, vol. 16, no. 3 (1988)
      reprinted in *Interviews*, Silet, p. 55
75   'On the one hand there were the lifers . . .' Oliver Stone quoted in
      'Oliver Stone goes to War', in *Icons: Intimate Portraits*, Denise
      Worrell (Atlantic Press, New York, 1989) p. 228
76   'The angry Achilles . . .' 'One From the Heart', Oliver Stone,
      American Film, Jan–Feb 1987
77   'I wanted to show that Chris . . .' Oliver Stone quoted in 'Oliver
      Stone goes to War', p. 249
79   'like the end of *Platoon*', Oliver Stone quoted in *Stone*, Riordan, p.
      52
80   'in an isolated part . . .' Oliver Stone quoted in '*Playboy* Inteview:
      Oliver Stone', Marc Cooper, *Playboy*, February 1988, reprinted in
      Interviews, Silet, p. 74
80   'like a rock star to me . . .' Oliver Stone quoted in 'Oliver Stone
      goes to War', p. 247
81   'contracted before *Platoon* . . .' '*Playboy* Interview: Oliver Stone',
      in *Interviews*, Silet, p. 89
82   'possibly the best work . . .' review of *Platoon*, Vincent Canby,
      New York Times, 19 December 1986
83   'People came out of *Apocalypse Now* . . .' review of *Platoon*, Mark
      Amory, *Daily Telegraph*, 26 April 1987

83 'Here is a movie that regards combat . . .' review of *Platoon*, Roger Ebert, *Chicago Sun-Times*, 12 December 1986

83 'The film is explicitly horrible . . .' review of *Platoon*, William Shawcross, *Times Literary Supplement*, 14 April 1987

83 '*Platoon* has no great truth about war . . .' 'America at War with Itself', Max Hastings, *Daily Telegraph*, 25 March 1987

83 'the first serious youth movie . . .' review of *Platoon*, Paul Attanasia, *Washington Post*, 16 January 1987

83 'very close to traditional Hollywood . . .' review of *Platoon*, Philip French, *Observer*, 26 April 1987

83 'Even if *Platoon* only spells out . . .' review of *Platoon*, Alexander Walker, *Evening Standard*, 23 April 1987

83 'a thinly conceived film . . .' review of *Platoon*, Nigel Andrews, *Financial Times*, 24 April 1987

83 'Just about everything in *Platoon* . . .' review of *Platoon*, Pauline Kael, *New Yorker*, 12 January 1987

83 'from a screenwriter . . .' review of *Platoon*, Attanasia

84 'The film concludes with a sanctimonious . . .' 'An absolute shower', Richard West, *Spectator*, 16 May 1987

84 'There have been reports . . .' 'Old passions reawakened by *Platoon*', Nena Darnton, *New York Times*, 20 March 1987

84 'had *Platoon* opened a decade ago . . .' 'Unwanted *Platoon* finds success as US examines the Vietnam War', Aljean Harmetz, *New York Times*, 9 February 1987

84 'if the Hollywood grapevine is correct . . .' *New York Times*, Aljean Harmetz, 16 March 1987

84 'Thank you for this Cinderella ending . . .' Oliver Stone quoted in *Inside Oscar*, Wiley and Bona, p. 697

Wall Street

89 'a Pilgrim's Progress of a boy . . .' Oliver Stone quoted in 'Oliver Stone Takes Stock', Cockburn

89 'He could have been a cop . . .' Oliver Stone quoted in 'Oliver Stone Takes Stock', Cockburn

90 'about 17 per cent . . .' *Stone*, Riordan, p. 240

93 'Half of me likes what [corporate raiders] do . . .' Oliver Stone quoted in 'Oliver Stone Takes Stock', Cockburn

97 'My father saw the world as a jungle . . .' Oliver Stone quoted in 'Oliver Stone Takes Stock', Cockburn

98 'We are making a movie about sharks . . .' Robert Richardson as quoted in *Oliver Stone*, Salewicz, p. 48

99 'In a gripping performance, Douglas . . .' 'Mike Makes Talk Money', Richard Berkley, *Sunday Express*, 1 May 1988

99 'Seldom since Orson Welles's day . . .' 'The Wall Street Smash', Shaun Usher, *Daily Mail*, 29 April 1988

99 'Such is the power of Douglas's . . .' review of *Wall Street*, Sue Heal, *Today*, 29 April 1988

100 'The entire film . . .' 'A Season of Flesh and Greed', Richard Corliss, *Time*, 14 December 1987

100 '*Wall Street* is inclined to see . . .' 'Father Figures' Richard Lambs, *Times Literary Supplement*, 29 April–5 May 1988

100 'a bull market in red braces . . .' news report, *Independent*, 7 April 1988

100 'is at its weakest when it preaches . . .' review of *Wall Street*, Rita Kempley, *Washington Post*, 11 December 1987

100 'Mr Stone's heart is in the right place . . .' review of *Wall Street*, Vincent Canby, *New York Times*, 11 December 1987

100 'ultimately [the film] gives the impression . . .' review of *Wall Street*, Ian Penman, *Face*, April 1988

100 '[Stone] can't decide . . .' 'Modern Times', Kathy Watson, *New Socialist*, March 1988

100 'The movie can be followed by anybody . . .' review of *Wall Street*, Roger Ebert, *Chicago Sun-Times*, 11 December 1987

100 'The film has such pace and style . . .' review of *Wall Street*, Hilary Mantel, *Spectator*, 7 May 1981

100 'The camera stalks through the film . . .' 'Wall Street Shuffle', Philip French, *Observer*, 1 May 1988

100 'constantly moving . . .' 'Father Figures', Lambs

100 'Oliver Stone has a knack for swimming against a tide . . .' 'Raiders of the Lost Market', David Edalstan, *Village Voice*, 15 December 1987

100 'The setting of *Wall Street* is hardly less male . . .' 'Valley of the Dulls', Adam Mars-Jones, *Independent*, 28 April 1988

101 'Oliver Stone, not only as the director . . .' Michael Douglas quoted in *Inside Oscar*, Wiley and Bona, p. 720

102 'I have not done movies about women . . .' Oliver Stone quoted in '*Playboy* Interview: Oliver Stone', Cooper, reprinted in *Interviews*, Silet, p. 89

Talk Radio

105 'Ed was there at the right moment . . .' Oliver Stone quoted in *Stone*, Riordan, p. 256

106 'I just remember a blur of very long days . . .' Eric Bogosian in *The Cinema of Oliver Stone*, Kagan, pp. 133–4

111 'It's my least favourite movie . . .' Oliver Stone quoted in 'The Dark Side', Gavin Smith, *Sight and Sound*, March 1996, reprinted in *Interviews*, Silet, p. 169

114 'Bogosian gives an outstanding performance . . .' 'Sitting on a Time Bomb', Nigel Andrews, *Financial Times*, 14 September 1989

114 'His Barry Champlain isn't just . . .' 'Freedom Now?' J Hoberman, *Village Voice*, 20 December 1989

114 'is probably [Stone's] best work to date . . .' review of *Talk Radio*, Ian Penman, the *Face*, April 1989

114 'crawls with a purpose . . .' review of *Talk Radio*, Richard Corliss, *Time*, 19 December 1988

114 'As in *Platoon*, Stone's camera . . .' 'Talking through the Long American Night', Kurt Jacobsen, *Guardian*, 2 February 1989

114 'Stone and cinematographer Robert Richardson . . .' review of *Talk Radio*, Hal Hinson, *Washington Post*, 21 December 1988

114 '*Talk Radio* may be one of the most lacerating . . .' 'Don't Touch that Dial', Derek Malcolm, *Midweek*, 14 September 1989

114 'Stone's most thoughtful film . . .' review of *Talk Radio*, Christopher Tookey, *Sunday Telegraph*, 17 September 1989

114 'A confused and flashy picture . . .' review of *Talk Radio*, Philip French, *Observer*, 17 September 1989

114 'For all the energy . . .' review of *Talk Radio*, Geoff Brown, *The Times*, 14 September 1989

Born on the Fourth of July

119 'We have a fascist security . . .' Oliver Stone quoted in *Inside Oscar*, Wiley and Bona, p. 759

119 'It was as if we had been linked by destiny . . .' Oliver Stone quoted in 'The War Within', Alan Mirabella, *New York Daily News*, 20 January 1990

120 'If I ever get the opportunity to direct . . .' Oliver Stone quoted by Ron Kovic in *Stone*, Riordan, p. 276

120 'I realised it was one of the great . . .' Tom Pollock quoted in *Stone*, Riordan, p. 276

121 'Get the girl at the end if you blow up the Mig . . .' Oliver Stone quoted in '*Playboy* Interview: Oliver Stone', Cooper, *Playboy*, reprinted in *Interviews*, Silet, p. 77

125 'We talked about the story while we were working . . .' Robert Richardson quoted in 'Born on the Fourth of July', Bob Fisher, *American Cinematographer*, February 1990

126 'My point was that . . .' Oliver Stone quoted in *Oliver Stone*, Salewicz, p. 65

127 'he passes from the private to the public . . .' Oliver Stone quoted in *Oliver Stone*, Salewicz, p. 66

127 'We chose a dream-like interpretation . . .' Robert Richardson quoted in 'Born on the Fourth of July', Fisher

127 'Stone originally planned . . .' 'Born on the Fourth of July', Fisher

129 'self-advertising flamboyance . . .' 'Born Bawling', Alexander Walker, *Evening Standard*, 1 March 1990

129 'If in doubt, Stone brings in a big crowd . . .' 'Telling it like it was', Hilary Mantel, *Spectator*, 10 March 1990

129 'As in *Platoon*, Oliver Stone seems unable . . .' 'Truth Mugged by Rhetoric', Nigel Andrews, *Financial Times*, 1 March 1990

130 'Stone may not be the most rigorous . . .' 'Raise the Flag and Dump the Dead', Derek Malcolm, *Guardian*, 1 March 1990

130 '[Stone's] contempt is made flesh . . .' review of *Born on the Fourth of July*, Gavin Martin, *NME*, 3 March 1990

130 'everything that was terrific . . .' 'Tom Terrific', Richard Corliss, *Time*, 25 December 1989

130 'arguably it comes the closest yet . . .' 'Return of the Unwanted Soldier', Hugo Davenport, *Daily Telegraph*, 1 March 1990

130 'what Cruise achieves . . .' 'Arms and the Man', Derek Malcolm, *Midweek*, 1 March 1990

130 'Willem Dafoe . . . puts more fireworks . . .' review of *Born on the Fourth of July*, Desson Howe, *Washington Post*, 5 January 1990

130 'Cruise has the right . . .' 'Potency', Pauline Kael, *New Yorker*, 22 February 1990

130 'at worst a pack of lies . . .' Pat Buchanan quoted in 'Into battle on political lines', John Cassidy, *Sunday Times*, 4 March 1990

131 'That politicised everything . . .' Oliver Stone quoted in *Stone*, Riordan, pp. 305–6

131 'your acknowledgement that the Vietnam War . . .' Oliver Stone quoted in *Inside Oscar*, Wiley and Bona, p. 777

132 'I think it's better to be wrong on the side of clarification . . .'
Oliver Stone quoted in *Stone*, Riordan, p. 305

The Doors

138 'the *Raging Bull* . . .' William Friedkin as quoted in *Cinema of Oliver Stone*, Kagan, p. 165

139 'It's like *Citizen Kane* . . .' Oliver Stone quoted in *Oliver Stone*, Salewicz, p. 69

141 'The more I studied it . . .' Oliver Stone quoted in *Stone*, Riordan, p. 312

145 'was bound up in so much legal red tape . . .' review of *The Doors*, Sue Heal, *Today*, 26 April 1991

146 'I do think that if you live fast . . .' Oliver Stone quoted in 'No One Here Gets Out Alive', Barry McIlheney, *Empire*, May 1991

146 'It never happened . . .' John Densmore quoted in 'Every Generation Need its Doors', Simon Garfield, *Independent on Sunday*, 7 April 1991

146 'It was in a hooch . . .' Oliver Stone quoted in 'The Man Behind *The Doors*', Jay Carr, *Boston Globe*, 1 March 1991

146 'The times in the field deadened me . . .' Oliver Stone quoted in *Stone*, Riordan, p. 46

146 'was over there in Vietnam . . .' Ray Manzarek quoted in *Stone*, Riordan, p. 313

146 'When Morrison died in 1971 . . .' Oliver Stone quoted in 'The Man Behind *The Doors*', Carr

147 'clearly . . . Stone wanted to *be* Jim Morrison . . .' review of *The Doors*, Neil Norman, *Evening Standard*, 25 April 1991

147 'There are so many different perspectives . . .' Oliver Stone quoted in 'Stone Unturned', Steve Grant, *Time Out*, 3 April 1991

147 'Some said she was a monster . . .' Oliver Stone quoted in 'When Meg met Oliver', Garry Jenkins, *Empire*, May 1991

147 'He's got it all down pat . . .' Jerry Hopkins quoted in 'Every Generation Need its Doors', Garfield

148 'on the more sensational side . . .' Bill Siddons quoted in *Stone*, Riordan, p. 312

148 '[Oliver Stone] had the making of a scene . . .' Patricia Kennealy speaking in the making-of documentary, *The Road of Excess*, Charles Kiselyak, 1997

150 'The film is an absurdity . . .' review of *The Doors*, Hal Hinson, *Washington Post*, 1 March 1991

151 'like being stuck in a bar . . .' review of *The Doors*, Roger Ebert, *Chicago Sun-Times*, 1 March 1991

151 'Visually and structurally . . .' '*The Doors* that lead to nowhere', Hugo Davenport, *Daily Telegraph*, 25 April 1991

151 'Stone . . . loads the film . . .' review of *The Doors*, Steve Grant, *Time Out*, 24 April 1991

151 'captured the snarling, provocative nature . . .' 'Destruction of Morrison myth', the *Sun*, 26 April 1991

151 'Val Kilmer has studied the records . . .' 'Only a burnt out Guitar Case is left', Philip French, *Observer*, 28 April 1991

151 'Stone's movie isn't really about The Doors', review of *The Doors*, *Rolling Stone*, 21 March 1991

151 'The spotlight is so firmly on Morrison . . .' '*The Doors* that lead to nowhere', Davenport

151 'Try as Val Kilmer does . . .' 'When the Music's Over', Derek Malcolm, *Guardian*, 25 April 1991

151 '[Stone's] sense of humour . . .' 'Riding out the Storm', Cathy Dillon, *Scotsman*, 26 April 1991

151 'There's the film about the rock-idol . . .' 'Through a key-hole', Sheila Johnston, *Independent*, 26 April 1991

JFK

158 'Eventually I read the book . . .' Oliver Stone quoted in *Screencraft: Directing*, Mike Goodridge (Rotovision, 2002), p. 106

159 'four DNA threads . . .' Oliver Stone quoted in *Oliver Stone*, Salewicz, p. 83

160 'Since *JFK* is a very cerebral movie . . .' Oliver Stone quoted in 'Clarifying the Conspiracy: An interview with Oliver Stone', Gary Crowdus, *Cineaste*, vol. 19, no. 1, 1992, reprinted in *Interviews*, Silet, p. 101

163 'Get me elected . . .' reported in 'Oliver Stone Talks Back', a self-penned piece printed in *Premiere* (January, 1992). Stone describes the line as originating in Stanley Kramer's *Vietnam: a History* (p. 326), and as spoken by LBJ at a 1963 Christmas drinks party. The actual quote was, 'Just get me elected, then you can have your war.'

165 'I do not think of myself . . .' 'Stone on Stone's image (As Presented by Some Historians)', Oliver Stone in *Oliver Stone's USA: Film, History and Controversy*, ed. Robert Brent Toplin (University Press of Kansas, 2000), p. 40

165 'I'm presenting what I call . . .' Oliver Stone quoted in 'Clarifying the Conspiracy: an interview with Oliver Stone', Crowdus in *Interviews*, Silet, p. 99

167 'I've taken the license of using Garrison . . .' 'Stone defends *JFK*: I've done all my Homework', Jay Carr, *Hollywood Reporter*, 15 August 1991

167 'There are many flaws in the real Garrison . . .' 'Oliver Stone Talks Back', Oliver Stone, *Premiere*, January 1992

170 'we created a strong documentary . . .' Robert Richardson quoted in 'The Whys and Hows of *JFK*', Bob Fisher, *American Cinematographer*, February 1992

171 'The verdicts in *JFK* . . .' 'Over-killing Kennedy', Alexander Walker, *Evening Standard*, 23 January 1992

171 'Yes, *JFK* is propaganda . . .' 'History in the Remaking', Shaun Usher, *Daily Mail*, 22 January 1992

171 'At least, he sets the stage . . .' review of *JFK*, Marjorie Baumgarten, *Austin Chronicle*, 27 December 1991

171 'It's more complex and intelligent . . .' 'Bullet Proof', Geoff Andrew, *Time Out*, 22 January 1992

171 'treats the riddles of history . . .' 'A Licence to Incriminate', Nigel Andrews, *Financial Times*, 23 January 1992

171 'Costner is simply not a layered enough . . .' 'Stunning Stone Shoots to Thrill', Sue Heal, *Today*, 24 January 1992

171 'many of Stone's dramatic efforts are dulled . . .' review of *JFK*, Desson Howe, *Washington Post*, 20 December 1991

171 'The camerawork of Robert Richardson . . .' review of *JFK*, Peter Travers, *Rolling Stone*, 27 December 1991

171 'in my view the writer-director . . .' 'Shots in the Dark', Anne Billson, *New Statesman*, 24 January 1992

172 'Sissy Spacek is virtually the only woman . . .' 'Conspiracy to Confuse', Mark Amory, *Spectator*, 25 January 1992

172 'The domestic side of Garrison's life . . .' 'Stoned on Symbols', Christopher Tookey, *Sunday Telegraph*, 26 January 1992

172 'the director of *JFK* is not . . .' journalist Tom Wicker's reply to 'Via the Director's Viewfinder', letter from Oliver Stone claiming the right to artistic licence to the *New York Times*, 5 January 1992

172 'Considered by itself . . .' Edward Bennett Williams quoted in 'Does *JFK* conspire against reason?' Tom Wicker, *New York Times*, December 22 1991

173 'Laughing all the way . . .' 'Overkill', Garry Trudeau, *New York Times*, 8 January 1992

173 'many young people . . .' Jack Valenti quoted in *Inside Oscar*, Wiley and Bona, pp. 850–1

Heaven and Earth

179 'It didn't work', Oliver Stone quoted in *Cinema of Oliver Stone*, Kagan, p. 209

179 'Obviously, I couldn't sit in the car . . .' Hiep Thi Le quoted in *Stone*, Riordan, p. 450

179 'a light around Hiep . . .' Oliver Stone quoted in *Cinema of Oliver Stone*, Kagan, p. 210

185 'heroic action in war . . .' 'Changing places', Margaret O'Brian in *Me Jane: Masculinity, Movies and Women*, ed. Pat Kirkham and Janet Thumin (Lawrence & Wishart, New York, 1995) p. 268

185 'hundreds of nameless, faceless . . .' 'Vietnam: the Reverse Angle' by Oliver Stone in *The Making of Oliver Stone's Heaven and Earth*, Michael Singer, from the screenplay by Oliver Stone with additional text by Oliver Stone, Le Ly Hayslip and Hiep Thi Le (Orion, London, 1993) p. 6

187 'I want . . . a good Oriental wife . . .' *When Heaven and Earth Changed Places*, Le Ly Hayslip with Jay Warts (Pan Macmillan, London, 1994) p. 435

189 'It's that unusual combination . . .' review of *Heaven and Earth*, Anne Billson, *Sunday Telegraph*, 23 January 1994

189 '*Heaven and Earth* is a very brave film . . .' review of *Heaven and Earth*, Quentin Curtis, *Independent of Sunday*, 23 January 1994

189 'Cry? I could have wept . . .' 'Oh, what a loveless war', Alexander Walker, *Evening Standard*, 20 January 1994

189 'the problem is not the story . . .' review of *Heaven and Earth*, Hugo Davenport, *Daily Telegraph*, 21 January 1994

189 'when you give in to the intensity . . .' 'Calling the Shots', Martin Woolacott, *Guardian*, 18 January 1994

189 'Humourless Stone makes a fiercely expert job . . .' 'Stone moves Heaven and Earth to show the torments of war', Angie Errigo, *Today*, 21 January 1994

189 'Stone films these domestic corridor scenes . . .' review of *Heaven and Earth*, Nigel Andrews, *Financial Times*, 20 January 1994

189 'In a time when few American directors are drawn . . .' review of *Heaven and Earth*, Roger Ebert, *Chicago Sun-Times*, 24 December 1993

190 'such thunderous brushstrokes . . .' 'The lie of the land', Derek Malcolm, *Guardian*, 20 January 1994

190 'Although Hiep Thi Le . . .' 'Stone moves Heaven and Earth to show the torments of war', Errigo

190 'the newcomer who plays Le Ly . . .' review of *Heaven and Earth*, Sheila Johnston, *Independent*, 21 January 1994

190 'Stone has scarcely turned into a caring . . .' review of *Heaven and Earth*, Geoff Brown, *The Times*, 20 January 1994

190 'I reckon Oliver Stone's *Heaven and Earth* . . .' 'Victory of the spirit in a land ravaged by war', Sheridan Morley, *Sunday Express*, 23 January 1993

190 'Stone isn't able to say much about Vietnam . . .' 'Promise her everything', Jonathan Romney, *New Statesman*, 21 January 1994

190 '*Heaven and Earth* isn't a tragedy . . .' review of *Heaven and Earth*, Johnston

Natural Born Killers

196 'Thom told me about the script . . .' Oliver Stone quoted in *Stone*, Riordan, p. 482

196 '[Stone] wanted to know if Sean Penn . . .' Don Murphy quoted in *Stone*, Riordan, p. 482

196 'I really wanted to do a combination . . .' Oliver Stone quoted in 'How a movie satire turned into reality', Bernard Weintraub, *New York Times*, 16 August 1994

196 'let's just lighten up and go . . .' Oliver Stone quoted in *Chaos Rising* (Charles Kiselyak, 1996)

197 'a fast road movie . . .' Oliver Stone quoted in 'Oliver Stoned', Gregg Kilday, *Entertainment Weekly*, 14 January 1994, reprinted in *Interviews*, Silet, p. 118

197 'quick, inexpensive project . . .' *Cinema of Oliver Stone*, Kagan, p. 228

198 'a Saturday night with Oliver Stone . . .' Robert Downey Jr quoted in 'Natural born director', Lynn Barber, *Daily Telegraph*, 25 February 1995

199 'I'm not the kind of director who likes to stop working . . .' Oliver Stone quoted in '*Natural Born Killers* Blasts Big Screen with Both

Barrels' by Stephen Piuzzello, *American Cinematographer*, November 1994

206 'I didn't want to portray realistic murder . . .' Oliver Stone quoted in '*Natural Born Killers* Blasts Big Screen with Both Barrels', Piuzzello

206 'We went to a very conservative approach in the prison . . .' Robert Richardson quoted in '*Natural Born Killers* Blasts Big Screen with Both Barrels', Piuzzello

206 'There are things in the movie that are still beyond my fingertips . . .' Oliver Stone quoted in 'Oliver Stone: Why do I have to Provoke?' Gavin Smith, *Sight and Sound*, December 1994

206 'under the knife of Brian Berdan and Hank Corwin . . .' 'Feed the Reaper', Chris Chang, *Film Comment*, July/August 1994

207 'Oliver would frequently have a song . . .' Jane Hamsher quoted in *Stone*, Riordan, p. 512

207 'amounts to a feature length. . . .' 'Oliver's Twisted Blood Fest', Christopher Tookey, *Daily Mail*, 24 February 1995

207 'Trailing hype and ludicrous tabloid . . .' review of *Natural Born Killers*, Geoff Andrew, *Time Out*, 22 February–1 March 1995

207 '*Natural Born Killers* is a passionately mad, frequently bad . . .' 'Big Bang movie', Nigel Andrews, *Financial Times*, 25 February 1995

207 'It's an impressive spectacle . . .' Desson Howe, *Washington Post*, 26 August 1994

207 'The main problem with *Killers* . . .' review of *Natural Born Killers*, Hal Hinson, *Washington Post*, 26 August 1994

208 'Though Stone holds up a mirror . . .' review of *Natural Born Killers*, *Rolling Stone*, 8 September 1994

208 'by muffing his point about the dehumanising . . .' review of *Natural Born Killers*, Quentin Curtis, *Independent on Sunday*, 26 February 1995

208 'it's a sustained assault on the senses . . .' 'Killing for the cameras', Hugo Davenport, *Daily Telegraph*, 24 February 1995

208 'Stone never fences with a rapier . . .' 'True Romance', J Hoberman, *Village Voice*, 30 August 1994

208 'Stone has never been a director known for understatement . . .' review of *Natural Born Killers*, Roger Ebert, *Chicago Sun-Times*, 26 August 1994

208 '*Natural Born Killers* plunders every visual trick . . .' 'Stone crazy', Richard Corliss, *Time*, 12 September 1994

208 'it certainly represents some breakthrough . . .' 'Virtual violence', Jonathan Romney, *New Statesman*, 24 February 1995

208 'by pushing an on-off button on an editing table . . .' 'This gun is overloaded', Alexander Walker, *Evening Standard*, 25 February 1995

'Mr Stone could well turn out to be . . .' review of *Natural Born Killers*, Janet Maslin, *New York Times*, 26 August 1994

208 '*Natural Born Killers*, alas, is satire on the media . . .' review of *Natural Born Killers*, Anne Billson, *Sunday Telegraph*, 26 February 1995

211 '*Natural Born Killers*'s secret Utopian ambition . . .' 'Exploding Hollywood', Larry Gross, *Sight and Sound*, March 1995

Nixon

217 'The tone of the piece . . .' Oliver Stone quoted in *Above the Line: Conversations About the Movies* (Da Capo, London, 2000) p. 88. Originally published in *Playboy*, August–September

218 'We had Brian [Berdan] in one room . . .' Oliver Stone quoted in 'The Dark Side', Gavin Smith, *Sight and Sound*, March 1996, reprinted in *Interviews*, Silet, p. 168

218 'taken the possibilities . . .' 'The Dark Side', Smith in *Interviews*, Silet, p. 167

218 'When I saw him in *The Remains of the Day* . . .' Oliver Stone quoted in 'Nixon, Lies and Audiotape', Anwar Brett, *What's on in London*, 13 March 1996

218 '[Hopkins] had that necessary roughness . . .' Oliver Stone talking on audio commentary, *Nixon* Special Edition US DVD

219 'I sensed that this wasn't just an opportunity . . .' Anthony Hopkins quoted in 'A Tricky Way to Play Dicky', Martyn Palmer, *The Times*, 14 March 1996

219 'But, Oliver, look no further . . .' Warren Beatty quoted in 'See Dick Run', Holly Millea, *Premiere*, December 1995

222 'a headless monster lurching through post-war . . .' 'The Year of the Beast', Christopher Wilkinson, *Nixon Annotated Screenplay*, ed. Eric Hamburg (Bloomsbury, London, 1996) p. 59

222 'The Beast also became a metaphor . . .' 'The Year of the Beast', Wilkinson, p. 60

222 'a giant of a tragic figure . . .' Oliver Stone in 'Interview with Oliver Stone', Michael Singer, *Nixon Annotated Screenplay*, p. xvii

225 'I was into more radical violence . . .' Oliver Stone quoted in 'Point Man', McGilligan

226 'the cowardice of the Eastern . . .' original quote in *The Final Days*, Bob Woodward and Carl Bernstein (Secker & Warburg, London, 1976) p. 192

226 'the tapes were like love letters', *Final Days*, Woodward and Bernstein, p. 166

227 'One of the year's best films', review of *Nixon*, Roger Ebert, *Chicago Sun-Times*, 20 December 1995

227 'Oliver Stone's bullying obsessive style . . .' review of *Nixon*, Desson Howe, *Washington Post*, 2 December 1995

227 'A great film then? Not quite . . .' review of *Nixon*, Alexander Walker, *Evening Standard*, 18 March 1996

227 'It is an extraordinary roller-coaster ride . . .' 'Sympathy for the devil', Derek Malcolm, *Guardian*, 14 March 1996

227 'Anthony Hopkins is miscast . . .' 'No brownie points for tricky Dicky', Anne Billson, *Sunday Telegraph*, 17 March 1996

227 'all too often looks more like Ed Sullivan . . .' 'It has all the charm of a lab rat', Barbara Shulgasser, *San Francisco Examiner*, 20 December 1995

228 'bum impersonation but a towering performance . . .' review of *Nixon*, *Rolling Stone*, 25 January 1996

228 'Film is not objective . . .' review of *Nixon*, Walker

228 'That this history is sometimes painted . . .' 'Sympathy for the Devil', Malcolm

228 'Stone's technique of intercutting . . .' 'Tricky Dicky meets a cold heart of Stone', Christopher Tookey, *Daily Mail*, 15 March 1996

228 'There is indeed something nauseating . . .' 'Too tricky by half', James Delingpole, *Daily Telegraph*, 15 March 1996

228 'would, it seem, consist of everyone . . .' 'Whitewash at the White House', Tom Shone, *Sunday Times*, 17 March 1996

228 'recast each of Stone's movies . . .' 'No brownie points for tricky Dicky', Billson

228 'concocted imaginary scenes . . .' Tricia Nixon's public statement as quoted in 'Stone raises storm with film on Nixon', Quentin Letts, *The Times*, 20 December 1995

229 'hatchet job . . .' William Safire quoted in 'Feud's Corner: Oliver Stone vs William Safire', *Sunday Times*, 3 December 1995

229 'whatever Nixon's problems . . .' *Nixon: the Triumph of a Politician, 1962–72*, Stephen E Ambrose (Simon & Schuster, London, 1989) p. 84

229 'There is much conflicting evidence . . .' Stephen Ambrose quoted in 'The Man, the movie, the muddle', Quentin Curtis, *Independent on Sunday*, 17 March 1996

229 'through Kennedy and Nixon . . .' 'Interview with Oliver Stone: America, Land of Failure', Michel Cieutat and Michel Ciment, *Positif*, April 1996, reprinted in *Interviews*, Silet, p. 182, trans. Nelle N Hutter-Cottman.

U Turn

233 'A story of bloodshed, passion . . .' *Irma La Douce* tagline reported in 'Deja View', *Empire*, December 1997

233 '*U Turn* was, in part . . .' Oliver Stone quoted in *U Turn* Production Notes

234 'It's a rule intended to protect the original . . .' Oliver Stone quoted in *U Turn Screenplay* and foreword by John Ridley, 'Introduction by Oliver Stone' (Bloomsbury, London, 1998) p. xviii

234 'as if architectural development . . .' 'How the Southwest was Redone', Andrew O Thompson, *American Cinematographer*, October, 1997

235 'I don't want to see this writer . . .' Oliver Stone and John Ridley quoted in 'Desert Rats', Anne Thompson, *Premiere*, September 1997

235 'It looked like it wouldn't happen . . .' quoted in 'Oliver Stone Visits the Heartland', *Premiere*, February 1997

236 'to convince the usual suspects we've worked with . . .' Clayton Townsend quoted in *U Turn* Production Notes

238 'At the end of the day . . .' Oliver Stone quoted in *U Turn* Production Notes

238 'the karma of six people . . .' Oliver Stone quoted in 'Oliver Stone takes a *U Turn* to sex, violence and action', Mark Egan, *Asian Age*, 2 October 1997

241 'had never seen it', Robert Richardson quoted in 'Desert Noir', Andrew O Thompson, *American Cinematographer*, October 1997

242 'It is clear from the first jazzy ominous . . .' 'What rough beasts', J Hoberman, *Village Voice*, 7 October 1997

242 'a jumpy neurotic thriller . . .' review of *U Turn*, Matthew Sweet, *Independent on Sunday*, 26 April 1998

242 'Under Stone's adept ministrations . . .' 'Stone takes another *U Turn* into paranoia', Ted Anthony, *Asian Age*, 14 October 1997

242 'For nearly two hours . . .' 'Oliver Stone makes a comedy, and the laughs don't stop there', Sam Taylor, *Observer*, 26 April 1998

242 'It's quite watchable, for a while . . .' review of *U Turn*, Tom Charity, *Time Out*, 22–29 April 1998

242 'This caricatural collection . . .' 'Raising hell in Arizona', Alexander Walker, *Evening Standard*, 23 April 1998

242 'Unfortunately Stone has seen fit . . .' review of *U Turn*, Quentin Curtis, *Daily Telegraph,* 24 April 1998

242 'homes in with unerring accuracy . . .' 'Creepy Crawlies', Tom Shone, *Sunday Times*, 26 April 1998

Any Given Sunday
246 'about an ageing linebacker . . .' Oliver Stone quoted in 'Stone's Throw', Peter Manso, *Premiere*, February 2000

247 'I wanted to tell a story . . .' Oliver Stone quoted in 'Calling the Plays', Chris Pizello, *American Cinematographer*, January 2000

247 'getting the black vernacular . . .' Oliver Stone quoted in 'Stone's Throw', Manso

248 'I don't think I've ever worked harder over a whole film . . .' Oliver Stone talking on director's commentary track, *Any Given Sunday*, Region 1 DVD

251 'scheduling and commitment problems . . .' Oliver Stone quoted in 'Calling the Plays', Pizello

251 '[Richardson] was becoming increasingly critical . . .' *Screencraft: Directing*, Mike Goodridge (Rotovision, London, 2002) p. 107

255 'everyone's a winner', Oliver Stone talking on director's commentary, *Any Given Sunday*

257 'Generally I didn't use any stadium light . . .' Salvatore Totino quoted in 'Smash Mouth Football', Chris Pizello, *American Cinematographer*, January 2000

258 'despite the film's multifarious faults . . .' review of *Any Given Sunday*, Clark Collis, *Empire*, April 2000

258 'a threat to sanity . . .' 'Never on a Sunday', Alexander Walker, *Evening Standard*, 30 March 2000

258 'It's a long, loud, grandstanding . . .' review of *Any Given Sunday*, Nigel Andrews, *Financial Times*, 30 March 2000

258 'all the elements are good . . .' review of *Any Given Sunday*, Lee Pinkerton, *Voice*, 27 March 2000

258 'exciting and involving . . .' 'Field of Conflict', Philip French,
     Observer, 2 April 2000

259 'there isn't really a single sequence . . .' review of *Any Given
     Sunday*, Roger Ebert, *Chicago Sun-Times*, 22 December 1999

259 'ultimately, Stone is just intoxicated . . .' 'A Whole Different Ball
     Game', Peter Bradshaw, *Guardian*, 31 March 2000

259 'compacts an epic vision . . .' review of *Any Given Sunday*, James
     Christopher, *The Times*, 30 March 2000

259 'hyper-macho vision . . .' review of *Any Given Sunday*, Stephen
     Holden, *New York Times*, 22 December 1999

259 'this is more than a film . . .' review of *Any Given Sunday*, Andrews

259 'is a big director . . .' 'Stone Raises his Game', Andrew O'Hagan,
     Telegraph, 31 March 2000

Two Documentaries

260 'If I hadn't gone to Vietnam . . .' Oliver Stone quoted in 'No One
     Here Gets Out Alive', Barry McIlheney, *Empire*, May 1991

261 'having approached . . .' 'Semper Fidel', Harlan Jacobson, *Film
     Comment*, May/June 2003

261 '[Stone] is no kind of . . .' 'Semper Fidel', Jacobson

261 'the subject is the only . . .' *Screen International*, 28 February 2003

Alexander

265 '[Vidal] offered to write . . .' Oliver Stone quoted in *Above the
     Line*, p. 96

265 'We came to believe that television viewers . . .' ABC spokesman
     quoted in 'TV network pulls plug on Oliver Stone air crash film',
     Ed Vulliamy, *Observer*, 8 November 1998

265 '*Gladiator* came out and worked . . .' Moritz Borman quoted in
     'Producer talks *Alexander*', *Filmforce.ign.com*, 2 May 2003

266 'The race for me has always been with my script . . .' Oliver Stone
     quoted in 'Stone says new film will be the challenge of his life',
     Ananova.com, 26 August 2003

268 'For historians one of the fascinations . . .' 'First action hero',
     Robin Lane Fox, *The Sunday Times*, 5 January 2003

269 'In Alexander's own untimely death . . .' 'It really is all a
     conspiracy', Oliver Stone, *The Sunday Times*, 8 November 1998

Index

Abdul, Paula 152
Adagio for Strings (Barber) 73, 81, 82
Aitken, Jonathan 226, 229
Alcacer, Santos 10
Alexander 21, 48, 49, 233, 263–271
Alexander the Great (book) 269–270
Alexander the Great (Luhrmann) 265, 266, 269
Allen, Joan 219, 229
Allen, Woody 84
Almost Famous 149
Alves, Joe 48
Ambrose, Stephen 226, 229
American Cinematographer 127–128
American Civil Liberties Union award 101
'American Dream' 38, 96
American President, The 218
Amory, Mark 171–172
anamorphic format 127
Andrew, Geoff 171
Andrews, Dean 163
Andrews, Nigel 65, 83, 129–130, 171, 189, 207, 258, 259
Ansen, David 158
Any Given Sunday 82, 152, 244–260
Apocalypse Now 71, 80, 81, 82, 83, 91
Arafat, Yasser 262
Ashby, Hal 14, 49
Asian Age 242
Asner, Ed 161
Attanasia, Paul 83
Aubuisson, Roberto de 61, 62
Austin Chronicle 171
auteur theory 14
Avary, Roger 195
awards
    BAFTA 84, 131, 173
    Born on the Fourth of July 131–132, 140
    Doors, The 152
    Golden Raspberry 40, 46, 242
    Heaven and Earth 190
    JFK 173

Midnight Express 22–23
Natural Born Killers 209–210
Nixon 229
Platoon 84
Salvador 66
Scarface 40
Talk Radio 114
Wall Street 101
Year of the Dragon 46

Baby Boy 26, 30
Bacon, Kevin 161
Bad Day at Black Rock 240–241
BAFTA awards 84, 131, 173
Baldwin, Alec 106–107
Barak, Ehud 262
Barkley, Richard 99
Barnes, Platoon Sergeant 79, 80
Barry, Raymond 121
Bauer, Steven 40
Baumgarten, Marjorie 171
Beatty, Warren 218, 219
Beck, Jeff 97
Belushi, James 55–56, 192
Ben-Hur 255, 269
Berdan, Brian 200, 206, 218
Berenger, Tom 72–73, 84, 121
Berg, Alan 108, 111, 112
Berkley, Elizabeth 249
Berlin Film Festival 114, 132, 259
Bernstein, Carl 226
Beswick, Martine 11
Billson, Anne 171, 189, 208
black and white photography 31, 228
Blessed, Brian 267
Block, Lawrence 49
Boesky, Ivan 97
Bogosian, Eric 104, 105, 106, 114
Boiler Room, The 98, 102
Bolt, Robert 18
Bonner, Raymond 54, 61, 63
Bonnie and Clyde 204
Boothe, Powers 237
Borman, Moritz 265
Born on the Fourth of July 4, 27–28, 30, 47, 67, 73, 81, 85, 105, 116–133, 152, 157, 164, 173

Born on the Fourth of July (book) 119, 126, 127
Boyle, Richard 51–67
Bradshaw, Peter 259
Brandel, Marc 24, 26, 31
Brazil Run (screenplay) 18, 62
Break (screenplay) 3, 71, 146–147
Bregman, Marty 35, 71, 119
Brenner, David 107, 131, 142, 161, 181, 199, 200
Bridges, Jeff 49
Brodie, Fawn 226
Broussard, Bill 162
Brown, Geoff 114, 190
Brown, Jim 249–250
Buchanan, Pat 130
Burman, Tom 26
Butkus, Dick 250, 252
Butterfield, Alexander 216, 218, 225
Byers, Patsy Ann 209
Byrne, David 99

Caine, Michael 26–27, 29
Canby, Vincent 15, 32, 82, 100
Candy, John 161
Capra, Frank 168
Carrillo, Elpedia 57, 66
Carter, Jimmy 52
Castro, Fidel 34, 37, 260–261, 262
Cattrall, Kim 192
Caviezel, Jim 253
Cazale, Frank 43
Charity, Tom 242
Chen, Joan 178, 180
Child of War, Woman of Peace (book) 177, 187
Child's Night Dream, A (book) 2, 233, 243–244
Christopher, James 259
Cienfuegos, Colonel Ricardo 54
Cimino, Michael 14, 42, 43, 44, 47, 71
Citizen Kane 226
Clainos, Nicholas 138
Comandante 260–261, 267
Coming Home 71, 127
Communism 60–61, 123
Conan the Barbarian 26, 29, 47–49, 269

Contra 62, 105
Copeland, Stewart 99, 113
Coppola, Francis Ford 133
Corliss, Richard 100, 114
Corwin, Hank 200, 206, 218, 251
Costner, Kevin 157, 160, 171
Courson, Pam 139, 140, 145, 147
Cover Up, The (screenplay) 18
Cox, Elizabeth *see* Stone, Elizabeth
Crossfire: the Plot that Killed Kennedy (book) 158, 169
Cruise, Tom 67, 90, 105, 120, 121, 129, 130, 131, 233, 265
Cuba 34, 37, 260–261, 263
Curtis, Quentin 189, 208, 229

Dafoe, Willem 72, 84, 121, 130
Daily Mail 50, 99, 171, 207, 209
Daily Telegraph 151, 198, 208, 229, 242
Dalby, Dave 256
Daley, Robert 46
Daly, John 54, 89
Danes, Claire 236
Dangerfield, Rodney 199
Dave 133, 166
Davenport, Hugo 130, 151, 189
Dawson, Rosario 267
Day-Lewis, Daniel 131
Day Reagan was Shot, The 133
De Laurentiis, Dino 42, 44, 53, 71, 73, 266
De Mohrenschildt, George 162
De Niro, Robert 43, 247
De Palma, Brian 19, 28, 35–36, 39, 40, 41, 138
De Vito, Danny 98
Dealey Plaza, Dallas 159–160
Dean, John 216, 218
Deer Hunter, The 43, 56, 71, 80–81, 127
Delerue, Georges 73, 82
Delillo, Don 168
Delingpole, James 228
Democratic Revolutionary Front (FDR), El Salvador 60
Denby, David 70
Densmore, John 134–135, 141, 146, 147, 148
Depp, Johnny 72, 74

Diaz, Cameron 249
DiCaprio, Leonardo 266
digital film techniques 49, 149–150, 269
Dillon, Cathy 151
Dillon, Kevin 141
Directors Guild of America 132
documentaries 260–263, 265
Dominique: The Loves of a Woman (film script) 3–4
Dooley, Richard 101
Doors, The 4, 26, 28, 122, 134–153, 240, 257
Doors, The (band) 134, 138, 146
Dornan, Robert 130–131
Douglas, Kirk 91
Douglas, Michael 90, 91, 99, 101, 102
Dourif, Brad 192
Downey Jr, Robert 198, 199
Drabinski, Garth 106
drugs
    Midnight Express 20, 21
    Scarface 37–38, 39
    Stone's involvement 1, 2, 21, 38
    Year of the Dragon 42, 45
Duchovny, David 248
Dye, Dale 70, 73, 81, 120, 161, 179, 181, 200, 263, 267

East Meets West Foundation 186, 187
Ebert, Roger 65, 83, 100, 151, 172, 189, 208, 227, 259
Edalstan, David 100
Ehrlichman, John 218, 219, 225
Eight Million Ways to Die 42, 49–50
El Salvador 51–67
Elias, Sergeant Juan Angel 79, 80
Empire magazine 233, 258
Eno, Brian 99
Entertainment Weekly 196–197
Errigo, Angie 189, 190
Escape 22
Estevez, Emilio 72
Evans, Josh 141
Evening Standard 171, 189
Evita 50, 217
Executive Action 168

Face, The 100
fantasy films 48

Farrell, Colin 265, 266, 267, 270
Fear and Loathing in Las Vegas (book) 63
Fear and Loathing in Las Vegas (film) 149
female roles 30, 57, 65–66, 91–92, 100, 171–172, 185, 190, 236, 249
Ferrell, Conchata 180
Ferrie, David 162
Film Comment 261
film noir 240, 243
film technique 14–15, 31, 64, 100, 113, 114, 127–128, 149–150, 169–170, 171, 188, 197, 199, 205–206, 226–227, 241, 248, 256–257
    digital effects 49, 149–150, 269
    hand-cam technique 32, 64, 256
    split-screen effects 99
Financial Times 258
Fitzgerald, Ben 79, 80
Flanders Film Festival 46
Fleischer, Charles 27
football 246–247, 255–256, 258–259
Ford, Corkey 121
Ford, Harrison 160
Fortune magazine 88, 90
Fox, Robin Lane 265, 267, 268, 269–270
Foxx, Jamie 249, 258, 259
French, Philip 65, 83, 100, 114, 151, 258
French Connection, The 46
French New Wave cinema 14
Frid, Jonathan 11
Friedkin, William 105, 119, 138

Gains, Herb 181
gangster films 35, 38, 39
Garcia, Risa Bramon 181, 220
Garrison, Jim 158, 159, 160, 161, 163, 164, 167, 168, 169, 172
Gershuny, Theodore 10
Ghia, Fernando 18
Gibb, Cynthia 57
Gibb, Tex Randall 253
Gibson, Mel 270
Gibson, William 192
Gladiator 265, 269

Goddet, Jacqueline (mother) 1, 2, 4, 175
Golden Raspberry awards 40, 46, 242
Goldsmith, Sir James 97
'gonzo journalism' 63–64
Goodman, Walter 65
Graham, Bill 138, 139, 141
Grazer, Brian 139
Green, Garrard 10
Green, Gerald 54
Greenburg, Harold 10
Greene, Ellen 107
Grisham, John 209
Gross, Larry 210–211
Guardian 114, 259
Guber, Peter 18

Hagman, Larry 219
Haig, General Alexander 225
Haldeman, Bob 225, 250
Halloween 11, 13
Halsted, Dan 217, 233, 237
Hamas 262
Hamburg, Eric 169, 217
Hamilton, Lee 169
Hamilton, Linda 198
Hamsher, Jane 196, 197, 207, 209
Hand, The 15, 23–33, 48, 66, 133, 233
hand-cam technique 32, 64, 256
Hanks, Tom 218
Hannah, Daryl 91–92, 140
Harari, Sasha 138, 139
Harden, Mike 256
Harrelson, Woody 195, 197, 198, 210
Hastings, Max 83
Hawks, Howard 35
Hayes, William (Billy) 16–17, 18, 22
Hayslip, Dennis 182, 186, 188
Hayslip, Le Ly 174–191, 198
Heal, Sue 99, 145, 171
Heaven and Earth 28, 59, 85, 174–191, 198, 204
Heaven's Gate 43
Hemdale productions 54, 66, 71–72, 89
Hemmings, David 54
Hendrickson, Stephen 90
Henry, David Lee 49
Heston, Charlton 250
Hinson, Hal 150–151, 207–208

Ho, Alex Kitman 42, 73–74, 92, 199
Hoagland, John 56, 63
Hoffman, Abbie 116, 121, 124
Holly, Lauren 249
Hollywood New Wave 14, 49, 204
Hope, Leslie 107
Hopkins, Anthony 216, 218–219, 226, 227–228, 229, 267
Hopkins, Billy 220, 267
Hopkins, Jerry 138, 147, 148
Horner, James 28, 32
horror films 10, 11–13, 26, 30, 32
Horror Movie (film script) 10
Horsley, Jake 20
Hoskins, Bob 220
Hot Shots! Part Deux 91
House Select Committee on Assassinations (HSCA) 164, 165, 169
Howard, Arliss 201
Howard, Robert 47
Howe, Desson 171, 207, 227
Hudson, Ernie 192
Hughes, Howard 158
Huizenga, Rob 247, 256
Hun brothers 201
Hunt, E Howard 216, 218
Hutshing, Joe 131, 142, 161, 171, 173

Idol, Billy 141
Illusion Entertainment 133–134, 217, 233
Illustrated History of The Doors (book) 148
image shakers 257
immigrants 38–39, 42, 45, 184–185
incest 4, 243
Independent 100, 190
Independent on Sunday 147, 189, 229, 242
Independent Spirit Awards 66, 114
Indictment: The MacMartin Trial 133
Industrial Light and Magic 139, 149–150
Israel 262–263
Ixtlan production company 133, 134, 192, 233

JD Productions 196, 209

JFK 62, 132, 152, 153–174, 191, 268
   screenplay 157–158
JFK in Vietnam (book) 159, 169
Johnson, Lyndon B 163, 169
Johnson, Randall 138
Johnston, David 10
Johnston, Sheila 151, 190
Jolie, Angelina 267
Jones, Jeffrey 181, 182
Jones, Tommy Lee 161, 173, 177, 180, 181, 183–184, 191, 199, 200
Joy Luck Club, The 133, 180
Judd, Ashley 200
Jungle, The (book) 61–62

Kael, Pauline 83, 130
Kapelman, Jeffrey 10
Kassar, Mario 139, 178
Kaufman, Larry 10
Kava, Caroline 121
Kempley, Rita 100
Kempster, Victor 161, 162, 178, 181, 234, 237
Kennealy, Patricia 139, 141, 148
Kennedy, John F 158–174
Kilday, Gregg 196
Kill Bill 206
Killer: A Journal of Murder 133
Killing Fields, The 64, 180
Kilmer, Val 135, 137, 140, 149, 150, 151, 152, 267
Kimball, Jeff 237
King of New York 39
Kissinger, Henry 219, 221, 224
Kitaro 188, 190
Kline, Robert 177
Klinghoffer, David 172
Knight, William G 143
Kopelson, Arthur 71
Kovic, Ron 53, 119–127, 153
Krieger, Robby 139, 141
Kurosawa, Akira 36, 234
Kustler, William 141

La Femme Nikita 22
Lardner, George 157, 172
Last Year in Viet Nam 3, 13
lawsuits 209, 233
Le Hiep Thi 177–191
Leary, Denis 201
Ledger, Heath 266
Lemmon, Jack 91, 161
Lerner, Stuart 24

Leto, Jared 267
Levitt, Heidi 220, 229
Lewis, Juliette 198, 210
Liddy, G Gordon 225
Life and Times of Deacon Davis, The (screenplay) 18
Limbaugh, Rush 111, 112
Ling, Barbara 142, 162
Lipper, Ken 89, 92, 97, 98
Lizard's Tail, The (book) 24, 26, 31
LL Cool J 249, 258
Logan, John 247
Loggia, Robert 192
Lombardi, Vince 245
Lone, John 46
Longest Day, The 160
Looking for Fidel 261
Lopez, Jennifer 236
Lord of the Rings, The 48
Ludwig, Tony 139
Luhrmann, Baz 265, 266, 269
Lumet, Sidney 35, 37
Lynch, David 192, 238

MacLachlan, Kyle 141
Mad Man of Martinique 3
Madonna 50
Madsen, Michael 141, 197
Mailer, Norman 172
Malcolm, Derek 65, 114, 130, 151, 190, 227, 228
Mantel, Hilary 100, 129
Manzareck, Ray 141, 146, 148
Marcos, Ferdinand 72
Marcovicci, Andrea 27
Marks, Richard 28
Marrs, Jim 158
Mars Jones, Adam 100
Marshall, EG 219–220
Martinez, Eugenio 216
Maslin, Janet 208
McEnroe, Annie 27–28
McGill, Bruce 27
McGinley, John C 74, 92, 106, 107, 121, 200, 220, 250
Medavoy, Mike 233
Menem, Carlos 50
Metcalf, Laurie 161
Miami Vice 38, 39
Midnight Express 16–23, 25, 46, 63, 66, 71, 210
Midnight Express (book) 18, 21–22
Midweek 114, 130
Milchan, Arnon 159, 178, 197, 217

Miles, Silvia 92
Milius, John 14, 48
Mirojnick, Ellen 90, 107
misogyny 30, 40, 57, 65–66, 102, 191, 236
Mitchell, John 225
Montana, Joe 246
Moon, Warren 250
Morley, Sheridan 190
Morocco 265–266
Moroder, Giorgio 22, 40
Morricone, Ennio 237, 241
Morrisey, Owen 89
Morrison, Jim 122, 134–153, 240, 268
Moscow Film Festival 152
Moses, Mark 121, 141
Mount, Thom 196
Mr Smith Goes to Washington 163, 168
Mulcahy, Russell 22
Murphy, Don 196, 197, 209
music
    Alexander 270
    Any Given Sunday 257–258
    Born on the Fourth of July 121–122, 128–129
    Doors, The 150
    Hand, The 28, 32
    Heaven and Earth 188–189, 190
    JFK 157, 170
    Midnight Express 22
    Natural Born Killers 206–207
    Nixon 220, 227
    Platoon 73, 82
    Salvador 64–65
    Scarface 40
    Seizure 15
    Talk Radio 113
    U Turn 241
    Wall Street 88, 99
    Year of the Dragon 46
My Left Foot 127, 131

National Football League 247, 248
Natural Born Killers 4, 23, 29, 49, 102, 152, 173, 193–211, 242–243
    screenplay 204–205, 209
Neidorf, David 121
Netanyahu, Benjamin 262
New Age, The 133
New Deal (Roosevelt) 94–95
New Jack City 39

New Socialist 65, 100
New Statesman 65, 190, 208
New York Daily News 15
New York Stock Exchange 89, 95
New York Times 15, 32, 65, 66, 70, 84, 100, 119, 196, 208, 259
New York University 1, 3
Newman, John 159, 169
Newman, Paul 66, 84, 105
Newsweek 158, 216
Ngor, Haing S 180
Nguyen, Ha 178
Nicholson, Jack 218
Nixon 4, 62, 74, 102, 133, 152, 173, 174, 211–230, 239
Nixon, Richard 95, 124, 153, 221–230, 268
Nixon, Tricia 228
NME magazine 66, 130
Nolte, Nick 236
Nordberg, Tom 218, 251, 267
Nothing but Trouble 238–239

O'Brian, Margaret 185
Observer 114, 242
O'Hagan, Andrew 259
Oldman, Gary 161, 163, 219
Oliver Stone's USA (book) 95
On Any Given Sunday (book) 256
On the Trail of the Assassins (book) 158, 159, 169
Oswald, Lee Harvey 160, 168
Other People's Money 98
Owens, Terrell 250

Pacino, Al 36, 40, 119–120, 217, 248–249, 250, 252
Palestine 262–263
Parente, William 65
Parker, Sir Alan 18, 19, 21, 50, 105
Pasztor, Beatrix Aruna 237
Paxton, Bill 235
Pederson, Chris 121
Penman, Ian 114
Penn, Sean 120, 196, 235
People versus Larry Flynt, The 133, 134, 233
Peres, Shimon 262
Peron, Eva 50
Persona Non Grata 262–263, 268
Pesci, Joe 161

Petrie, Dan 119
Pfeiffer, Chuck 121, 220
Pfeiffer, Michelle 50
Philippines 72, 82, 120
Phoenix, Joaquin 236
Phoenix Pictures 233
Pierce, David Hyde 219
Pinkerton, Lee 258
Pitt, Brad 269
Plana, Tony 161, 220
Platoon 3, 18, 30, 42, 54, 57,
    66, 67–85, 97, 100, 102,
    120, 122, 123, 128, 174,
    234
Plimpton, George 220
Pollock, Tom 120
Pressman, Edward 26, 28, 35,
    47, 89, 105, 106
Prieto, Rodrigo 267–268
Private Parts 111
product placement 90, 101, 248
Prouty, L Fletcher 158, 159,
    167–168, 172
Psycho 13
Puff Daddy 248
Puttnam, Lord David 18, 19
Pyne, Daniel 247

Quaid, Dennis 250
Quinlan, Kathleen 148, 182
Quinn, Francesco 74

racism 19–20, 23, 40, 44,
    66–67, 247, 255
Rascals, The (screenplay) 18
Ray, Ellen 158
Reagan, Ronald 38, 52, 59, 61,
    102
Rebozo, Bebe 225
Red Rock West 241
Reidy, Joe 181
Renna, Chris 161, 181
Reservoir Dogs 195, 196
Return, The (book) 22
Return to Paradise 22
Reversal of Fortune 133
Reynolds, Debbie 180
Reznor, Trent 207
Rhames, Ving 248
Richardson, Robert 55, 57, 64,
    72, 73, 82, 84, 92, 98, 100,
    107, 114, 125, 127, 142,
    162, 170, 171, 173, 178,
    181, 198, 199, 206, 227,
    237, 241, 251, 267
Riders on the Storm (book)
    135, 148

Ridley, John 233, 235, 239
Riefenstahl, Leni 173
Rimbaldi, Carlo 26
Riordan, James 1, 30, 90
Riva, J Michael 28
Rivele, Stephen 216, 217, 222
road movies 196–197, 204,
    238
Rock, Dr 51–53, 55, 62–63
Roelfs, Jan 268
Rolling Stone magazine 138,
    151, 171, 208, 228
Romero, Archbishop 62
Romney, Jonathan 190
Rooker, Michael 161
Roosevelt, Franklin 94–95
Rosenfeld, Robert 256
Roth, Steve 49
Rothchild, Paul 141
Rubeo, Bruno 73, 107, 113,
    120
Rubinek, Saul 220
Ruby, Jack 163
Rusconi, Jane 158, 159
Russo, Perry 161, 167
Rutowski, Richard 26, 142,
    149, 161, 181, 197, 200,
    234, 237, 240
Ryan, Meg 140, 147, 249

Safire, William 229
Saloman Brothers 89
Salvador 14, 32, 39, 51–67, 72,
    92, 102, 132, 173, 188,
    229
San Francisco Examiner
    227–228
Sanders, Jay 161
Sarkis, Najwa 3, 18
Sarris, Andrew 32
Savage, Bill 209
Savage, John 56
Savinar, Ted 105
Saving Private Ryan 81, 257
Saviour 133
Scalia, Pietro 161, 171, 173,
    199
Scarface 4, 19, 23, 29, 33–41,
    42, 66–67, 98, 101, 210,
    250
Scheer, Bob 217
Scheer, Christopher 217
Schwarzenegger, Arnold 47,
    196
Scorsese, Martin 3, 14, 142, 267
Scotsman 65, 151
Scott, Ridley 48

Scream 98
Screen International 261
Seizure 7–16, 30, 66, 132, 208
Semel, Terry 158
Shaw, Clay 158, 162–163, 164,
    167, 168
Sheen, Charlie 72, 73, 80, 89,
    90–91, 92, 120
Sheen, Martin 55, 80, 91
Siddons, Bill 147–148
Simpson, Claire 73, 92, 107
Simpson, OJ 203
Simpsons, The 81, 169
Sinclair, Upton 61
Sizemore, Tom 198, 199
Sklar, Zachary 159
Sorvino, Paul 219
South Central 133
Spacek, Sissy 161, 172
Spectator 84, 129
Spider-Man 72
Spielberg, Steven 133
split-screen effects 99
Spy Game 105
St Clair, Bob 250
Steadicam 128, 149
Steenburgen, Mary 220
Stern, Howard 111, 112
Stigwood, Robert 50
Stone, Elizabeth (wife) 28, 31,
    35, 54, 103, 186, 204
Stone, Jacqueline *see* Goddet,
    Jacqueline
Stone, Lou (father) 1–2, 21, 62,
    79, 89, 96–97
Stone, Michael (son) 220, 251
Stone, Oliver
    drugs 39–40, 270
    early life 1–3
    marriage to Najwa Sarkis 3,
        18
    marriage to Elizabeth Cox
        28, 35, 186, 204
    production work 133–134,
        192, 233
    Vietnam experience 1, 2–3,
        13, 78–79, 125, 173
Stone, Sean (son) 54, 92, 101,
    142, 161, 181, 200, 220,
    237, 251
Stone, Sharon 236
Stray Dogs (book) 233, 239
Streep, Meryl 50
Sugar Cookies 4, 10
Sugerman, Danny 138, 148
Summer, Edward 47
Sun 151

Sunday Express 99, 190
Sunday Telegraph 83, 114, 189, 208, 227
Sunday Times 172, 228, 242
Superior, Arizona 234
Sutherland, Donald 161
SWAT 134, 266
Sweet, Matthew 242

takings 15, 65, 82, 99, 129, 150, 171, 189, 207, 227, 241, 256, 258
Talk Radio 102, 103–115, 132, 203, 210
Talked to Death: the Life and Murder of Alan Berg (book) 105, 112
Tarantino, Quentin 47, 195, 197, 204–205, 206, 208–209, 267
Taylor, Lawrence 249
Taylor, Sam 242
Technocrane 149
Thailand 178, 179, 266
themes 13, 33
  anger 29, 30, 32, 76–77
  the 'Beast' 222, 224, 228, 229
  greed 93–96, 98
  immigrants 38–39, 42, 44–5, 184–185
  incest 4, 243
  paranoia 242
  politics 58–64, 164–169, 216–217, 260–263
  prisons 22, 203
  racism 19–20, 23, 40, 44, 46, 247, 255
  violence 23, 36–37, 200–203, 209, 210–211
  war 75–78, 122–126, 132–133, 185, 191, 259
Thomas, Roy 47
Thompson, Hunter S. 63
Thomsen, Moritz 64
Thornton, Billy Bob 236
Throne of Blood 36
Time magazine 100, 130, 208, 216
Time Out 151, 171, 207
Times, The 114, 172, 259
Times Literary Supplement 83, 100
Titanic 235
Tittle, YA 250
Today 99, 145, 171, 189, 190
Tookey, Christopher 114, 172, 207, 228

Toomay, Pat 250, 256
Totino, Salvatore 251, 256–257, 267
Towne, Robert 49
Townsend, Clayton 199, 235–236, 237
Traffik (TV programme) 46
Travolta, John 138
Troy 269
Trudeau, Gary 172–173
Trump, Donald 97
Twentieth-Century Fox 89
Twin Peaks 180, 192
Tyler, Liv 242

U Turn 4, 23, 26, 57, 115, 133, 230–243, 255
Union City Blue 32
Unitas, Johnny 250
Upton Sinclair Award 173
Usher, Shaun 99, 171

Vajna, Andy 217
Valenti, Jack 173
Vangelis 270
Variety 15
Vassler, Rand 196
Veloz, David 197
Venice Film Festival 210
Vernieu, Mary 220, 237
Vidal, Gore 265
Vietnam war 43, 46–47
  Born on the Fourth of July 116–133
  Heaven and Earth 174–191
  JFK's involvement 159, 166, 169, 172
  Nixon 222
  Platoon 68–85
  Stone's experience 1, 2–3, 13, 78–79, 125, 173
Viglietta, Rocky 135
Village Voice 32, 114, 208, 242
Villechaize, Herve 10–11
Voice 258
Voight, Jon 236, 242
Vossler, Rand 51

Wagner, Bruce 192
Wagner, Paula 120
Walker, Alexander 83, 129, 171, 189, 208, 227, 228, 242, 258
Wall Street 27, 39, 40, 85–102, 140, 238
Walsh, JT 219
Warner Brothers 158, 178, 197, 209, 217, 265

Warren, Earl 161
Warren Commission Report 158, 159, 164, 165, 169, 172, 174
Washington Post 83, 100, 114, 130, 150–151, 171, 172, 207
Washington Times 172
Watergate 212, 218, 221, 224
Waterston, Sam 27, 221
Waynes World 2 149
Weakness and Deceit (book) 54, 63
Webber, Andrew Lloyd 50
Weil, Robert 243
Weiner, Richard 246
Weisburg, Harold 172
Weiser, Stanley 3, 89, 101
Welcome to Collinwood 22
Whaley, Frank 141, 161, 162
When Heaven and Earth Changed Places (book) 177, 187
Whitaker, Forest 72
White, Robert 62
White, Stanley 45, 73, 220
Wild Palms 133, 192
Wilkinson, Chris 216, 217, 222
Williams, Edward Bennett 172
Williams, Jamie 247, 250
Williams, John 122, 129, 131, 157, 170, 220, 227, 229
Willow 140
Wincott, Michael 106, 121, 141
Windsor-Smith, Barry 29
Winston, Stan 26
Wolves, The (film script) 4
Woods, James 55, 56, 66, 67, 133, 220, 250, 252
Woodward, Bob 226
Woolacott, Martin 189
Woronov, Mary 11
Wright, Steven 201
Wright, Travis 101
Writers Guild of America 66, 132, 234

Yale university 1, 2
Yang, Janet 133
Year of Living Dangerously, The 64
Year of the Dragon 19, 23, 29, 41–47, 66, 71, 73
Yolocamba 65

Zapruder, Abraham 160, 170
Ziegler, Ron 225
Zophres, Mary 251